Murder Most Foul

MURDER
Most Foul

THE
KILLER
AND THE
American Gothic
Imagination

KAREN HALTTUNEN

HARVARD UNIVERSITY PRESS
Cambridge, Massachusetts
London, England

Library of Congress Cataloging-in-Publication Data
Halttunen, Karen, 1951–
Murder most foul : the killer and the American
Gothic imagination / Karen Halttunen.
p.   cm.
Includes bibliographical references and index.
ISBN 0-674-58855-X (cloth)
ISBN 0-674-00384-5 (pbk)
1. Murder—United States—History.
2. Murder—United States—Case studies.
3. Murder in literature.
4. Gothic revival (Literature)—United States.
I. Title.
HV6524.H28   1998
364.15′23′0973—dc21   98-22624

Designed by Gwen Nefsky Frankfeldt

In memory of Jo, and for Deb

Acknowledgments

My debts are many. They begin, as always, with my teachers, John L. Thomas at Brown University and David Brion Davis at Yale. They guided this project through professional example, unfailing support, and their own superb scholarship: most notably Jack's path-breaking essay on "Romantic Reform in America, 1815–1865," which first set me to thinking about the dark underside of theological perfectionism; and David's *Homicide in American Fiction, 1798–1860: A Study in Social Values,* a creative work well ahead of its time, without which this book could not have been formulated.

Many colleagues and friends have read part or all of this manuscript in various stages, offering invaluable criticisms and suggestions along the way. I would like to thank Joel Bernard, Daniel A. Cohen, Patricia Cline Cohen, Robert Finlay, Richard W. Fox, George M. Fredrickson, Lisa Halttunen, T. Walter Herbert, Joy Kasson, Jackson Lears, Sarah C. Maza, Michael Meranze, Lewis Perry, Michael S. Sherry, Daniel Singal, Amy Gilman Srebnick, Alan Trachtenberg, Clarence Walker, and my late colleagues Paul Goodman and Roland Marchand, gentle men and scholars both. I am also grateful for comments by lecture audiences and seminar participants at a number of colleges and universities. My fellow fellows at the National Humanities Center in North Carolina, "class" of 1995, offered criticism and encouragement, food and drink, and lasting friendship: my warmest thanks go to Charles Capper, Rhonda Cobham-Sander, Pat

ACKNOWLEDGMENTS

Cohen, Robert and Priscilla Ferguson, Jonathan Freedman, Barbara
Harris, Ellen Schrecker, Luise White, Margery Wolf, and to Kent
Mullikin for making it all happen. I am very grateful to my research
assistant, Jill Hough, for invaluable help with a bibliographic data-
base. At Harvard University Press, Joyce Seltzer gave the manuscript
a close and intelligent reading, and helped me see my way to cutting
it by some 150 pages, for which I am (finally) very grateful; and Anita
Safran edited it with a fine and careful hand.

For fellowship support, I would like to thank the National En-
dowment for the Humanities, the National Humanities Center, the
President's Office of the University of California, the American Antiquarian Society, the Huntington Library, the Davis Humanities
Institute, Northwestern University, and the University of California,
Davis. The librarians who made this project possible are many. My
greatest debt is to the American Antiquarian Society in Worcester,
Massachusetts, whose superb holdings in early American and nineteenth-century materials, combined with the considerable expertise
of its staff, make it a very special place to work; I would like to thank
in particular John Hench, Nancy Burkett, Joanne Chaison, Marie
Lamoreaux, and Georgia Barnhill. I am grateful as well to the Boston Public Library, Houghton Library, the Huntington Library, the
Library of Congress, the Newberry Library, and the Yale Law Library.

My greatest personal debts are acknowledged in my dedication.
Betty Jo Teeter Dobbs shared with me the early and middle years of
this project, offering her wisdom, warmth, and a gentle wonderment
that anyone could be so interested in matters so violent. After Jo's
death in 1994, Deborah Elizabeth Harkness renewed my life and saw
me through. This book is for both of them.

Contents

Illustrations

All illustrations are courtesy of the American Antiquarian Society.

FOLLOWING P. 32

The coffins of Beadle's victims, his murdered wife and four children, float above his corpse.

[Stephen Mix Mitchell], *Narrative of the Life of William Beadle* (Hartford: Bavil Webster, 1783), frontispiece.

Richard Johnson shoots his pistol at Ursula Newman.

A Correct Copy of the Trial & Conviction of Richard Johnson, for the Murder of Ursula Newman (New York: Christian Brown [1829?]), title page.

Thomas Topping beats his wife to death.

Annals of Murder, or, Daring Outrages, Trials, Confessions (Philadelphia: John B. Perry; New York: Nafis & Cornish, 1845), p. 31.

Arthur Spring's murderous assault on Ellen Lynch.

Horrible Murder of Mrs. Ellen Lynch, and Her Sister, Mrs. Hannah Shaw (Philadelphia: A. Winch, 1853), front cover.

Two murderers dismember their victim.

An Account of the Apprehension, Trial, Conviction, and Condemnation of Manuel Philip Garcia and José Demas Garcia Castillano (Norfolk: C. Hall, 1821), title page.

John Haggerty kills his neighbors, the Fordneys, with an ax.

Testimonium Dr. Baker et aliorum fecit in the trial, in quaem est confession of John Haggerty (Lancaster: J. S. Jones, 1836), front cover.

Michael McGarvey flogs his wife to death with a horsewhip.

Tragedies on the Land, Containing an Authentic Account of the Most Awful Murders (Philadelphia: A. Winch, 1853), frontispiece.

Margaret Howard, the wronged wife, pleads with her husband not to abandon her.

Trial of Mrs. Margaret Howard for the Murder of Miss Mary Ellen Smith (Cincinnati, 1849), frontispiece.

The house where the two sisters were murdered by Arthur Spring.

Horrible Murder of Mrs. Ellen Lynch, and Her Sister, Mrs. Hannah Shaw (Philadelphia: A. Winch, 1853), inside front cover.

Courtroom scene at the trial of Professor John Webster.

Trial of Prof. John W. Webster, for the Murder of Dr. George Parkman (Boston: Daily Mail Office [1850]), title page.

Mary Cole hangs for the murder of her mother.

The Confession of Mary Cole (New York [1812]), title page.

The handsome, boyish face of murderer William Teller, signed by a reader.

Confessions, Trials, and Biographical Sketches of the Most Cold Blooded Murderers (Boston: George N. Thomson, 1837), p. 255.

The murderer of prostitute Helen Jewett.

"Richard P. Robinson" (New York: Alfred Baker, 1836), color lithograph.

The murder trial report as literature.

Trial of Henry G. Green, for the Murder of His Wife (New York, 1845), n.p.

The bludgeon that was used to kill Captain White.

Trial of John Francis Knapp as Principal in the Second Degree for the Murder of Capt. Joseph White (Boston: Dutton & Wentworth, 1830), n.p.

Murder as mystery: the veiled murderess.

Life and Confession of Mrs. Henrietta Robinson, the Veiled Murderess! (Boston: Dr. H. P. Skinner, 1855), title page.

The murderess unveiled.

Life and Confession of Mrs. Henrietta Robinson, the Veiled Murderess! (Boston: Dr. H. P. Skinner, 1855), back page.

Map of the murder scene.

Trial of Reuben Dunbar, for the Murder of Stephen V. Lester and David L. Lester (Albany: P. L. Gilbert, 1850), p. 2.

The midnight murder of Joseph White.

Confessions, Trials and Biographical Sketches of the Most Cold Blooded Murderers (Boston: George N. Thomson, 1837), frontispiece.

The home where Alfred Fyler killed his wife, Ruth.

The Fyler Murder Case (Syracuse: Smith & Hough, 1855), opposite p. 122.

Diagram of the Fyler house interior.

The Fyler Murder Case (Syracuse: Smith & Hough, 1855), opposite p. 122.

The Harvard Medical College building, the site of the Parkman murder.

Awful Disclosures and Startling Developements [sic], in Relation to the late Parkman Tragedy (n.p., 1849), title page.

Ephraim Littlefield, the amateur sleuth, and sketch of the evidence produced in court.

Trial of Prof. John W. Webster, for the Murder of George Parkman (New York: Stringer and Townsend, New York Daily Globe, 1850), p. 79.

Parkman's skeleton, reconstructed.

Trial of Professor John W. Webster, for the Murder of George Parkman (Boston: John A. French, 1850), p. 25.

The floor plan of Webster's laboratory.

Trial of Professor John W. Webster, for the Murder of George Parkman (Boston: John A. French, 1850), p. 14.

FOLLOWING P. 134

Adam Horn dismembers the corpse of his wife.

Annals of Murder, or, Daring Outrages, Trials, Confessions (Philadelphia: John B. Perry; New York: Nafis & Cornish, 1845), p. 52.

Joel Clough stabs the woman who rejected his courtship.

Trial, Sentence, Confession and Execution of Joel Clough for the Wilful Murder of Mrs. Mary Hamilton (New York: Christian Brown, 1833), inside front cover.

Murder Most Foul

Introduction

A DOMESTIC servant kills her newborn infant, the fruit of an illicit sexual liaison, and when her crime is discovered, confesses to killing an earlier child by the same man to conceal her fornication. A twelve-year-old girl chokes and batters to death the six-year-old girl who had reported her theft of some strawberries. A wealthy elderly man is bludgeoned and stabbed to death in his bed by a contract killer hired to secure an inheritance. A beautiful young woman is found dead in the Hoboken River, her body injured by either a botched abortion or a violent rape, and her killer is never identified. A seventy-year-old man shoots his twenty-three-year-old wife out of fear that she is a witch, who summons her lover by touching the kitchen sieve, and blows unseen poisons onto her husband's food, shirts, and bedclothes. Accounts of these murders, from the late seventeenth century through the mid-nineteenth, captured the American popular imagination in ways that reflected the changing cultural constructions of the crime.

"Other sins only speak; murder shrieks out," wrote playwright John Webster in 1623, in *The Duchess of Malfi* (IV. ii. 261). The act rends the community in which it takes place, calling all relationships into question—mother and infant, husband and wife, lovers, friends, strangers, and mere acquaintances—and posing troubling questions about the moral nature of humankind. Murder thus demands that a

{1}

community come to terms with the crime—confront what has happened and endeavor to explain it, in an effort to restore order to the world. In literate societies, the cultural work of coming to terms with this violent transgression takes crucial form in the crafting and reading of written narratives of the murder, the chief purpose of which is to assign meaning to the incident. As Hayden White has observed, every narrative account, even the purportedly "nonfictional," is an artificial construct, for the world does not just "present itself to perception in the form of well-made stories, with central subjects, proper beginnings, middles, and ends."[1] Any story of murder involves a fictive process, which reveals much about the mental and emotional strategies employed within a given historical culture for responding to serious transgression in its midst.

In American culture, the dominant narrative expressing and shaping the popular response to the crime of murder underwent a major transformation in the late eighteenth and early nineteenth century. For a century after their earliest appearance in late seventeenth-century New England, printed responses to the crime tended to take the form of the execution sermon, preached shortly before the convicted criminal was put to death for his or her offense. The execution sermon was a sacred narrative which focused not on the bloody deed or the judicial process which had brought the murderer to the scaffold, but on the spiritual condition of the condemned criminal. What course of smaller sins had brought this sinner to the terrible transgression for which she or he was about to be hanged? What was her spiritual state now, and where would she spend eternity? These were the central concerns of the execution sermon. But in the late eighteenth and early nineteenth centuries that sacred narrative was gradually replaced by a variety of secular accounts—criminal biographies and autobiographies, journalistic narratives, and, most important, printed transcripts of murder trials—which turned attention to the crime itself and its unfolding within worldly time. What was the nature of the violence; when and where had the crime taken place; what were the murderer's motives; and just how had he or she been brought to worldly justice?

Previous scholars have explained the new genre of criminal narratives as an expression of "sensationalism," a degraded pursuit of the thrill of sensation for its own sake, which accompanied the emergence of a mass readership. The more people read, within this view, the more they flocked to purchase a seamy, pulp literature devoted to scenes of dramatic violence, strong emotions, illicit relationships, and other titillating transgressions. This argument works somewhat like Abraham Lincoln's reported response to a popular work on spiritualism: "Well, for the sort of people who like that sort of thing, that is about the sort of thing they would like." My own premise is that, though salvation history was losing cultural power in the late eighteenth century, the search for meaning in the face of violent transgression did not disappear with that older framework. The new secular accounts of murder endeavored to replace the sacred narrative with a new mode of coming to terms with the crime. And the extreme violence of the new accounts was not "gratuitous" in the meaningless present usage of that term; rather, it represented a significant new strategy for confronting the crime of murder.

The emerging secular literature organized the popular response to murder within a set of narrative conventions that are most usefully characterized as Gothic, the term assigned by literary historians to their contemporaneous fictional expression. The first of these conventions was *horror*, which employed inflated language and graphic treatments of violence and its aftermath in order to shock the reader into an emotional state that mingled fear with hatred and disgust. The new murder stories explicitly instructed readers to experience horror in the face of the crime, and didactically explained the precise nature of that emotional state, which typically rendered the person experiencing it speechless and unable to assign meaning to the event in question. The second convention was *mystery*, which used incomplete, fragmented, and chronologically confused narratives (influenced by murder trial reports) to impress upon readers the impossibility of achieving a full knowledge and understanding of the crime. Well before what literary historians have called the "invention" of detective fiction by Edgar Allan Poe in 1841, the nonfictional literature of murder was presenting the crime of murder as fundamentally a matter of mystery.

{3}

It was thus the peculiar nature of the Gothic narrative of murder to try *and fail* to come to terms with the shocking revelation that murder had been committed. For Gothic mystery and Gothic horror affirmed the ultimate incomprehensibility of any given crime of murder, in sharp contrast to the execution sermon's unproblematic acceptance of the nature of the act and the guilt of the condemned murderer. It was a dramatic departure from the execution sermon's formulaic demonstration that all murders were simply natural manifestations of universal depravity, and its tendency to express surprise, not that one sinner had committed this crime, but that everyone else in the community had not.

The Gothic tale of murder repeatedly and ritualistically failed to assign meaning to the crime because it sought to comprehend radical human evil within the larger intellectual context of Enlightenment liberalism, which did not recognize radical human evil. In contrast to the earlier belief in man's innate depravity, Enlightenment liberalism understood human nature as essentially good, rational, and capable of self-government. How then to explain murder? The new secular narratives routinely invoked liberal explanations of the crime: the murderer had been the victim of childhood neglect or abuse; the murderer had misapplied his powers of reason by acting upon an unfortunate "motive"; the murderer had neglected self-government and had permitted his passions (the dangerous emotions) to overwhelm his sentiments (the inborn guarantors of virtue). But again and again, such liberal explanations of the crime failed: some men and women murdered despite their good religious and moral upbringings; some murdered without any discernible motive; and some killed coolly and dispassionately. In the face of such explanatory breakdowns, the new murder narratives had ritual recourse to the Gothic conventions of the fundamental mystery of murder—its intrinsic unknowability—and its fundamental horror—the inhuman nature of the act.

The most important cultural work performed by the Gothic narrative of murder was its reconstruction of the criminal transgressor: from common sinner with whom the larger community of sinners were urged to identify in the service of their own salvation, into

{4}

moral monster from whom readers were instructed to shrink, with a sense of *horror* that confirmed their own "normalcy" in the face of the morally alien, and with a sense of *mystery* that testified to their own inability even to conceive of such an aberrant act. The new Gothic murderer—like the villain in Gothic fiction—was first and last a moral monster, between whom and the normal majority yawned an impassable gulf. The Gothic narrative of criminal transgression proved central to the modern liberal construction of the concept of criminal deviance—the view expressed by Charles Dickens that the "criminal intellect" was nothing like "the average intellect of average men" but "a horrible wonder apart." That view was eventually to shape modern social-scientific views of the criminal in such fields as psychology, sociology, criminology, and criminal law.

In its primary concern for the condemned murderer as exemplary sinner, the early New England execution sermon gravitated to murders committed under the influence of the most widely shared sins of the community, such as drunkenness, unchastity, or religious neglect. The nineteenth-century Gothic narrative also tended to focus on certain types of crime, along new lines of selectiveness. Most broadly, the new narrative sought out especially shocking or bloody murders, and cases that proved unusually resistant to full and certain resolution, for representation. In addition, certain categories of story-line lent themselves particularly well to Gothic narration. Tales of domestic murder evoked a powerful sense of horror over the crime's shocking violation of the new sentimental domesticity, and of mystery at the unusually hidden nature of murder in the private sphere. Similarly, tales of sexual murder received a seemingly disproportionate attention in nineteenth-century murder literature, due to the special possibilities they presented for horror and mystery. Each of these story-lines—the domestic and the sexual—put its own particular twist on the Gothic reconstruction of the murderer as monster.

One last category of murder lent itself with peculiar power to Gothic narration. By the early nineteenth century, legal narratives of the crime were crafting an insanity defense that reveals much about the historical relationship between the Gothic imagination and the Enlightenment liberal view of human nature. For the insanity defense attributed the crime to disease, a somatic distortion of the mental faculties, thus effectively denying the evil of the primary identity by laying blame on an alien persona that had somehow invaded it. The Gothic narrative of criminal transgression proved central as well to the dominant liberal disposition of the convicted criminal deviant, namely, segregation in a penitentiary or mental hospital, institutions which hid the horrors of moral monstrosity from the sight of normalcy. For the criminal's moral otherness was deemed to require his or her full separation from normal society, within an institution which, though expressly designed for rehabilitating inmates and restoring them to society, in fact constructed impassable barriers between the normal and the abnormal. Once constructed, such institutions helped perpetuate the central Gothic conventions of evil, socially reinforcing both the horror at the criminal deviant's radical otherness, and the sense of the mysterious, hidden nature of human evil.

This book focuses on the changing cultural construction of criminal transgression, using printed accounts of murder to address the larger question of what happened to the popular understanding of human evil after the doctrine of innate depravity began to weaken in the context of Enlightenment liberalism. My aim is to shed new light on the historical significance of the Gothic imagination in constructing a set of conventions surrounding the collective response to murder—conventions that run so deep in modern liberal culture that they appear to be natural, instinctive, when in fact they are historically contingent. The Gothic imagination has proved a major factor in shaping the modern liberal concept of criminal and mental "deviance" and what should be done about it.

CHAPTER ONE

The Murderer as
Common Sinner

ESTHER RODGERS was born in Kittery, Maine, in 1680, and was apprenticed at the age of thirteen to a religious family. Four years later, she committed her first murder, stopping the breath of her newborn child, the fruit of an illicit liaison with a Negro serving in the same household in Newbury, Massachusetts. She buried the body, and her crime went undetected. But when Rodgers again became pregnant a few years later, and secretly delivered and then buried the infant—who she thought might have been still-born—neighbors discovered her deed. She was charged with murder, under a seventeenth-century English law that held any woman guilty of infanticide who buried a newborn child in the absence of witnesses to its natural death. It was then that Rodgers confessed to the earlier killing. She was convicted of the crime of infanticide and, after eight months' imprisonment, she was executed.

These are the basic facts of the crime and punishment of Esther Rodgers. But to tell the story in this fashion, with primary attention to mundane events arranged in chronological order, is to diverge dramatically from the story formally told to Rodgers's contemporaries. The format of that telling was the execution sermon—more precisely, the three sermons preached on the infanticide's behalf by the Rev. John Rogers shortly before her execution, and subsequently printed, along with her "Declaration and Confession," under the title

Death the Certain Wages of Sin, in 1701.[1] Whatever tales of such a crime might have passed by word of mouth, whatever form the case may have assumed during judicial proceedings against the accused, the story of the murder formally entered print within the framework of the execution sermon, which frequently included the confession or last words of the condemned criminal. The execution sermon shaped the official narrative of the event along highly formulaic lines.

Death the Certain Wages of Sin showed relatively little concern for the details of the crime itself: it offered no dramatic reenactment of the crime, and paid limited attention to such matters as time and place or the precise nature of the violence. Instead, it focused on the spiritual pilgrimage of Esther Rodgers as she moved from a state of religious indifference to overwhelming conviction of sin to a strong hope, as her execution drew near, in her salvation. At the hands of the Rev. John Rogers, various other clergmen, and the "certain Gentlewoman of the Town" who visited and comforted the condemned criminal in prison, and with the active cooperation of Esther Rodgers herself, the story of this murderer's crimes was shaped into a triumphant narrative of spiritual transcendence, of victory over sin and eternal death. Once an irreligious, unchaste woman willing to destroy her own child to conceal her vicious conduct, she had been spiritually transformed during her eight months of bondage, and had emerged from prison "Sprinkled, Cleansed, Comforted, a Candidate of Heaven." This condemned young servant demonstrated God's mercy to even the greatest of sinners: if an infant-killer could emerge from her spiritual struggles as a "Candidate of Heaven," so too could any sinner who undertook to confess, repent, and hope in Christ.

In offering up condemned murderers as models for more ordinary sinners to empathize with and emulate, the execution sermon was a distinctive response to dramatic acts of criminal transgression in early New England culture. Witnesses to Rodgers's life and death were expected not to shrink from the condemned murderer in moral repugnance, but to identify with her moral condition and imitate her spiritual progress. The editor of *Death the Certain Wages of Sin* reported that Esther Rodgers's cheerfulness and composure while en route to her execution "melted the hearts of all that were within seeing or hearing, into Tears of affection." The condemned murderers who emerged from the pages of New England execution sermons bore very different moral features from those of the murderers who would replace them in the pages of popular American criminal literature after the late eighteenth century. The early American murderer was regarded as a moral representative of all of sinful humanity, and was granted an important spiritual role in the early New England community.

———————

Before the sixteenth century in Western Europe, casual violence was a way of life for people of all social ranks. Small insults led easily to physical assault, family rivalries took form as vendettas, and personal scores were frequently settled through extra-legal violence. Aggressive behavior and the willful infliction of pain on others were largely tolerated, and bystanders, rather than intervene to end an altercation, were likely to stand around and cheer it on. Most homicides were committed against neighbors and friends, or among strangers who met accidentally, rather than against blood relatives, a fact suggesting that sudden passions rather than long pent-up tensions lay behind many fatal assaults. But in the early modern era, with the emergence of nation-states and their monopolization of violence and supreme rule, the violence of individual persons became restrained, and casual physical assault grew less common in daily interaction. English homicide rates declined by some fifty percent between the thirteenth and the seventeenth centuries, and then dropped dramatically again between 1660 and 1800. The gradual extension of the "civilizing process," with its demands for a rational civic order and emotional self-control, the slow shift from a feudal culture founded on concepts of personal honor to a modern bourgeois culture more attuned to property values, and the emergence, especially in the seventeenth and eighteenth centuries, of a new humanitarian sensitivity to cruelty and violence, all contributed to a social order in which people were more willing to negotiate differences than to take up arms to settle them.[2]

Accompanying this decline in the incidence of fatal assault was a gradual change in the popular perception of murder. The crimes considered most heinous in the Middle Ages had been heresy against God and treason against the state. But by the sixteenth and seventeenth centuries, the murder of an individual had largely surpassed these as the most serious of crimes. The English came to regard murder as a "crying sin" that defiled the Land, bringing guilt to the collective community, until the crime's call for justice was heard.[3] Popular belief held that God actively interposed in the discovery of murders, ensuring that "murder would out": under His providential detection the ghosts of victims appeared to tell the story of their violent deaths, corpses bled in the presence of the guilty party, and murderers changed physically in ways that revealed their guilt. Within a culture deeply fearful of sudden, unprepared death— "Cut off even in the blossoms of my sin," complained the ghost of Hamlet's murdered father—the untimely death of a murder victim was deemed particularly terrible.[4]

An extensive popular literature emerged to address a heightened English interest in criminality in general and murder in particular. By the mid-seventeenth century, sales of chapbooks, broadsides, "small histories," jest-books, and "small godly books" were booming. A previously oral society was turning into a semi-literate society in which schooling to the level of reading literacy was commonplace, and some members of even the humblest social groups could read. From the outset, a significant portion of this popular literary market was devoted to crime. By the late seventeenth century, much popular criminal literature fell into one of two narrative patterns. The first was the picaresque tale of criminality, a loosely structured, amoral, escapist kind of narrative which was typically used to capture, in light-hearted fashion, the roguish life of the highwayman. The second was the spiritual biography of the criminal-as-sinner, a tightly structured moral tale of sin, confession and repentance, conversion, and finally judicial death, which charted, in appropriately somber tones, the life-course of the murderer. In a variety of forms including criminal lives, last dying speeches, and the printed accounts of the Ordinary or prison chaplain of Newgate, spiritual biography contributed to the widening popular belief that murder was one of the most terrible crimes known to humankind.[5]

In late seventeenth- and early eighteenth-century New England, the predominant form of criminal narrative was the execution sermon. These sermons were delivered on the Sabbath preceding or on the morning of the appointed day of execution, and sometimes on both occasions, with the condemned criminal sitting, guarded and in chains, in the front of the church below the pulpit. An integral part of the execution ritual, they were well-attended events: as the Rev. Eliphalet Adams observed in 1738, "When the Day of Execution comes, then, Multitudes, Multitudes flock together." Four or five thousand people gathered for the execution of Esther Rodgers; and five thousand for the last execution sermon delivered for murderer James Morgan.[6]

As the hour of execution drew near, the condemned criminal was led from prison to gallows in a solemn procession, sometimes wearing the halter with which he or she was shortly to be hanged. On the way, the murderer was accompanied by clergymen who continued their task, begun months earlier with the judicial conviction of the felon, of examining the spiritual state of this soul on the brink of eternity. Once the small party had mounted the gallows, a clergyman or the condemned criminal would read the confession, to which the prisoner might add some final remarks: Esther Rodgers addressed the crowd from the ladder just before receiving the halter around her neck; Katherine Garret, a Pequot Indian servant convicted of infanticide, died with her hands upraised in prayer. Final prayers were offered by the clergy and sometimes by the prisoner, and at last, the executioner proceeded with the hanging. Beginning in the 1670s, clergymen and printers collaborated to produce published texts of the sermons preached for condemned murderers, sometimes accompanied by the criminals' conversion narratives, confessions, last words, and conversations with their clerical advisers. As Cotton Mather didactically observed, "One sayes well, That *Sermons Preached,* are like Showres [sic] of *Rain,* that Water for the Instant; But *Sermons Printed,* are like *Snow* that lies longer on the Earth."[7]

In form, the execution sermon was much like any other: opening with a biblical text, it went on to propound a doctrine based on that text, subdivide that doctrine into a number of discrete propositions, and set forth the applications and uses of those propositions by the congregation. The formal presentation of God's Word by the clergy was deemed crucial to every significant event in the life of New England communities, including election days, militia musters, fast days appointed in response to special judgments of God, and thanksgivings called to acknowledge special blessings, as well as public executions. As the only regular means of public communication in colonial New England, the sermon was a powerful force in shaping that culture's values and sense of corporate purpose for a century and a half. In the hierarchical system that characterized early American culture, public ceremonies (such as executions) assumed considerable importance for transmitting information down to the common people, in a face-to-face communal setting that reinforced the social deference of listener to speaker.[8] But as printed texts, too, execution sermons wielded great authority in a highly literate early New England culture, in which reading and piety were inseparable. Sacred texts were often read aloud, and even silent reading was intensive—close, repetitious, reverential—a practice which tended to invest the written word with the authority of divine truth that clerical authors intended. Lay men and women in early New England generally "respected what the clergy wrote, preferring 'godly' books to any other kinds of reading matter."[9]

In keeping with the new view of the crime that had emerged in the early modern period, the clergy pronounced that "Murder is an exceeding great Sin," "a Sin of a very hainous [sic] and heavy guilt."[10] Execution sermons spelled out in some detail the grounds for their emphatic condemnation of the crime. They generally began by exploring biblical law on murder, pointing to the prominent position of the commandment "Thou shalt not kill" at the head of the second table of Mosaic law, and citing a wide range of texts calling for the execution of convicted murderers. But they went on to observe that murder is "against the Law of man, as well as against the Law of God: All Nations that have any thing of Civility among them, do abhor the crime." Indeed, murder was so contrary to "the Light of

Nature" that "the very Heathen" regarded it as "great and heinous."[11] New England execution sermons voiced the English view of murder as a sin that "defiles the Land, where it is committed." But this view took on even stronger significance in the Holy Commonwealth: as Increase Mather sadly observed, even though "no convicted Murderer did ever escape the stroke of Justice in this Land (which is a matter of rejoycing), yet it is a very sad thing, that any in such a place as this should be found guilty of such a Crime."[12] In the Holy Commonwealth, murder represented a dramatic eruption of evil in a society deeply committed to doing battle with sin.[13]

But if the crime of murder tended to evoke statements of shock and outrage in New England execution sermons, the murderer himself generally did not; execution sermons drew a clear distinction between the sin and the sinner. No matter how terrible the crime, New England clergymen believed that its underlying cause was the same as that of every other sin known to postlapsarian humanity: innate and total depravity. "The Venemous Hearts of Men," Cotton Mather explained in 1713, "have in them the Root, which all *Murders* grow upon."[14] New England clergymen before 1750 overwhelmingly embraced the doctrine of original sin set forth in the Westminster Confession of Faith and its constituent Larger and Shorter Catechisms. According to this "federal" or "covenant" doctrine of the Fall, God had made a covenant of works with Adam, offering the first man life in return for perfect obedience. But when Adam and Eve disobeyed God, they "fell from their original righteousness and communion with God, and so became dead in sin, and wholly defiled in all the faculties and parts of soul and body," and all of their descendants fell with them into a sinful estate consisting in "the guilt of Adam's first sin, the want of original righteousness, and the corruption of his whole nature, which is commonly called original sin; together with all actual transgressions which proceed from it."[15] As John Rogers explained, "Every Child of *Adam* is born a Leper, all over defiled, from the Crown of the Head to the sole of the Foot." The source of murder, as of all human wickedness, was "that *Original Sin*, which the hearts of all men are by nature full of, and is a fountain that is always sending forth its bitter streams."[16]

Because the doctrine of original sin provided a universal explanation of the roots of murder, there was little need to pay attention to
what later generations would call "motive." Instead, execution sermons explored the patterns of sinful conduct that paved the way to
murder. The act was merely the culmination of a long course of
sinfulness whose prevailing pattern was that "Little Sins make way
for greater" down a slippery slope leading to "a great Transgression."
In this fashion, for example, a young woman might move from "*little*
Follies" to "solitary Filthiness" to "secret *Fornications*" to "secret *Murders.*"[17] Many execution sermons offered catalogues of the lesser sins
that could lead to murder, such as "your pride, your disobedience to
your Parents, your impatience of Family Government, your company
keeping, your Whoredoms, and your despising of Christ." Even such
a sin as habitually saying, "I'll be hang'd if a thing be not thus or so,"
could pave the road to murder; and convicted murderer James Morgan was said to have "murdered many a man with his bloody tongue,
before he was left of God to murther any with his hand." Execution
sermons often dwelled at greater length on the "besetting sin" leading to murder than on the final crime of violence: as Cotton Mather
explained to an infanticide in 1693, "Your *sin* has been *Uncleanness;*
Repeated *Uncleanness,* Impudent *Uncleanness,* Murderous *Uncleanness.*" In Mather's treatment, the crime for which this woman was
about to die—killing her newborn twins—was secondary to those
sexual activities which he insisted had set her irreversibly down the
road to murder.[18]

The effect of the execution sermon's treatment of criminal causality was to establish a strong moral identification between the assembled congregation and the condemned murderer. For the doctrine
that the root of the crime was innate depravity undercut any notion
of the murderer's moral peculiarity, with all humankind bound in
that original sin committed by the first parents of the race. In the
presence of condemned infanticide Rebekah Chamblit in 1733, the
Rev. Thomas Foxcroft intoned, "The sorrowful Spectacle before us
should make us all reflect most seriously on *our own* vile Nature;
which the Falls of others are but a Comment upon: and should excite
us to humble ourselves under a sense of the Corruption of *our Hearts,*

{14}

which are naturally as bad as the worst." The only difference between the condemned murderer and the rest of humanity was "the restraining grace of God, to whose Name alone belongs the Praise, that any of us have been with-held from the grossest and most horrid Acts of Wickedness."[19]

Not only were all women and men equally burdened by that original sin which was the root cause of murder; all were guilty as well of committing those besetting sins which could lead ineluctably to that worst of crimes. The moral kinship of the larger community with the condemned murderer was strengthened by the execution sermon's emphasis on the progressiveness of sin, for what unchaste woman could deny that her course might lead to infanticide? What drunken man, what disobedient servant could be certain that he had not placed his foot on the road to murder? Under a New Testament understanding of the law, furthermore, the sixth commandment could be broken quietly in the private heart of the sinner as well as publicly in the flesh: as the Rev. John Williams said, "I would fain have charity, that there is but one in this Assembly, that hath been guilty of Murder in the highest degree of it; yet I fear there are several that have Murdered in their hearts, and some who have been guilty of interpretative Murder." The category of "interpretative murder" covered a multitude of sins, including sexual uncleanness, drunkenness, anger, hatred: "And if he that hateth his Brother, be a Murderer," according to the Rev. Samuel Moody in 1726, "how many Murderers be there that go about our Streets, and joyn in the publick Worship." How many, indeed. According to Cotton Mather, even husbands who spoke harshly to their wives were guilty of murder.[20] No one, it appeared, was innocent of the crime.

Significantly, this moral identification of ordinary sinners with condemned criminals was a feature of religious discourse more generally. The Rev. Thomas Shepard once likened sinners to criminals awaiting execution on the scaffold: "Thou art condemned, and the muffler is before thine eyes, God knowes how soon the ladder may bee turned, thou hangest but by one rotten twined thread of thy life over the flames of hell every houre." Samuel Sewall, for one, took this lesson to heart, reporting in his diary that he fell asleep one night and dreamed "a very sad Dream that held me a great while. As I remember, I was condemn'd and to be executed." For devout New Englanders, the moral predicament of the condemned murderer was essentially indistinguishable from that of the rest of sinful humanity.[21]

The moral and spiritual parity of ordinary sinners and the convicted murderer was encouraged in execution sermons through the clergy's careful delineation of how the audience was supposed to feel when confronting an exemplary sinner. Repeated references to "the sorrowful object before us" and the "unhappy Malefactor" invited hearers and readers to respond to the murderer with a compassionate fellow-feeling bordering on the modern psychological concept of empathy. "With the tenderest Bowels of Compassion, and the deepest Concern of Soul," said William Shurtleff in 1740, "I would apply myself to the poor Prisoner, whose Miserable Case has occasion'd this vast and numerous Assembly." Compassion, not hatred or contempt, was the appropriate response to the condemned murderer: "None of us all have any reason to despise you, in your present deplorable Circumstances . . . Your Case might have been my Case or the Case of any other person here, if the Sovereign Lord of all had so pleased." As Esther Rodgers's pastor warned his readers, "he must needs want Faith for himself, that wants Charity for such an one" as that unhappy baby killer. A lack of Christian love for the murderer, far from being a stamp of righteousness, showed a failure of Christian faith, suggesting the damnation not of the condemned criminal but of the spectator at the scaffold.[22]

To dwell on the specific act of physical violence that had brought this felon to the scaffold, rather than on the innate depravity and the small or "besetting" sins that all men and women shared with the murderer, was to risk generating a sense of revulsion and moral superiority among the audience. Most execution sermons proffered only limited accounts of the crimes for which their subjects were about to suffer the extreme penalty of death. Some never referred directly to the murder: preaching before infanticide Rebekah Chamblit, Thomas Foxcroft alluded to her crime only by saying that "Pride has tempted many a young Woman to destroy the Fruit of her own

{16}

Body, that she might avoid the Scandal of a spurious Child." Other sermons offered strikingly brief tales of murder, sometimes comprising a single sentence: "A Man whose Name was Jeremiah Fenwick, was upon a Fair Trial brought in GUILTY of having Murdered his Neighbour with an Axe, which he took up, and Employed a repeted [sic] Blow thereof, at the Person at whom his Anger was Enraged."[23] The murder of their master by Nicholas Feavour and Robert Driver was summarized in one sentence, following which the next five paragraphs explored the sinful course of pride, idleness, and disobedience to parents that had led to the murder.[24] Because murder was an exceptional sin, while pride, idleness, and disobedience were frequent, a sermon on the dangers of the lesser sins could work greater spiritual effects among a sinful congregation than any undue attention to the terrible details of the "great Transgression."

More detailed stories were offered by convicted murderers themselves, such as Rebekah Chamblit's "Declaration, Dying Warnings and Advice," or Patience Boston's *Faithful Narrative*. Even in these accounts, however, primary attention was paid not to the crime itself but to the course of sinfulness that had preceded it and the religious conversion that followed.[25] Occasionally, an exceptionally shocking murder seemed to mandate more details, such as when pirates refused to grant a sea captain's request for a little time to prepare his soul before they killed him, or when the black man Joseph dispatched his wife with an axe followed by a razor (intended to make her death appear a suicide).[26] But even these accounts lack the intense concentration on the nature of the violence and the dense social and physical contexts of the crime familiar to later murder stories. What was the sequence of events leading up to the crime in the days and hours preceding it, and what thoughts, words, or actions had immediately triggered the violence? No precise descriptions were offered in early New England criminal literature, no dramatic reenactments of the struggle, no dying words of the victim. Sometimes, as in the case of Joseph, the weapons were cited, but execution sermons avoided characterizing the wounds inflicted or the state of the corpse.

Execution sermons employed a common rhetorical device to obvi-

{17}

ate any undesirable attention to the social and physical realities of murder: they expressly redirected readers' attention from "the blood of Abel"—the murder victim—to the "blood of sprinkling"—Christ the Savior. "'Tis true, the innocent Blood cries from the Ground for Vengeance," said Mather Byles in his execution sermon for a black servant who had poisoned an infant, "But yet, the Blood of Sprinkling speaketh better Things than the Blood of *Abel*, and this lifts up a prevailing cry for Pardon & Forgiveness for you." Theologically, Byles was urging his listeners to turn from thoughts of vengeance to thoughts of salvation. At the same time, he was inviting them to transcend any worldly interest in the nature of the violence and replace it with a concern for eternal matters. Execution sermons ran red with the blood of the crucified Christ, not that of murder victims: "Now humbly betake your self to the blood of sprinkling; come to the fountain opened, to be washed in; there is enough in the blood of Christ for your pardon and healing."[27] What was offered here was pardon and healing—for the condemned criminal as well as for the entire New England community.

By emphasizing that the fundamental cause of murder was universal depravity and its course the slippery slope of common sinfulness, by arguing that all of sinful humanity was guilty of murder under a rigorous application of God's law, by summoning the sympathy of pious listeners/readers for the condemned murderer, and by granting only minimal attention to the violent act that threatened to place the murderer in a separate category of sinners, the execution sermon identified the spiritual predicament of the condemned criminal with that of the larger community. New England clergymen set forth this understanding of the murderer's status within a clear religious purpose: to put the salvation drama of the murderer in the service of the community's own salvation. The congregation—all innately depraved sinners, according to early New England belief—stood to learn from the repentant criminal something about the power of divine grace.

Shaped by the combined efforts of legal and religious authorities, then by editorial hands, the lives of most condemned murderers in early New England were represented as models of religious conversion. The criminals' pilgrimage in grace began with the court's pronouncement of sentence, which prescribed a set period before execution as "a space to repent," "commonly a Month at least" but often longer: Katherine Garret was granted almost six months before execution, and Esther Rodgers was given eight.[28] During that period, the prisoner received visits from ministers and other pious persons, sometimes daily, for instruction, spiritual direction, scriptural reading, and prayer. Condemned murderers were also permitted to attend Sabbath meetings and lecture days in order to participate in the ordinances of Christ, and hear prayers and sermons explicitly directed to their own circumstances. With some justification did the Rev. Foxcroft proclaim, "It may be there is no Place in the World, where such Pains are taken with condemn'd Criminals to prepare them for their Death; that *in the Destruction of the Flesh, the Spirit may be saved in the Day of the Lord Jesus.*" The prisoner was expected to be grateful for this "precious Season of Grace" and for the divine Providence that had arrested him in his course of sin to grant him that season.[29]

The condemned murderer's "Season of Grace" provided the presiding minister with plenty of material by which to track and report on the criminal's spiritual progress right down to the moment of execution. Printed execution sermons sometimes included separate accounts concerning the prisoner's conduct between sentencing and execution, or transcripts of conversations that had taken place between the minister and the condemned murderer in prison or on the way to the gallows. The Rev. William Shurtleff's *The Faith and Prayer of a Dying Malefactor* (1740), for example, was accompanied by "A Brief NARRATIVE Concerning the CRIMINALS" (Sarah Simpson and Penelope Kenny), which reported that their behavior offered grounds for hope in their salvation. John Rogers's extensive account of Esther Rodgers's execution offered a transcript of the close spiritual questioning to which she was subjected on the morning of her execution, including such queries as, *"Whether, when her Coffin was brought in, it did not daunt her?"* On the way to the gallows, the prisoner was asked where she placed her hopes that she was about to die in Christ, and when she briefly faltered in her steps was quickly asked, how she was doing now? It was with a note of relief as well as triumph that the clergyman finally reported that Esther Rodgers met her death with a "Composure of Spirit, Cheerfulness of Countenance, pleasantness of Speech, and a sort of Complaisantness in Carriage towards the Ministers who were assistant to her," and thus gave all present reason to trust in her salvation.[30]

New England clergymen generally shied away from flatly announcing that any sinner was clearly and unequivocally among God's elect. But under their doctrine of the Atonement, a repentant murderer enjoyed the same access to free grace as any other sinner. "Tho' no Murderer hath eternal Life abiding in him, yet they, that have Grace given them to Repent of their Murders, with Unfeigned Repentance, will have their Souls cleared from the guilt of their Murders by the Righteousness of Christ, and so shall be blessed with Life Eternal." When ordinary New Englanders heard their clergymen assuring murderers that "there is Life to be had for such an one as *thou* art; yea even for *thee* there is Life," they experienced renewed hope that they too might be saved.[31]

During these final months and especially moments of their lives, exemplary criminals played an active role in dramatizing their prospects of salvation for the benefit of a large audience. "*I* James Morgan, *being Condemned to die, must needs own to the glory of God, that he is Righteous, and that I have by my Sins provoked him to destroy me before my time,*" confessed that murderer in 1686. Such confessions and dying warnings, usually read publicly at the last Sabbath before the execution or at the gallows on the day of execution, were a central part of execution ritual. "I heartily mourn for all the Sins of my Life; and above all for the Fountain of all Sins, which I have in an Heart that is desperately wicked. I most particularly confess and bewail my Blood-Guiltiness," said Jeremiah Fenwick in 1717, thus proclaiming penitence not just for the murder of his neighbor, but for all the sins he had ever committed, and above all for the intrinsic depravity of his original nature that was the source of all his evil deeds. Clerical coaching and even spiritual bribery clearly helped shape such exemplary confessions, as when the Rev. Samuel Moody unabashedly told Joseph Quasson that "God might yet do more for

{20}

him" if he gave his own account of his sinful ways to the world in a written confession.[32] But given the power of shame in Puritan culture—the extreme sensitivity to the opinions of others that shaped the lives of early New Englanders—such confessions reflected the convicted sinner's desire to be restored, in the role of repentant sinner, to membership in the larger community before his death.[33]

The printed confessions of condemned murderers were meant to serve as models for the rest of the sinful New England community to emulate. The repentant murderer willingly offered herself as a cautionary example for others to heed: as the Rev. Thomas Foxcroft said of Rebekah Chamblit, "It appear'd to me one of the best Symptoms upon this poor Criminal, that she seem'd desirous her Example might be a Warning to others." Many condemned murderers took the hint and explicitly directed their audience to contemplate their own miserable example of a life gone bad. In "The Last Speech of Hugh Stone," the condemned wife-killer said, "O thou that takest no care to lead thy life civilly and honestly, and then Committest that Abominable Sin of *Murder*, here is this *Murderer*, look upon him; and . . . take example by *me*." Significantly, Stone's major warning did not concern the extraordinary sin of murder; it was directed at the lesser sin of his habitually saying, when provoked by a companion, "I will kill him." Most dying speeches echoed execution sermons in focusing on the more common sins that prepared the way to murder. Some elaborated on a particular sin such as drunkenness, while others ran the gamut from Sabbath-breaking to keeping bad company—thus reminding listeners and readers that their own mundane sins might also be paving the road to murder. It was the hope of the clergyman who helped to orchestrate such confessions that the assembled congregation would "hearken to the solemn Warnings that have been frequently given, by Condemned Criminals, at the Time and Place of their Execution."[34]

In the end, the murderer's offense against society was recast into a service: the killer was to serve not just as an example of the vileness of sin, but as a dramatic public demonstration of the redemption of an exemplary sinner. Esther Rodgers's model conversion made her, in John Rogers's apt metaphor, "*a* Pillar of Salt *Transformed into a*

Monument of Free Grace." The execution sermon was a major expression of the jeremiad, the predominant literary form of the late seventeenth and early eighteenth century, which lamented declension in the Holy Commonwealth and exhorted the people of New England to restore their special relationship with God by returning to moral righteousness and spiritual awakening.[35] The jeremiad often directly addressed particular social groups whose sinful habits were regularly deplored: young people notorious for disobedience, lust, and neglect of God's ordinances; servants deplored for disobedience and their besetting sin of night-walking; Indians charged with drunkenness; blacks with savagery; and sailors infamous for cursing, drinking, and whore-mongering.[36] As Thomas Foxcroft wrote in his *Lessons of Caution to Young Sinners,* "You have now in your hands a very serious and pathetical SERMON, preach'd on a solemn & awful Occasion, which it is wish'd and hop'd may, by the Efficacy of the Spirit of Grace, prove a Means of Awakening, of Restraint, and of Conversion to many of you."[37]

This central religious purpose shaped early New England execution ritual along lines different from those of Michel Foucault's influential model for understanding public executions in early modern Europe. In this view, public execution was a ceremony designed to "inscribe" the power of the state on the suffering body of the individual, and thus publicize the advisability of obedience. The "spectacle of suffering," which was enjoying its classic age in the seventeenth and most of the eighteenth century, served to underline the power of rulers at a time when the state's authority was not fully consolidated and bureaucratized, and its powers of physical coercion were relatively weak. The role of condemned criminals within this "theater of punishment" was to acknowledge the enormity of their crimes and the justice of their punishment, thus testifying publicly to the authority of the power which had brought them to the scaffold. And the role of gathered crowds was to be deeply impressed with the state's displayed power over life and limb, and to respond with an appropriate degree of fear and awe (though crowds did not always behave as the authorities wished, occasionally displaying an unseemly sympathy with the plight of the condemned criminal; at Tyburn, they sometimes threw flowers and kisses to the condemned). The popular literature of broadsides and chapbooks generated by specific executions "constituted an important point of contact between official ideas on law and order and the culture of the masses."[38]

Public executions in early New England clearly did participate in the theatrical nature of early modern punishment. The "Wretched Spectacle" was spatially organized with an eye to visibility: the three thousand people who gathered to witness Joseph Quasson's execution found that the gallows had been set in a valley with hills on either side so they could have "an advantageous Prospect." As a result, "the great Assembly of Spectators, were generally much affected, perhaps almost beyond Example."[39] But how exactly were they affected, and to what ends? True, the power of the state was clearly at work in the system of justice that convicted a felon and put him to death. But the explicit purpose of the spectacle, as expressed in the execution sermons, was the moral and religious edification of the community, not the display of political power. As the Rev. John Rogers announced at Esther Rodgers's execution, *"Reader, This Serves only to draw the Curtain, that thou mayst behold a Tragick Scene, strangely changed into a* Theater of Mercy." In early New England, the "theater of punishment" was actually a "Theater of Mercy," demonstrating the path to salvation for all sinners. Instead of reflecting a distant state and an isolated victim in a drama of monarchical authority before terrified witnesses, the New England execution sermon shaped a more intimate drama of an exemplary sinner standing before compassionate spectators who joined with him in a collective struggle against sin. Whereas sympathy for the condemned criminal was deplored by the powers-that-be at Tyburn as the crowd's defiant challenge to the authority of the state, it was encouraged by New England clergymen as the community's ritual acknowledgment of a shared sinfulness. Of James Morgan's execution in 1686, a visiting London bookseller reported, "I think, during this Mournful Scene, I never saw more serious nor greater Compassion."[40]

In keeping with this purpose, printed execution sermons typically recorded as little about the actual execution as they reported of the murder itself. Some works ended at the moment when the rope was placed around the neck of the condemned; at least one printed sermon concludes with the clergyman's physical departure from the gallows at this dramatic moment, just before the judicial death. When the execution was recorded, it was usually with brevity and indirection: "the Executioner did his Office." Even when one clergyman provided details of the murderer's death, he did so for spiritual purposes: the infanticide Mary Martin had to be "turned off" the death cart twice before she died, by providential direction, since her own first attempt to kill her child had failed.[41] A standard rhetorical device was to redirect readers' attention from the first death, that of the body, to the second death, of the soul: "But verily, There is nothing in the *First Death*, which may be compared unto the *Destructive Miseries* in that *Second Death*. DEATH is the *King of Terrors;* But in comparison of the *Second Death*, it is but a *Shadow of Death*." Clergymen deliberately contrasted the levels of physical pain involved in the two deaths: as one told James Morgan, "You are in danger of being now quickly cast into those exquisite amazing Torments, in comparison of which, the anguishes which your body ever did feel, or shall feel before night, or can ever feel, are just nothing at all."[42] The tortures inflicted by the state upon the criminal's body were expressly not the focus of this execution ritual, but rather the torments of hell that awaited all unrepentant sinners. The transcendent drama of collective sin and redemption took clear precedence over the worldly performance of the power of the state.

The New England execution aimed ritualistically to achieve a reconciliation between the criminal and the community whose most powerful mores he or she had violated. The prisoner's part was to be offered as a moral example for the congregation and to assume a sacrificial role analogous to that of Christ by dying publicly and ignominiously for an act rooted in a sinfulness that was shared by all. The community's part was to acknowledge that they shared in the convicted criminal's moral and spiritual condition, thereby crossing the illusory divide between themselves and the condemned man or woman standing before them on the gallows. In so doing, they symbolically closed the social fissure opened up by the grave crime of murder, "recementing the social bond" both between the criminal and the community, and within the community itself.[43] Having crossed that divide to stand figuratively side-by-side with the criminal at the scaffold, the people affirmed their shared hope that they too might yet be saved.

Public execution was a ritual response to the problem of evil. Execution sermons began by acknowledging the reality of essential human evil, admitting that the crime of murder was heinous, pointing to the total depravity of the murderer, and, most important, asserting the moral identification of the murderer with every other innately sinful member of the New England community. But execution sermons then moved to transcend that evil by putting it to the service of salvation, setting up the murderer as an example not only of deep depravity but of spiritual hope, pointing to her spiritual progress and dying confession as a model for the larger community to emulate, and harnessing both her extraordinary sinfulness and her dramatic demonstration of repentance and spiritual awakening to restore a backsliding New England people to their earlier relationship with God.

The practice of execution proved consistent with the larger pattern of ritual responses to the problem of evil in seventeenth-century New England. Early New Englanders lived in a world they believed to be pervaded with evil, and they devoted much cultural energy to acknowledging and explaining its active presence. This took place on three different levels. First and foremost was the inescapability of moral evil arising from the innate depravity of humankind, polluted with sinfulness since the Fall of Adam and Eve. From this derived the natural evil that had been introduced into the creation by that same Fall: Adam's first sin was "the source of all the disorders and miseries that any part of this lower creation groans under," including death, disease, and such natural disasters as crop failures, plagues, earthquakes, fires and floods.[44] Underlying both the moral evil of humankind and the natural evil of the lower creation was the third and most dangerous form of evil, the supernatural evil worked by God's age-old enemy: "But yet beware of Satans wylye baites/ He lurkes amongs yow, Cunningly hee waites . . ."[45] New England cosmology taught that the ordinary everyday world was the site of an invisible ongoing battle between the forces of darkness and the forces of light. The activities of good and evil spirits, demons and ghosts and witches, were just as real and immediate to these New Englanders as their own houses and fields and livestock.[46]

Early New England culture was thus pervaded with an acute sense of the ever-present danger of evil, regarded not as extrinsic, occasional, accidental, but as intrinsic, endemic, radical, "always present in the flow of daily life."[47] But if Puritan culture promoted an intense awareness of the problem of evil, it also generated a multitude of ritual practices for dealing with it: not to avert it—an impossible task—but to seek safety in the terrible face of it. These included such widely diverse practices as private prayer and ritual humiliation, church discipline and excommunication, the care of the sick and dying, covenant renewal and the communal fast day, the judicial witch trial and the clerical exorcism. And all these practices conformed to the same basic structure as the public execution: first, fully acknowledging the power of evil, usually in the form of a confession of sin, individual or collective; and then, moving to transcend that evil through an act of reconciliation that mended both the breach between the sinner and God and that between the sinner and the community.[48]

At the center of Puritan religious experience was a cyclical movement from conviction of sin to spiritual hope, and back again. The believer's first step toward salvation was a full recognition of his total depravity: as the Rev. Thomas Hooker explained, "It's one thing to say sin is thus and thus, another thing to see it to be such; we must look wis[e]ly and steddily upon our distempers, look sin in the face, and discern it to the full." But this full acknowledgment of sinfulness did not mire the sinner in helpless misery. Rather, it signalled the beginnings of a spiritual journey out of sin toward sanctification and salvation. The central theme of Puritan autobiographical narratives was not a mere cataloguing of sins but a joyful celebration of God's free grace in the face of human depravity, as when Thomas Shepard reported, "When I was on my bed in Monday morning the Lord let me see I was nothing else but a mass of sin and that all I did was very vile, which when my heart was somewhat touched with, immediately

{26}

the Lord revealed himself to me in his fullness of goodness with much sweet affection." This movement was never definitively completed; the cycle from moral misery to the stirrings of grace was cyclically repeated again and again in the lives of hopeful saints.[49]

The same spiritual dynamic of first "looking sin in the face" and then seeking reconciliation with God shaped early New Englanders' ritual response to natural evil. Because sickness and death had been introduced into the world by Adam's Fall, both were regarded as powerful reminders of human depravity and as occasions for the confession and repentance of sin. When Cotton Mather's children fell sick, for example, he reminded them of "the analogous Distempers of their Souls" and instructed them "how to look up unto their great Saviour for the Cure of those Distempers." Natural disasters, ranging from plagues of caterpillars to Indian attacks, prompted a similar response in more communal forms, such as official fast days and rituals of covenant renewal, which lamented the collective sinfulness that had unleashed God's wrath and formally renewed the community's commitment to the godly life and hope in Christ. The captivity narrative, a specialized literary response to Indian warfare, was structured along similar lines: it traced the removal of the white captive—figure of the soul in bondage to sin—by demonic henchmen into the dark chaos of the wilderness, where she is brought to full recognition of the depravity of her own heart, and then finally restored to Christian civilization and hope for salvation.[50] Within the New England theodicy, natural evil served the greater good of salvation; the direct confrontation with evil, both moral and natural, made possible the ultimate transcendence of evil through the sinners' reconciliation with God.

This same ritual structure shaped New Englanders' response to the witches and demoniacs whose activities made visible and immediate the power of supernatural evil. Witchcraft and demonic possession were a critical part of Satan's "horrible plot against the country." But Satan was powerless to launch his terrible assaults without God's permission, which was periodically granted so that the people might be chastised for their waywardness and brought to recognition and repentance of sin—often on specially designated communal

fast days—in service of their salvation.[51] When Elizabeth Knapp of
Groton, Massachusetts, fell victim to demonic possession, the Rev.
Samuel Willard called her "a monument of divine severity," and
invited the townspeople to search their own souls for those sins "that
have given Satan so much footing in this poor place."[52] Willard's call
for repentance reflected the Puritan sense of the risks of "imputing
to the Devil too much of our own sin and guilt"; in the image of
Satan, early New Englanders recognized "a portrait—horrifying in
its familiar pride—of themselves." Despite the Rev. Willard's confusion as to whether Elizabeth Knapp was Satan's innocent victim or
active accomplice, he affirmed that "She is an object of pity, and I
desire that all that hear of her would compassionate her forlorn
state."[53] A similar compassion was summoned for the approximately
fifty people who confessed to entering pacts with the devil at Salem:
most escaped trial altogether, and were received back into the larger
community of sinners for fulfilling its demand to acknowledge their
sinful failings.[54]

Even early New England church-discipline aimed at the ultimate
reconciliation of sinner and community: church members who violated their covenant obligations through such sins as drunkenness,
fornication, theft, or assault were first given every opportunity to
confess and repent and remain members in good standing; those
who refused to confess were formally admonished and temporarily
barred from Communion. Only those who persisted in hardened
indifference were excommunicated, and then less for the initial offense than for their refusal to acknowledge their sinfulness: as the
Rev. Robbins of Plymouth explained, "the *falling into Sin* is just
Cause of Shame—but 'tis *no Shame to Confess it* but a lasting shame
not to confess it." Even then, excommunication was intended to
bring the reprobate to repentance and full restoration to fellowship.[55]

Punishment practices in early New England in general reflected
the goal of social reconciliation, which emphasized "contrition, rec-
lamation, and reintegration." Most criminal punishments consisted
in fines or public whippings, followed by restoration to the community; long-term imprisonment was rare, as was the permanent stig-
matization of branding. Criminals were expected and sometimes

required to offer full confessions of their sins. As one trial witness observed, "The more sensible you are of sin, the more hopes there is of marcy [sic]": contrition publicly and properly performed often resulted in commutation of sentence.[56] Most significant, some offenders were sentenced—not to penitentiaries, the invention of a later generation—but to residence in orderly households where their conduct might be supervised and corrected by the same social discipline that shaped the lives of all. To a striking degree, former offenders were successfully reintegrated into their communities, as evidenced in their common appointment or election to positions ranging from fence or highway surveyor, tythingman, or constable, to town clerk or selectman, church deacon or deputy of the General Court.[57]

This system placed significant limits on the degree to which criminal offenders were stigmatized by their misconduct and the ensuing punishment: when a criminal publicly confessed his transgression and proclaimed his penitence, received his commutation or alternatively paid his fine or endured his lashes, and then went to live in a well-governed household, eventually to be appointed or elected to positions of service and trust, the community received him back in its midst. Even when the offense was capital, the New England execution ritual sought to restore the condemned criminal to symbolic membership in the community before his or her death. When it was reported of Patience Boston that, after her final pious words, "the Executioner did his Office, and the dear Saint I doubt not quietly slept in Jesus," that egregious sinner—an Indian servant who had murdered her master's grandson—was spiritually embraced by the Holy Commonwealth even as she was physically removed from it.[58] The execution sermon invited all New Englanders to look sin in the face—the face of the convicted criminal before them—and see in that face a mirror image of themselves, with their rages and lusts, wayward impulses and vicious inclinations, small sins and great. "There but for God's restraining grace go all of us" was the only spiritually acceptable response to this powerful encounter.

The larger spiritual purposes of the execution sermon distinguish this early American literary form from the later genre of "sensationalism," a popular literature which stimulates emotional excitement as a pleasurable end in itself.[59] Though in some historical sense a predecessor to the popular "thriller," the execution sermon did not seek to arouse terror for its entertainment value. On the contrary, it deliberately avoided dwelling on the blood and gore of the murder, and the suffering and death of the condemned criminal at his execution. Nor did execution sermons constitute a literature of *horror* (in the modern usage of that term), which claims a powerful revulsion from blood, death, and the sudden revelation of evil experienced by those who discover or hear of the crime. Most commonly, the "horror" of execution sermons captured the terrible guilt that overwhelmed murderers themselves once they realized how deeply they had sinned. Nathaniel Clap observed that because murder is "against the Natural Conscience," "it brings horror upon the minds of them, that are guilty of it." Esther Rodgers reported from prison that "All the Sins of my Life came to my Remembrance: I fell into great horrours, and was in great distress & perplexity about my condition." The underlying nature of horror lay in the murderer's anticipation of hell: "the Murderers [sic] Soul is filled with hellish horror of heart; so that he is as it were Damned above ground, and in Hell whilst he is yet alive."[60] Nor was such usage limited to execution sermons: when the ruling elder of the Salem church inadvertently picked up a conjurer's book, when a Roxbury woman died in spiritual despair after the stillbirth of her child, and when a confessing witch admitted to falsely charging two members of her family with witchcraft, all reported their "horror" in terms of their fears of the devil and of everlasting torment.[61]

Not until the late eighteenth century, with the advent of a humanitarian sensibility, did predominant attention turn from the murderer's "horror" in contemplating his own damnation, to the "horror" experienced by the onlookers in contemplating the murderer's crime. The readiness of early New Englanders to imagine themselves bathing in the blood of Christ points to the pre-humanitarian sensibility that shaped the clergy's representations of both the crime of murder and its judicial consequence, public execution. When execution sermons directed readers' and listeners' attention from the blood of

Abel to the blood of Christ, and from the death of the body to that of the soul, they did not do so out of any squeamishness about carnage or delicate sensitivity to pain and suffering. In their world, pain was not only accepted as a feature of life after the Fall, it was embraced as a useful instrument of social discipline, in the corporal punishment of children, servants, and slaves, criminals and mad people—a discipline that was routinely displayed on the public stage of the scaffold, where whippings and executions could be witnessed by all and sundry. Such practices bred a mundane familiarity with blood and pain.

In this world, death itself was a constant, intimate presence. From the fifth through the late eighteenth century, Western death practices promoted a "promiscuity" of the living and the dead: dying involved attendance at the deathbed by large groups of family and friends; corpses were laid out and prepared for the grave by the women of the neighborhood; interment was in burial grounds located at or near the center of the community, which were routinely used for other public purposes; and no one seemed particularly troubled by either the sight of graves or the smell of corpses. A common penal practice was to display the cadavers of executed criminals: dangling from the scaffold, hanging in chains, harnessed upright on the wheel. In keeping with traditional attitudes, early New Englanders buried their dead in churchyards and town commons, and erected tombstones decorated with skeletons and skull-and-crossbone designs, whose epitaphs referred matter-of-factly to moldering dust, worms, and decay. Only with the privatization of death, beginning in the second half of the eighteenth century, did the physical fact of death begin to evoke the revulsion and squeamishness which continues to characterize the modern response to it.[62]

In its treatment of horror as more a spiritual than a secular concern, the central movement of the early New England execution sermon was, once again, one of transcendence. It pushed through the crime itself, past the physical blood of the murder victim to the metaphorical saving blood of Christ, to remove attention from the murderer's past transgression and focus it on the future state of his soul. Similarly, the sermon moved beyond the imminent judicial death of the condemned criminal to express greater fear of his possible "second death," eternal death in hell. The primary purpose of depicting the horrors of hell was to remind both the condemned criminal and the assembled congregation to look to the state of their souls. But the refusal to dwell on the more worldly horrors of the murder was also part of the ritual's larger strategy to effect a moral reconciliation between the condemned criminal and the community.

Early Americans' understanding of human depravity instilled in them a powerful sense of the moral precariousness of all women and men, a conviction that anyone could be struck with criminality at any moment should God momentarily withdraw His sustaining grace and permit people to act upon their universally intrinsic nature. Humankind was not divided into rigid categories of normalcy and deviancy, but strung out along a moral continuum, on which all were equally vulnerable to slippage in the direction of major transgressions such as murder.[63]

As a popular criminal genre, execution sermons had a transcendent purpose: to induce a strong sense of moral and spiritual identification with the condemned criminal, then urge the listener/reader to look beyond the bloody crime to the triumphant conversion of the murderer and follow his spiritual example. This was not a literature of sensationalism in any meaningful historical sense—not an early American variety of thriller, melodrama, or sensationalistic journalism. Such thrill-seeking sensationalism would emerge later, in a modern cultural convention which shifted attention away from the criminal's own internal sense of guilt and fear of hell to the community's powerful sense of revulsion from the crime and its perpetrator.

A HORRID MASSACRE!

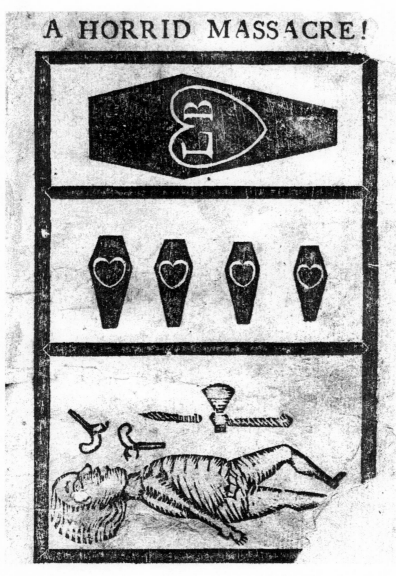

William Beadle's 1783 murder of his wife and four children, followed by his suicide, prompted this stylistic representation of his victims' coffins and his own corpse, with the weapons of his violence floating over it. This is an early example of how the cult of horror redirects readers' attention from the spiritual destiny of the convicted murderer to the crime itself, in all its bloody violence.

Trial & Conviction of
RICHARD JOHNSON,

FOR THE

MURDER
Of Ursula Newman,

On the 20th Nov. 1828, by shooting her with a
pistol loaded with buck shot or slugs,
NINE OF WHICH ENTERED HER BODY;
TOGETHER WITH THE

Charge of the Court,

AND THE

CONFESSION OF THE PRISONER

Of his entention to have added Suicide to the Horrid and Appalling Murder for which he is to suffer an ignomenious
death, and his letter to a friend in Philadelphia previous to his Conviction.

◦◦◦◦◦◦◦◦◦◦◦

NEW-YORK:
PRINTED AND SOLD WHOLESALE AND RETAIL, BY

CHRISTIAN BROWN.
No. 211 WATER-STREET, N. YORK.

Richard Johnson shot his paramour, Ursula Newman, for
rejecting his proposal of marriage, in 1828. In the
nineteenth century, murder illustrations moved beyond
stylized references to the crime to capture the violence in
progress, here indicated by Johnson's smoking pistol.

Thomas Topping beat his wife to death with a
variety of domestic objects—chair, stool, broomstick,
fire tongs—after she refused to fetch a pail of water
at his command. This illustration accompanies a
narrative account that is strikingly specific about the
complex choreography of his fatal assault.

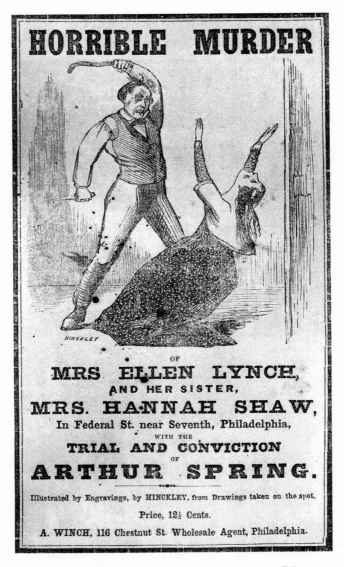

The horror of Arthur Spring's murderous assault on Ellen Lynch is captured in the visual melodrama of his violent, aggressive stance over his helpless victim, and in the monstrous distortion of his facial features.

AN
ACCOUNT
OF THE

APPREHENSION, TRIAL, CONVICTION, AND CONDEMNATION

OF

MANUEL PHILIP GARCIA

AND

JOSE DEMAS GARCIA CASTILLANO,

Who were executed on Friday the 1st of June, 1821, in the rear of
the town of Portsmouth, in Virginia, for a most horrid
murder and butchery, committed on

PETER LAGOARDETTE,

IN THE BOROUGH OF NORFOLK ON THE 20th OF MARCH PRECEDING.

TOGETHER WITH AN

APPENDIX,

CONTAINING THEIR CONFESSIONS, &c.

Norfolk.

PUBLISHED BY C. HALL,

And sold by most of the Booksellers in the United States.

June, 1821.

In the emerging cult of horror, the dismemberment of the
victim's corpse became an important feature of popular
murder literature, as in this graphic illustration on the title
page (1821). Note once again the exaggeratedly sinister faces
of the two "monstrous" murderers in this case.

John Haggerty, who pleaded not guilty on grounds of insanity, axed to death his neighbors, the Fordneys, in an effort to precipitate the Last Judgment. The sensationalism is heightened by the presence of two children: one kneeling on the floor with upraised hands pleading for mercy, the other watching from the open window through which another intended victim is carrying the child to safety.

The pornography of violence. Michael McGarvey beat his wife to death with a leather horsewhip after tying her to the bedpost by her hair. The woman in the doorway, who stands transfixed and watches passively, personifies the reader-as-voyeur, the guilty imaginative spectator to the crime of murder.

"My God, my God! what shall I do? my children: give me back my children," she pleads (in the original caption) with her husband, who is taking them away to live with him and his paramour. The wronged wife later stabs the mistress to death. The heightened emotionalism of this case is captured in this stock scene from theatrical melodrama, with its overcharged language attributed to the woman soon to commit murder.

The public excitement of the crowd gathered at the scene of Arthur Spring's double murder in Philadelphia reflected the more private sensations of the readers, who could vicariously visit the scene of the crime by gazing at illustrations such as this.

The Parkman Murder.

TRIAL

OF

PROF. JOHN W. WEBSTER,

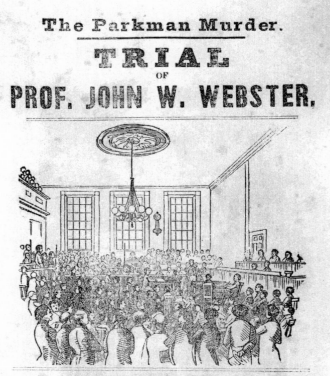

For the Murder of

DR. GEORGE PARKMAN,

November 23, 1849.

Before the Supreme Judicial Court, in the City of Boston.

With Numerous Accurate Illustrations.

BOSTON :

PRINTED AT THE DAILY MAIL OFFICE,

14 & 16 State Street.

Large crowds flocked to the courtrooms when accused murderers stood trial. Readers of murder trial reports—such as this one of Professor John Webster's trial for killing Dr. George Parkman—were implicitly invited by such illustrations to imagine themselves present in court.

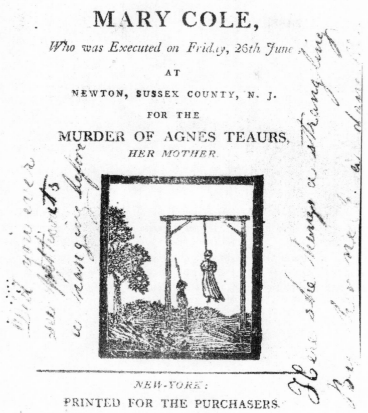

THE

CONFESSION

OF

MARY COLE,

Who was Executed on Friday, 26th June ,

AT

NEWTON, SUSSEX COUNTY, N. J.

FOR THE

MURDER OF AGNES TEAURS,

HER MOTHER.

NEW-YORK:

PRINTED FOR THE PURCHASERS.

The cult of horror focused new attention on the judicial death of
convicted murderers such as Mary Cole, who killed her mother in 1812.
A contemporary reader has scrawled on this title page a prurient and
openly voyeuristic delight in the image of a hanged woman: "Did you
ever see petticoats a hanging before . . . Here she hangs a strangling by
her neck a dangling."

Here is an example of the reader's identification with the murderer. J. R. Moore, who in 1865 signed his copy of the criminal anthology *Confessions, Trials, and Biographical Sketches of the Most Cold Blooded Murderers* (1837), wrote his name and initials repeatedly throughout the book. Here, significantly, he has twice signed the handsome, boyish face of murderer William Teller, characterized admiringly in the text as a criminal "of bold and cunning daring."

Hero-worship of the murderer was not uncommon. This fine lithograph of Richard Robinson, the nineteen-year-old clerk and young-man-about-town who murdered prostitute Helen Jewett in New York City in 1835, portrayed him as good-looking and nattily attired. His supporters wore caps similar to his to the trial, and cheered the jury's verdict of "not guilty."

CHAPTER TWO

The Birth of Horror

B ARNETT DAVENPORT was born in New Milford, Connecticut, in 1760. As a boy, he acquired a reputation for using bad language; put out as a servant at age nine, he began pilfering green corn and watermelons, ran away from his master under pretense of having been abused, and had to be placed with a second master. Early in the Revolutionary War, he enlisted with a Massachusetts regiment and served for three years at Ticonderoga, Valley Forge, and Monmouth before deserting; hired to reenlist, he did so and then deserted again. At the age of nineteen, he went to live with Caleb Mallory, his wife, daughter-in-law, and three grandchildren. Though treated with great kindness, he resolved to kill the entire family and rob the house. From the moment of this decision, he was "haunted and possessed with the thoughts of murder." Davenport decided on the night of February 3, 1780, to carry out "my bloody, land-defiling, soul-ruining, and heaven-daring plan." He waited for the family to retire, made a knapsack to carry his loot, and began plundering the house. He beat to death Caleb Mallory, his wife, and a granddaughter whom he found in their bed, then grabbed some money, donned some of the dying Caleb's clothing, set fire to the house (with the remaining two grandchildren in it), and departed.[1]

In a first-person account of his crimes, published after his execution, Davenport offered dramatic details concerning the precise se-

quence of his violent actions, the weapons used, the wounds inflicted, the "shrieks, cries, and doleful lamentations" of his victims,
and how the scene looked when he was finished. When he began
striking Caleb Mallory with a swingle (a wooden tool for beating
flax), his victim fought back, knocking the candle out of his assailant's hand and asking "who I was? what I meant? and said, tell me
what you do it for?" Caleb called to his wife for help, as she shrieked
and cried out. Davenport pounded Caleb until the swingle split, then
grabbed a gun and used it to batter husband and wife until they were
still. When the seven-year-old girl woke up and began to cry, asking
"what is wrong with grandmother?" Davenport beat her to death.
The room, he reported, was "now besmeared with blood, and filled
with horrendous groans," as he used a pestle to smash open a chest in
search of valuables. But Caleb and his wife revived, and Davenport
"mashed his head all to pieces" with the pestle, and beat her again
until her face was "swoln to twice its common bigness, disfigured
with wounds, and covered with gore and streaming blood." Davenport offered abundant evidence to support his claim that he had
perpetrated "the blackest crimes that ever mortals committed."[2]

A Brief Narrative of the Life and Confession of Barnett Davenport
differed strikingly from the execution sermons for infant-killer Esther Rodgers published some three-quarters of a century earlier.
While the Rodgers sermons had addressed transcendent matters
of salvation—both hers and the larger community's—the Davenport narrative focused on worldly particulars: his biographical background, the social context of his crimes, the precise sequence of
events culminating in the murders, and specific details of time and
place. While the Rodgers confession referred only briefly to the
murder itself, in a flatly matter-of-fact tone, the account of Davenport's crime paid extensive attention to the violence of his assaults,
self-consciously enlisting overblown language to maximize his readers' emotional response: "My heart trembles and is moved out of its
place, at the relation of this most tremendous, cruel, bloody, and
amazing scene." The Rodgers sermons had avoided any suggestion
of the peculiar heinousness of her sins; the Davenport narrative
deliberately emphasized the extraordinary nature of his—"the most

{34}

awful crimes that ever were perpetrated in this land, or perhaps any other."[3]

By 1780, American murderers such as Barnett Davenport were beginning to assume dramatically different moral features from those of an earlier period. Whereas Esther Rodgers had been represented in popular print as an example of a universally depraved humankind, Barnett Davenport depicted himself as set apart from the rest of humanity, perpetrator of the worst crimes in all human history, from whose remorseless savagery readers were expected to shrink with revulsion. Around mid-century, the popular literature of murder in America began a major reconstruction of the murderer, from common sinner into moral alien, in response to the new understanding of human nature provoked by the Enlightenment. To impress upon readers the vast moral gulf separating them from the exceptionally vile transgressor before them, that new murder literature shaped a recognizably modern, Gothic sense of horror. When Barnett Davenport announced that February 3, 1780, was "A night big with uncommon horror," he was not invoking his ancestors' transcendent horror of the sinful conscience anticipating hell, but a worldly horror in the face of pain, carnage, and violent death; this declaration strengthened his claim to matchless evil.[4]

The execution sermon survived through the end of the eighteenth century. When a drunken Moses Paul murdered Moses Cook in 1771, when Abiel Converse committed infanticide in 1788, and when Caleb Adams killed the boy Oliver Woodworth in 1803, the executions of the condemned criminals became the occasion for sermons which largely conformed to the conventions that had prevailed for a century and more. Clergymen continued to urge sympathy for "the poor Malefactor," pointedly observing, "He that is to suffer this day, is not the only one in this assembly under the sentence of death," for "all have sinned."[5]

But in the second half of the century, the popularity of the sermon came under challenge from a number of alternative literary forms. Descriptive narratives of murders, such as *Account of a Horrid Murder*,

Committed by Captain William Corran (1794) began to appear, and were sometimes anthologized in collections like *The American Bloody Register* (1784).[6] Some writers cast their accounts in poetic form, in such works as *A Poem on the Execution of Samuel Frost,* convicted of the murder of his master Elisha Allen, or *A Tribute to the Memory of Catherine Berrenger,* believed to have been poisoned by John Benner, her betrothed.[7] Increasingly popular was the first-person account, such as *A Narrative of the Life of John Lewis,* who murdered his wife in 1760, and *An Authentic and Particular Account of the Life of Francis Burdett Personel,* who murdered Robert White in 1773.[8] Among the new types of murder narratives, the one that achieved cultural dominance was the printed report of the murder trial, such as *The Trial of Alice Clifton, for the Murder of her Bastard-child* (1787). Though only a few trial accounts were printed in America before 1750, by the end of the century they were being published in numbers comparable to execution sermons. And in the first decades of the nineteenth century, their volume swelled, swamping all other forms of narrative and demonstrating the historical triumph of the legal discourse of murder over the theological.[9]

A dramatic expansion in the world of print facilitated the proliferation of new murder accounts. In the late eighteenth and early nineteenth centuries, the number of book titles expanded, the average size of print editions swelled, and new print centers sprang up to meet a growing popular demand. The sharp rise in elementary literacy prompted John Adams to boast that "a native American who cannot read and write is as rare as a comet or an earthquake." Bookstores became a common feature of the commercial landscape, and their inventories grew over time, especially after book prices fell in the early nineteenth century. Subscription libraries, which had first appeared in the 1760s, doubled in number in the last decade of the century; social libraries emerged; and individual family libraries grew larger. Expanding transportation and communication networks carried books, pamphlets, broadsides, and newspapers to even the most remote areas of the rural hinterland. And among the most popular categories of print available were books on death, violence, and crime.[10]

{36}

The expansion in the world of print transformed the nature and significance of reading as a cultural practice. Traditional reading, shaped by print scarcity, had been *intensive* in nature, involving a slow, deliberate, and respectful reading and rereading of just a few books, notably the Bible, a practice that charged the printed word with a sacred character. New readers, by contrast, read *extensively*, moving quickly through a wide range of available books, seeking amusement more than edification, and regarding a text as a commodity that could be casually taken up, discarded, and replaced by the next, in a restless quest for the "latest intelligence."[11] The reading revolution contributed to the desacralization of the printed word, as the rapid consumption of many books decreased the significance of any one in particular, and as the practice of reading aloud gradually yielded to silent reading by individuals, which invited personal responses to the printed word. These changes dissipated the sacred aura that had surrounded The Book in traditional societies. Secular works—with their attention to newness and change—were dominant by the 1790s, while sacred works—with their relatively stable concern with the wisdom of the ages—were significantly outnumbered.[12]

The new murder narratives were overwhelmingly secular works, written by a diverse array of printers, hack writers, sentimental poets, lawyers, and even murderers themselves, who were displacing the clergy as the dominant interpreters of the crime. Ministers were losing their cultural monopoly over the popular literature of murder at a time when their larger professional authority was in serious decline. In 1740, the clergy had composed 70 percent of all learned professionals in the colonies, and expressed the leading ideas of their culture through one of its most influential rituals, the sermon. But in the half century that followed, the clerical sphere of influence steadily narrowed under the combined impact of religious disestablishment, vigorous denominational competition, and growing competition for cultural authority from other professional groups. By 1800, the clergy had been reduced to only 45 percent of learned professionals. John Trumbull's poem, *The Progress of Dulness*, showed how far the profession had sunk by 1773, with its spoof of the

Reverend Tom Brainless, whose ministry "does little good, and little harm."[13]

As the clergy's cultural authority diminished, so too did that of the sacred masterplot they had crafted to explain the crime of murder. The new tales of murder practiced what novelist Samuel Richardson called the "new species of writing" that was revolutionizing English literature by mid-century—a form of storytelling that shaped not only the novel but poems, plays, history, autobiography, journalism, political pamphlets, religious treatises, and legal discourse. This species of writing, which literary critics (with varying degrees of enthusiasm) have labelled *realism*, reflected not merely an innovative literary style but "an entire paradigm of knowing."[14] Realist narrative aimed at the representation of "real life," the day-to-day activities of ordinary persons. It was "densely particularized," committed to details. Realism showed a special interest in private life, peering through the keyhole into the proliferating private spaces of eighteenth-century life.[15] Stories were organized into carefully sequenced representations of human events in worldly time; plot—"the intelligible whole that governs a succession of events in any story"— emerged from the implicit causality at work in the temporal unfolding of events.[16] Realist plot was moved not by the universal human nature of the depraved Everyman, but by unique, idiosyncratic individuals whose distinct identities were themselves understood to have been shaped, in Hume's formulation, as a "chain of causes and effects."[17]

Between 1750 and 1820, nonfictional murder literature grew steadily more realistic in its detailed attention to the events leading up to a murder. *The Life of John Lewis,* for example, described a day in the life of his household—offering scenes of his very pregnant wife fetching water from the spring to wash clothing at her tub, himself making a plow, their sharing the mid-day meal, his invitation to her to lie down with him on the bed after dinner—before detailing how he strangled her to death on their bed. The new murder accounts abounded with information about private lives which helped explain the crime. Readers learned that the slave Alice Clifton's married lover had promised to buy her and make her as fine a lady as his wife;

that Mary Cole's mother had shared a bed with Mary and her
husband, Cornelius, for the first year of their marriage; that John
Banks's wife, Margaret, was a poor cook who served her husband
pot-liquor when he asked for coffee.[18]

Observing that murders "are often committed in secret—sometimes in dark and gloomy recesses," the new tales of murder invited
readers to peer into those secret spaces, such as the bedchamber of
the Caleb Mallorys. Some accounts offered the story of what a
concealed witness saw, such as the neighbor who watched from her
yard John Graham's habitual battering of his wife, Phoebe, in the
bedchamber of their home, in the months before he finally beat her
to death.[19] One murder narrative literally provided a "keyhole" view
of the crime: thirteen-year-old Anne Messenger, on her way to buy
licorice at Sarah Cross's shop in Philadelphia, found the door locked
and looked through the keyhole to see John Joyce murdering the
shopkeeper. Others offered more than a keyhole, opening windows
onto whole worlds of complex social and personal relations. When
the black servant, William Hardy, was accused of killing his infant
child by Elizabeth Valpy, a white servant in the same household, trial
witnesses included the respectable master of the two servants, the
Salem selectman who had known Elizabeth during her stay in that
town's poorhouse, and the disreputable Irishwoman in whose "disorderly" house Elizabeth had given birth. This murder trial report
ushered the reader into a world of masters and servants, respectable
houses and poorhouses and houses of assignation, illicit sex, attempted abortion, and finally murder. Its social density was a new
feature in American murder literature, as it was a growing feature of
American life.[20]

The new murder literature carefully presented the sequence and
causes of events in worldly time. James Johnson invited his friends to
a party where all got drunk; guest Lewis Robinson danced with his
host's wife and stepped on her toes; she challenged her husband's
manhood for allowing Robinson to insult her; Johnson stabbed his
guest to death. Captain Edward Tinker initially protected his ap-
prentice crewman Edward from the ill use of others at sea; but when
Tinker scuttled a ship for the insurance money and Edward refused

to take an oath denying his master's criminal action, Tinker killed him. In August 1805, James Purrinton moved his family to Augusta, Maine, and worked contentedly and hard on his new farm for nearly a year; but a serious drought depressed him, he grew anxious about his family's welfare, and on July 9, 1806, between two and three in the morning, he slaughtered his pregnant wife, seven of their eight children, and himself.[21] This designation of the precise date and hour of the crime—unknown to the execution sermon—gradually became a commonplace of the new literature. Locating the crime in worldly time demanded a degree of precision previously considered unnecessary.

Above all, the new murder accounts evinced a great interest in the narrative act of defining the individual person by his or her distinguishing characteristics and tracing personal development over time. Readers learned that James Purrinton was an affectionate man and obliging neighbor, easily elated or depressed by the vicissitudes of economic fortune, a man "of the middle size, rather dark complexion, grave countenance, and reserved in company," who "never looked the person in the face he was addressing." Ebenezer Mason had an "odd disposition," never laughed, and showed no attachment to the female sex; Thomas Starr had been a promising, bookish, and well-mannered youth who excelled in music and psalmody, before he sank into intemperance and debauchery.[22] Two newly popular forms of literature, the autobiography and the epistolary narrative, were enlisted to enhance the subjective, introspective treatment of the murderer's personal traits.[23]

Some murder accounts offered close explorations of the murderer's biographical background. Born in Ireland, Francis Burdett Personel had attended school for eight years and was then apprenticed to a trade, eventually becoming a master and working for a time in England. When his father died, his mother summoned him home, and in the face of her steady dissatisfaction with everything he did, Personel turned to drink and the company of sinful women. He went to America for eighteen months, until financial distress drove him home. But when his mother chose a woman to be his wife, Personel returned to America, entering indentured service in Maryland to pay for his passage. Eighteen months later, he ran away, to work as a schoolmaster in Virginia, where he was converted by Baptist New Lights. Suspected of being a runaway, he took a horse from the widow he had planned to marry and ran away again, to New York, where he married a prostitute. One night, learning that she was in the company of two men, he decided to demonstrate to his neighbors "that I was an honest man, and innocent of her doings" by assaulting and killing one of her clients. While awaiting execution for murder, Personel again turned to Christ, and delivered a righteous diatribe against all society's sinners, especially those "daughters of hell," the prostitutes of New York. His conversion notwithstanding, Personel was one of a new breed of worldly criminals, and his account focused more on his picaresque experiences in this world than on his hopes for the next.[24] These late eighteenth-century and early nineteenth-century murderers, unlike their early American predecessors, emerged from such biographical narratives as unique criminal personalities with distinctive life histories.

In replacing the declining cultural power of the sacred masterplot, the secular accounts tried to assign meaning to the crime of murder by treating each case as an extraordinary event, a peculiar episode demanding a unique explanation. The execution sermon had offered a simple and universally applicable answer to the question of causality, but the ideas about human nature that were at the core of the Enlightenment took a toll on orthodox Christian views of human sinfulness, and popular murder literature was being significantly reshaped as a result.

Enlightenment thinkers on both sides of the Atlantic were applying the basic assumptions of the Scientific Revolution to the study of human nature, with particular attention to the moral life. John Locke's view of the mind as *tabula rasa*, a blank slate on which external impressions are inscribed by experience, struck the first serious blow to the doctrine of innate depravity, and generated a sustained interest in the influence of environment on character development.[25] Scottish moral philosophers reaffirmed Locke's view that men and women were not born inherently evil, but argued that humankind was endowed at birth with a moral sense, analogous to the five senses. Though the moral sense required proper nurture and instruction, human nature was endowed with an instinctive love of virtue, a matter not of reason but of innate feelings or "sentiments." Morality was thus conceived as not only natural but pleasurable. Eighteenth-century American philosophers and educators were attracted to the new moral philosophy of the Scottish school, and traditional Calvinism began to look "cold and lifeless"[26] by comparison. At mid-century, opponents of the Great Awakening moved easily into the Enlightenment camp, sermonizing on "The Absurdity and Blasphemy of Depretiating Moral Virtue."[27] Even the followers of revivalist Jonathan Edwards placed increasing emphasis on human freedom and abilities at the expense of God's total sovereignty. God's purpose was coming to be seen as the happiness of humanity.[28]

This fundamental shift in eighteenth-century views of human nature had a pronounced impact on popular murder literature. As one attorney put it, man "has the lamp of reason and conscience lighted in his heart, by which he distinguishes between *good* and *evil*"; and human nature, far from being hopelessly depraved, is marked by dignity, nobility, benevolence, compassion, and even an inward "divinity,"[29] wrote another. Though the late execution sermons, and some of the new narratives as well, continued to invoke intrinsic human evil as the ultimate cause of the crime, popular murder literature began to cast about for explanations more in keeping with a rational understanding of human nature. Life-histories of criminals offered environmental explanations of the murderer's actions. "The Confession of Winslow Russell" blamed his criminal conduct on parental indulgence, charging that his parents did not make him attend school. Seventeen-year-old Cato told a tale of abandonment by African parents, who purchased their own freedom from slavery and left him behind to follow an ungoverned course, culminating in his murder of Mary Akins. Mary Cole reported that her mother had refused her the breast when she was two months old, leaving Mary's father to place the infant with her grandmother until she could eat solid food; Mary endured her mother's cruelty for twenty-three years, and finally murdered her. Caleb Adams was said to have been damaged in mind and body while still *in utero,* when his father installed his mistress and her child in the Adams home.[30] The new life histories explained the causes of murder to a generation increasingly more inclined to the view of human nature espoused by John Locke than to that preached by John Calvin.

Enlightenment ideas focused attention on *motive.* What idea or purpose had prompted this action by the murderer, a creature of presumed reason and volition? Initially, this concern was addressed in a general way: John Lewis killed his wife out of sexual jealousy; Bathsheba Spooner hired men to kill her husband because her marriage was not agreeable to her.[31] But in the first decade of the nineteenth century, as printed trial reports came to dominate the literary response to murder, the term "motive" came into common use. "No crime ever was committed without some motive," argued the defense attorney for Captain Edward Tinker. In 1807, when accused wife-killer Alpheus Hitchcock's defense argued that he had no motive to murder "his bosom companion," the prosecution proved that he had transferred his affections to another woman. Though motive alone did not prove guilt, "we shall the more readily believe it, when we see some strong motive to the commission of the act."[32] In the sacred masterplot of the execution sermon, "motive" was rendered unnecessary by the conviction that all acts of murder sprang from the same source, innate depravity. The enlightened view of human nature as essentially free, reasonable, and inclined to virtue demanded inquiry into a murderer's motive.

In the late eighteenth century, the most frequent explanation for acts of murder was uncontrolled passion. Within Enlightenment moral philosophy, the driving force of human affairs was the emotions, which were divided into "sentiments" (source of virtue) and "passions" (enemies to reason and moral self-government). Many a murderer was said to have been driven to the crime by uncontrolled passion "whether of envy, malice, or revenge," a "tempest of the soul" which drowned out "the voice of reason" in a man, leaving him with "a thirst, which nothing but blood can satiate." The Negro youth Bristol killed out of "cruel Rage and Passion"; the pirate Joseph Andrews killed when "governed by the furious Impulses of his disorderly Passions"; twelve-year-old Hannah Ocuish killed because she had been left "to the uncontrouled [sic] influence of the direful passions, malice and revenge." As one historically minded defense attorney explained, human passions had replaced demonic intervention to explain the causes of crime: since "the Arch Fiend has ceased to walk abroad in his infernal majesty for the purpose of instigating mankind to the commission of crimes, his diabolical purposes are, in *these days,* accompanied by the agency of his fell missionaries, the passions of man."[33]

From 1750 to 1820, American murder literature commonly cited three interrelated factors—environmental influences on character, the motive to murder, and ungoverned passions—in an effort to explain the causes of murder for an increasingly secular age. But none of these factors, whether cited singly or combined, proved as intellectually satisfying as the earlier invocation of innate depravity. Readers learned that John Joyce had been born in slavery in Maryland, served in the U.S. Navy, married and had two children in wedlock and two outside, divorced his unfaithful wife, worked at a variety of jobs, and sold his horse eighteen months before he killed shopkeeper Sarah Cross. All of this testified to an unstable life, but did not add up to an explanation of his sudden urge to murder. Accounts pointing to the murderer's excellent upbringing suggested that his crime could not be explained by environment alone. Thomas Starr had been a promising, well-mannered youth with a taste for books and music, but unspecified ungentlemanly conduct had cost him the love of his intended wife, and he had turned to intemperance, debauchery, and finally murder. Some men were surprise murderers, who showed few advance signs of the danger they posed to their fellow beings. When Abel Clemmens killed his wife and eight children in 1805, one observer reported, "what is very remarkable he had always lived with them in a most affectionate manner."[34]

Just as the environmentalist explanation of murder sometimes failed, so too did efforts to identify the murder motive. Some "motives" were patently inadequate, as when Stephen Arnold brutally beat to death his six-year-old niece Betsey Van Amburgh because she could or would not pronounce properly the word "gig" (it came

{44}

out at the trial that Arnold, a teacher, did not tell her how to pronounce the word until he had whipped her the seventh and final time). Barnett Davenport admitted to readers that he beat to death Caleb Mallory's family "without the least provocation, or prejudice against any of them." Some murderers killed out of unexplainable compulsion: Henry Halbert confessed that he had murdered his randomly chosen victim because "I began to be tired of my Life and I was determined to kill some body." The apparent purposelessness of such murders was dramatized in reports of the victim's last words. "Lord, John, what did you do that for," Sarah Cross asked her killer, who had decided first to murder her, and only as an afterthought to rob her shop. To readers he reported only that "I felt tempted to commit the act."[35]

Some of the era's most notorious criminals murdered dispassionately, on the basis of carefully reasoned theological error (the Deist disbelief in future punishment). "Where have we read of such deliberate and dispassionate murder!" exclaimed the Rev. James Dana of the William Beadle familicide. "Murder upon principle! . . . What violence to reason!—to all the tenderest ties in life!—to humanity itself!"[36] In the second half of the eighteenth century, the "cold-blooded killer" became a common fixture in American murder literature. The three "hard-hearted" men hired by Bathsheba Spooner killed her husband "in cool blood," after patiently awaiting the "opportunity to put their bloody design in execution." "Nor was Pharoah's heart harder than mine," was Barnett Davenport's confessed state while he was beating to death the Mallory family. "To an heart not past all feeling what could have been more shocking!" than the sight and sounds of his victims, "But how unmoved was I, who now set myself to searching for the money of the dead."[37] The hard-hearted murderer of the new accounts committed the crime out of "a cool deliberate wickedness of thought," with a "heart obdurate to all the feelings of nature," and remained an "unfeeling fiend," "insensible" of wrong-doing after the deed was done.[38]

The new crime narrative focused on a question that had not been necessary within the sacred masterplot: what went wrong? Within the Enlightenment world view, murder was caused by some combination of environmental influence, motive, and uncontrolled passion. Yet a significant number of murder narratives printed between 1750 and 1820 demonstrated the inadequacy of all these attempts to explain the crime, as some men and women murdered against character, or from an inexplicable compulsion to kill, or in cold-blooded insensibility. These crimes challenged the prevailing rational view of human nature, with its attention to character as a developmental product of environmental influences, its emphasis on the powers of human reason, and its reliance on sentiment, the inner moral sense, as the ultimate guarantor of virtue.

Printed accounts of such inexplicable murders in the late eighteenth and early nineteenth centuries were narratives of incomprehension, whose common pattern was to try *and fail* to come to terms with the crime within the contemporary liberal view of human nature. Many narrators simply characterized the murderer as monster, a terrible aberration from normal human nature. "What a monster of a man was this!" was the Rev. John Marsh's reaction to William Beadle's slaughter of his wife, four children, and himself. John Battus, who raped and murdered a young girl, actually applied this characterization to himself, writing to the victim's parents from his prison cell, "I am fearful you will not have hearts to forgive such a wretched creature, such a monster as I have been."[39] The term sometimes connoted physical ugliness, characterizing the murderer as "a hideous ugly looking monster" in hell; or invoked actual physical deformity, such as the distinctive facial features and physical movements of Caleb Adams. Courtroom lawyers occasionally approached the "monstrosity" of the murderer through the popular science of physiognomy, which affirmed that character was written into the facial features; Edward Tinker's prosecutor pointed to his countenance and observed, "On it, in strong and burning characters are portrayed, I AM NOT CAIN; YET AM I TINKER THE MURDERER!"[40]

For the earlier clerical interpreters of the crime, it had been sufficient to acknowledge that the murderer had acted upon his intrinsic nature of total depravity.[41] But late eighteenth-century narrators had to make a different kind of sense of the murderer, as someone who had dramatically deviated from a nature conceived as inherently good and self-governing. As Cambridge Platonist Benjamin Which-cote explained, "Nothing is more certainly true than that all Vice is unnatural and contrary to the nature of Man . . . A depraved and vicious Mind is as really the Sickness and *Deformity* thereof, as any foul and loathsome disease is to the body."[42] Evil was not natural; it represented a monstrous distortion of our intended nature. The guilt of Captain Tinker was represented as a "shocking deformity"—his crime was said to "blur the face of Nature"—because his conduct placed him outside human nature. The new murderer could only be understood as "inhuman," a "fiendlike *foe* to man."[43]

This delineation of the murderer paralleled the treatment of the villain in the popular Gothic fiction that was sweeping the Anglo-American book market at that period. Gothic fiction was closely related to sentimental literature, which aimed at arousing readers' feelings in order to refine them, to nurture the moral sense by arousing sympathy. While sentimental fiction explored the benevolence of "human nature," Gothic fiction focused on the place of evil within it, treating wickedness as a warped distortion of humankind's original goodness. The villainous Manfred in *The Castle of Otranto* (1764) and Ambrosio in *The Monk* (1795) were examples of such distortions. Their "monstrosity" was more metaphorical than real. Other Gothic works more literally employed the sentimental aesthetics of Adam Smith, who decreed that virtue was physically lovely and evil was monstrous, twisted, ugly. Mary Shelley's monster is the best-known example of such physical laws. But American Gothic writers contributed many similarly misshapen villains: Charles Brockden Brown's Carwin, George Lippard's Devil-Bug, Edgar Allan Poe's Hop-frog, and Nathaniel Hawthorne's Chillingworth.

In seventeenth-century New England, monstrosity had been a manifestation of the "world of wonders," an awe-inspiring reminder of God's providential power.[44] But in the late eighteenth century, Gothic fiction made monstrosity "the outward show of the terrible inner distortion of man's innate good nature into evil." The Gothic novel's treatment of the villain pointed toward the emergence of the nineteenth-century understanding of evil as psychological monstrosity, an unhealthy aberration from the natural mind.[45] The image of

Gothic fiction [margin annotation]

the murderer as monster expressed the incomprehensibility of murder within the rational Enlightenment social order. In effect, this Gothic emphasis on the monstrosity of the evil-doer served to protect the secular faith in human reason by treating profound evil as an unnatural perversion. The moral monstrosity attributed to the murderer effectively placed him beyond the pale of normal humanity.

Such was the narrative treatment of Samuel Frost, who was executed in 1793 for killing his master, Captain Elisha Allen, by beating him to death with a hoe while Allen was setting out cabbage plants. As a boy, Frost had killed his own father (by beating his brains out with a handspike), in retaliation for the victim's abuse of Samuel's mother, but had been acquitted for that crime on grounds of mental incapacity. Frost's own *Confession and Dying Words* offered abundant material for an environmental explanation of his crimes. His mother had died, he thought from his father's abuse, when he was fourteen years old; he had then lived in a succession of families until he arrived at Captain Allen's, where he was treated like a slave; he had repeatedly run away, and been flogged for it every time; and finally he decided to kill his master (in a manner chillingly reminiscent of his murder of his father).

Significantly, the "Account of Samuel Frost," which accompanied this first-person narrative on the same broadside, did not seize the opportunity to cite Frost's difficult upbringing as the cause of his crimes. The anonymous narrator chose rather to emphasize that Frost's "mind was evidently not formed altogether like those of other persons." Frost "thought it no great crime to kill such as he supposed treated him very ill—and did not appear to have a just conception of the heinous crime of Murder." He "had a most savage heart which nothing could meliorate, and would talk with the same calmness and composure of the horrid Murders he had committed, as though the persons who fell a sacrifice to his fury, had been of the brutal creation." He was "savage—void of all the finer feelings of the soul, and destitute of the tender affections of filial love and gratitude." The narrator concluded, "He appears to have been a being cast in a different mould from those of mankind in general, and to be the

connecting grade between the human and brutal creation." Samuel
Frost was a moral alien, set apart from the run of humankind by his
inexplicable moral otherness.[46] !!! moral alien

This new stance towards the condemned criminal was enforced by
the Gothic cult of horror that was beginning to shape popular murder literature. Popular usage of the term "horror" began to turn
attention away from the murderer's anticipation of damnation and
eternal torment, and toward the emotional response prompted by a
confrontation with the crime. As the Rev. Charles Chauncy wrote in
1754, "It is indeed a Crime that is *shocking* to the human Mind, unless
when abandoned to all Sense of what is right and fit," a crime "so
associated with *Dread* and *Horror,* that we should tremble at the
Thought of committing it." "There is something so unnatural, so
awful, so shocking to the mind, so grating and painful to all the
feelings of the human soul, in deliberate murder," echoed the Rev.
Nathan Fiske in his response to the Spooner murder.[47] Not God's
law but "the feelings of the human soul" were now the standard by
which the gravity of the crime was to be judged. After 1750, the view
that "a deed so monstrous" as murder "cannot fail to excite in every
human bosom" the powerful emotional response of "horror" was
repeatedly elaborated.[48]

As the concept of horror moved into a secular world of meaning,
printed murder accounts became oriented to the "horror" at work
in specific crimes. "The bloody Murder of Miss Elizabeth McKin-
stry," an appendix to an execution sermon, recounted in graphic detail how the Negro youth Bristol struck his victim with a flatiron,
then knocked her into the fire where her face was burned, and
finally dragged her downstairs to finish her off with an axe. The
author observed pointedly, "One cannot call to Mind the particular
Circumstances of this tragic Scene, without the deepest Emotions
of Horror." Bathsheba Spooner's murder-by-hire of her husband
Joshua prompted the claim that this was the most horrible crime in
American history: "So premeditated, so aggravated, so horrid a mur-

der was never perpetrated in *America,* and is almost without a parallel in the known world." Such superlatives quickly became a standard formula in American murder literature.[49]

The competitive claim to "the most horrible murder ever committed" shifted cultural attention from the exemplary sinner to "the most shocking, inhuman and unnatural"[50] murderer ever. Whereas execution sermons focused on murders that best illustrated various "besetting sins" such as drunkenness, unchastity, or neglect of religion, narrators now were being drawn to crimes with the greatest shock value. Domestic murders, in particular, claimed attention within the literature. In works such as *A Narrative of the Life of John Lewis* (1762), the murderer himself referred to the strangling of his pregnant wife on their conjugal bed as a "horrid and devilish Jobb." But not all of the most shocking murders were domestic: accounts of twelve-year-old Hannah Ocuish's murder of six-year-old Eunice Bolles, Henry Halbert's random murder of the Woolman boy, and Jason Fairbanks's killing of his sweetheart, Eliza Fales, after she rejected his romantic suit, represented these murders as crimes so abominable as to defy any sympathetic identification by the reader with the convicted killer.[51]

Horrifying murder narratives exhibited intense interest in the nature of the criminal violence, a concern almost wholly absent from earlier execution sermons. Late eighteenth-century literature was filled with close descriptions of weapons, wounds and bruises, the site of the carnage, the nature of the assault, and the last words of the victim. Descriptions of the crime scene—the deck of the *American Eagle* after pirates murdered shipmaster William Little in 1797, the inn room where Samuel Mayo and William Love killed lodger David Whittemore in 1807, the hat shop where James Anthony murdered Joseph Green in 1814—extensively documented the victim's blood on floors, clothes, bedsheets, weapons.[52] At one murder scene, a bloody head mark was discovered on the ceiling; at another, "the distinct impression of a bloody hand" was found over the fireplace.[53] Graphic language was enlisted to heighten readers' horror: the murderer "imbrued" his hands in the blood of his victim, acting

{50}

the part of a "butcher"; his weapon was "bath'd all o'er with reaking gore!" and he himself was "wet with blood."[54]

Full descriptions of the "shockingly mangled" body of the murder victim became increasingly common. The body of Joseph Porter, murdered by Captain William Corran on board the brig *Falmoth* in 1794, was described as having "large gashes about the hips, above a foot long and three or four inches deep, one ear totally cut off, the nose almost cut through, the right eye forced out of the socket and hanging down the cheek suspended by a bloody membrane; the arms had upwards of twenty wounds from one to three inches deep: the sheet was very bloody, and much clotted blood on the cabin floor."[55] More clinically but no less graphically, printed murder trials opened with indictments that closely described the violence done to the victim, elaborated upon in the medical testimony at the trial: Alice Clifton inflicted a wound four inches long and one inch deep on the throat of her infant daughter; Susanna not only cut the throat of her new-born son, but broke his jaw with her hands and nearly cut his tongue off close to the root. Whereas early American execution sermons had explicitly directed attention away from the blood of the murder to the blood of Christ, the new horror accounts centered directly on the "mangled remains" of the murder victim.[56]

The first full-blown horror account in American murder literature appeared in 1783. William Beadle had been born in Essex, England, some fifty-two years before the events of December 1782 plunged him into infamy. He moved first to Barbados, then to the mainland colonies in 1762, eventually settling in Wethersfield, Connecticut, where for a time he made a good living as a shopkeeper. But during the Revolutionary War, Beadle's acceptance of Continental currency plunged him into economic distress, which he proudly tried to conceal from his neighbors behind a facade of prosperity. He began to while away his idle time by reading works of rational theology, which weakened his belief in hell. He decided that the best way out of his difficulties would be to kill his entire family—his thirty-two-year-old wife Lydia and their four children, ages six to twelve—and then take his own life, thus sending his family united into a happier state.

In the gray of the morning on December 10, 1782, he awakened the maid, who shared a room with the children, told her that Mrs. Beadle was ill, and sent her off with a letter for the physician. When she was gone, he carried out the murders and suicide as planned.

The printed response to the Beadle murders was swift and extensive, and the story's shifting emphasis over time provides a case study in the transformation of the sacred literature of murder into secular narrative. Two of the earliest printed responses to the murders were sermons, both published in 1783: James Dana's *Men's Sins Not Chargeable on God, But on Themselves* essentially took the place of the execution sermon which had been denied to the community by Beadle's suicide; while John Marsh's *The Great Sin and Danger of Striving with God* was the funeral sermon for Lydia Beadle and her children. But appended to Marsh's sermon was the secular narrative that would quickly eclipse both these works in popular appeal: "A Letter, from a Gentleman in *Wethersfield* to his Friend, containing a Narrative of the Life of William Beadle, (so far as it is known) and the Particulars of the Massacre of himself and Family," written by Stephen Mix Mitchell, who was almost certainly one of the first to discover the crime.[57] This work was also published separately in 1783 under the title *A Narrative of the Life of William Beadle*, which added a significant adjective to its subtitle, offering "the Particulars of the *'horrid* Massacre.'"[58] While the Beadle *Narrative* went through several reprintings, neither of the sermons on the case was ever reprinted in full.

The *Narrative* focused on the peculiar horror of the Beadle familicide. Its cover illustration, headed "A HORRID MASSACRE," consisted of three pictorial frames vertically stacked: at the top was a large coffin adorned with a black heart (Lydia), in the middle were four small coffins with black hearts (the children), and at the bottom was a supine body with a hatchet, knife, and two pistols floating above it (Beadle himself)—all iconographic references to the specific murders at hand. Mitchell also staked out a competitive claim for the special horror of the Beadle murders, saying, "'Tis doubtful whether any history of modern times can afford an instance of similar barbarity, even in the extreme distress of war." He related in detail how

Beadle had struck each of his victims with an axe, then slit their throats with a carving knife. He described the almost ritualistic positions of the victims' bodies: Lydia and her son had been laid with their heads hanging over the side of their beds, "as if to prevent the bedding from being besmeared with blood," and Lydia's face had been covered with a handkerchief; the three daughters had been removed from their beds and "laid on the floor side by side, like three lambs, before their throats were cut," and then had been covered with a blanket. He noted that the front stairway of the house was "marked with blood from the steps of the perpetrator of the dreadful acts." And he described the corpse of Beadle himself, who had finally seated himself in the kitchen, with the axe and the carving knife at his side, then placed two pistols in his ears and pulled the triggers, blowing his brains onto the walls and wainscoting of the room.[59]

The *Narrative* paid close and explicit attention to the emotional impact of the crime scene on those who came to view it. It focused less on the sequence of actions taken by Beadle than on the step-by-step discovery of the murders by those who first entered the house, and on their horrified responses. The revised work's new section, "A true account of the situation of the house on the morning after the dreadful catastrophe," expanded the earlier treatment of the discovery from four sentences to seven or eight pages, offering a closer treatment of the emotional responses of the first people on the scene. The editorial alterations in the successive reprintings of the Beadle murder narrative offer dramatic evidence of the rapid growth of the cult of horror in the last decades of the eighteenth century.

The discovery of the murder began when the family physician read the letter brought to him by the Beadles' maid, which notified him of Beadle's "dreadful purpose." Asking "Esquire Mitchell" to accompany him, the doctor returned with the maid to the house. The two gentlemen (with either an excess of delicacy or a want of courage) sent the maid into the house first. She, "with trembling limbs," went upstairs and opened the door to the children's chamber. Upon seeing the contents of the room, "her horror was so great that she fainted and fell down stairs backward"; the doctor caught her in his arms and she "recovered her senses; but horror stopped her utterance." Mitchell excused himself from further exploration, going outside to lean against the garden fence. The doctor then tried to persuade two nearby workmen to go "see what the dreadful spectacle could be," but they agreed only to follow him upstairs. "Surely a more distressing sight never agonized the human feelings than now presented itself to their view: the floor was swimming with blood." The three men next went to Mrs. Beadle's room; another corpse was discovered and described in grisly detail. Finally, they descended to the kitchen and confronted the sixth and final corpse. "Such a tragical scene filled every mind with the deepest distress; nature recoiled and was on the rack with distorting passions": the emphasis was on the power of murder to assault the feelings of those forced to confront it.[60]

"Nature recoiled" from William Beadle because his own "nature" was unnatural. "What a monster of a man was this!" A central purpose of the Beadle *Narrative,* as of the sermons preached around these murders, was to try to explain why Beadle had done what he did: the biographical treatment accorded him clearly pointed to the effects of economic difficulties and theological errors on his state of mind. With his business in trouble, he had turned to heretical works which led him to believe that all worldly actions were predetermined and therefore right; that a man's killing his entire family was no different from "a man's destroying a nest of wasps," and that both were "as much directed by the hand of heaven as the making this whole world was—And if this is the case there is no such thing as sin."[61]

But despite such attempts at explanation, the narrators of Beadle's crime could not overcome their profound sense of shock at the slaughter. "That a person, favoured with Christian light and liberty, who appeared to be an affectionate husband, and a tender fond parent, should, with deliberation and in cool blood, massacre an amiable wife, and four lovely and promising children, and then take away his own life, is an event so extraordinary, surprizing, and unheard of, that we can scarcely believe it a reality."[62] William Beadle was a surprise killer, an affectionate husband and fond parent who suddenly, and virtually without warning, massacred his entire family. No amount of biographical or theological explanation, this account implied, could reason away the ultimately unexplicable nature of Beadle's actions.

The corpse-discovery scene so prominent in the Beadle *Narrative* was becoming central to murder accounts, and they began to open with such a discovery. "On the 21st of July, 1786, at about 10 o'clock in the morning," the appendix to an execution sermon began, "the body of the murdered child was found in the public road leading from *New-London* to *Norwich*, lying on its face near to a wall." Similarly, the story of the Mary Cole matricide opened with the announcement that "The most shocking, inhuman and unnatural murder has lately been discovered near this place," and went on to relate how the body of Agnes Teaurs had been found, skull fractured and throat cut, buried beneath the floor boards of the murderer's house. The emphasis of such treatments was on the horror evoked by the discovery of the corpse: it was "with horror of soul" that searchers removed Marcus Lyon's murdered body from the Chicopee River.[63] It was calculated to induce a horror-stricken response in the reader that would replicate that of the crime's discoverers. Such a response involved a numbing of the sensory faculties. The corpse of Sarah Cross was said to "petrify with horror" those who gazed upon it. A violent murder "freezes the mind with horror." When the soul is filled with horror, "its active and reasoning powers are for a moment suspended"; its "faculties" are "benumbed and petrified."[64] This understanding of horror was consistent with that set forth by English Gothic novelist Ann Radcliffe, who distinguished between terror, which expands the soul and opens the faculties in a state of apprehension of an unknown threat, and horror, which contracts the soul and freezes the faculties in response to a direct confrontation with what is repellently evil.[65] Within Lockean psychology, horror involved a shutting down of those sensory faculties through which experience impinged upon the mind to become knowledge. In the face of what was overwhelmingly, repugnantly evil, the Enlightenment liberal mind refused to accept the evidence of the senses, in an act tantamount to moral denial.

A major part of this shutting down of the faculties in horror was speechlessness. The response of the Beadles' maid to the revelation of domestic massacre proved prototypical: "her horror and affright was [sic] so great that she fainted," and even when she regained consciousness, "horror stopped her utterance."[66] The failure of language in the face of horror quickly became one of the most pervasive conventions of the new murder literature. "No words can describe the horrors of my situation," reported one survivor of a murderous piracy in 1800. When the first outsider arrived at the scene of the Purrinton familicide, "a scene was presented which defies the powers of language, and beggars all description." At the Fairbanks trial, the Attorney General referred to the scene of the murder as "an image from whence the eye turns with horror, and of which language refuses a description." The narrator of the murder of Marcus Lyon in 1806 tried to convey his own speechlessness with creative punctuation: "I—now—proceed—but—language fails me—terms cannot paint this doleful tragedy," he wrote, early in the account.[67]

To be petrified with horror was to experience a shutting down of the sensory faculties and mental powers that would ordinarily process the sensory impressions passing through those faculties; to be rendered speechless in the face of horror was to lose the capacity to articulate a coherent response based on such ordinary mental processing. The convention of speechlessness indicated an inability to assign meaning to the transgression. To be suddenly deprived of all language by the sight of a dead body was to be rendered incapable of rationally coming to terms with it. Horror was about the essential meaninglessness of evil within an Enlightenment world view committed to the basic goodness of humankind.

Even as horror pointed to the intellectual failings of the liberal response to murder, it shaped a well-defined emotional response to the crime. "Human nature recoils with horror" in the face of murder; "the bare mention" of the crime, admitted one defense attorney, "carries terror to the honest mind, and necessarily excites some degree of abhorrence and detestation, towards that being, who is suspected of imbruing his hands in the blood of a fellow-creature."[68] The earlier encouragement of moral identification with the murderer began quietly to disappear. In his execution sermon for William Shaw in 1771, the Rev. Moses Baldwin charged the condemned murderer with intemperance, swearing, quarreling, and domestic abuse; but instead of extending the moral lesson to all listeners, he called upon the magistrates to suppress vice, and the masters of public houses not to serve vicious men, implying that Shaw's besetting sins were not shared by the entire community but practiced by a vicious subgroup. Charles Chauncy reassured his congregation that he had no "Apprehension, as tho' there was any one here present, upon whom this *inhuman Crime* could be justly fastened . . . I would rather hope, the Idea of this Sin, is, in all our Minds, so associated with *Dread* and *Horror,* that we shold tremble at the Thought of committing it."[69] In Chauncy's treatment, horror was a mechanism for emphasizing the distance between the murderous and the morally normal.

By the end of the century, the cult of horror was replacing an earlier, sympathetic view of the condemned criminal as moral exemplum with a view of the murderer as moral alien. The new model sinner did not claim to exemplify a sinful humanity, but instead acknowledged his nature as a deviant, and even played up his monstrosity for the benefit of his reading public. Such a sinner was John Battus, the indentured servant who in 1804 raped and then murdered thirteen-year-old Salome Talbott. *The Confession of John Battus, A Mulatto* offered a highly melodramatic account of Battus's crimes, the tone of which was calculated to maximize the reader's moral horror. Out of a "worse than brutal lust," Battus had assaulted a "lovely and blooming damsel" and "disrobed her of that virgin purity, which is the flower and pride of her sex!" Then, "blind to the ruins of beauty!" and "deaf to the plaints of innocence and humanity!" he beat her with a stone, threw her into a pond, and struck her with a rail until she sank. His was a "barbarity, unknown among savages or beasts"; he was "a monster" who had committed "the most horrid crimes ever done in this christian country"; he was "too disgusting and dangerous to intermix with civilized society!" Battus's editor agreed, observing that his execution was lamentable but necessary "to rid the world of a monster, too overgrown in iniquity, too pestilential to society, to live in it."[70]

By inducing horror in the reader, the Gothic account of murder managed to arouse the proper feelings assigned to normality in the face of moral monstrosity. The literature presented a new relationship to the criminal, in which "nature recoils" from an evil that was defined as unnatural, alien, nonhuman. The emotional instructions conveyed were to shrink from the murderer with revulsion. John Battus's close description of his murderous assault on Salome Talbott was not gratuitous: it was intended to demonstrate his monstrosity, and to evoke from readers the proper response of "I am normal/moral, you are abnormal/evil." The cult of horror contributed to a general hardening of social lines between "normality" and "abnormality" which was locking such social types as criminals, mad persons, and homosexuals into closed categories of deviancy.[71]

Over the course of the eighteenth century, a view of instinctive human virtue arising from the moral sense was joined by a new view of the natural world, which took the place of the orthodox Christian view that nature had "fallen" with Adam and Eve. The American Enlightenment affirmed that the universe was an orderly, purposeful, and intelligible world regulated by natural law—not a coldly mechanical system that ran largely by itself, as some European skeptics would have it, but a moral order governed by a benevolent God, whose existence and works might best be understood through a study of Nature as the truest Scripture. This understanding of the natural world in turn transformed the understanding of the supernatural, regarded by early New Englanders as the site of an ongoing battle between God and the prince of darkness. Eighteenth-century rationalism gradually relegated belief in demons and witches to a medieval superstition. "The devil, like an old actor whose declamatory style has become comic, was losing his audience." By 1780, New England Arminians were beginning to deny the existence of hell, and even the Rev. Joseph Bellamy, heir to the revivalistic tradition of Jonathan Edwards, was explaining that the ultimate ratio of the saved to the damned would be at least 17,000 souls to one.[72]

The implications of this reorientation to the problem of evil were worked out by Benjamin Franklin, who reasoned that if God is both omnipotent and benevolent, then evil is logically impossible: "If He is all-powerful, there can be nothing either existing or acting in the Universe against or without His Consent; and what He consents to must be good, because He is good; therefore Evil doth not exist."[73] Such an extreme theodicy did not, of course, represent the beliefs of most Americans, but it did indicate the direction of eighteenth-century ideas about the problem of evil. Those ideas were undermining the earlier conviction of the reality and presence of evil, and thus contributing to the decline of the whole array of rituals enlisted by early Americans to combat the problem. Public confession, church discipline, covenant renewal, fasting, and witchcraft accusations gradually lost cultural power over the course of the eighteenth century. Into the vacuum left by these practices flowed the cult of horror. The liberal response to the crime was to assert that human evil was not radical but extrinsic, alien, a monstrous distortion of normal human nature, and then to invite individual readers to experience the horror of it. Through this private emotional experience of horror, isolated readers did not transcend the evil, but rather were mired down in it, immobilized and speechless in their alienation and disgust, without even the possibility of assigning meaning to it.

Modern Gothic horror was the characteristic response to evil in a culture that provided no systematic intellectual explanation for the problem. The Gothic view of evil at work in the cult of horror was not an irrational reaction against an excess of Enlightenment rationalism, but an indispensable corollary to it, which ultimately served to protect the liberal view of human nature. The prevailing concept of human nature as basically good, free, and self-governed in the light of an innate moral sense, was protected from the potential threat of major transgressions by the imaginative creation of a monstrous moral alien, separated from the rest of humankind by an impassable gulf. And the key to the monstrosity of the Gothic murderer was his willingness to visit "unspeakable" pain and ultimately death on his victims.

Gothic murder as monster

CHAPTER THREE

The Pornography of Violence

O N THE night of April 6, 1830, eighty-two-year-old Captain
Joseph White, a wealthy and respectable citizen of Salem,
Massachusetts, was murdered in his bed. "The annals of history and
fiction furnish nothing—which for its cold-blooded and deliberate
atrocity can be compared" with this crime, reported one chronicler.
The assailant climbed into White's mansion through an unbarred
window, crept up the stairs to his chamber, struck him one blow in
the head with a wood bludgeon loaded with lead, then stabbed him
thirteen times with a dirk. That an "aged and respectable citizen,
living in the centre of this populous town, so long remarkable for its
tranquility, peace and order" could be murdered in his sleep "produced uncommon excitement" in the community. A committee of
vigilance was formed to track down the killer, and their efforts led
to the arrest of Joseph Jenkins Knapp, Jr., husband of the victim's
grandniece, along with his brother, John Francis Knapp, and Richard
and George Crowninshield. In an effort to inherit the old man's
money, Joseph had offered his brother $1,000 to kill White, and John
Francis had subcontracted the job to the Crowninshield brothers.
Dick Crowninshield apparently did the killing, and subsequently
hanged himself in custody. The state engaged Daniel Webster to
help try the remaining defendants, and his eloquence secured the

convictions of both Knapps, who were executed for their part in the crime (George Crowninshield was acquitted).[1]

Daniel Webster's closing speech at the two trials of John Francis Knapp was called by one contemporary "the greatest ever delivered to an American jury."[2] In it, Webster invoked astonishment that "in this age so enlightened, and in this country so civilized, in the midst of society so refined, and in a family so respectable," there could have been someone willing to plan murder for money. "There was no burst of passion in the perpetrator to soften the atrocity of the deed; all was done calculatingly, calmly, coolly and skillfully." Yet despite the atrocity of the crime, and the "universal alarm" it sent "through every fibre of the community," Webster regretfully reported a popular "morbid interest in the fate of the bold, daring and resolute perpetrators." The "very horridness of the crime rendered it attractive. The monster presented to us, was rendered beautiful by its superlative ugliness." Webster attributed this strange "admiration" in part to the dangerous influence of popular crime writer Edward Bulwer-Lytton, "whose genius had endowed vice with attraction." But at a deeper level, he faulted the peculiar workings of the human mind: "So strangely was the mind of man constructed, that pleasure could be gathered from the elements of pain, and beauty seen in the Gorgon head of horror."[3]

Webster's formulation of this paradox captured an increasingly powerful feature of popular murder literature after 1800: its deliberate use of pain and horror to generate readers' *pleasure*, the peculiar "dreadful pleasure" of imaginatively viewing terrible scenes of violent death. According to Dick Crowninshield's biographer, "every thing connected with this horrid transaction is read with avidity," an assertion borne out in the dozen different publications on the case.[4] Nineteenth-century readers of popular murder literature avidly sought pleasure in pain, and beauty in horror. Why they did so eluded Webster's attempt at a timelessly psychological explanation, for this response to murder was strikingly absent from early American execution sermons. Whereas the execution sermon had been a morally legitimate popular literature, controlled by the clergy and

{61}

aimed at readers' salvation, the murder narratives of the expanding nineteenth-century print culture were borderline-illicit literary productions, catering to their readers' questionable pleasure in vicarious violence.

What explains the historical emergence of the "dreadful pleasure" of reading horror? How did repellent descriptions of violence, suffering, and death—such as Webster's own close account of the bludgeoning and stabbing to death of Joseph White—come to exercise such a powerful hold over readers in the first half of the nineteenth century? And why was this form of reading entertainment so laden with guilt, as reflected in Webster's lament for the public's "morbid interest" in the crime and its perpetrator? The answers to these questions lie in a revolution in sensibility we may call humanitarian, which in shaping dramatically new responses to pain and death gave rise to a pornography of violence that both fed a new taste for body-horror, and confirmed the guilt attached to that taste. Nineteenth-century murder literature set up a very troubled relationship between the violence of murder and the reader as imaginative spectator to that violence. Though the literature continued to construct the murderer as monstrous moral alien, it ultimately worked to implicate the crime-reader in the murderer's terrible guilt.

———⋗●⋖———

"It is grievous to see or hear (and almost to hear of) any man, or even any animal whatever, in _torment_." With these words, written in 1724, William Wollaston captured the culture of sensibility that was emerging in eighteenth-century England, a new set of attitudes and emotional conventions at the heart of which was a sympathetic concern for the pain and suffering of other sentient beings. The culture of sensibility revolutionized the meaning of pain in Anglo-American culture. Orthodox Christianity had traditionally viewed pain not only as God's punishment for sin (the English term is derived from the Latin _poena_, punishment), but also as a redemptive opportunity to transcend the world and the flesh by imitating the suffering Christ. "Preanesthetic cultures responded to pain not with denial but with curious forms of affirmation" that were rooted in a premodern acceptance of its inescapability. The eighteenth-century cult of sensibility redefined pain as unacceptable and indeed eradicable, and thus opened the door to a new revulsion from pain which, though now regarded as "instinctive" or "natural," has in fact proved to be distinctively modern. In the context of the bourgeois "civilizing process," compassion and a reluctance to inflict pain became identified as distinctively *civilized* emotions, while cruelty was labelled as *savage* or *barbarous.*[5]

The intellectual origins of the humanitarian sensibility lay with the Latitudinarian divines of the late seventeenth and early eighteenth centuries. In reaction to English Puritanism and the harsh Hobbesian view of human nature, the Latitudinarians argued that humankind is instinctively sympathetic, naturally inclined to virtuous actions because of the pleasurable feelings such actions generated.[6] The Latitudinarian tradition exerted an important influence on the third Earl of Shaftesbury, who learned from John Locke the importance of sensation to knowledge, but diverged from his tutor by positing an innate "moral sense," capable of distinguishing good from evil through an intuitive grasp of the beauty of virtue, and inclined to the good through innate sympathy.[7] The philosophers of the Scottish Enlightenment developed further Shaftesbury's views on human benevolence. Francis Hutcheson, for example, posited a "sense of the soul we may call the sympathetick" such that "When we see or know the pain, distress or misery of any kind which another suffers, and turn our thoughts to it, we feel a strong sense of pity, and a great proneness to relieve, where no contrary passion withholds us."[8]

The moral philosophy of sympathy shaped a literature of sensibility, which undertook to teach virtue by softening the heart and eliciting tears of tender sympathy with pitiful tableaux of poverty, imprisonment, slavery, the aftermath of war, tormented animals, women in distress.[9] And this literature, with its central conviction that the pain of others is and ought to be obnoxious to us, contributed to eighteenth-century humanitarian reform, which identified a range of formerly unquestioned social practices as unacceptable cruelties and demanded that men and women of sensibility put a stop to them. Among the earliest beneficiaries of the new vogue for compassion were animals, as humanitarians called for an end to such blood sports as cock-fighting and cock-throwing, bull- and bear-baiting, and stag-hunting.[10] The early modern "spectacle of suffering," the public infliction of pain or death on the bodies of criminal offenders, came under criticism and was gradually replaced with the penitentiary system.[11] The brutal treatment of the insane was challenged by a generation of asylum-keepers who worked to replace the physical coercions and heroic medical procedures of "terrific" mental healing with "moral treatment," based on the humanitarian conviction that the insane were entitled to the same benevolent sympathy as the rest of humanity.[12] The violent punitive practices of the armed services (English reformers focused on the army, Americans on the navy) were criticized on the grounds that flogging was "a disreputable, cowardly, unmanly, unfeeling, brutal, inhuman and bloody mode of punishment."[13] The corporal punishment of children fell into disfavor among liberal Lockeans and Romantics.[14] War, duelling, prizefighting, even "football" (a term covering a range of games in which serious injuries and occasional deaths occurred) were all objects of reform concern.[15]

The increasing sensitivity to pain contributed as well to intensified medical efforts to discover an effective anesthesia. Traditionally, Western medicine had joined with orthodox Christianity in regarding pain as inevitable, and had tended to discourage efforts to interfere with it on the grounds that suffering was a vital part of the body's natural healing process. But in the eighteenth century, physicians and surgeons grew increasingly sensitive to the pain they inflicted on their patients until, "By the 1750s, the man of feeling had truly entered the operating room." The medical establishment's systematic search for a painless surgical technique began with Joseph Priestley's discovery of nitrous oxide gas in 1773, and culminated in Boston dentist William T. G. Morton's successful administration of ether anesthesia to a surgical patient at Massachusetts General Hospital in 1846. The "preanesthetic era" (1754–1846) also saw efforts to alleviate surgical pain by refrigeration techniques, nerve compression, hypnosis, subcutaneous injection of morphine (first isolated in

1806), controlled asphyxia, and drastic bleeding to the point of syncope just before operating. In the early eighteenth century, the term "anesthesia" had referred to a defective lack of feeling; by the end of the century, it connoted a "positive medical relieving of feeling, a blessing rather than a defect." By 1845, the American patent medicine business had discovered (and to some extent helped create) a lucrative national market for general pain cures, with the registered trademark for a "Celebrated Pain Killer" which promised to treat not disease but pain itself.[16]

The search for surgical anesthesia both reflected and reinforced "that dread of pain—that 'instinctive' revulsion from the physical suffering even of others," which has in fact proved to be "uniquely characteristic of the modern era." The modern sensibility, which averts its eyes from pain whenever possible or approaches it with fear and trembling, was well expressed by British anti-vivisectionist Francis Power Cobbe: "The infliction of pain is a thing naturally so revolting to the cultivated mind, that any description of it inevitably arouses strong sentiments of dislike, if not of horror."[17]

This new significance of the body in pain was accompanied by a new significance of the body in death. In the late eighteenth century, a changing attitude towards death became evident in the desire to segregate the dead from the living. Not only the cemetery, but the deathbed scene and the funeral were privatized, concealed from public view. Graveyards came to conjure images of despair and decay, and complaints were voiced about their revolting state as stinking quagmires where the miasma of putrefaction threatened the health of the living. The practice of opening old graves to commit new corpses to the earth aroused new fears; some reformers went so far as to argue against family tombs altogether, because of "the forbidding and repulsive conditions which attend on decay." As the smell of corpses grew offensive, the practice of displaying dead criminals grew just as unacceptable as the public torture of living bodies. In New England, gravestone carvers gradually abandoned skeletal designs, replacing them successively with winged angels, the urn-and-willow design, and realistic portraits of the deceased in life or afterlife. By the 1820s and 1830s, the rural cemetery movement was

death as privatized [margin annotation]

separating the dead from the living in new cemeteries outside cities and towns. At the same time, professional undertakers began to take over from the family and friends of the dead the task of preparing the body for burial; and the traditional eight-sided coffin, whose shape conformed to the human body, was replaced by the casket with its less corporeal design.[18] The relatively easy social familiarity with death common in the premodern period was being replaced by a powerful sense of alienation from the dead.

The same generation that discovered pain to be intolerable and death repulsive, discovered their pornographic possibilities as a source of dreadful pleasure, precisely because their unacceptability made them obscene. By the late eighteenth century, "In the world of the imagination, death and violence have merged with desire." Sentimentalists themselves constructed sympathy as a "dear delicious pain," "a sort of pleasing Anguish"; their critic William Godwin went further, calling sensibility a "moon-struck madness, hunting after torture."[19] The emerging pornography of death took shape in such varied cultural expressions as Baroque tomb sculpture, the popular obsession with cadavers and their dissection, the Gothic theme of the living corpse, and the Romantic tendency (best exemplified by Edgar Allan Poe) to represent the dead body as an object of beauty and desire. In relabelling violence, pain, and death as obscene, the humanitarian revolution conferred a new imaginative significance on the body *in extremis* as illicit, titillating, prurient.

Gothic fiction, which emerged in the last decades of the eighteenth century as one of the most popular literary genres in England and the United States, explored both the horror and the allure of the body in pain and in death. Gothic fiction embodied Burke's aesthetic theory of the sublime and beautiful, first published in 1756: "Whatever is fitted in any sort to excite the ideas of pain, and danger . . . is a source of the *sublime;* that is, it is productive of the strongest emotion which the mind is capable of feeling." Pain and danger were abundantly present in such Gothic works as William Beckford's *Vathek* (1786), Ann Radcliffe's *The Italian* (1797), and Charles Robert Maturin's *Melmoth the Wanderer* (1820). Over time, the genre shifted from the gloomy but veiled terrors of earlier works towards ever-cruder and more lurid representations of violence. The *Schauer-Romantik* school, as exemplified by Matthew Lewis's *The Monk* (1796), revelled in scenes of rape, torture, and charnel-house corruption and decay. Gothic fiction in general showed a marked predilection for scenes of torture, sexual violation, and murder, and treated such subjects in a manner calculated to arouse maximum revulsion and disgust. And its treatment of torture closely linked pain with beauty, and cruelty with sexual desire, articulating an erotic sensibility that exerted a powerful influence on English Romanticism from the late eighteenth century through the Decadents. The literature of "romantic agony" carried forward the Gothic exploration of the newly discovered bond between pleasure and suffering.[20]

Gothic fiction exemplified a broader literary trend in the late eighteenth and early nineteenth century that was captured in the neologism "sensationalism." According to the *Oxford English Dictionary*, the earliest usage of the term "sensation," meaning "an excited or violent feeling" or "the production of violent emotion as an aim in works of literature or art," was in 1779. Over time, the term increasingly lent itself to what was perceived to be a degraded commercial tendency to pander to public excitement in the face of particularly terrible or shocking events, to what William Wordsworth in 1801 characterized as a "craving for extraordinary incident" and "degrading outrageous stimulation." Wordsworth attributed the phenomenon to urbanization and modern information technology, which were intensifying the popular desire to be shocked or thrilled so long as the beholder could remain safe. Within fifty years of Wordsworth's lament, the English periodical *Punch* was blaming the very term "sensation" on the Americans.[21] In American popular literature, captivity narratives and their literary successors the dime novels, the popular "mysteries of the city" genre, historical works on the Inquisition, the literature of "counter-subversion" produced by social opponents of Mormonism, Masonry, and Catholicism, the semi-sociological literature of exposé, which purported to unveil the evils of mental institutions and prisons—all were sensationalistic in nature; all appealed to a popular voyeuristic taste for scenarios of suffering. "Reader," wrote James Brice in *Secrets of the Mount-Pleas-*

ant State Prison, "if you could but once witness a state prison flogging. The victim is stripped naked and beaten with a cruel instrument of torture called a cat, from his neck to his heels, until as raw as a piece of beef."[22]

Perhaps most revealing, a growing predilection for scenarios of suffering was becoming increasingly central to pornography *qua* pornography. Traditional English erotica had been dominated by bawdy, an innocent and unselfconscious kind of sexual writing, especially attentive to themes of cuckoldry and scatology, which tended to treat sex as an uncomplicated animal act and a source of ribald humor. But in the second half of the seventeenth century, English booksellers and printers began to translate from French and Italian a more modern kind of sexual writing, pornography, which meant to arouse lust and encourage sexual fantasies. Pornography has been defined as "the written or visual presentation in a realistic form of any genital or sexual behaviour with a deliberate violation of existing and widely accepted moral and social taboos."[23] Not until the eighteenth century did those taboos include, on any significant scale, the infliction of pain.

Sexual flagellation apparently interested few readers and authors before the eighteenth century. But in 1718, Edmund Curll published an English translation of a Latin medical work, entitled *A Treatise of the Use of Flogging in Venereal Affairs,* with a voyeuristic frontispiece illustration of a woman flogging the bare buttocks of a man while a variety of spectators looked on. By the 1730s, the respectable *Gentleman's Magazine* was including some essays and letters on the art of flogging, and when John Cleland proffered up his tale of *Fanny Hill, or Memoirs of a Woman of Pleasure* (1748–49), he included a scene of mutual flagellation between Fanny and Mr. Barvile. The flagellation mania significantly increased in the late eighteenth century—just at the time the Marquis de Sade was producing his works associating torture and murder with sexual arousal, which would earn him the distinction of having his name assigned to the genre. The pornography of sadism entered its heyday in the nineteenth century, when "the English vice" became the central convention of English pornography. In such works as *The Rodiad* (c. 1820) and *The Merry Order of*

St. Bridget (1868), various combinations of sexes and (often ambiguous, due to cross-dressing and role-playing) genders participated in the flagellation mania.[24] And from its earliest appearance, the pornography of pain was highly voyeuristic in nature, dependent not only on the implied spectatorship of the reader/viewer, but also on the inclusion in the material of witnesses to the sexual infliction of pain.

The key to the advent of sadomasochistic pornography is the changing attitudes towards pain in the late eighteenth and early nineteenth centuries. If pornography is best defined as the representation of sexual behavior *with a deliberate violation of moral and social taboos*, then the growing violence of it in this period is attributable to the new shock value of pain within a culture redefining it as forbidden and therefore obscene. In a similar fashion, the new shock value of pain and death defined by humanitarianism reshaped murder literature into a pornography of violence.

———

After 1820, the expansion in the popular literature of murder continued at an increasing pace. Propelled by new republican ideals of an informed citizenry and by commercial development, American culture was moving out of the information scarcity of the colonial period into an era of information abundance. The invention of steam printing and other technological innovations made it possible for publishers to print more titles and larger editions and sell them at a cheaper price, while advances in transportation enabled them to peddle their wares in a mass consumer market. The nineteenth-century communications revolution transformed "the dynamics of contagious diffusion," the process by which news of exceptional events—such as wars, the deaths of famous people, or murders—moves from person to person and place to place. The diffusion of news, which in the eighteenth century had been a relatively slow, local, face-to-face process, grew swifter, wider, and more impersonal as new regular channels of mass communication became available in the form of commercial networks, more frequent newspaper publication, and eventually the telegraph. Popular murder accounts—trial reports, criminal biographies, and other secular narratives, generally printed in octavo-sized pamphlets, often twenty-four or forty-eight pages in length—were part of the new communications system that routinely spread the word as far and as fast as commercial networks could carry it.[25]

The diffusion was reinforced in the 1830s with the emergence of the penny press, cheap daily newspapers whose circulation was five to ten times larger than that of the older, more expensive papers. Eighteenth-century newspapers had been devoted primarily to government proclamations, European politics, and notices of ship arrivals and departures, with only an occasional paragraph of crime coverage; early nineteenth-century journalism had added only the political party organ. But the penny daily offered a mix of scandals, sports, and above all, crime coverage, intended to appeal to a mass urban readership. Leading the field were two New York papers, *The Sun,* founded by Benjamin H. Day in 1833, and *The Herald,* founded in 1835 by James Gordon Bennett. Even their crime coverage remained generally limited to short reports on crimes and trials, until the murder that irrevocably altered the nature of American journalism: the 1836 axe-murder of the beautiful and notorious prostitute Helen Jewett by her lover Richard Robinson, a young clerk in a New York firm. During two months of extensive front-page coverage of the murder and the ensuing trial, *The Herald* and *The Sun* took opposing positions on Robinson's guilt and dramatically expanded their circulation. In 1845, the *National Police Gazette* followed the penny dailies' successful lead with a weekly periodical devoted to crime coverage, and watched its own subscriptions skyrocket in just a few years.[26]

In the cultural context of humanitarianism, the crime of murder was increasingly deemed a sensational event, capable of generating great public excitement. Popular murder literature began to make special note of the "extraordinary degree of feeling and excitement" that affected "all ranks and classes of people" when news of a murder first broke. When Lucius Foot was found beaten to death in a horse stall at the Litchfield Church in Connecticut, the community was "shocked to its very heart"; when Andrew Alger was killed on the

{70}

road for the money he carried, the "community was thrilled and electrified." News of murder generated "a thrill of horror," "a chill of horror."[27] Excited crowds quickly gathered at the scene of the crime. Thousands reportedly swarmed the house in Portsmouth, Virginia, where two men had killed and dismembered Peter Lagoardette, coming "to see the horrible sight, or to hear the particulars, if they could, of the murder." After Daniel Davis Farmer's fatal assault on Anna Ayer at Goffstown, New Hampshire, one of the many visitors who trooped past the dying woman to view her head wound wrote to the convicted killer that he had seen "the place of carnage, the bloody house and bed of the poor victim, her garments rolled in blood, yea, the fatal club, the stone, and all the blood-besmeared weapons of death," and finally "the corpse of her whose death stamped your crime with the hue of murder."[28]

Later, large crowds attended the murder trial, sometimes arriving hours before the courthouse opened, obstructing traffic for blocks, creating scenes of "awful tumult and confusion." The "courtroom, the moment it is opened, is crowded almost to suffocation," with women and men of "all classes."[29] They came, reportedly, "to become acquainted with the details of this fiend-like massacre," and "to get a sight of the fiend in human form, who perpetrated the foul and heartless deed." Once packed into the courtroom, these crowds responded emotionally to the proceedings. At the trial of Joel Clough, who had stabbed Mary Hamilton to death for rejecting his romantic suit, the display of her bloody garments accompanied by a physician's description of her injuries "produced a gust of feeling and emotion in the crowded audience," and "every eye was suffused with tears." At the trial of John Webster, the display of a box of bones found in his laboratory furnace "created a thrilling sensation, and a general buzzing noise in the gallery." A printed report of Albert Tirrell's trial for murdering his paramour, prostitute Maria Bickford, noted every "sensation" that swept the courtroom in response to testimony.[30]

Subsequently, public excitement prompted great crowds to gather for the executions of convicted murderers. A reported 12,000 attended Joel Clough's hanging; 30,000 (an estimated one-third of them women) watched Jesse Strang's execution for the love-triangle murder of John Whipple; 50,000 showed up to watch John Johnson die.[31] The privatization of execution in various states after 1830 hampered but by no means halted such interest (and indeed might have stimulated it). When Peter Robinson was executed in New Brunswick, New Jersey, in 1841, huge crowds surrounded the prison and commandeered the rooftops of adjacent houses and a church. Disappointed when Robinson's body was not exhibited to them, some swarmed the prison yard, cut up the hanging rope, and threw it to the mob outside. Alexander Anderson's and Henry Richards's death sentences prompted a petition to have Pennsylvania's privatization law suspended for the occasion. When it failed, people pressed against the wall nearest the scaffold, climbed ladders and trees to peer over the jail's walls, positioned themselves on rooftops and at garret windows, and purchased tickets for seats on a nearby barn and an elevated platform built for the occasion. Such interest reportedly pervaded all social classes: the curious drove to Robinson's hanging in vehicles ranging "from the humblest milk-cart, to the smart 'two-horse wagon.'"[32]

The public excitement stimulated by a murder went hand in hand with the popular demand to read all about it. After the Rev. Ephraim Avery's arrest, every available press was "made to teem with pamphlets, and essays, and placards and caricatures, and songs" which were "hawked about both city and country, while the movers in the business rejoiced to see the excitement extended." As early as 1821, defense attorneys were routinely claiming the impossibility of their clients' receiving a fair trial because of the advance publicity: "An account of a murder is always seized upon, and circulated with the greatest eagerness and avidity" and "the more shocking the circumstances, the greater the relish and curiosity."[33] Nineteenth-century murder literature regularly recorded the speed at which the news of murder spread. After Sarah Furber's incompetent physician delivered her body for dissection to the Harvard medical faculty, who refused to believe that her death had been natural, "What terrible suspense now filled the public mind! . . . Every word in regard to her, went, as if on telegraphic wires, and was sought more eagerly than the record of European revolutions."[34]

Once a sacred literature controlled by a clerical elite in the interests of moral order and spiritual salvation, murder narratives were now a sensationalist literature that appealed directly to an expanding popular readership in quest of entertainment. This literature did not simply report "intense excitement"; it actively sought to stimulate it, intentionally sending a "thrill of horror" to readers' hearts. Its sensationalism was evident in such volume titles as *Murder Most Foul!* (1836) and *Awful Disclosures!* (1849), and in the growing popularity of murder anthologies such as *Annals of Murder, or, Daring Outrages, Trials, Confessions &c.* (1845).[35] Though the Gothic convention of speechlessness continued—"Language is incapable of giving utterance to the feelings that shock the soul as its horrors and enormities are brought before us"—this disclaimer typically preceded a torrent of highly charged language, self-consciously addressing the powerful emotions assumed to have been aroused by crimes of murder. Authors informed readers of their own emotional response to the crime: "Who can portray the dire scene of blood-shed and death, without its exciting within him the creepings of his agitated frame, and sensations poignant?" They advised readers what their emotional response should be: "The cruel murder of an amiable woman . . . is calculated to excite the utmost horror in the breasts of the virtuous and humane"; while a murder-dismemberment was "calculated to inflame the public feeling with horror and disgust."[36]

Most important, murder literature after 1800 focused overwhelmingly on images of the body in pain and death. The primary technique of sensationalism was body-horror, the effort to arouse the reader's repugnance (and excitement) in the face of the physiological realities of violent death. After 1800, popular murder literature practiced new and increasingly extreme strategies to evoke readers' fascinated revulsion and disgust in the face of murderous violence. Tales of murder grew precise about the weapons used: Anna Ayer died of wounds inflicted by a maple club "two and a half feet long or more, one inch and a half in diameter." Some accounts offered illustrations of the weapon. The injuries of the murder victims were described in detail: "The throat was cut from ear to ear, severing the jugular veins, carotoid arteries, windpipe, muscles and nerves, leaving the neck-bone entirely bare." Lavinia Bacon's daughter returned from church one Sunday in 1843 to find her mother "a mangled corpse on the floor of the parlor. Her skull was literally broken to pieces—one of her eyes knocked completely out of sight and her face mutilated beyond the possibility of recognition."[37] The "wholesale butchery" of mass murders and of assaults involving a variety of weapons and types of injuries received extensive attention.[38] Increasingly, accounts focused on the pain endured by the victim before death. The judge who sentenced James Eldredge for administering arsenic to his fiancée, Sarah Jane Gould, in 1857, emphasized, "For five full days, you stood by and saw her writhe in agony and sink in death."[39]

In many murders, body-horror took the form of specific details about the state and fate of the victim's corpse: dead bodies whose damage testified to long-term abuse, dead bodies gnawed by wild creatures or infested with scavengers, dead bodies in an extreme state of putrefaction.[40] Unusual and macabre methods of corpse disposal received special attention; readers learned how Edward Donnelly burned his wife Catharine's body in the fireplace, pounding her more recalcitrant bones with an axe, smashing the remnants, and finally throwing her ashes outside. Mary and Cornelius Cole buried the body of Mary's mother, Agnes Teaurs, below the floor of their house, where it was found a few months later by tenants who "perceived an unusual and unpleasant smell" and pulled up the floorboards to discover the body covered with ashes and some tow. Extensive attention was paid to the murder of banker Abraham Suydam by his desperate mortgagee Peter Robinson, who buried his victim in the cellar of his (mortgaged) house and then laid a new wood floor over the grave; to the horror of all, Robinson confessed that he "dug the grave before his still living victim, threw him into it alive, and then struck him over the head with the spade, dashed in his skull, and thus killed him." *The Manchester Tragedy,* which recounted the abortion-death of Sarah Furber, reported that "the most revolting scene" of the entire tale took place after her death at the hands of her inept physician: "When life became extinct, immediately, before the blood had become cold in the veins, he who had caused her death, deposited, with his own guilty hands, the dead body, embedded in straw

{74}

and charcoal, in a coarse, rough box, marked 'glass,' and conveyed it, as *baggage*, to Boston and offered it to the Medical College for dissection."[41]

The most horrifying cases of corpse disposal involved corpse dismemberment, which had the effect of graphically prolonging the violence of the murder beyond death. Indeed, these accounts tended to relate the murder quickly, then take their time in tracing the dismemberment and, typically, burning of the corpse. When Manuel Philip Garcia and José Demas Garcia Castillano killed Peter Lagoardette in Norfolk, Virginia, in 1821, the printed account of their crime focused on their dismemberment of the corpse (illustrated on the title page), explicitly invoking the reader's "horror and *disgust*" and "sentiment of *abhorrence*" in the face of such *"revolting"* action. *The Confession of Adam Horn* (1843) detailed how he had killed his wife with two blows of a stick, then chopped off her head and burned it, scattered her teeth in the woods, severed her limbs and buried them under an old bake oven, buried her trunk in the peach orchard, then, under fear of discovery, moved her limbs from bake oven to orchard to the attic of the house. In 1857, the "triple murderer" J. M. Ward of Sylvania, Ohio, detailed at great length "my disgusting work" of killing, dismembering, burning, and scattering the remnants of his wife's corpse. According to the judge who presided over Ward's preliminary hearing, "the body was disposed of in a manner still more revolting" than the "horrible murder" itself.[42] Accounts such as these suggest that the nineteenth-century cult of horror quickly generated a demand for variety and a taste for the bizarre for a soon-jaded popular appetite.

A widely available technique for enhancing and prolonging the horror of the crime was provided by forensic medicine, which increasingly involved dissection of the murder victim. The earliest printed treatments of medical postmortems, which appeared around the turn of the century, were brief and offered minimal technical information with little fanfare. They simply confirmed that Matthias Gotlieb's wife had died of three stab wounds he inflicted upon her; that Timothy Kennedy died of the axe blow to the head delivered by Michael Powers.[43] By the 1830s, however, printed accounts of medical postmortems, especially in murder trial reports, had grown significantly longer and more detailed. When Dr. Samuel Johnson testified to the state of Salem murder victim Joseph White, he reported three different levels of examination: the initial visual inspection of the corpse; the probing of the stab wounds in the heart region and a manual examination of the victim's fractured forehead; and finally, the dissection of the head and chest. Some postmortem reports offered virtually textbook explanations of autopsy procedure. Dr. James Dougal related in detail how he and the coroner exhumed Catharine Earls's coffin, carried it into the nearby church, removed the body, and undressed it; then visually examined it for signs of decay (arsenic delays putrefaction), opened the body from neck to pelvis with a two-part incision, surveyed all the internal organs, and removed the stomach and intestines to be tested for poison.[44]

As medical examinations of the victims grew central to popular murder literature, they became a crucial part of the criminal narrative, uniquely illuminating the nature and extent of the violence and underlining its horror. Dr. Joseph H. Streeter examined the corpse of rape-murder victim, Mrs. Houghton, and reported the severe bruising of her jaw, right arm, chest, and neck; the skin torn from her face, elbows, and shoulder-blades; and the internal coagulation of blood around her neck and shoulder. Though his official conclusion was death by strangulation, his testimony suggested far more about the struggle between the victim and her assailant. As the editor of another trial report noted, "the reader's imagination will involuntarily picture a most terrible contest between the murderer and his victim" in reading a physician's testimony about the knife wounds found on the victim's hand, probably incurred as she grappled with her husband in self-defense. The judge who sentenced John Earls for the murder of his wife Catharine used medical testimony to support a sentimental story of the dead woman's wounded *heart:* "The grave gave up its contents—that heart whose affections had clung around you for more than fifteen years, was the first to proclaim, by its ventricles filled with blood, that its pulsations had been suddenly arrested by the operation of some sudden, violent and unnatural cause."[45]

Medical testimony contributed significantly to the steady intensification of body-horror in popular murder literature. Sometimes medical examiners introduced body parts into the courtroom, such as the skull of Lucius H. Foot, and skull fragments from the corpse of Reuben McPhetres. Some autopsy reports spoke to the pain endured by the murder victim: Dr. James Rush, who examined Eliza Sowers after her fatal abortion, explained that "death is not often accompanied with the agonies which this girl suffered." Most medical testimony was delivered in tones of clinical detachment: Dr. William Wallace reported that the mortal blow inflicted on Anna Ayer broke off a piece of her skull "nearly as large as a cracker"; Dr. Garwood H. Atwood observed that the wound in Lucius H. Foot's forehead was large enough for him to "put two fingers right into the brain." But such language may have enhanced readers' sense of horror by virtue of its coolness in the face of terrible physiological damage. So too did some of the details of what went on in dissecting rooms. At the trial of Edward Bradley, Dr. Pliny Jewett testified, "I have broken skulls with a hammer in the dissecting room"; at the trial of Professor John Webster, Dr. Woodbridge Strong explained how he had once dissected a pirate and then burned his body for the bones.[46]

The simple fact of medical dissection was sufficient to induce horror in this period, as evidenced in the judicial practice of adding dissection to the death sentence to enhance the punishment. Several murderers expressed their "great aversion" to being dissected. Suicide Richard Crowninshield's "last request" to his father was that his body be "decently buryed, and have it protected from the dissecting Knife"; the body of executed murderer Jesse Strang was conveyed to his family for burial, "to spare his respectable connexions the additional agony they would have experienced had his body been consigned to the dissecting-knife." But the same accounts that reported the aversion of condemned murderers and their families to dissection, described the autopsies performed on the victims. James Eldredge's prosecutor tried to arouse the jurors' outrage by regretting that "we could not leave [Sarah Gould] to the undisturbed repose of the grave," because it was necessary for her to be "eviscerated, mutilated by the surgeon's knife, that her decaying members might yield to scientific skill, irrefutable proofs of *that* man's damning guilt." The damage inflicted on the corpse by the forensic physician, he implied, was a horrifying extension of the damage done to her living body by her murderer, who must be held responsible for both acts. This conflation helps explain the special horror attached to the case of Dr. Valorous P. Coolidge, who poisoned his friend Edward Mathews and then coolly performed the postmortem examination of his own victim: "I do not believe," wrote this crime's chronicler, "that in the whole annals of crime, any thing like a parallel to this can be produced."[47]

Nineteenth-century murder literature focused on "the revolting ceremony" of execution with a degree of physiological detail missing from early American execution sermons. Readers learned that blood and mucus flowed from the hanged Henry Leander Foote's mouth, that the pirate Gibbs "died hard," that the lynched body of David Mayberry was "a ghastly, horrible sight." *The Manheim Tragedy* offered a minute-by-minute medical analysis of the hangings of Alexander Anderson and Henry Richards, describing their muscular contractions, bursts of air from their windpipes, and urinary, rectal, and seminal discharges. Many accounts elaborated on the "mortal agony" suffered by the dying criminal: "his sufferings were apparently long and painful," "he was horribly convulsed," and "His face after death showed signs of agony, and pain in dying." One author enhanced the horror of execution by reporting the galvanic experimentation performed on a murderer's corpse; evoking comparisons with Mary Shelley's fictional monster, he observed that "*When a dead man opens his eyes and looks about, moves his limbs, throws his arms on his breast, grinds his teeth, and tries to catch you,* it requires strong nerves to witness the spectacle."[48]

The humanitarian revolution in sensibility, which introduced a whole range of new attitudes towards violence, pain, and death, provided the necessary cultural context for sensationalistic murder literature. In an era when willful violence was coming under censure, murder stories turned from matters of salvation to scenes of violent assault. In a period when pain was being redefined as an intolerable aspect of the human condition, popular murder narratives came to pay close attention to the agonies of murder victims. At a time when the sight and smell of human corpses were becoming repugnant to the living, popular murder literature lingered on their putrefaction. Dissection of the human body had become so offensive by the early nineteenth century that even condemned murderers were sometimes spared that final punishment, but popular murder literature represented the dissection of murder victims with growing detail. The carving of meat for dinner was increasingly deemed an unappealing sight, to be relegated to the kitchens, pantries, or sideboards of genteel homes; the butchering of human bodies was, by contrast, a central concern of murder literature. More generally, in an era when many mundane bodily practices—elimination, noseblowing and spitting, sexual activities, dying itself—were being privatized in service to the civilizing process, the literature of body-horror fully exposed the process by which murder victims' bodies were damaged, dismembered, and medically disembowelled.

By the early nineteenth century, the "refinement of America" had been under way for a century, and was extending outward and downward from the aristocratic elite of the colonial period to shape the lives of the expanding middle classes. One hallmark of the refined man or woman was "delicacy" of feeling, a humanitarian sensitivity to precisely the sort of thing addressed in popular murder literature: violence and bloodshed, pain and suffering, death and decay—all held to be ugly and in poor taste.[49] In this context, the more sensationalistic murder literature became, the more its authors and editors formulaically denied their own sensationalism. Typically, they claimed to be publishing their works, not to generate public excitement, but in conscientious *response* to public "alarm" and "anxiety," which they hoped "a correct report" of the case would help lay to rest. In recounting the violence inflicted by John Joyce on Sarah Cross, one author paused to explain, "It is not, however, our intention to elicit more feeling on this melancholy occasion, than has been publicly expressed—nor could we, were we even disposed, do it with propriety." With a similar concern for "propriety," the preface of an account of John Johnson's bloody murder of James Murray proclaimed the author's intent "to make the sketch he has undertaken, in some degree worthy of the perusal of the enlightened and intelligent portion of the community, instead of the vulgar and commonplace history of 'a *most bloody murder.*'" The editor of *The Manheim Tragedy* assured readers that "We are not of the class who take pleasure in the reading or circulation of the details of the horrible in crime," and promised that "the more revolting details . . . have been touched as lightly as was deemed consistent with narrative truth."[50]

Authors and editors addressed endless explanations and apologies to the presumedly delicate sensibilities of middle-class readers, anxious to hear some moral rationale for their choice of reading material. In proclaiming the "propriety" of their works, and disclaiming to be "of the *class* who take pleasure" in such literature, the publishers revealed their own assumption of the middle-class character of their readership. They substantiated their claims of offering a high-minded form of entertainment to respectable readers by presenting a wide range of arguments in support of the moral value of their publications. Variously, they expressed hopes that their murder accounts would discourage vice, drunkenness, uncontrolled passion, and seduction. They promised to promote the moral education of children and emphasized the importance of religion as the only true foundation of public virtue. They expressed concern about the incidence of crime in the new republic, and hoped that their depictions of criminal punishment would serve as an effective warning to all potential offenders. They suggested that the technical information, legal and medical, offered in their trial reports would assist lawyers and physicians in future judicial proceedings.[51] The preface to one murder anthology likened its function to surgery: "No one imagines that the surgeon's duty, when called to probe disgusting or painful wounds, is a pleasant one—but nobody denies its necessity and usefulness . . . Our publication is to the moral what the surgeon's is to the physical man."[52]

But such repeated claims to higher moral purposes, respect for delicate sensibilities, and an enlightened readership actually high-lighted the illicit qualities of popular murder literature—the titillat-ing prurience of its treatment of violence, pain, and death. The dreadful pleasure was a prurient pleasure, which rested on the knowledge, shared between author and reader, that tales of murder dealt with matters of questionable taste. The standard formula was to denounce "that depraved taste" which hungered for murder sto-ries, and then proceed to feed it. Despite all denials, sensationalism did induce pleasure in its readers: as attorney John V. L. McMahon stated at the murder trial of George Swearingen, "We gather with joy, even in our infancy, around the tale of horror, which makes each particular hair stand on end."[53] But this joy was a "dreadful pleasure" laden with guilt. Authors and editors of crime literature tried to disclaim the very thing Daniel Webster assumed was behind the intense public excitement surrounding the White murder: pleasure in pain and beauty in horror. But the more they apologized the more guilt they expressed, and the more dreadful pleasure they structured into the description of pain. No matter how loudly a given murder narrative protested its concern for delicacy of feeling, its substance gave the lie to its claims. By playing off the tension between refine-ment and coarseness, gentility and vulgarity, this literature revealed its nature as a pornography of violence.[54] Popular murder literature did not pander to the lower social orders so much as it addressed the "lower" part of human nature as understood within Victorian moral psychology, a nature being restructured by the growing requirements of the civilizing process.

In the late eighteenth and early nineteenth centuries, the cultural meanings of pain and death were being reshaped by a heightened awareness of the close relationship between the revulsion and the excitement or desire aroused by pain and death. But to call this sensibility pornographic does not in itself explain why nineteenth-century readers actively sought out the horror experience, rather than avert their newly sensitized eyes from violence, pain, and death. Literary criticism may offer a useful approach to explain this paradox. Horror literature presents images of the culturally forbidden and invites readers to give free play to their illicit desires in the realm of the imagination. In so doing, it permits readers to triumph over forbidden impulses by suppressing them again. Having met the repressed and reasserted the power of the conscious self over it, readers take pleasure in repeating the process because it reinforces our mastery over the dark forces which constantly threaten to seize the upper hand.[55] This helps explain the fundamental ambivalence of murder literature. For the central concern of horror is taboo (the culturally forbidden), and taboo generates ambivalence, an emotional state "in which the mind oscillates between attraction and repulsion."[56] It is thus significant that Gothic horror literature emerged in the midst of the humanitarian revolution, which was constructing historically new taboos from a wide range of pain practices formerly accepted as natural and inescapable.

The experience of dreadful pleasure arose from new reading practices (a connection confirmed by murder literature's growing assumption that *horror* was something *read*).[57] Gothic literature was part of the "comparatively new world of silent literary communications" that was gradually replacing the oral-aural orientation of pre-literacy, and even of early literacy with its reliance on reading aloud, with the modern practice of solitary reading. Modern reading is a private activity conducive to the psychic process of "interiorization," the creation of a secluded inner realm of silent thought where individual selfhood can be generated, free from the pressures of the immediate presence of others. The dramatic expansion of "interiorization" in eighteenth-century Anglo-American culture was most evident in the rise of the novel, with its focus on the private and the inner life. Interiorization created an inner psychic arena for both the imaginative exploration of forbidden desires and for their repression.[58] Reading horror literature thus helped enforce the rising levels of repression demanded by the growing humanitarian sanctions against violent impulses and actions. Significantly, a concept of the unconscious began to take shape in the seventeenth and eighteenth centuries, a development which has been historically linked to the rise of Gothic literature. In this sense, horror literature contributed not only to the *discovery* of the unconscious, but to the actual *making* of the modern unconscious, into which all the desires and practices newly condemned by humanitarianism were to be relegated by repression.[59]

The popular literature of murder in the nineteenth century was a major expression of the new pornography of pain and violence, providing both an abundance of body-horror to cater to the new excitement and a steady stream of disclaimers and apologies for its own sensationalism, which merely reinforced the illicit thrill of reading such literature. Murder literature was closely related to sexual pornography, through its tendency to fuse sex with violence on the grounds of their common obscenity, and its special interest in crimes of passion, rape-murders, prostitute-killings, and abortion-homicides. But in a broader sense, the pornography of violence was at work in the growing voyeurism of popular murder literature. Humanitarians urged men and women of sensibility to gaze upon scenarios of pain in the virtuous effort to stimulate their sympathy for the sufferings of others. Sentimental art—fictional, visual, and dramatic—focused on tableaux of pain and death; humanitarian reform appealed for support by presenting terribly graphic images of suffering prisoners and slaves. Both sentimental art and humanitarian reform literature aroused serious concerns about the sadism implied in such representations. And in such expressive forms as sexual pornography, Gothic fiction, and a wider range of sensationalist genres, that dark corollary of the humanitarian sensibility took form as a more overtly sadistic voyeurism that revelled in the illicit pleasure of imaginatively watching others suffer.

Murder literature too focused on the *spectacle* of murder, treating violence as something that must be imaginatively *seen* by readers. Murder was a "bloody spectacle," a "shocking scene," a "horrid drama" to be watched in the private theater created by interiorization.[60] Nineteenth-century accounts offered detailed visual descriptions of murder, carefully sketching what might be called the choreography of the crime. Note, for example, this account of Thomas Topping's murder of his wife Elizabeth, which began with a dispute over whether she would fetch a pail of water:

This terminated in his giving her a blow with his fist, when she again endeavoured to leave the room. He then locked the door, and commenced beating her with a chair, which he broke to pieces over her head, and then took a broomstick, and broke it up by striking her on various parts of the body. Having so disabled her that she could not stand, he threw her on a bed in the room, took a knife and fork, and stabbed and cut her head, body and face, in six or seven places. Not having finished his brutal work, he then caught hold of a shoemaker's hammer, with which he deprived her of the little life that was remaining. He then stamped upon her with his feet, and threw her on the floor.[61]

Such detailed textual descriptions were often reinforced by visual illustrations: a fiendish-looking Peter Robinson grasps Abraham Suydam by the throat and raises a heavy mallet over his face; Richard Johnson shoots his pistol (from which smoke is pouring at the hammer and barrel) at Ursula Newman; Adam Horn stands, bloody knife in one hand and his wife's severed head in the other, with her mutilated corpse and a hatchet at his feet.[62]

The literature did not leave it to readers to figure out their designated role as imaginative spectators to the crime. Instead, it issued repeated, direct invitations to look at the crime imaginatively, to reconstruct it in their mind's eye and watch the violence unfold. "See his fallacious foe behind him uplifted raise the *axe*, and with the fell, fatal blow, prostrate the youthful KENNEDY!" The editorial preface to the trial of Thomas Barrett invited readers to "Imagine a pious old lady, of 70 years, sitting in her lonely cottage, by her little stand, with the word of God before her . . . Barrett, reeling from the dram-shop, enters her dwelling, and, with a lustful passion that would disgrace a brute, drags the old lady to the bed, and forcibly violates the chastity of her person; and then, to conceal this abominable crime, commits a greater, by seizing her by the throat and strangling her to death." Another account commanded, "See the besotted countenance of the drunkard as exhibited in this [illustration at the top of the page]—he has tied his wife to a chair, has communicated fire to her clothes, and is standing with fiendish delight to witness the destruction that he has attempted!"[63] This entry in the anthology *Annals of Murder* offered a double viewing frame, instructing readers to watch the murderous husband watch his wife burn to death.

This visual technique was often enlisted by prosecuting attorneys eager to help juries mentally reconstruct the crime just as the state represented it. In his closing at Knapp's trial, Daniel Webster coached the jurors:

> The villain could almost be seen entering the house, treading the deserted rooms, ascending on feathers, alone, the noiseless stairs; opening with stealthy and velvet tread the chamber of his sleeping victim; watching beneath the moonlight the gray hairs of the sleeper, visible in the breeze; we could almost hear the fatal blow; witness the poignard repeatedly driven to his heart; the aged arm raised by the assassin to repeat his aim; its restoration to its original position; the smoothing of the bed clothing; the feeling of the pulse to be certain that all was safe.

Webster thus invited jurors (and readers of the printed trial) actually to accompany the murderer into the house and up the stairs into the bedchamber of the victim, to witness the crime in all its detail. "Whilst his unsuspecting victim is partaking of the food, and drinking of the poisoned bowl, see [John Earls] lying upon a bed, on the opposite side of the room, watching his prey, like some ferocious monster!" commanded the prosecutor in that murder trial.[64]

In the relatively rare cases involving eyewitnesses to the murder, printed trial reports contributed to the construction of murder as spectacle by presenting a range of different vantage points on the crime. At the trial of Joel Clough for murdering Mary Hamilton in her mother's boardinghouse, family members, servants, boarders, taproom customers, and neighbors came forward to testify to the sequence of events surrounding the assault, offering four accounts of the stabbing, six of the victim's last words accusing Clough of the crime, and ten of her actual death. One eyewitness testified to what he called "the horrid scene" of the stabbing: "I saw the handle of some instrument in his right hand, the blade of which, was in her breast or side . . . up to the guard; as he held it in his hand he gave it a prying motion laterally with the appearance of wishing, to push it further in." One illustration represents the wounded Hamilton, arms outstretched like an opera diva, standing on the staircase landing, with Clough at the top of the stairs clutching his dirk, her mother beginning the ascent from the ground floor, and three witnesses clustered around the central action.[65]

Like the sentimental novel, the murder account revealed an intense concern for private space and private experience that testified to the growing cultural power of interiorization. This literature crafted the reader's role as voyeur to the crime, a figure that has gained cultural power in Western art and literature (including pornography) since the sixteenth century.[66] Such a person seems to hover in one murder illustration. It depicts Philadelphia carter Michael McGarvey murdering his wife: he has tied her to the bedstead by her hair and is flogging her to death with a whip. At a half-open doorway just behind McGarvey (where neither he nor his victim can see her) is a woman who, though presumably just discovering the crime, appears to be standing by and passively watching.[67] The illicit and secret nature of her spectatorship made her a voyeur like the reader who observes her.

Film critics argue that horror movies force us "to confront the relationship between watching and participating," making casual detachment impossible. A similar dynamic shaped nineteenth-century murder literature, with its many techniques for transforming readers into spectators to the violence. Like modern horror films, these narratives promoted an "aggressive and voyeuristic spectatorship" which implicated readers—figured in the female spectator in Michael McGarvey's doorway—in the violence. The horror image proffered in the texts and illustrations of nineteenth-century murder narratives embodied a way of seeing that was fundamentally pornographic, in its self-conscious representation of a culturally forbidden act.[68]

Aggressive spectatorship was especially pronounced in the rising popularity of first-person accounts by the murderer himself, which anticipated by more than a century Alfred Hitchcock's cinematic technique of identifying the spectator's gaze with that of the killer. "He fell, stunned and lifeless to the ground, looking up imploringly in my face, quivered and trembled like a leaf," confessed Reuben Dunbar after murdering his stepfather's two nephews. "I kept tightening the cord until her cheeks assumed a purple hue," read one false confession of the unsolved murder of Mary Cecilia Rogers. "I stood long side of her body, her heart's blood gushing out and running under my feet," reported wife-killer John Cowan. "Perspiration rolled from my brow in chilling drops, as I looked upon the awful deed, and that lovely form, which less than one hour before had been so active," wrote rapist-murderer Henry Foote. "My hands being wet, I did not know whether it was blood or dew, but by smelling, I found it blood," confessed Andress Hall after killing Noah and Amy Smith.[69] Readers of such passages as these witnessed the murder through the eyes of the killer: seeing the victim fall, watching her face change color, seeing her blood flowing under the murderer's feet, even feeling the murderer's perspiration running down his face and smelling the blood on his hands.

Did readers actively identify in any meaningful sense with the murderers they read about? A clerical commentator on the Webster-Parkman case thought so: "The public mind becomes fearfully familiar with blood, and runs with eagerness, often with criminal sympathy, into the very channels of thought and feeling which before had polluted only the mind that formed them." He was responding to a popular cult of the murderer in the nineteenth century. Visitors—including journalists who reported their experiences to readers—went to the prison cells of murderers, and often reported on the condemned men's attractiveness.[70] Romantic tales were told of certain murderers: of the love that prompted Jereboam Beauchamp to avenge his wife's dishonor by killing her seducer, and her suicide in his cell before his execution; of the prison-cell marriage between Caroline M. Henshaw and condemned murderer John Colt, the day before he cheated the hangman by taking his own life. A following of young men flocked to support Richard Robinson, accused of murdering prostitute Helen Jewett: during his trial, when the defendant took to wearing a cap (presumably to hide the bald spot by which the brothel keeper had identified him), his fans adopted the same cap as the badge of their allegiance, and burst into applause

{ 87 }

when the defense suggested that the brothel keeper was herself the murderer.[71] Albert Tirrell's fans similarly applauded at his verdict of "not guilty" for the murder of prostitute Maria Bickford; and wax figures of both murderer and victim were displayed by a traveling wax museum, which advertised that the dress and jewelry adorning its model—Bickford's extravagance, suggested Tirrell's defense, had driven him to justifiable homicide—had actually belonged to the victim. In 1827, the New York Museum advertised a wax tableau of Jesse Strang shooting John Whipple, assuring audiences that the rifle in the exhibit was the actual murder weapon.[72]

Despite Daniel Webster's attempt to blame the "morbid interest" in murderers on the fiction of Edward Bulwer-Lytton, the novelist's works were just one more expression of the growing allure of the murderer. Ironically, Peter Robinson had a cast of his head made by the same phrenologists who boasted that they had also cast Webster himself, along with Clay and Van Buren. The convicted killer responded to their request, "I know what you want to do with it; you want to hawk it about the streets of New York, and cry out, 'Here's the head of Peter Robinson the murderer, only half a dollar.'"[73] One enthusiastic reader of a grisly murder anthology repeatedly wrote his name and initials throughout the book, and twice signed the face of William Teller, who killed a prison guard while escaping from prison; he also copied in pencil a portrait of accused murderer Joseph Jenkins Knapp, whose first name he shared.

Perhaps the most suggestive evidence of readers' sense of moral complicity with the murderer's crime was the appearance of a guilty belief that reading murder literature could actually stimulate similar acts of violence in the reader. In June 1833, Sally Cochran was murdered by the Cochrans' servant, Abraham Prescott. The two had gone strawberry-picking together; he asked for sex and, when she refused, struck her with a stake and killed her. The center of Prescott's defense was a plea of insanity, on the grounds that he had been in a somnambulistic state at the time of the murder. Prescott, his attorney explained, was at an age (eighteen) "when the vivid affections were most operative, when whatever the imagination took hold of, it seized with force." And the "mental irritant, that excitement of the imagination" that had triggered his insanity was the 1833 trial of Ephraim Avery, a married Methodist minister accused of seducing and impregnating a millworker, then hanging her to conceal his lust. The Avery-Cornell murder "engaged the thoughts of the whole community" and more particularly, "every member of this family," since Sally's husband was reading a copy of the Avery trial on the afternoon of his own wife's murder. It was probable, according to the defense, that Sally and Abraham were discussing the case as they walked to the strawberry patch. The "excitable and astounding thought" that "a minister of a holy religion should have been on trial for so monstrous a crime"—

> it was this agitating thought, that helped unman [Prescott's] diseased intellect and led him without consciousness, whither it would,—and the effect was precisely such, as would be likely to result from such causes, and with such immediate previous mental associations. We all know, that the subject of our recent thoughts are [sic] often the subject of our dreams, and so it is in somnambulism and insanity; well, acts of violence, killing a female, having got firm possession of his diseased intellect, (by means of the Avery trial,) and in fact aiding or causing a manifestation of insanity, the act was such as medical men would have foretold, for similar cases are recorded.[74]

Within this tale of murder, a man who became an imaginative spectator of another man's dreadful violence was so thoroughly implicated in the crime that he was driven to commit a murder of his own. For Prescott, interiorization had not led to greater repression of forbidden impulses, but had unleashed them.

Sensationalism was a complex historical phenomenon. In eluding the grip of clerical control that had constrained the early American execution sermon, nineteenth-century murder literature offered readers a new kind of excitement and pleasure in the imaginatively voyeuristic entertainment of impulses newly forbidden by humanitarianism. But that pleasure was fundamentally a guilty pleasure, as evidenced in the constant moral apologies and rationales issued by the editors and publishers of popular murder literature. In crafting the role of the reader as onlooker to the violence, nineteenth-century murder literature explored the problematic relationship between watching and participating in such violence, thus suggesting the reader's moral complicity in the murderer's terrible crime. Though the initial impulse of the cult of horror was to establish an insurpassable moral distance between the murderer and those who read of his crime, its ultimate tendency was to implicate the readers in the murderer's guilt. And this guilt was far more terrible than the earlier sense of commonly shared sinfulness preached in early American execution sermons, for this guilt remained a matter of moral monstrosity. Perhaps this is why the techniques of body-horror grew ever more revolting over time: bringing the viewer closer to the murderer's violence heightened the need to vilify the killer in an effort to reassert a reassuring moral distance from evil. And that need for distance simply ratcheted up the horror, implicating the viewer ever more deeply in the murderer's terrible guilt.

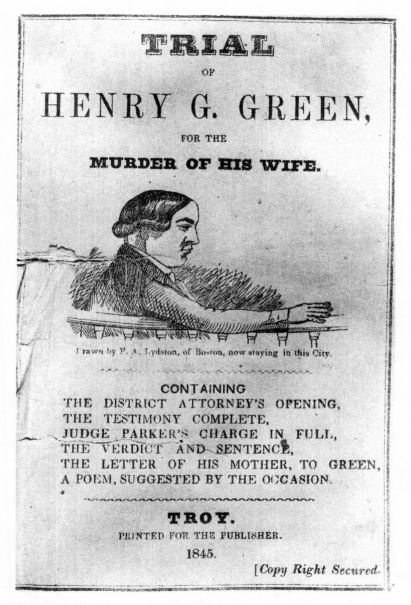

TRIAL

OF

HENRY G. GREEN,

FOR THE

MURDER OF HIS WIFE.

Drawn by F. A. Lydston, of Boston, now staying in this City.

CONTAINING
THE DISTRICT ATTORNEY'S OPENING,
THE TESTIMONY COMPLETE,
JUDGE PARKER'S CHARGE IN FULL,
THE VERDICT AND SENTENCE,
THE LETTER OF HIS MOTHER, TO GREEN,
A POEM, SUGGESTED BY THE OCCASION.

TROY.
PRINTED FOR THE PUBLISHER.
1845.

[*Copy Right Secured.*]

The dominance of the trial report in American murder literature after 1800 shaped a popular understanding of the crime as a *mystery* to be solved. This literature targeted, not a narrowly professional audience of lawyers, but a broader readership, as indicated in this title page for the *Trial of Henry G. Green,* which included a letter to the condemned man from his mother and a poem prompted by his crime.

BLUDGEON

FOUND UNDER THE STEPS OF HOWARD STREET CHURCH.

† Loaded with Lead.

Trial transcripts, like detective fiction, presented bits of evidence from which the larger narrative of the crime needed to be pieced together. Readers, like jurors, were invited to examine the exhibits in order to reconstruct the murder. Herewith the wooden bludgeon loaded with lead that was used to kill Captain Joseph White in 1830.

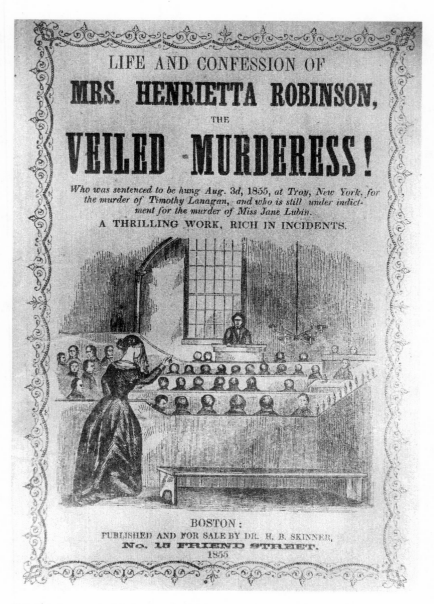

LIFE AND CONFESSION OF

MRS. HENRIETTA ROBINSON,

THE

VEILED MURDERESS!

Who was sentenced to be hung Aug. 3d, 1855, at Troy, New York, for the murder of Timothy Lanagan, and who is still under indictment for the murder of Miss Jane Lubin.

A THRILLING WORK, RICH IN INCIDENTS.

BOSTON:
PUBLISHED AND FOR SALE BY DR. H. B. SKINNER,
No. 18 FRIEND STREET.
1855

Murder as mystery. The title page of this work depicts the accused woman as symbolically shrouded in mystery. Her back is to the viewer, her face hidden beneath the veil she wore in court, her hair is primly pinned on top of her head, and she is fully clothed.

THE VEILED MURDERESS UNVEILED

The back-page illustration from *The Veiled Murderess!* literally removes the veil of mystery. The now-convicted killer's face is turned towards the viewer, disclosed in its implausible beauty, hair falling loosely onto her naked shoulders, and her body is not clothed but merely draped to a provocatively low line on her bust.

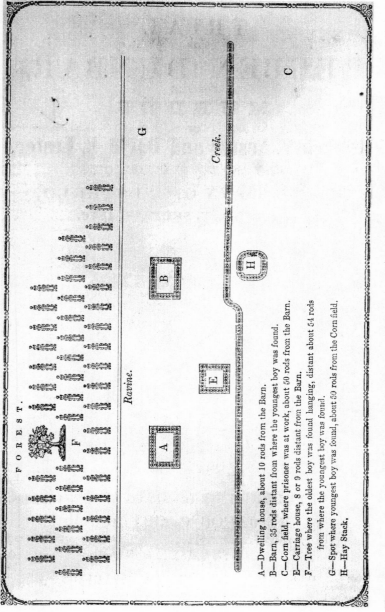

FOREST.

Ravine.

Creek.

A—Dwelling house, about 10 rods from the Barn.
B—Barn, 35 rods distant from where the youngest boy was found.
C—Corn field, where prisoner was at work, about 50 rods from the Barn.
E—Carriage house, 8 or 9 rods distant from the Barn.
F—Tree where the oldest boy was found hanging, distant about 54 rods from where the youngest boy was found.
G—Spot where youngest boy was found, about 50 rods from the Corn field.
H—Hay Stack,

The cartography of murder. The murder mystery required that the crime be visually mapped, so the reader could imaginatively reconstruct it by tracking the murderer's evil path. This chart marks the cornfield ("C") where Reuben Dunbar was working on the day he murdered his two step-cousins and the locations of the two bodies ("F" and "G"), and charts the various distances traveled by the killer.

This illustration of the Joseph White murder captures the essential elements of the "mystery": the private bedchamber with its heavily draped bed where the elderly victim slept, the stealthy advance and furtive glance of his killer, and the midnight hour when the full moon was partially obscured by clouds.

Unroofing the murder. Readers of the murder mystery were invited to the scene of the crime: to examine, for example, the external facade of Alfred and Ruth Fyler's home near Syracuse, New York—

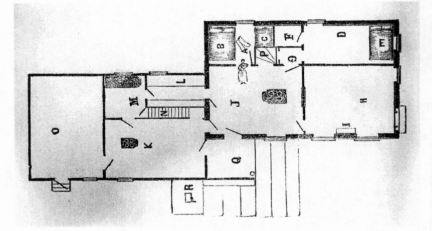

—and then imaginatively remove the roof of the Fyler home to uncover its interior layout, the family's sleeping arrangements, and the position of Ruth's recumbent body. This floor plan was accompanied by an elaborate key (not shown), explaining each letter, to "enable the reader to perfectly understand the location and relative positions of the several apartments, and to better comprehend the testimony."

AWFUL DISCLOSURES

AND

STARTLING DEVELOPEMENTS,

IN RELATION TO THE LATE

PARKMAN TRAGEDY.

A VIEW OF THE MEDICAL COLLEGE IN NORTH GROVE STREET, BOSTON,
WHERE THE HORRIBLE TRAGEDY IS SUPPOSED TO HAVE
BEEN PERFORMED.

WITH A FULL ACCOUNT OF THE DISCOVERY OF THE REMAINS OF THE
LATE DR. GEORGE PARKMAN, AND THE SUBSEQUENT ARREST OF

PROFESSOR JOHN W. WEBSTER.

Gothic space. The murder mystery's fascination with private spaces and their
secret evils is suggested in this 1849 title-page illustration, in which the facade
of Harvard Medical College implicitly invites readers to penetrate to its inner
precincts where "the horrible tragedy" took place.

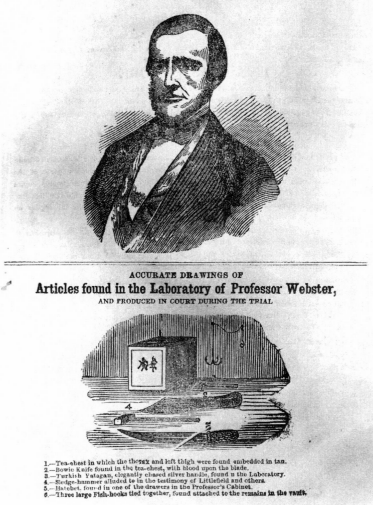

EPHRAIM LITTLEFIELD,
JANITOR OF THE MEDICAL COLLEGE,
Who discovered the Remains in the Vault of Professor Webster.

DRAWN BY ROWSE, FROM A DAGUERREOTYPE BY CHASE.—ENGRAVED BY MARSH, EXPRESSLY
FOR THE NEW YORK GLOBE.

ACCURATE DRAWINGS OF
Articles found in the Laboratory of Professor Webster,
AND PRODUCED IN COURT DURING THE TRIAL

1.—Tea-chest in which the thorax and left thigh were found embedded in tan.
2.—Bowie Knife found in the tea-chest, with blood upon the blade.
3.—Turkish Yatagan, elegantly chased silver handle, found n the Laboratory.
4.—Sledge-hammer alluded to in the testimony of Littlefield and others.
5.—Hatchet, found in one of the drawers in the Professor's Cabinet.
6.—Three large Fish-hooks tied together, found attached to the remains in the vault.

The Webster-Parkman mystery. This trial report offered its readers a portrait of the amateur sleuth, Ephraim Littlefield, who would not rest until he had discovered Parkman's dismembered body, and a still-life sketch of the physical evidence produced in court to convict Webster of the crime.

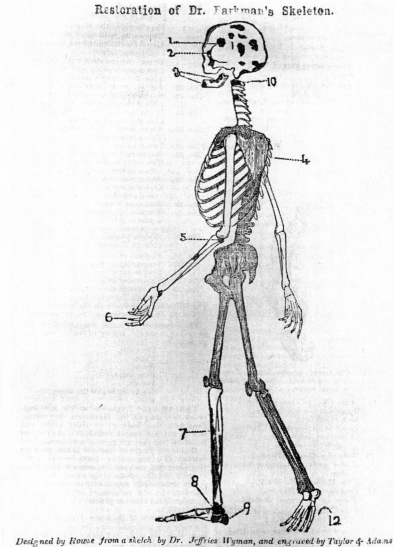

Designed by Rowse from a sketch by Dr. Jeffries Wyman, and engraved by Taylor & Adams Especially for the Boston Herald.

The do-it-yourself kit for the Webster-Parkman murder. Several trial transcripts offered readers this sketch of Parkman's skeleton, indicating which parts were found in the privy vault and tea chest (shaded), which parts in the furnace (black), and which parts were never found (white)—

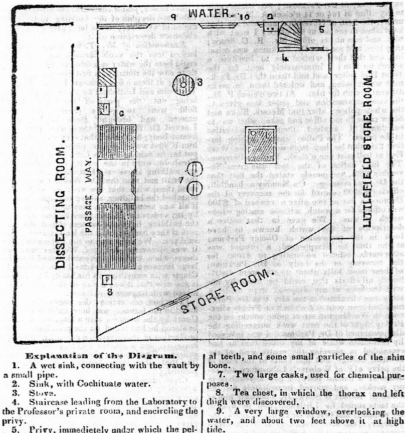

—and this floor plan of Webster's laboratory, indicating the various locations of the privy vault, tea chest, and furnace. Readers were thus invited to reconstruct the *crime* by looking first at the skeleton, and to reconstruct the *investigation* by looking first at the plan.

CHAPTER FOUR

The Construction of Murder as Mystery

W HEN twelve-year-old Hannah Ocuish killed six-year-old Eunice Bolles in New London, Connecticut, in 1786, the Rev. Henry Channing delivered her execution sermon, warning parents and masters not to neglect the religious and moral instruction of children. When it was printed, the editors appended a brief account which began, "On the 21st of July, 1786, at about 10 o'clock in the morning, the body of the murdered child was found in the public road leading from *New-London* to *Norwich,* lying on its face near to a wall. Its head was covered with stones, and a number lay upon its back and arms. Upon examining the body the scull [sic] appeared to be fractured; the arms and face much bruised, and the prints of finger-nails were very deep on the throat." In the investigation that followed, the neighborhood turned out to look for the murderer; Hannah was questioned, and tried to divert suspicion by claiming she had seen four boys near the scene of the crime. When a search failed to turn them up, she was questioned again, then taken to the Bolles home to be charged with the murder in the presence of the dead child. Hannah burst into tears and confessed. Only at this point in the story was the reader offered a sequential account of the crime, based on the "particulars which she then gave, and which appeared in the course of the trial." Five weeks earlier, Eunice had reported Hannah for stealing fruit at "strawberry time," and Hannah had plotted revenge. Catching sight of her young enemy headed for school, Hannah lured Eunice from her path with a gift of calico, then beat and choked her to death, finally covering the body with stones to make it appear that Eunice had been killed by a falling wall.[1]

The volume that included Hannah's story, entitled *God Admonishing His People of Their Duty*, marked a literary boundary between the early American execution sermon and a strikingly new way to tell the tale of a murder, based on that "peculiar distortion of more usual narrative conventions" which characterizes detective fiction. The "characteristic action of all detective fiction" is to "begin with the recent impact of a crime and work backward to restructure the incomplete fragments of present knowledge into a more intelligible whole and consequently to explain the past."[2] On the surface, the story of an investigation is narrated, while on another level, the hidden story of the crime is brought to light.[3]

But the Ocuish narrative, unlike the detective story, was not fiction. It concerned an actual murder, the nature of which was fully understood at the time of publication, and it focused on a real murderer, whose identity was known—not just to the volume's editors, but to readers who had read the execution sermon. Nor did the Ocuish narrative set forth a character resembling a detective, a single organizing intelligence to conduct the investigation and make sense of the crime. In 1786, before the professionalization of law enforcement in America, the townspeople of New London had solved the murder of Eunice Bolles.

The term that best captures the nature of the Ocuish account is *murder mystery*, a narrative that approaches the crime as a mystery, a problem to be solved. The cultural construction of murder-as-mystery was already under way in 1786, over half a century before Edgar Allan Poe's "invention" of detective fiction with "The Murders in the Rue Morgue" in 1841.[4] The murder mystery was a by-product of the new legal discourse on crime that was replacing the earlier theological discourse. As the popularity of execution sermons yielded to trial reports, and lawyers seized from clergymen the cultural task of shaping crime stories, the moral certainty of the early American murder narrative was displaced by a new understanding of the crime as fundamentally resistant to full knowledge, moral comprehension, and narrative closure.

USE

———————

Early American execution sermons assigned no mystery to the crime of murder. Their guiding assumption was a centuries-old proverb, "Murder will out." Just as the blood of Abel had cried from the ground, calling God to bring Cain to justice for his terrible crime, so the blood of every murder "cries from the Ground, and brings down Vengeance from Heaven."[5] Early New Englanders brought suspected murderers to touch the corpse in the presence of the coroner's jury, and if "the *Blood* came fresh into it"—as when Mary Martin touched the face of her dead newborn child—the guilt of the murder was proved.[6] The corpse-touching test "mimicked the archetypal structure of confession—the revealing of the hidden, the up-welling of a sin that God alone can see and forgive," and pointed to the widespread New England belief that God knows all secret crimes.[7] Sometimes, the clergy conceded, "the Murders themselves are concealed, or if discovered, yet it is not known who committed them: Nor can they be found, tho' the strictest Search be made for them." But even in these cases, God knew the secret murderers, and God would, in His own time, bring them to light.[8]

Before the mid-eighteenth century, the Anglo-American criminal trial was not adversarial. It worked as an inquisitorial procedure conducted by a judge whose job was to ferret out God's truth, considered to be single and uncontestable.[9] The conviction rate of criminals brought to trial in seventeenth-century New England was extraordinarily high—around ninety percent—because the magistrates had already established blame at the preliminary examination. Few trials resulted in acquittals, not because magistrates treated defendants as guilty unless proved innocent, but because they avoided raising criminal charges that could not be substantiated by two witnesses, as required by biblical law. The purposes served by the trial were to convince spectators of the defendant's guilt, educate townspeople in the evils of crime, and inflict a ritual humiliation on the criminal to induce confession and repentance. The strikingly high rate of confession among those brought to trial further discouraged any popular sense of the problematic nature of criminal guilt.[10] Virtually all of the subjects of execution sermons had confessed their crimes.

There was little room for mystery here. In the legal world of early New England, indicted criminals were guilty criminals, convicted criminals obligingly confessed their guilt, and the public assumed without question that such moral certainty was guaranteed by God's active presence throughout the entire process. As convicted wife-murderer Joseph explained, "But GOD has now brought me out."[11] The execution sermon rarely mentioned the process of criminal justice that had brought the condemned malefactor to the scaffold, but simply accepted without qualification his or her guilt. Significantly, early New England culture had no print format for addressing unsolved or unproved murders.

Though the execution sermon survived into the nineteenth century, its dominance in American murder literature gradually yielded to the murder trial account. Few murder trial accounts were printed in the colonies before the American Revolution, and these tended not to be formal trial transcripts.[12] In 1770, a transcript of the trial proceedings for the eight soldiers charged with murder in the "Boston massacre" was printed. Several others followed before the end of the century, and the extremely successful *Narrative of Whiting Sweeting*, printed in 1791 and reprinted at least thirteen times by 1797, included an account of his trial for the murder of Darius Quimby.[13] The many reprintings of the Sweeting narrative in the 1790s proved to be the beginning of the sustained dominance of legal discourse within nineteenth-century murder literature.

Some legal narratives treated the trial as one of several points of interest in a crime, which might include a narrative of the murder, the life-history of the murderer, the convicted criminal's confession, the execution.[14] Another category of legal narratives, which first appeared after 1800 and became more common after 1830, consisted of selected portions of the judicial proceedings—the preliminary examination of a suspect, the closing for the defense or prosecution, the judge's charge to the jury or sentencing speech, the petition for clemency, the commutation of sentence—or of legal commentaries on those proceedings.[15] Comprising about 15 percent of murder narratives printed before 1789, this legal literature steadily rose in proportion after 1790, reaching a level of 66 percent in the 1820s and staying there for the duration of the nineteenth century.[16]

The emergence of the murder trial report signaled the gradual breakup of the clerical monopoly over the public discourse of murder. Rising generations of intellectuals increasingly embraced law over theology. Still a weak and widely despised corporate guild in the early decades of the eighteenth century, the legal profession gradually gained in strength and status as lawyers emerged as spokesmen and agents within the commercializing trans-Atlantic economy. "Lawyer or merchant," wrote Hector St. John de Crevecoeur, "are the fairest titles our towns afford." After 1760, lawyers launched their astonishingly rapid rise to political leadership, which would soon place them in the forefront of the Revolution and secure their position as the preeminent profession in America. New political power brought with it a broader intellectual ascendancy, most evident in the close connection between law and letters in early republican culture, which produced an impressive number of lawyer-writers, including Noah Webster, Charles Brockden Brown, Washington Irving, Richard Henry Dana, Sr., and William Cullen Bryant.[17]

The rising professional status of lawyers accompanied the emergence of the adversarial trial in Anglo-American criminal justice. After the mid-1730s, English judges began to allow defendants the help of counsel, and the "rambling altercation" of the earlier criminal trial was gradually replaced by the sequence of the prosecution followed by the defense.[18] With this restructuring, the role of lawyers in the criminal trial was broadened, and their powers extended at the expense of the presiding judge. In revolutionary and early republican America, courtroom speeches by attorneys and judges, whose educational training typically included English and classical literature as well as Blackstone's *Commentaries,* emerged as a crucial form of cultural expression. "The trial in republican society was a central ceremony and the courtroom speech its most visible ritual." Crowds packed the courtrooms to hear their favorite legal orators, while newspapers and journals gave extensive coverage to trials and related legal matters. In their drive for professional ascendancy, lawyers took good advantage of the widespread familiarity with legal conceptualization and language in revolutionary culture, to gain significant control over public discourse in the early republic.[19] In this context popular murder literature turned increasingly to the trial report as the most appropriate narrative form for exploring the nature of the crime.

Most trial reports purported to be transcripts which recorded all trial testimony, the closings of counsel, the judge's instructions to the jury, the verdict, and, when the defendant was found guilty, the sentencing. Some were only eight or twelve pages in length; others ran into the hundreds of pages.[20] They varied greatly in accuracy and completeness. While the *Report of the Case of John W. Webster* ran to 628 pages, the pointedly titled *Full and Correct Report of the Trial and Conviction of Prof. John W. Webster* was, at 64 pages, only one-tenth as long; though the *Report of the Trial of Jason Fairbanks* was 84 pages in length, *A Deed of Horror! Trial of Jason Fairbanks* (which claimed to have been "Correctly taken down by a gentleman on the spot") was only 8 pages.[21] Trial reports were variously compiled by clerks of the court, members of the bar, attorneys involved in the trial, one entrepreneurial jail warden, and newspaper reporters;[22] many, like that by the "gentleman on the spot," were reported anonymously; some observers took notes "in shorthand" or used "phonographic" or "stenographic" methods.[23]

Some editors explicitly offered their publications to lawyers interested in "arguments and decisions upon important points of law." But the editorial practice of omitting technical treatments of case law (or using shorthand references) suggested a desire to reach a wider readership. As one editor explained, his was "a plain and simple statement of the evidence" which omitted "all technicalities."[24] Published trial reports bore the marks of a popular literature: cheaply printed, usually between paper covers, and cheaply sold, often illustrated, and, especially in the more sensational crimes, printed in competing editions by several publishers. The murder of John

Whipple by his wife Elsie and her lover Jesse Strang generated seven trial reports; the murder of Dr. George Parkman by Professor John Webster prompted nine, plus three trial-related accounts. Many editorial prefaces appealed explicitly to a wider reading audience, justifying publication of the trial with reference to public curiosity and alarm, the exclusion of would-be spectators from packed courtrooms, the desirability of giving "the poorer classes of inquisitive citizens" an opportunity "to learn how their lives and liberties are protected," and the usual moral value of a work on the wages of crime. The *Trial of Lucretia Chapman* expressly offered "to the reading community at large" a story of "romantic character."[25]

The major effect of the transition from a religious to a legal discourse on murder was moral uncertainty about the nature of the crime and the assignment of guilt. The early American execution sermon had assumed that worldly justice matched divine justice, and all that needed to be known about the crime had been providentially brought to light. In contrast, the trial report did not assume the guilt of the accused murderer, but rather made that guilt its central problem. And the new adversarial trial made legal truth a matter of formal argument rather than inquisitorial determination.

Moral uncertainty first appeared, revealingly, in the legal turn taken by late eighteenth-century execution sermons. A waning clergy began to make reference to the "Bar of Justice" that had brought their convicted criminals to the scaffold, and some editors began to include legal materials with their printed execution sermons.[26] For the most part, the clergy cited the condemned murderer's trial in order to reaffirm his guilt of the crime. But the moment they began to *argue* the murderer's guilt, they implied the possibility of his innocence, as when the Rev. Moses Baldwin contended that William Shaw had to be guilty because his various alibis had contradicted each other. The Rev. Enoch Huntington in 1796 actually acknowledged that "Human judicatories, and the judgments and executions dependent upon them, may be erroneous"—though he affirmed that Thomas Starr's trial had been fair. By 1805, the Rev. Moses Welch was willing to admit, shortly before Samuel Freeman's execution, that he did not know the truth concerning the guilt of the

{97}

convicted murderer (who continued to proclaim his innocence), but warned him against lying just before death.[27]

These legal inclusions in the execution sermons revealed the encroachments of the system of worldly justice upon the theological interpretation of murder. Criminal trials normally begin with an accusation of guilt—in legal terms, an indictment—which must then be persuasively argued ("proved") by the prosecution if guilt is to be found. Formal guilt thus does not initiate the trial report, but can only conclude this genre of narrative. And some accusations of guilt do not hold up in court: from their earliest inception, many printed trials ended in acquittals which offered no formal narrative closure. The murder trial of the soldiers charged in the "Boston massacre" resulted in six acquittals and two convictions of manslaughter; John Graham was acquitted of the murder of his wife Phoebe in Baltimore in 1804. Even more problematically, William Hardy was first convicted of the murder of his illegitimate infant child in Boston in 1806, then acquitted in a new trial granted on a legal technicality.[28] Editors learned to refer to the "supposed murder" and the "alleged murderer" in titles of cases resulting in acquittal.[29] The trial report proved an important print format for addressing unsolved or unproved murders.

But the main way in which the trial report made guilt problematic was through its narrative qualities. It represented a distinctive mode of addressing the crime of murder: the effort to reconstruct the events surrounding a violent death by sorting through those fragments of the past that lawyers called *evidence*. The emergence of the adversarial trial generated the strong and self-conscious concern for evidence which ran through the pages of murder trial reports. Before the mid-eighteenth century, with a few minor exceptions, there was no law of evidence establishing the rules excluding certain kinds of evidence—such as hearsay or character evidence based on past convictions—from being heard by the jury. But as English judges began to allow defendants the help of counsel, the courts began to develop rules of evidence such as the corroboration rule and the confession rule; treatises on evidence began to appear, to assist lawyers eager to learn the art of adversarial trial work.[30]

Murder trial reports presented readers with a range of evidence used to reconstruct the events surrounding a violent death. Most prominent was the physical evidence, often introduced in court with a melodramatic flourish: the blunted hatchet and blue cloak found near Rosina Townshend's brothel after the murder of Helen Jewett, the note left by Sarah Cornell before she was found hanging from a hayrick, the distinctively striped bloody glove discovered at the scene of the murder of Anna Ayer, the arsenic found locked in James Eldredge's satchel after Sarah Jane Gould's agonized death.[31] Some murderers were convicted in part by the tracks of their boots at the murder scene.[32] Trial witnesses sometimes brought forth crucial aural evidence: the overheard threat of violence, the barking of dogs which suggested the time the crime was committed.[33] Medical evidence was introduced with increasing frequency during the first half of the nineteenth century. Though John Hendrickson had chosen the vegetable poison aconite for its difficulty of detection, medical and chemical investigators claimed successfully to have uncovered the cause of his wife's death and thus helped secure his conviction of murder. By mid-century, trial attorneys were beginning to address such forensic questions as, how does impact alter the shape of a bullet? Can human blood be distinguished from chicken blood? How long does a dead body take to grow cold? And how does the pattern of blood shed on a shirt by a spontaneous nose-bleed differ from blood shed during a deadly assault?[34]

Rarely were murderers convicted on the basis of eyewitness testimony: as prosecutors routinely explained, "When a murderer has resolved upon his deed, he does not call out his neighbors to witness it; his intention lurks in the dark chambers of his heart, until it conducts him to the secluded scene of its action." It was thus necessary for prosecutors to turn to circumstantial evidence to build their cases against defendants. And circumstantial evidence, as prosecuting attorneys well knew, left troubling gaps in the story of a murder. The prosecuting attorney who claimed that circumstantial evidence needed no apology, went on immediately to apologize for it as "the only evidence by which secret crime can ever be detected." Thus was it necessary, for example, to convict murderer Lucian Hall on the basis of the blood found on the clothes he wore on the day of the murder, his inability to explain his absence from home or to produce an alibi, the cut on his hand and his discrepant accounts of it, his suspicious behavior between the time of the murder and his arrest, and the testimony of several witnesses that someone of his size and peculiar gait had been seen near the victim's home around the time of the murder. Such evidence was considerable—it "left *scarcely any* doubt in the minds of the public about his guilt"—but it remained incomplete.[35]

The trial reports' extensive reliance on circumstantial evidence constructed murder *stories* that were usually fragmented, chronologically jumbled, and incomplete. Evidence concerning the discovery of a murder or the state of the corpse might be introduced before evidence of the events that led up to the murder, and most trials doubled back on themselves once the defense began its case. And circumstantial evidence left significant gaps in the narrative. The Rev. Ephraim Avery's claim to have been wandering alone around Portsmouth, Rhode Island, at the time of Sarah Cornell's death in Tiverton, could not be corroborated by the two people he said he encountered on his rambles, the man with the gun and the boy with the sheep, who were never found. And where was the body of nine-year-old Charles Stevens, whose father was charged with battering the boy to death in 1823? The prosecution charged that the body had been boxed and dumped into the ocean, but it was never found and Charles Senior was acquitted.[36]

Further confusing the coherence of the trial report's narrative was its piecemeal reconstruction of events from multiple and often conflicting perspectives. Was Eliza Fales still romantically involved with Jason Fairbanks at the time of her death, or had she lost interest in his romantic suit? Was John Graham a drunken philanderer who habitually beat his wife, Phoebe, out of malicious cruelty, or a loving, tender-hearted husband who became intemperate and violent only when driven to despair by her drunken and indecent conduct?[37] Witnesses at these trials disagreed. Even expert witnesses sometimes testified at cross purposes.[38] And some witnesses and defendants contradicted their own previous testimony: James Anthony, charged with murdering Joseph Green in a hatter's shop in Vermont in 1814, offered conflicting alibis concerning his whereabouts on the night of the crime, saying variously that he had been in bed at the shop, that he was out at the time, that he was out and another man was present, and that he was present when another man committed the murder.[39]

In fact, the formal indictment which initiated most trial reports often offered several different versions of what had happened, thus throwing readers into serious confusion from the outset. In the trial of John Francis Knapp for the murder of Captain Joseph White in 1830, the indictment charged Joseph J. Knapp (the defendant's brother) and George Crowninshield with contracting for the killing, with the following variations: John Francis Knapp committed the act alone; he killed White but was aided or abetted by Richard Crowninshield, Jr. (George's brother); Richard Crowninshield committed the murder aided and abetted by John Francis Knapp; and a person unknown killed White aided and abetted by John Francis Knapp (the involvement of two Knapps and two Crowninshields in the White murder added complexity to this multi-layered narrative).[40] Such multiple indictments were drawn up to follow a legal imperative to cover all possible variants of the crime, to prevent the defendant from going free. But standing as they did at the head of printed accounts of the murder, they compounded the narrative uncertainty structured into these legal stories.

Chronologically disjointed, fragmentary, internally inconsistent, incomplete: the new adversarial trial was challenging to follow and difficult to interpret. For that reason, criminal lawyers were developing an important technique for helping their most immediate "readers"—the jury—to retain, organize, and interpret the chaotic stream of information coming at them from witnesses. Criminal trials are organized around storytelling, the construction of clear, "common-sense" narratives which assist jurors in their arrangement of time frames, characters, motives, means, and settings—stories which cut through the confusions generated by trial testimony to achieve narrative clarity. In the story lines set out by attorneys, murder trials achieved their greatest degree of narrative coherence.[41]

But it is the peculiar nature of adversarial courtroom storytelling to be competitive: first the prosecution and then the defense takes up the chaos of details provided by witnesses and shapes it into as clear and compelling a narrative as possible, in an effort to persuade jurors to choose that side's plot line.[42] Though a significant degree of implicit plotting went on in the choice of witnesses by both prosecution and defense, it was in their summations that they explicitly and didactically set forth their competitive stories. There they shaped chaos into plotted narrative through a close attention to sequence and consequence, characterization and motivation, plausibility and point of view. And there they contested most directly the true nature and meaning of the events that had taken place.

Two dramatically different stories were told, for example, by the prosecution and the defense in the trial of Lucretia Chapman for the murder of her husband in Andalusia, Pennsylvania, in 1831. William Chapman died of arsenic poisoning some six weeks after the arrival of a stranger to the Chapman home, a Spanish-speaking youth, Mina, who boasted of his wealth and position as son of the governor of California and quickly launched a romantic courtship of the matron of the house, twenty years his senior. Eleven days after William's death, Lucretia and Mina were secretly married. Subsequently, suspicion arose concerning the cause of William's death; Lucretia learned that Mina (the "Spaniard") was a confidence man, an impoverished Cuban recently released from the Philadelphia penitentiary after serving time for larceny; and it was discovered that he had purchased arsenic the day before his host's final illness.

Lucretia Chapman's trial involved testimony from servants, boarders, Chapman children, pupils from the Chapmans' school, neighbors, an itinerant bookseller, Lucretia's clergyman and the family's personal physicians, a tailor, a pharmacist, the undertaker, the Mexican consul in Philadelphia, police officers, and sundry medical experts. The prosecution shaped the chaos of all this testimony into a story of a lustful, avaricious matriarch who had eagerly responded to the blandishments of her young lover and, monstrously, helped him season her husband's sickroom soup with arsenic. Using the same testimony, the defense wove a tale of a pious and tenderly devoted wife and mother who had, through feminine passivity and trust,

{102}

fallen victim to a diabolically clever seducer, married Mina only because it was her dying husband's final wish, and played no part in poisoning the soup. Lucretia Chapman was acquitted of murder; Mina, whose trial soon followed, was convicted and hanged.[43]

The Chapman trial pitted the prosecution and the defense against one another as duelling storytellers. More commonly, the prosecution told a coherent story of the crime and the defense countered with an anti-narrative, aimed at unravelling the prosecution's story by any and all means available—even presenting its own set of mutually inconsistent story-lines—to arouse jurors' reasonable doubt. Such was the strategy of attorneys Andrew Dunlap and Jonathan H. Cobb in defending John Boies, on trial for the murder of his wife, Jane, in 1829. Prosecution witnesses testified that, for six months before Jane's death, the defendant had repeatedly battered her (breaking several bones), openly claimed his prerogative to beat her, and once threatened her life; and that she had died as a result of "several mortal wounds" out of fifteen inflicted on her with the bloody axe found in the Boies home after her death.[44]

To this narrative of murder, the defense responded with an anti-narrative which included the following elements. First, the prosecution had failed to demonstrate that Jane Boies had been murdered: a chronic drunkard subject to fits, she may have died of alcohol-induced apoplexy, or from injuries suffered during a fall from a wagon nine days before her death (which Jane had reported to her husband's sister to explain a wound in the side of her head). Second, even if she was murdered, the prosecution had failed to demonstrate that John Boies was the murderer: no one witnessed the crime, and the dying woman did not accuse her husband. Third, even if she was murdered by John Boies, the prosecution had failed to demonstrate the manner of death cited in the indictment: if she died not from axe wounds but from his extended abuse, then the jury must acquit John as formally charged. Fourth, even if she was killed by John Boies with an axe, the defendant might have assaulted his drunken and ill-tempered wife in self-defense, in the heat of passion, without malice aforethought, in which case the jury should convict him not of murder but of manslaughter. The defense attorney sought to generate reasonable doubt with a multiplication of alternative story lines. Nonetheless, John Boies was convicted of murder.

The overall effect of this common defense strategy was to reduce the pieces of evidence to their original chaos. At their greatest level of narrative coherence, murder trial reports proffered two conflicting but plausible stories of what had taken place; more commonly, they offered one reasonably persuasive narrative and one willfully confusing anti-narrative. Within the trial report, some narrative closure was usually offered in the jury's decision. But the publication of the trial transcript clearly permitted readers to draw their own conclusions or, alternatively, to remain in a state of indecision about the events in question. And the new genre of trial commentary was sometimes enlisted to issue formal challenges to trial outcomes on various legal, procedural, and medical grounds.

When the secular narrative of murder replaced the religious narrative, uncertainty arose, ironically, not from a poverty of information about the crime, but from a welter of testimony and detail which lent itself to various interpretive treatments. The problem with the new legal narratives was that they no longer spoke in the name of an omniscient authority. As Judge Marvin explained in sentencing John Hendrickson to death for the murder of his wife, Maria, "It is not given to mortal man to look into the thoughts and the hearts of his fellow men . . . we are unable to speak with unerring certainty of 'hidden things.' That power and that knowledge rests with and belongs to God alone; and He alone, beside yourself, *knows* whether you are or are not guilty."[45]

Trial lawyers made a major effort to restore to their legal narratives the moral certainty of the earlier theological tale of the crime. Most crudely, they did so by raiding the execution sermon for its providential language: "Murder will out!" claimed one prosecutor after another, as well as an occasional judge; "The blood of the sacrifice at last spoke from the ground"; "Sirs, a detecting and avenging Providence, appears to have attended this homicide."[46] Prosecuting attorneys echoed earlier clergymen in referring to Providence as that "eye which seeth in secret," which would "bring the offence and the offender to the light and condemnation of the world" by an operation that remained vaguely "miraculous."[47]

But these men of the law adapted divine Providence to courtroom use by explicitly connecting it to circumstantial evidence. Divine Providence, they explained, was responsible for the trail of evidence that enabled them to reconstruct the murder.[48] Reshaped by the lawyers, divine Providence acted through circumstance: "But, that Being who rules the universe, and who has commanded 'that whosoever sheddeth man's blood, by man shall his blood be shed,' has *by many circumstances,* brought this crime to light, and caused the prisoner's own acts, and conduct, to lead to his conviction."[49] The providential power actively intervened (almost like an overzealous policeman) to plant evidence against the murderer: the "finger of Providence was visible" in James Eldredge's accidental dropping of the key to the satchel where he had stashed his arsenic; the "hand of Providence was visible" in permitting Anna Ayer's daughter to survive the attack which killed her mother; "the mysterious ways of divine Providence, which lead to the detection of secret murderers" were at work in the discovery of the letter implicating the murderers of Joseph White.[50]

Nineteenth-century lawyers did not rest their claim to providential intervention on miracles. Theirs was an Enlightenment God who worked through natural laws—this-worldly ways and means of detection. Though the presiding judge in the murder trial of John Hendrickson identified as "a Providence!" the clot of blood found in the victim's heart at the autopsy, he went on to summarize the physician's testimony that such clots appeared in all victims of aconite poisoning, and explained, "Nature follows the course which the great artificer has laid out for her, and God works by given laws." Similarly, the judge sentencing John Earls for the murder of his wife, Catharine, announced that "the finger of Providence had interposed, in accordance with that well established truth that 'murder will out,'" to arouse public suspicion; he then went on to explain how the autopsy had definitively revealed the murderous cause of death.[51] Even in cases which involved little forensic medicine, legal language emphasized the intrinsic interconnectedness of all occurrences both human and natural. Seemingly discrete events were actually "links" in the "chain of circumstances." By 1850, such courtroom language was sufficiently powerful to influence the language of the pulpit: the Rev. Edward Kirk, preaching for the condemned Prof. John Webster, referred to the "web of circumstances" that had "entangled" this suspect, and explained that "A thousand unseen sentinels keep watch for God."[52]

Perhaps the most frequently cited natural law through which Divine Providence worked was psychological: the revelatory inclinations of the guilty conscience. One of the most famous passages in nineteenth-century criminal literature—Daniel Webster's closing for the prosecution of John Francis Knapp—addressed this phenomenon. Webster proclaimed that "the guilty secret of murder never can be safe" because "the general administration of Providence forbids it." The murderer "lives at war with himself" until "his bosom's secret over-masters him," and he either confesses or commits suicide.[53] Recalling John Hendrickson's statement, after his wife's death ("One thing I know, they won't find arsenic"), his prosecutor exclaimed, "Murder will out, and in such cases as this Omnipotent Wisdom effects the revelation; and this man's conscience was then crying, 'I murdered my wife! It was I who murdered her!'"[54]

Within their legalistic version of "Murder will out," prosecution lawyers assured jurors that Providence—the all-seeing and all-powerful divine agency—was present in every small link in the chain of circumstantial or "moral" evidence (as it was alternatively called). This was a remnant of sacred storytelling rattling around within the larger secular narrative of the crime, a legal fiction that provided an argument not just for the guilt of any given defendant, but for the legitimacy of circumstantial evidence, and in the largest sense, for the cultural authority of legal narrative. But the lawyers could not fully close the gaps that opened up in their circumstantial narratives of criminal guilt. No dropped key, no incriminating note, no clot of blood could take the place of the providential eye and hand. Lawyers then resorted to a language of *mystery*.

"Much of the case," they acknowledged, "must remain a mystery."

Sometimes prosecutors invoked the term in strategic concession that their stories of the defendant's guilt had left some questions unanswered. Lucretia Chapman's prosecutor referred to a private conversation between the defendant and her alleged accomplice as one of "the unexplained mysteries of this singular history." More commonly, it was the defense attorneys who brought out the mysterious nature of the crime, to emphasize the inadequacy of the prosecution's case. The death of Maria Bickford "may remain in mystery till the heavens are no more, and the sea has given up its dead," said Rufus Choate in defense of Albert Tirrell. "The government has not reached the bottom of this transaction." Without eyewitnesses to Lucius Foot's murder, no one would ever fully know "the secrets of that awful night"; the court could only "see through a glass darkly." Addressing the jury in defense of accused wife-killer George Swearingen, John V. L. M'Mahon spoke on the limits of circumstantial evidence: "you cannot trace out all the shadowy forms, with which human events are clothed—you cannot follow with unerring steps, through all their devious windings, the secret purposes and actions of men . . . you cannot call up as the dead are called from the grave, all the circumstances of human actions, and give to each its proper place, and clothe it with its proper intent."[55] Whatever their strategic legal purposes, such statements underlined the crime's ultimate unknowability, its final resistance to seamless and omniscient narrative.

As murder-as-mystery spilled over from legal narratives of the crime into the larger popular literature, growing interest in the "mysterious" nature of murder was evident in titles such as "Mysterious Murder," "Misterious [sic] Abduction and Murder," and "Mysterious Affair."[56] Mystery, like horror, generated a competitive sensationalism: no murder was "more enveloped in the shades of mystery" than the Sarah Cornell murder; the Boorns-Colvin case was "one of the most mysterious events recorded in the annals of time." With increasing frequency, murder accounts opened by presenting the crime as a puzzle to be solved: "On Friday, the 17th of September, 1841, Mr.

Samuel Adams, a highly respectable printer, residing at No. 11 Elizabeth street, New York, of the firm of Scratcherd & Adams, of No. 59 Gold street, suddenly and mysteriously disappeared."[57]

The narratological structure of the nonfictional murder mystery, first prompted by the Ocuish case, echoed the structure of the trial report. It began with the *corpus delicti*, the fact of the crime, usually established by the dead body; then moved through the investigation, citing the fragments of circumstantial evidence uncovered by that investigation; pulled those fragments together within a narrative that usually remained incomplete; and only at the end identified the murderer. In 1821, the account of Peter Lagoardette's murder opened as follows: "On Tuesday, the 20th of March, about two o'clock, P.M., Josiah Cherry, a police officer, was informed, on coming home to his dinner, that something like a murder must have been committed that morning in Mrs. Hetherington's house, as a considerable noise like scuffling, and screams, had been heard there by some of the neighboring women and children."[58] The narrative followed Officer Cherry's movements as he climbed through a window, went up the stairs, entered the room at the eastern end of the second floor, and discovered a dismembered body. After describing the murder scene in some detail, this account related the community's response to the crime, recorded the launching of an investigation, and finally reported that two Spaniards had been seen near the house on the day of the murder. Brief summations of the trials were then offered. Finally, the narrator backtracked to discuss the killers' criminal careers before the murder, and their connection with their murder victim.

Like classic detective fiction, this tale of murder operated on two separate levels—the murder investigation and the crime itself. This layered quality was highlighted in the three-part title of another account: *Narrative of the Murder of James Murray,/and the Circumstances of its Detection/With the Trial of John Johnson.* The story begins: a corpse is discovered in New York and publicly displayed so it can be identified. A Catholic priest recognizes sailor James Murray; he is traced to his vessel, which he had left in the company of a man who kept a sailors' boarding house in lower Manhattan. The police examine several such houses and find John Johnson. They take him back to the sailing vessel, where he is identified as the victim's companion on the day of his disappearance; and when he denies any knowledge of Murray, his house is searched. Under a board in the cellar are found a sheet, an axe, and other articles stained with blood. Authorities then locate the cartman who had conveyed Murray's trunk, subsequently found hidden under Mrs. Johnson's bed. Finally, a trail of blood is traced from a bedroom through the cellar and up the steps to the street, and Murray's blood-stained clothes are found in Johnson's yard. Working backward from the corpse, this narrative first tracked the victim to his entry into the city, then traced his steps to Johnson's boarding house, and finally followed the bloody trail to the place where the corpse was discovered, thus coming full circle to its own starting point: the dead body. "Here then was developed, by a most singular and almost irresistible chain of circumstantial evidence, a crime which was perpetrated at the dark and silent hour of midnight."[59]

Literary historians have traced the origins of detective fiction to three short stories by Edgar Allan Poe—"The Murders in the Rue Morgue" (1841), "The Mystery of Marie Roget" (1842–43), and "The Purloined Letter" (1845)—and cited the remarkable range of conventions invented by Poe in these stories: the characters of the brilliant, eccentric detective and his admiring, less sharp-witted companion; the blunderings of the police; the locked-room murder; the wrong suspect to whom all evidence seems initially to point; concealment by means of the obvious and solution by means of the unexpected; the aphorism that once all impossibilities have been eliminated, whatever remains, however improbable, is the truth; the aphorism that the more bizarre the case, the easier it is to solve.[60]

Poe's stories appeared in the historical context of the professionalization of law enforcement in the early nineteenth century. Eighteenth-century American communities (such as Hannah Ocuish's New London) were largely self-policing: though constables often helped keep the peace, communities still depended on the volunteer night-watch and the hue and cry or *posse commitatus* for the arrest of criminals. By 1821, when Officer Cherry investigated the Lagoardette murder, some American cities had added a day-watch to their night-watch force, but these policemen remained untrained, often unsala-ried, and understandably reluctant to take on criminal cases that offered no reward money. The model for the modern metropolitan police force was established by Sir Robert Peel (whose name pro-vided members of that force with their nickname), in the London Metropolitan Police Act of 1829, which assigned officers to walk regular patrols or "beats" as a deterrent to crime and urban unrest. London's example was imitated by Philadelphia in 1833, Boston in 1837, and New York in 1845. But the primary concern of these new police forces was the prevention, not detection, of crime. Though they gradually introduced detective divisions in the 1850s, detectives continued to operate on the traditional model of the eighteenth-cen-tury "thief-taker," who did not actually arrest thieves but rather re-turned stolen property, acting as the middleman between the crimi-nal and the victim, for a private fee.[61]

But the murder-mystery narrative that was reshaping tales of murder in the late eighteenth and early nineteenth centuries actually anticipated both the appearance of the professional detective and Poe's "invention" of detective fiction. Indeed, in at least one case, the murder-mystery narrative mandated the invention of the detective, rather than vice versa: the unsolved murder of Mary Cecilia Rogers in New York in 1841 proved a major factor in the formation of the New York police department in 1845.[62] The more important factor in the emergence of this new narrative was the growing dominance of the legal discourse of the crime. Significantly, the editorial prefaces to some trial reports enlisted the murder-mystery format for a pre-liminary version of the crime story. The introduction to the report of Alfred Fyler's trial offers a case in point. The subsection entitled "The Murderer's Work" described the "blood-smeared apartment" and "mangled corpse" as they had been first discovered. "First Ru-mors and Suspicions" threw out the red herring of Alfred Fyler's hired men, upon whom he had tried to cast suspicion. "Effects upon the Public" reported the "thrill of horror" that swept the community when the murder became known. At length, "Suspicion Resting against Fyler" revealed that "The deep mystery that at first enveloped the bloody transaction, speedily gave way to strongly grounded suspicions against Fyler, the husband, as the perpetrator of the murder," after which "Investigations Commenced" reported the thorough investigations made before Fyler's indictment.[63] Only then, after the reader had been led through the maze of the murder-mystery narrative to arrive at a point clearly indicated in the title of the work ("A Full Report of the Trial of Alfred Fyler"), did the trial report commence.

Other narrative forms both reflected and contributed to the growing moral uncertainty surrounding the crime of murder. Whereas earlier first-person accounts consisted overwhelmingly of confessions by condemned murderers, those appearing in the late eighteenth century—such as *The Narrative of Whiting Sweeting* (1791) and *The Address of Abraham Johnstone* (1797)—frequently denied guilt. The fictional *Life of Ambrose Gwinett* (1784), who escaped from hanging to locate his supposed murder victim, claimed its "Demonstratively proving, that Condemnations upon circumstantial Evidence are injurious to Innocence, incompatible with Justice, and therefore ought always to be discountenanced, especially in Cases of Life and Death."[64] In 1825, the final words of convicted murderer John Dahmen forever muddled moral certainty about his crime: "he had told many stories, some of them true and some of them false," and "there was a book of his *adventures* published—but that they must not believe it." *The Confession of Jereboam O. Beauchamp* (1826) offered a different sort of moral ambiguity: though the convicted murderer, himself a lawyer, admitted his crime, he used the "confession" format to explain in endless detail that the prosecution lacked evidence against him and to claim that he had been framed.[65] Other purported "confessions" printed in the nineteenth century actually blamed the murder on someone else.[66]

Another expression of murder-as-mystery was the growing attention to murders that ultimately eluded solution. The body of Mary Cecilia Rogers was found in the Hudson River near Hoboken in July 1841, three days after she had disappeared from her mother's boarding-house on Nassau Street. The coroner's inquest found that she had been bound and gagged, raped by several men, then strangled (though the New York City Coroner recorded the cause of death as drowning). But public rumors circulated that "the Beautiful Cigar Girl" (who had tended counter at a popular tobacco shop, where she was well known to participants in New York's sporting culture), had taken her own life, or died of complications following an abortion, or been strangled by a single male companion with whom she was seen at a roadhouse near the Weehawken, New Jersey, shore (where items of her clothing were found in a thicket). One suspect after another was identified—including Rogers's betrothed, Daniel Payne, who soon committed suicide—then cleared. And the press followed it all, reporting all rumors, printing coroner's reports, quoting depositions, covering police investigations, and spinning purported solutions in stories with titles such as "The Mary Rogers Mystery Explained."[67]

But printed coverage did more to sustain the impenetrable mystery than to dispell it.[68] The fact that no one was ever brought to trial for the crime proved an irresistible opportunity for contemporary writers to offer their own solutions. Edgar Allan Poe, in "The Mystery of Marie Roget," claimed to have solved the murder simply by reading all newspaper accounts of the case: the victim was raped and then strangled by a young naval officer (though, in response to late-breaking evidence, Poe awkwardly revised his tale to suggest death by abortion). Ned Buntline's *The Mysteries and Miseries of New York* (1848) laid the crime to a "hag" and "she devil" abortionist modelled on the notorious Madame Restell. Joseph Holt Ingraham, in the sequel to *La Bonita Cigarera; or the Beautiful Cigar Vender [sic]: A Tale of New York* (1844), explained that "Maria" was not murdered at all, but spirited off to England to rejoin her aristocratic British family, from whom she had been kidnapped in childhood. Pulp-master E. E. Barclay published a phony confession in 1851.[69] But the entry in *Annals of Murder*, entitled "The Mysterious Fate of Mary Cecilia Rogers, The Beautiful Cigar Girl of New York," acknowledged that here was a murder mystery that defied solution: "Time passed without unveiling the mystery connected with the fate of the Beautiful Cigar Girl . . . here we leave it, leaving the reader to draw his own inference from the facts as we have presented them."[70] If the printed trial report provided a kind of scaffolding for the cultural construction of murder as mystery, the Mary Rogers case demonstrated that the scaffolding might be taken down and the structure would stand. The many fictions prompted by this murder mystery provided a substitute for the multiple and competing narratives that a trial would have afforded, had anyone been indicted for the crime.

The impulse to construct murder as mystery was not limited to those crimes which ultimately defied solution. On the surface, there was little mystery to the crime committed by Henrietta Robinson in Troy, New York, in 1853: in the presence of eyewitnesses, she added arsenic to grocer Timothy Lanagan's beer to punish him for bouncing her from one of his parties. Robinson was duly convicted of murder and sentenced to be hanged, though her sentence was commuted to imprisonment at Sing-Sing. But her origins and identity became the subject of much speculation. Conflicting stories were told: she was the seduced and abandoned daughter of a high-ranking family in Ireland; she was born in Quebec to English aristocracy with lineage (on the wrong side of the blanket) to George III; she was the daughter of a poor Irishman in Vermont; she was the cast-off mistress of a politician in Troy. "She was a mystery, a problem, which nobody could unravel or explain."[71]

Robinson's elusive identity was dramatically signalled by the blue veil which the insane defendant insisted on wearing at her trial, over the protests of the jury and judge and against the advice of her own counsel. *The Life and Confessions of Mrs. Henrietta Robinson, the Veiled Murderess!* presented readers with a front-cover illustration of the veiled Harriet Robinson, her back to the viewer, her hair pinned in a bun, standing in court during her sentencing. Its back cover offered a portrait of THE VEILED MURDERESS UNVEILED, showing an implausibly beautiful young woman facing the viewer, with long hair flowing loosely around her shoulders, naked to a pruriently low line on her bust, below which she is apparently not clothed but merely draped.[72] The implication of this pair of illustrations is startlingly clear: in physically moving through this text from the front cover to the back, the reader has participated in the process of removing the veil (and, it is suggested, the clothing as well) from a murderess, and thus in uncovering the mystery of her crime.[73]

{113}

Some murders were labelled mysteries because the corpse was missing. Edward Rulloff was suspected of killing his wife and child at Ithaca, New York, but was convicted only of kidnapping since the bodies were never found. His crime prompted references to "shrouds of mystery" and "veils of secrecy." The "barrel mystery" of 1859 and the "great trunk mystery" of 1871 were named after the murderer's method of temporarily concealing his victim.[74] Some tales of murder enhanced the mystery surrounding the crime by reporting supernatural visitations to either the victim or the murderer. An alleged biography of murder victim Maria Bickford reported that upon the Maine housewife's arrival at a Boston brothel, "a raven, so unusual in that place, darted by so close to her that its pinions brushed the ribbons of her bonnet." Murderers themselves frequently reported supernatural episodes associated with their sense of guilt over their crimes. John Lechler, convicted of strangling his wife, Mary, reported, "But scarcely had I completed the horrid deed till I became sorry for what I had done. I thought that I saw something flying through the room nearly touching the ceiling—it appeared very terrific, and told me what I had done." Andress Hall, en route to his murder of Noah and Amy Smith, heard "a strange, unearthly noise" and saw a large "bird of warning"; when it followed him, he realized that "if I commit this murder, I shall surely be betrayed in some way."[75] Adam Horn, after burying portions of his wife in his peach orchard, thought he saw a lantern moving from his neighbor's house towards her grave; when he panicked and left town, the murder was discovered.

The editor of Horn's confession equivocated on whether the lantern was supernatural or a psychological "visitation of the fancy."[76] He thus directed readers' attention to the single unanswered question of the murder, casting an aura of mystery over a crime which was otherwise fully solved. This story plays on the distinction between faith in the supernatural and superstition, best understood as a belief adhered to loosely or uncritically, which provides no clear explanations because it is not part of a coherent, internally consistent world picture.[77] No superstitious intrusions had occurred in early execution sermons: within their supernatural cosmology, providential activity was structured into every worldly occurrence and posed no mystery demanding explanation. When superstition was invoked in nineteenth-century murder literature, within the context of a post-Enlightenment, naturalistic world view, the sense of mystery was intended to prevail.

One of the best-known murder "mysteries" of the early nineteenth century included a significant dose of superstition: the supposed murder of Russell Colvin by Stephen and Jesse Boorn, in Manchester, Vermont. Colvin, the mentally deficient brother-in-law to the Boorn brothers, disappeared in 1812, following a violent argument with them. In the years that followed, local rumors arose that the Boorns had killed him because he was a burden to the family. Then, in 1819, the Boorns' uncle reportedly received a visitation from Colvin's ghost, who told Amos that he had been murdered and then led him to his grave, a cellar hole in Manchester. Others in the community began to report similar visions of Colvin's ghost. A jackknife and a button found in the cellar hole were identified by Colvin's wife as his (though the bones found proved not to be human). The Boorn brothers were arrested for Colvin's murder, and both eventually told stories that implicated them. Jesse Boorn's confession followed a prison-cell night-terror he experienced after a visit from his father: "he was frightened about something that had come into the window, and was on the bed behind him."[78] Despite the absence of the *corpus delicti*, both brothers were convicted and condemned to death (Jesse's sentence was commuted to life imprisonment) in 1819.

But the Boorns were saved by the discovery that Russell Colvin was alive, still mentally befuddled, and working as a hired man in Monmouth County, New Jersey. The long, unexplained absence, the seven-year gap between his disappearance and the trial (which permitted many stories and rumors to circulate), the indecisive physical fragments from the cellar hole and other supposed burial sites, the conflicting and ultimately false "confessions" (one prompted by a supernatural visitation), the series of ghostly sightings in the community—all lent themselves to narrative mystery. Most notable were *Mystery Developed*, printed in Hartford in 1820, and *The Dead Alive* by English mystery writer Wilkie Collins, published in Boston in 1874. Even the reappearance of the supposed victim did not dispel the view of the case as "one of the most mysterious events recorded in the annals of time."[79]

All these conventions—veiled ladies, disappearing corpses, intrusions of the supernatural, the dead returned to life—were drawn from Gothic fiction to lend meaning and coherence to nineteenth-century murder narratives. But it was a peculiar kind of coherence, which arose from the exigencies of narrative incoherence and moral uncertainty stemming from the new legal discourse. As lawyers took over from clergymen the primary responsibility for crafting tales of murder in American culture, and as the powers of the providential detective weakened within their legal narratives of guilt, the old moral certainties about the nature of the crime and the identity of its perpetrator were lost.

The new murder mystery required that readers play an active role in shaping the narrative and assigning guilt for the crime. Execution sermons had required only that readers accept on clerical (and ultimately divine) authority their official version of a unified and uncontestable truth. But the new legal narratives effectively treated readers as jurors who had to take an active role in crafting the murder narrative.[80] Just as jurors were expected to actively sort through the chaos of trial testimony and physical evidence to make sense of what really happened, so too were readers.[81] One reader of the trial of Daniel Corey noted, in a tiny nineteenth-century hand, several minor errors in the printed transcript with a care that demonstrated extremely close reading. Another reader wrote in the margin of a convicted murderer's claim to innocence, "This statement is universally regarded as a lie from beginning to end." James Holden of Philadelphia, who in 1834 presented his brother George with a copy of the Lucretia Chapman trial, filled a front leaf with his firm belief that "the witch" was guilty, and professed his delight that she was reduced to social outcast after her acquittal: "Thus we see How muchsoever we may deceive Man and so elude the grasp of the Law the Hand of Retributive Justice will eventually grasp us and in the end we shall meet with our Reward!!"[82]

Murder mysteries required that readers actively shape the narrative by sifting through evidence, piecing together fragments of the past, tracking, detecting, probing, "unveiling." As one account of the Mary Rogers case concluded, "This is all that has ever been discovered of the fearful mystery—and here we leave it, leaving the reader to draw his own inference from the facts as we have presented them." Murder mysteries effectively required readers to take upon themselves the responsibility of crafting the master narrative of the event after the withdrawal of the "providential narrator," through a "process of detection" that was now more human than divine.[83] The mystery narrative's invitation to the reader to participate was all the more compelling in the absence of any single organizing intelligence in the early nineteenth-century nonfictional accounts. The ordinary reader was the primary "detective" in the new legal narrative of the crime.

The murder-mystery narrative formalized the new demands placed on readers by pulling them immediately into the investigative process. The new format invited readers to follow the townspeople of New London, Connecticut, as they scoured the neighborhood in search of Eunice Bolles's murderer; to share with the people of Onandaga County, New York, the suspicion of Alfred Fyler's two hired men, before discovering that Fyler himself had murdered his wife, Ruth; to join in the crowd's interrogation of the two men seen loitering in Lavinia Bacon's neighborhood at the time of her murder.[84] Only occasionally did a police officer provide readers with a professional vantage on such investigation. More commonly, it was neighbors and townspeople whose investigative efforts were recorded for readers to follow: people like Captain Farmer, who first discovered the dying Anna Ayer, initiated the search for evidence which turned up a bloody mitten, and then required Daniel Davis Farmer to try on the mitten.[85]

Trails of blood were reported, not solely to horrify readers, but to enable them to participate in the investigation of the crime. The discovery of David Whittemore's blood on the headboard of his bed, his bedroom window, and the siding below, indicated that he had been assaulted in bed and then dragged out the window to the river where his corpse was found; blood found on the bed, stairway, garret, woodbox, and shed of the Return J. M. Ward home suggested where he had stowed the body of his wife, Olive, while gradually destroying it through dismemberment and burning.[86] By mid-century, the tracking of the murderer's footsteps—by ordinary civilians who were first at the scene—was common.[87] A growing popular awareness of such forensic concerns became evident: in one case, the victims' neighbors carefully measured the footsteps they found, hoping "it might lead to something towards the detection of the murderer"; in another, one witness warned his companions, as they approached the victim's body, "to be very careful and keep outside the road so as not to disturb the tracks."[88] Readers of such trial testimony were implicitly invited (with the jurors) to follow closely in the tracks of the violence.

But the tracks of crime were not limited to the literal blood-trails and bootmarks left by the murderer. They included a widening range of what were coming to be called "clues." Broken lamps, dying ducks and chickens, the sound of chopping meat, a wounded nose, a stolen necklace, a "pallid face, and quaking knees": all enabled readers of murder literature to trace the murderer's violent actions through detective semiotics.[89] Courtroom language framed the process of deductive reasoning from the evidence, as in one attorney's didactic explanation (anticipating the fictional Sherlock Holmes), "Taking all these facts in connection, the barking of the dogs, the noise heard by Mrs. Candee, the noise heard by Mrs. Harriman, the tracks leading to and from the church, the outer pool of blood; and how can we escape the conclusion, that the murder took place at 2 o'clock in the morning, rather than at an early hour in the evening."[90] By 1843, the editor of wife-killer Adam Horn's confession felt compelled to warn readers against the "erroneous conclusions of witnesses from appearances," observing that, in judicial testimony, "every circumstance and every appearance that presents itself in the scene of inquiry, and in the site of supposed crime, takes the hue, and becomes the indication and the proof, of the ruling idea of the guilt," until "every plank is expected to speak the murder."[91] Such a warning to readers testifies to the assumption that they were actively participating in their own reconstruction of the crime, based not solely on a straightforward confession of guilt, but on fragments of presumed evidence.

The figurative "tracking" of the crime often led readers on an evidentiary trail directly to and even into the body of the victim.[92] In printed trial reports and other legal narratives, dead bodies spoke in medical forensics. Readers, along with jurors, were told that "the secrets of the dissection room have been disclosed to you," in service to their powers of detection.[93] Though postmortem reports spoke most directly to cause of death and the nature of the assault, they sometimes offered far more complex narratives of death, which enabled readers to track the violence through the silent witness of the victim's body.

The murder trial of John Hendrickson offers a rich example of the narrative possibilities of medical autopsy. Prosecutors addressed at length the defendant's suspicious movements and actions before and after his wife's death. In addition, expert medical witnesses offered an organic account of what had happened inside Maria's body after she ingested the poison. Her stomach lining had produced a protective mucous membrane "as if nature . . . had made an extraordinary effort to protect and defend the stomach from the deadly effects of the substance or poison which had been introduced into it . . . preventing it from coming in contact with the tender coats of the stomach, and from entering into the system and destroying life." Within this medical melodrama, Maria's internal organs had tried to repel her husband's assault. And her heart identified the poison as aconite, by producing "that clot of blood" which the prosecutor likened to "the 'damned spot' on the hand of Lady Macbeth; 'it would not out.' There it stands, an imperishable monument of this mode of death." The autopsy even suggested a motive for the crime: Maria was so severely afflicted with venereal disease that "the power to minister to [her husband's] unrestrained passions was, beyond all doubt, greatly impaired, if not altogether destroyed; and this, to a lustful and depraved young man, was motive enough."[94]

After the jurors had found John Hendrickson guilty, Judge Marvin in his sentencing speech referred to "the scorched path which has been traced out by science in the alimentary canal—a path scorched by the liquid poison which you administered," and warned his listeners that the advancements of science "enables its votaries to detect the most subtle poisons, and to *trace the very footsteps of crime.*"[95] The "scorched path" of aconite through Maria Hendrickson's gastrointestinal track enabled—indeed required—both jurors in the courtroom and readers beyond it to mentally reconstruct the murder by "tracing the very footsteps of crime."

To assist such active reconstruction, popular murder literature offered detailed descriptions of the evidence. Readers of the Boorns-Colvin case learned much about the minimal physical evidence used to establish the *corpus delicti:* the knife, button, hat, bones, and fingernails that allegedly demonstrated Colvin's death. *The Life of Michael Powers* described the broadaxe found at the house where Timothy Kennedy was killed: though it appeared "newly washed," the axe was speckled with blood, and a single sandy hair of the same color as the victim's was found adhering to it.[96] The editors of printed murder trials often added their own detailed descriptions of physical evidence introduced in court, where it had, of course, been immediately visible to those present. More significant, they sometimes offered readers graphic illustrations of key physical evidence. The bludgeon "Loaded with Lead" that was used to murder Joseph White, the cut on the hand of accused murderer Lucian Hall (an illustration highlighted in the trial report's title and identified in a caption as "a very exact representation"), facsimile copies of eight letters from the Rev. Ephraim Avery to his alleged victim, Sarah Cornell, and of her final note blaming him for her death: all were made visually available to readers.[97] And the practice of publicly exhibiting key pieces of evidence—letters between Richard Robinson and his victim, the extravagant dress worn by victim Maria Bickford, the rifle used by Jesse Strang to shoot John Whipple—was another means to assist such popular armchair detection.

In their self-conscious concern for the detection process, murder-mystery narratives were geared to assisting readers' visual reconstruction of the murder. The literature was highly attentive to the spatial dimensions of the crime. It offered extensive descriptions of the crime scene. The *Trial of James Anthony, for the Murder of Joseph Green* (1814) opened with a lengthy description of the hatter's shop where the crime took place, which included the building's siting relative to the buildings around it and the street, its access and visibility from the street, its dimensions, the names and layout and dimensions of the three rooms on the ground floor, with explanations of windows, doors, the chimney and its operations, the staircase ("under which the body of Mr. Green was discovered"), and the upstairs room ("in which is the *basin* where Anthony's neck handkerchief was found"). As the editor explained, "Those who have not examined the place where the unfortunate Green was murdered, will perhaps be better enabled to understand the evidence for a brief description."[98] The house where Peter Lagoardette died had brick piers eighteen inches high; the Fyler house was constructed, not of cobblestone as indicated in the main text of *The Fyler Murder,* but of Onandaga blue limestone as explained in an editorial erratum: such details were intended to help readers reconstruct the crime in full and accurate visual detail.[99] Some accounts included line drawings of the building where the murder took place.[100]

Even more important than simply illustrating the scene of the crime was the effort to help readers determine precisely how the murder had taken place in three-dimensional space. What was the layout of the neighborhood and of the building where the crime occurred? What was the murderer's mode of access to the victim? Where and in what position was the body found? These were questions that a growing number of printed accounts addressed. Even before Anglo-American detective fiction began to include diagrams of the crime scene, American nonfictional murder narratives were providing readers with maps and floor plans to assist their visual reconstruction of the crime.[101]

A map of the streets and major buildings, including the home of murder victim Joseph White, of Salem, Massachusetts, accompanied the printed trial of John Francis Knapp in 1830. By 1844, the report of Lucian Hall's trial for the murder of Lavinia Bacon included a foldout map of Meriden, Connecticut, which was significantly more detailed—charting four roads, a railroad, thirty-four houses, and various other buildings and topographic features of the area—and which served a more direct purpose—to map the country between the residence of the accused murderer and that of his victim, thus enabling readers to track the murderer's movements to and from the scene of the crime. By 1850, the printed map of the farmstead where Reuben Dunbar killed his two nephews marked where the boys' bodies had been found, and estimated several distances—50 rods from the cornfield where Dunbar had been working to the body of the younger boy, 54 rods from his body to that of his older brother— that were crucial to the spatial reconstruction of this double murder. Some maps actually traced the perpetrator's route to the murder: on the map of State Street in Boston, where Thomas Selfridge murdered Charles Austin in 1806, a "Dotted line shows Mr. Selfridge's Track bearing towards the Branch Bank." A detailed map included with one report of the Rev. Ephraim Avery's trial carefully plotted two different routes: the guilty route he must have taken if he in fact killed Sarah Cornell, and the innocent route he claimed to have taken.[102] Once again, it was the reader's task to choose between them.

Even more than maps, architectural floor plans were offered to "afford our readers a more correct and intelligible idea of the scene and theory of the murder." In 1826, the report of Jereboam Beauchamp's trial included a floor plan of victim Solomon Sharp's house, indicating the window where Mrs. Sharp had seen someone peering in, and the door through which the murderer had entered. In one extant copy of this work, a nineteenth-century hand has labelled three rooms ("Bed Room," "Passage," "Parlour") which had not been identified by the editor—a work of marginalia demonstrating the reader's active mental participation in reconstructing the crime. The floor plan of Joseph White's house indicated the "Gate through which the murderer is supposed to have passed to gain access to the house" and "The window at which he entered." One trial edition added a dotted line from that window to Joseph White's second-story chamber to "show the track of the Murderer, who had to pass up one pair of stairs to arrive at the room." Increasingly, the murder diagrams revealed the location of the victim's body: a straight line marked "the position of Mrs. Bacon's body when first discovered, her feet being towards the kitchen door"; the tiny figure of a recumbent woman indicated where Ruth Fyler was found.[103] Many accounts offered detailed sketches of the murder in its immediate interior setting.[104]

All these maps, architectural sketches, and floor plans point to a powerful spatial sensibility at work in the murder-mystery narrative. The literature evinced a special fascination with closed, private spaces, ranging from a Vermont hatter's shop to a fancy New York brothel, from a boarding-house room in Bordentown, New Jersey, to "the recess" of a wealthy man's bed-chamber in Salem, Massachusetts.[105] Locked satchels, closed trunks, and "mysterious chambers" were ubiquitous in this literature, which frequently invoked "the mysteries of that room" where a murder had taken place.[106] Attorneys metaphorically suggested that mystery itself was a locked room, by referring to crucial evidence as the "key, which unlocks the whole mystery."[107] Gothic murder was "perpetrated in secrecy and in private," "in dark and gloomy recesses, unfrequented by man"; in murder, "all is dark, all secret, all mysterious."[108] In the murder-mystery narrative, private space was mysterious space, the site of secret evils demanding to be penetrated, investigated, exposed, and mapped out by the reader. The need to exert mental surveillance over secret spaces was evident in the advertising logo chosen by the Pinkerton Detective Agency, established in 1855: it was a single large eye surrounded by the words "The Eye that Never Sleeps."[109] The growing perception of the hidden quality of murder, the cultural imperative to reconstruct what happened by tracking down the perpetrator, helped shape a diffuse conviction that evil was something demanding to be mapped out.

The nineteenth-century murder mystery participated in a pervasive cultural idiom which treated human transgression as a dark secret lying buried beneath the deceptively serene surface of American social life. Its literary origins lay in eighteenth-century Gothic fiction, with its central image of the haunted castle, a place of dark winding passageways, trapdoors with rings, secret doors, and vaults under ground—fantastic, Piranesian architectural spaces whose terrified visitors can never quite make out the floor plan.[110] This Gothic spatial sensibility in turn influenced the "mysteries of the city" fiction initiated with Eugene Sue's *Les Mystères de Paris* (1842–43). This genre, which achieved great American popularity in the 1840s, rested on the conviction that the visible city conceals an invisible, even subterranean city of darkly depraved "mysteries."[111] The Gothic attention to the terrible evils practiced in private space was evident in a broad range of reform literature, which exposed such mysteries as a secret criminal underworld, secret houses of sexual assignation, secret gambling "hells," and the "subterranean" operations of intemperance.[112] It also shaped the polemical literature attacking Catholics, Mormons, and Masons as practitioners of terrible secret rituals. Maria Monk's *Awful Disclosures of the Hotel Dieu Nunnery of Montreal* (1836), for example, purported to expose the evil practices of a Catholic convent—including rape, torture, and murder—by providing readers with verbal tours and visual maps of the convent, with its Gothic dungeons, torture chambers, and underground passageways.[113]

The Gothic spatial sensibility represented an important new effort cognitively to come to terms with the expanding urban world of the early nineteenth century. As cities underwent dramatic growth, both horizontally and vertically, they became the sites of "an increasingly complex array of structures, spaces, institutions, and social types," which were readily interpreted as presenting "to the unknowing viewer a deceptive surface appearance."[114] The city was coming to be seen as primarily unknown and perhaps unknowable social space. Nonfictional urban writers echoed "mysteries of the city" fiction in representing it as a world of subterranean labyrinths and secret passageways, trapdoors and sliding panels, where terrible evil lurked unseen. "What a task have we undertaken!" wrote George Foster in *New York by Gas-Light* (1850), "To penetrate beneath the thick veil of night and lay bare the fearful mysteries of darkness in the metropolis . . . all the sad realities that go to make up the lower stratum—the under-ground story—of life in New York!" Invoking the same urban idiom, a letter attributed to acquitted murderer Richard Robinson exclaimed, "Could the secret transactions of the city of New York be exposed, what a scene of depravity would be exhibited!"[115]

Inviting his readers on an underworld tour of New York's oyster cellars, gambling dens, dance halls, and whorehouses, George Foster intoned, "Let us make use of our Asmodean privilege." He was invoking a favorite figure of city writers in the period: the demon Asmodeus, the evil spirit whose particular form of mischief was to lift the roofs off urban structures to discover the secret evils below.[116] The Asmodean impulse—the growing popular need to imaginatively enter and explore the secret spaces of the new urban world—also shaped the nonfictional literature of murder in the early decades of the nineteenth century. When a dentist named Harvey Burdell was found murdered in the New York boarding-house where he and several companions had engaged in some highly unorthodox sexual arrangements, the *Herald* reported that "We have had a house unroofed before our eyes."[117] The word "detection" actually means "'taking the roof off,' i.e. uncovering what is hidden," a meaning illuminated by Sherlock Holmes's expressed wish to "fly out of that window hand in hand [with Watson], hover over this great city, gently remove the roofs, and peep in at the queer things which are going on, the strange coincidences, the plannings, the cross-purposes, the wonderful chains of events, working through generations, and leading to the most *outré* results."[118]

This same Asmodean impulse helps explain the power of the architectural diagrams included with nineteenth-century murder literature: they visually removed the roofs of murder scenes, so that readers' eyes might penetrate into the secret spaces where evil lurked. The murder mystery regularly and ritualistically marvelled at the privacy of evil in densely settled areas, in small villages as well as cities. In his opening charge to the Grand Jury concerning the Salem murder, Chief Justice Parker expressed astonishment that an "aged and respectable citizen, living in the centre of this populous town" could be "assassinated in his bed . . . with such secrecy that not a trace for a long time appeared." In sentencing two men for the murder of Peter Lagoardette in Portsmouth, Virginia, the judge described their crime—murder followed by dismembering and burning the corpse—and then observed, "The scene of this bloody and diabolical transaction was a house in the thickly settled part of our town, and the time, *day*." Most surprising, in sentencing Return J. M. Ward for the murder (also followed by dismemberment and burning) of his wife in Sylvania, Ohio, the judge said, "This is alleged to have been done, *in a quiet village*, in your own dwelling, and within a few feet of other inhabited houses. The act was done in secret." City or village, the tale was the same: a closely settled population was no defense against terrible acts practiced in private spaces. These legal narratives of murder affirmed the spatial secrecy of the crime even as they formally exposed it through the revelatory ritual of the murder trial: "We draw aside the veil which hides the secret acts of this [murderous] husband from the gaze of the world."[119]

The classic case that illustrated the murder mystery's demands on the reader, especially with respect to spatial reconstruction, was the murder of Dr. George Parkman by Professor John Webster at the Harvard Medical College.[120] On the afternoon of Friday, November 23, 1849, Parkman disappeared, and when an initial search failed to turn him up, "the most horrible apprehensions—fears of a secret murder—filled the public mind."[121] Boston's recently formed police force, headed by Marshal Francis Tukey, launched a search of the city on Saturday, placing an ad in the evening papers, offering a $3,000 reward for information regarding Parkman's whereabouts, and dragging the Charles River and Boston Harbor in search of his body. It soon emerged that Parkman had last been seen entering Webster's laboratory at the Harvard Medical College. Quick and careless police searches of the College turned up nothing suspicious.

Ultimately, it was not the new breed of police professionals who uncovered the crime but a persistent amateur named Ephraim Littlefield, the College janitor, who lived with his family in a basement apartment. Struck by some irregularities in Webster's conduct during the week following Parkman's disappearance, convinced that the chemistry professor must have killed the missing man, and motivated perhaps by the reward money, Littlefield launched an independent search for the body, focused on a privy which he knew opened into a large vault beneath Webster's laboratory. On November 29, Thanksgiving Day, Littlefield used a trapdoor in the basement to descend into the crawl space of the building, advanced on hands and knees sixty feet to the brick wall of the privy vault, then began laboriously drilling a hole through its five courses of masonry while his wife stood lookout. The following day, "Having made an orifice and lighted a candle, he perceived under the floor of the privy what appeared to be the lower half of a human body." That evening, John Webster was taken into custody and charged with murder. He was taken to the Medical College (in a faint echo of the corpse-touching test) to witness the removal of a pelvis, right thigh, and lower left leg from the privy vault. These were laid on a board, and "Dr. Webster was led forward to confront the mangled parts of a human body. On coming in sight of the horrid spectacle, his agitation was intense—the sweat rolled in big drops from his forehead, and he would have sunk to the ground had he not been supported."[122]

Police authorities now made a thorough search of Webster's rooms at the College, and this time they uncovered a great deal: blood stains on the floor, Webster's blood-stained pants and slippers, blankets from Webster's home that had been used to screen the laboratory windows, and miscellaneous bone fragments (including several pieces of jawbone) and a partial set of false teeth in the furnace. Most important, under the flooring of Webster's private back room, they found a tea chest and in it, under a layer of geological specimens labelled by Webster, was a layer of body parts packed in tan: a headless and armless trunk, partially burned, empty except for the lungs and left kidney, and a left thigh that had been forced into the chest cavity, accompanied by a blood-stained bowie knife. When these new body parts were laid out with those from the privy vault, "it was at once seen that they belonged to the same body—all parts being in the same state of decomposition."[123] The Coroner's Jury determined that the body parts found in Webster's vault could not have migrated there from the separate vault used for dissection subjects by the anatomy students. And the body parts were identified by the victim's wife and friends as those of the late George Parkman.

The enormous popular attention to the Webster-Parkman murder owed much to the high social station of the two major players: Webster was the Erving Professor of Chemistry at the medical school; Parkman was a wealthy real-estate speculator and benefactor to the College. The two had known one another for forty years, since they had been undergraduates together at Harvard. The murder was notorious as well for its grisly horror. But the strongest appeal of this case was the mystery of the crime, enhanced by the Gothic precincts of the Harvard Medical College. On the day after Webster's arrest, 2,000 people gathered outside the College, and within a week, 5,000 had toured its interior. One of the earliest printed accounts of the murder, significantly entitled *Awful Disclosures and Startling Developments, in Relation to the Late Parkman Tragedy,* appealed directly to this popular curiosity with a front cover "view of the medical college in North Grove Street, Boston, where the horrible tragedy is supposed to have been performed."[124]

In most of the printed accounts of the Parkman murder, the Medical College building played a role closely resembling the haunted castle of Gothic fiction, easily rivaling the Castle of Otranto, the Palace of Vathek, and the House of Usher for its mysteriously evil atmosphere. Just as the Gothic novel invited readers to enter and explore the haunted castle, printed accounts of the Parkman murder drew readers into the nether regions of a secretive building, with trapdoors and subterranean passageways, corpses and bottles of human blood, where violent death and dissection awaited the unwary. When the author of *Awful Disclosures* praised Harvard and Boston for their tireless efforts "to probe the matter to the bottom,"[125] he chose his words wisely, for this murder mystery literally involved subterranean probing to uncover the evil.

The peculiar spatial qualities of both the murder and its investigation were dramatized throughout the eleven days of Webster's trial. Because the prosecutors remained ignorant of how Webster had killed Parkman, they focused on the discovery of his dismembered body in an effort to induce jurors to reconstruct mentally just how those body parts came to be deposited throughout the Medical College. It was a highly visual strategy, producing a map of the area, various interior sketches and floor plans, a jury tour of the scene of the crime, and a three-dimensional wooden model of the College, with movable walls, stairs, and furnishings, constructed so that it could be taken apart.[126] Medical witnesses provided a sketch of the major body parts that had been found, laid out in their proper relations to one another; and Parkman's dentist fitted some jaw fragments and false teeth into the dental molds he had taken several weeks before his patient's death.[127] The *pièce de resistance* was the life-size drawing of a human skeleton (sneakily drawn to resemble Parkman with his vigorous pedestrian stride and protruding lower jaw), with its parts variously shaded and keyed to the architectural floor plan of Webster's laboratory, so that viewers could see at a glance which portions of Parkman were found in the furnace (marked black), which were found in the privy vault and the tea chest (shaded)—and which parts of Dr. Parkman were never found at all (white).[128]

Laid side by side, the anatomical sketch and the architectural drawing provided jurors and readers of the nine printed versions of the Webster trial with an imaginative do-it-yourself kit for the two layers of narrative involved in all murder mysteries: the story of the investigation and the story of the murder itself. When the viewer's eye moved first to the skeleton, imaginatively pulling it apart and depositing its pieces in the various parts of the College identified by the floor plan, the viewer reconstructed the murder itself. And when the viewer's eye went first to the floor plan, locating the various pieces of Parkman and reassembling them into the skeleton, the viewer—juror or reader—mentally reenacted the murder investigation.

The court-appointed defense attorneys responded with a poor and brief showing, taking only two days after the prosecution's seven. "The fearful chain of circumstantial evidence"[129] surrounding Webster had been too much for the defense, and the jury delivered a verdict of "guilty" on March 30. Webster was sentenced to die for the crime of first-degree murder. Shortly thereafter, he delivered a confession of sorts to the Reverend George Putnam, who took it to the Committee of Pardons of the Massachusetts Governor's Council. Parkman, claimed the convicted murderer, had come to his rooms at the College to threaten him concerning an outstanding debt, and Webster, in a burst of anger, had picked up a piece of wood and struck him, killing him with a single blow.[130] He was guilty, in short, not of first-degree murder but of manslaughter. But Webster's plea for clemency, and the many letters written to the Governor by ordinary citizens pleading that he be pardoned, ultimately went unheard. Webster was duly executed and buried under a nameless stone at Copp's Hill Burying Ground, instead of Mount Auburn Cemetery as he had requested and the public had been led to expect, because his attorney feared a body-snatching.[131]

The public and legal hullabaloo following the verdict highlighted the degree of moral uncertainty surrounding the case. Newspapers all over the country proclaimed Webster's innocence, or contended that his guilt was inadequately proved.[132] Chief Justice Lemuel Shaw's final words to the jury were more appropriate than he perhaps intended: "Gentlemen, when it is said that we may err, it is true. But it is nothing more than to say that we are human. On a subject where absolute certainty cannot be obtained, where moral certainty must always govern, it is always possible to fall into error."[133] Shaw's own legal errors in the trial proved so egregious that he doctored the trial transcript for print, in order to justify the verdict and sentence. In a strange twist of legal history, his amended version has been cited by generations of lawyers as offering the classic definition of the requirements of circumstantial evidence: each of the circumstances in the chain of evidence must be separately proved, then all must be proved consistent; and if the chain holds, all evidence taken together must produce "a reasonable and moral certainty."[134] But "reasonable and moral certainty" was precisely what was missing from the Webster-Parkman case. In all likelihood, the body fragments discovered at the Medical College were Parkman's; he probably died a violent death (whether murder or manslaughter) at the hands of Webster. But the chain of evidence was not unbroken; the *corpus delicti* was insufficiently proved; the greater plausibility that Webster acted without premeditation was not effectively resolved; and no single transcript of the trial was accepted as accurate by all participants. "What passed within the walls of that private room, no man may ever know"; the "dreadful mystery" of the Webster-Parkman case remained.[135]

The Webster-Parkman case captured the core dynamic of the new murder-mystery narrative. It placed the burden of moral knowledge on the reader, transferring narrative responsibility from the providential eye to the readers' own, requiring them to reconstruct the crime and to assign guilt for it. Readers were invited to consult area maps, architectural sketches, and floor plans; to visit the scene of the crime, examine sketches of the evidence provided by trial-report editors, and use the do-it-yourself kit of the shaded skeleton and College floor plans to reenact both the murder and the investigation. But the murder-mystery format itself ensured that there would be no moral certainty about either the nature of the crime or the assignment of guilt. There could be no clear narrative closure, no omniscient account, because legal truth was problematic, contestable, and reasonable doubt worked like an acid on coherent narrative. Significantly, even Webster's "confession"—unlike its early New England antecedent—did not clear up the mystery surrounding the crime, but rather kept it open and unsolved.[136]

The transfer of the burden of moral knowledge from the providential eye to the private eyes of readers helps explain the deep power of detective fiction in modern secular culture. Once we recognize that the cultural construction of murder-as-mystery preceded the "invention" of detective fiction, the way is cleared to understanding detective fiction as a fantasized solution to the problem of moral uncertainty in the world of true crime. For the Heroic Detective of detective fiction did exercise providential powers of vision and agency. His French prototype, Sûreté head Eugene-François Vidocq, boasted in his heavily fictionalized memoirs in 1829, "Nothing escaped me . . . I knew all that was passing or projecting." His American prototype, Poe's Auguste Dupin, read the minds of those around him and solved the mystery of Marie Roget without ever leaving his own armchair. The English Inspector Bucket, from Charles Dickens's *Bleak House,* also read people's minds, entered rooms magically, and seemed to be, in the words of Jo the crossing-sweeper, "in all manner of places, all at wanst." Omnipresent, omniscient, all-powerful: a clear line of descent linked the providential eye of the execution sermon to the "private eye" of nineteenth-century detective fiction (the name was coined after the Pinkerton logo). The Heroic Detective was equal to the task of reconstructing a full and authoritative narrative of the crime, thus removing the narrative burden from the shoulders of ordinary readers and restoring moral certainty to the world.[137]

But the Heroic Detective was, after all, just a fiction.[138] Auguste Dupin did not in fact solve the real-life mystery of Mary Rogers: Poe's attempted armchair solution was proved wrong even before his story went to print. True crime persists, and the nonfictional murder mystery lacks moral certainty. These facts have shaped both the nature and the quantity of true-crime literature in American print culture since the early nineteenth century. As a result, it is a literature obsessive about details, insistent in its imperative need to reenact, endlessly fascinated with physical evidence, time tables, crucial gaps and missing pieces, and the spatial reconstruction of the crime. And for the same reason, the quantity of true-crime literature seems to be infinite. Most early American murders received one printed treatment, the sacred narrative of the execution sermon, and one truth, God's truth. But many nineteenth-century murders generated multiple narratives, multiple interpretations, because their truth was contestable, fluctuating, uncertain. And some nineteenth-century murders received new narrative attention decades after their occurrence, including Mary Rogers, Lizzie Borden, and Webster-Parkman, because in the murder mystery, truth is open-ended; there is no closure.

For early New Englanders committed to a doctrine of innate depravity, evil had posed no mystery, because it was acknowledged as an intrinsic and ineradicable aspect of human nature. Within that religious world view, it was self-evident that all men and women were capable of, and effectively guilty of, the crime of murder. The Gothic understanding of evil emerging in late eighteenth- and early nineteenth-century America, by contrast, rested on the elusiveness of evil within an enlightened liberal culture that treated evil as extrinsic, inessential, and environmental in origin. In the secular world view, evil was not self-evident but puzzling and problematic. And the legal culture treated every individual charged with criminal transgression as innocent unless proved guilty, in an adversarial procedure incapable of achieving the moral certainty of the earlier inquisitorial method. As criminal truth became a matter for legitimate professional contestation, human evil grew elusive. The Gothic murder narrative repeatedly affirmed "the thick, murky darkness of unnatural crime"—crime that violated, not confirmed, the prevailing understanding of human nature.[139]

The mystery of murder combined with the horror of murder to constitute the larger Gothic response to the crime. Just as Gothic horror made murder unspeakable, incomprehensible, inexplicable, Gothic mystery made the crime unknowable, incomprehensible, inexplicable. And just as horror resisted moral closure, requiring that readers engage in an endless ritual repetition of shock and speechlessness, mystery resisted narrative closure, constructing an open-ended and ultimately doomed effort to achieve moral certainty concerning what happened and who was responsible. Together, Gothic horror and Gothic mystery joined to make the liberal confrontation with the crime of murder an endless ritual, without narrative closure and without moral comprehension.

But just as horror ultimately undermined the reader's comfortable sense of distance from the murderer as moral alien, so too did the convention of mystery. The cult of horror subverted moral distance by commanding readers to act as passive spectators to the murder in a way that implicated them in the murderer's own terrible evil. The cult of mystery subverted readers' sense of the murderer's otherness by requiring them to reenact the crime, following in the murderer's footsteps, accompanying him through the first-floor window, up the stairs, into the bedchamber, weighing all evidence both physical and circumstantial, even thinking their way into his twisted mind to

{ 133 }

imagine his thoughts and motives to murder. Just as Sherlock Holmes had to think like Moriarty to catch that master criminal, nineteenth-century readers of nonfictional crime literature were invited to think like the murderer to reconstruct the crime. In mystery as in horror, the deepest and most terrifying evil ultimately resided in the readers of true-crime literature themselves.

This sketch of Adam Horn dismembering the corpse of his wife visually casts him in the role of Perseus decapitating Medusa. Averting his own eyes, he holds up the head of the slain female monster, streaming with blood, by its snaky locks of hair so the viewer can witness its horror.

Sexual murder and the chaste female victim. Joel Clough stabs to death his sweetheart, Mary Hamilton, after she had spurned his romantic suit. The canopied bed featured so prominently in this crude illustration economically conveyed to readers the sexual undercurrents of this crime.

Sexual murder and the seduced female victim. The "Beautiful Cigar Girl," found dead in the Hoboken River, is here manhandled by two assailants at cliff's edge. Though the "mystery" of her death was never solved, rumors circulated that she had been either gang-raped and strangled, or killed by an incompetent abortionist. This ambiguous image allows for both scenarios, depicting the victim with a skirt hiked well above her ankles and clinging pruriently to her legs.

Sexual murder and the depraved female victim. Richard Robinson approaches his paramour, New York prostitute Helen Jewett, to kill her with a hatchet. Her luxurious sleigh bed and the elaborately ornate mirror, sign of her sexual vanity, offered readers an exciting glimpse into the bedroom arrangements of the notorious "Palace of the Passions" brothel.

The eroticization of the female corpse. When the murder victim was known to be sexually fallen, it became permissible to portray her corpse as an object of erotic desire, as in this color lithograph of the dead Helen Jewett, prone on her bed, breasts and legs presumably exposed by the fire set by her killer.

"She had it coming." In cases of murder involving unchaste female victims, the evil of the crime was attributed not to the murderer as monster, but to the sexual monstrosity of his victim. Here, Helen Jewett is portrayed as a combination of Eve and Medusa, with a foul snake entwined around her neck, and the letters of her infamous name dripping blood.

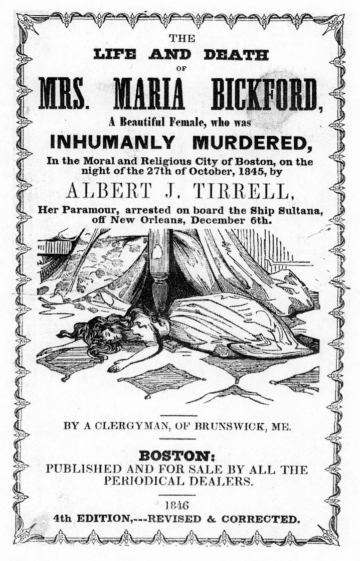

THE

LIFE AND DEATH

OF

MRS. MARIA BICKFORD,

A Beautiful Female, who was

INHUMANLY MURDERED,

**In the Moral and Religious City of Boston, on the
night of the 27th of October, 1845, by**

ALBERT J. TIRRELL,

**Her Paramour, arrested on board the Ship Sultana,
off New Orleans, December 6th.**

BY A CLERGYMAN, OF BRUNSWICK, ME.

BOSTON:

PUBLISHED AND FOR SALE BY ALL THE
PERIODICAL DEALERS.

1846

4th EDITION,---REVISED & CORRECTED.

The other notorious prostitute-killing of the early nineteenth
century was the murder of Boston prostitute Maria Bickford.
Albert J. Tirrell slit her throat with a razor, nearly decapitating
her, in a boarding-house room they shared. But this illustration of
her corpse suggests that she was fatally impaled by the bed in
which she had sexually sinned.

An illustration from a fictitious biography of Maria Bickford depicts her as a sexually ripening adolescent, here asleep in the woods and dreaming of her first seducer. The black imp that hovers over her head is aiming a stick or weapon at her throat, prefiguring the fatal wound that would be administered by Albert Tirrell, and thus casting the guilt of her murder onto the victim herself, by linking her initial sexual fall to her violent end.

CHAPTER FIVE

Murder in the Family Circle

I N Edgar Allan Poe's "The Black Cat" (1843), the criminal narrator sets forth what he calls "a series of mere household events."
Falling under the grip of the "fiend Intemperance," he develops a
savage dislike to his pet cat, and one day takes up an axe to kill the
beast. When his wife stays his hand, he buries the weapon in her
head instead.[1] Poe's phrase, "mere household events," captures a
central characteristic of the nonfictional literature of domestic murder in the same period. Printed accounts of such crimes offered
not just stories of murder, but tales of the family: of marriage, par-
enthood, siblings and in-laws; romantic love and sexual infidelity,
physical abuse and domestic rebellion, separation and reconciliation.
These tales of the family drew cultural power from a major transition
in American domesticity: the shift from the traditional patriarchal
family, with its central concerns for economic productivity and hierarchical order, to the modern sentimental family, with its central
concerns for emotional closeness and mutual affection. The popular
literature of family murder affirmed the new domesticity in terrifying
tales of people who violated its tenets. It also appealed to a backlash
against the new ideal by providing readers with the pornographic
pleasure of witnessing those violations. The literature of domestic
murder revealed a deep sense of unease with the new norms of
American domesticity in the nineteenth century.

The powerful narrative impulse at work in this literature of family life gone badly awry points to an underlying conviction that mystery and horror attached not solely to the crime of murder, but to the family itself, which was represented as a place of dark secrets and endemic violence. Popular stories of domestic murder fundamentally altered the broader Gothic narrative, which constructed the murderer as moral monster outside the bounds of human normalcy. For the domestic-Gothic tale of murder quite literally brought the horror and the mystery *home,* showing readers that sometimes the moral monster was not an alien creature of the wicked world outside, but an intimate companion at the family fireside.

Early American murder narratives had paid no particular attention to crimes of domestic murder. Though a significant number of execution sermons concerned infanticides, clerical tales of this crime were expressly not domestic: single mothers killed their newborn children to conceal the sin of fornication, precisely because there was no family to receive the child. The "besetting sin" with which such exemplary sinners as Esther Rodgers were charged was not any familial failing—no monstrous deviation from maternal love—but rather sexual uncleanness. Even married infanticide Sarah Smith, executed at Springfield in 1698 for smothering her infant conceived in adultery while her husband was held captive in Canada, was chastised for her sins of "Lying, Stealing, Adultery, and Murder," but not for want of maternal feeling.[2]

A handful of New England execution sermons before 1750 did concern wife-murders. In 1690, Hugh Stone slit the throat of his pregnant wife during a dispute over the sale of some property. In 1715, Jeremiah Meacham attacked his wife and her sister with an axe, then set fire to the house to avoid being taken into custody. In 1721, the African-American Joseph killed his wife with an axe, as he self-righteously explained to the Reverend Cotton Mather, because "she told me, that she had as liev talk with the Devil, as talk with any of GODS Ministers." Rev. Mather, who preached sermons for both Hugh Stone and Joseph, pointed out the peculiar heinousness of domestic murder, charging Stone, "You have Murdered *Her* whom you should have Loved above all the world"; and telling Joseph that "To see a *Man hanged for Murdering his Wife;* 'Tis a fearful Spectacle!"[3]

But none of the execution sermons for these wife-murderers elaborated on the specifically domestic contexts of their crimes. Though Stone's wife was pregnant at the time of her murder, no domestic circumstances were cited beyond their property dispute. Though Meacham's double-murder of his wife and sister-in-law, followed by his torching the house, might seem to invite attention to his family situation, the Rev. Nathaniel Clap attributed his actions to Meacham's failures of religious observance, vicious habits, and mental disturbance. The case that prompted greatest attention to the domestic nature of the crime was that of Joseph: he was cast as a husband who employed harsh language and "vile Carriage" towards his wife, and his victim—labelled "a very *Insupportable Wretch*"[4] by the Rev. Mather—was implicitly charged with some responsibility for her own death. But here too, domestic detail was limited, and Joseph's chronic mistreatment of his wife was addressed more generically as besetting sin than as the intimate tale of a specific marriage gone bad. Execution sermons did not use the occasion of domestic murders to tell tales of family life.

Beginning in the late eighteenth century, nonfictional accounts of domestic murders grew increasingly popular, expanding in both number and variety. Wife-murder remained common in the literature; printed accounts of this crime grew increasingly versatile, coming to encompass, for example, the murder of common-law wives of many years and legitimate brides of one week.[5] In 1778 the first husband-murder received printed attention: Bathsheba Spooner hired two British soldiers to assist her lover, Ezra Ross, in beating to death her husband, Joshua Spooner. Others followed in the nineteenth century, including Lucretia Chapman's alleged conspiracy with her lover, the "Spaniard" Mina, to administer arsenic to her husband, William, in 1831, and Hannah Kinney's alleged poisoning of her husband, George T. Kinney, in 1840.[6] Even as infanticides were largely disappearing from the literature, child-murders began to appear: in 1806, Jesse Wood shot his grown son, Joseph, in a drunken disagreement over a debt; Amos and Abigail Furnald murdered Amos's illegitimate son, Alfred, in 1827. A handful of parent-killings entered the literature: Mary Cole in 1813 murdered her mother, Agnes Teaurs, to whom Mary and her husband, Cornelius, owed money; and Benjamin White killed his father in 1843.[7] The full array of nineteenth-century domestic murders included a wide range of domestic relationships between murderer and victim. Nieces, stepdaughters and sons, stepcousins and nephews, mothers-and brothers-in-law were killed by their respective relations, and the stories of their murders were told in rich domestic detail.[8]

The new direction of this literature was first evident in the *Narrative of the Life of John Lewis* (1762). Lewis, twelve years married, killed his pregnant wife not long after she had refused to lie down with him in mid-afternoon. He was subsequently tempted to kill two of his children, but resisted the impulse. In contrast to earlier execution sermons preached for wife-murderers, this account set forth the home setting of the crime, detailing the victim's work over her washtub and the murderer's making a plow, the family's mid-day dinner and mid-day rest, the couple's children and their ages, and such domestic artifacts as the bed on which Lewis strangled his wife, the pillow he placed under the corpse's head, and the blanket he finally drew over her. The *Narrative of John Lewis* explained that, though he had initially told the judge that differences of religion had prompted his crime, the truth was that he had killed his wife out of sexual jealousy, suspecting her of infidelity both before and after their marriage. John Lewis's shifting story about his motive reflected in microcosm the shift from earlier religious explanations of the crime to domestic explanations.[9]

Accounts of the William Beadle case in 1782 similarly opened up the Beadle home and its operations for popular inspection. Readers learned that the family consisted of 52-year-old William Beadle, his 32-year-old wife Lydia, their four children—one boy, at age 12 the oldest of the four, and three girls, of whom the youngest was six—and a maid who slept in the room with the children. Beadle had been a prosperous merchant who had fallen on hard times during the

War, but insisted that the family keep up the appearance of prosperity. He had initially planned the massacre a month before he committed it, and had served a fine oyster dinner to his family that November evening, but the maid's premature return to the house forced him to reschedule the murders. For some time before that final night, Beadle carried an axe and a carving knife to his bedside each night. He had shown a marked carelessness about his children's safety, uncapping a well near the house where they played, and frequently urging his son into deeper water when he went swimming in the river. But readers also learned that Beadle was "an affectionate husband" and "a tender, fond parent."[10]

The Beadle murders fell into an expanding category of familicides, the slaughter of an entire family by its patriarchal head. Between 1780 and 1850, a significant number of these massacres made their way into print, beginning with James Yates's slaughter of his wife and four children in Tomhannick, New York, in 1781.[11] Some of these cases were distinguished from other domestic homicides only by scale: John Cowan's murder of his wife and two children, for example, revealed a pattern of chronic abuse, intemperance, and sexual jealousy increasingly typical in the literature of wife-murder. But several of these family-murders (including the Beadle case) conformed to a story line unique to this category of crime, in which a loving husband and father came to believe that killing his family would be an act of kindness and patriarchal duty, in some cases commanded by God. James Purrinton was a "uniformly tender and affectionate" husband and father, who was "often heard to express his fond anticipations of the moment when [his family] would all be happy; and has sometimes added, how greatly it would enhance his happiness if they could all die at once." When a severe drought threatened their prosperity, he killed his wife and seven of his children (the eighth Purrinton child escaped), and cut his own throat.[12]

The attention given to domestic homicide expanded as a result of the emergence of a new set of ideas and practices of family life. The traditional family had been a "little commonwealth," an integral part of the larger social and political world, serving as the main site of economic production as well as school, hospital, prison, and welfare institution in one. Though essentially nuclear in structure, its household might include servants, convicts, apprentices, unrelated single persons, and recent immigrants. But by the mid-eighteenth century, in the commercial cities on the Eastern seaboard, specialized public institutions such as hospitals, schools, and almshouses were absorbing traditional family responsibilities; workshops were emerging as new centers of economic production; and the family accordingly began to lose a number of its larger social functions. Middle-class families in particular grew more private, closing off from the larger world and retreating from older practices of communal surveillance and supervision over domestic matters.[13]

By the nineteenth century, these economic and social changes were idealized in a vision of the "family circle" as a private and protected place, the peaceful repository of higher moral and spiritual virtues deemed to be threatened by commercialization—a safe arena for the sentiments and affections of family members. The doctrine of separate spheres represented the family as a sanctuary from the evils of the world outside, and the cult of true womanhood asserted that women were peculiarly suited to their new role as priestesses of the sanctuary by their unique qualities of passionlessness, piety, passivity, and domesticity, which rendered them morally superior to men. "The family state then, is the aptest earthly illustration of the heavenly kingdom, and in it woman is its chief minister," explained domestic reformer Catharine Beecher. Woman was pronounced "God's appointed agent of MORALITY," whose major responsibility was to use her power within the family to refine man's "human affections and elevate his moral feelings."[14]

Sentimental domesticity involved a reconfiguration of power relations within the family, based on an emerging critique of patriarchy. The legitimacy of the traditional family had been established, theoretically, on the conviction that the patriarch's authority derived from God, and materially on his control over landed property and productive skills, which gave him the power (enforced by law in seventeenth-century New England) to determine when and whom his children might marry. But Enlightenment ideas about the rights of the individual challenged patriarchal theory, while the gradual erosion of fathers' economic power by shrinking land holdings in the eighteenth century undermined their power to choose their children's marriage partners.[15] Marriage was coming to be seen less as a property arrangement made by fathers than as an emotional bond to be forged by couples who were increasingly likely to take their courtship into their own hands. By the last decades of the eighteenth century, American magazine literature, sentimental fiction, and personal diaries and correspondence were affirming that romantic love was the proper foundation of marriage. As one suitor wrote to his beloved, "If the Ardor of my Affections and the sincerity of a heart wholly devoted to you can inspire you with a Tender Sentiment towards me, suppress not the Emotion."[16]

If romantic love was increasingly seen as marriage's proper starting point, strong affection and mutual respect between interdependent partners were to be its driving force. In correspondence, marriage partners began to address one another as "Friend," and to write in increasingly romantic terms of their longing for reunion. The focus of marital sexuality shifted from reproduction towards emotional intimacy and physical pleasure, a tendency reinforced by a decline in the birth rate that was severing sex from its reproductive consequences. The new companionate ideal of marriage set limits on the patriarchal power of the husband over his wife, as evidenced in the rising success rate of women's petitions for divorce, and the growing willingness of courts to accept such grounds as loss of conjugal affection, the adultery of the husband, intemperance, incompatibility, and physical abuse. In the traditional family, patriarchal anger was accepted as an appropriate enforcement of sexual hierarchy; though colonial statutes prohibited husbands from striking their wives except in cases of self-defense, the punishment for the offense was mild, and even in cases of known abuse, the authorities tended to command wives to be submissive and obedient to their husbands. With the emergence of the companionate marriage, husbands were instructed to conquer their anger in the interest of marital harmony. As William Alcott advised *The Young Husband* in 1840, "The reign of gentleness is very much needed in this jarring, clashing, warring world," and "no quarrels . . . are so bitter as family quarrels."[17]

Sentimentalism shaped a new approach to child-rearing within the American family. In the traditional family, the child was regarded as a miniature adult, whose innate depravity was to be subdued through the "rod of correction," which was viewed as an "ordinance of God." But gradually over the course of the eighteenth century, childhood came to be viewed as a unique stage of life worth cherishing. The Romantics contributed heavily to the new view of the child as innocent, malleable, naturally social and affectionate; as Lydia Maria Child wrote in 1831, "They come to us from heaven, with their little souls full of innocence and peace; and, as far as possible, a mother's influence should not interfere with the influence of angels." For such angelic creatures, corporal punishment was increasingly regarded as inappropriate, even harmful. The new goal of child-rearing was not to frighten children into obedience through physical chastisement, but to use the powers of persuasion and parental example—as well as social isolation, the withholding of love, and manipulation through guilt—to prepare children for rational self-government, regarded by liberals as "the only effective and lasting government—the one that touches the springs of action, and in all circumstances controls them."[18]

This approach meshed well with woman's growing role as primary child-rearer, for women were believed to be naturally better than men at the fine art of moral suasion: "Because her voice is gentlest, her eye beams with fondest affection . . . These silken threads are harder to burst than the iron chains of authority." Accompanying all this new attention to the special nature and needs of childhood was a steady decline in the white native-born birthrate, from an average of seven or eight children born to each family before 1800, to an average of five or six by 1850, to an average three or four by 1900. Child-rearing replaced child-bearing as the most time-consuming aspect of women's lives, as children ceased to be economic assets and emerged as economic liabilities in need of education and skilled job training, and as parents grew increasingly committed to the demanding new form of child-nurture.[19]

Against a backdrop of ideological and social change, accounts of domestic murder took shape as self-conscious explorations of real families in deep trouble. The new domestic ideology shaped a sub-genre of Gothic murder narrative in which the new ideas and practices of family life enhanced the conventions of both mystery and horror. Privatization and the decline of communal surveillance over the family made the home an ideal setting for the murder mystery. The domestic murder in particular was committed "in secret," "in your own dwelling, and within a few feet of other inhabited houses." In the trial of John Hendrickson, the prosecutor referred to the testimony of the victim's mother saying, "By the mother, we expose the privacy of domestic life. We draw aside the veil which hides the secret acts of this husband from the gaze of the world" and examine his conduct "in those more secret hours, hidden from all eyes (save one)."[20] The power of the story was enhanced by the excitement of uncovering appalling evil in that very place where evil was theoretically to be least expected: the holy temple of home. An additional appeal resided in the rich details about how other people conducted their private domestic lives. Peter Lung called his mother-in-law a "damned bitch"; Alfred Fyler was having an affair with the family's Irish servant; Maria Hendrickson and George Kinney (both victims of spouse-murder) had venereal disease. Such information would probably not have come before the public eye, had the crime of murder not opened these homes to the public gaze.[21]

In the 1860s, English sensation fiction achieved popularity by transposing "the disruptive and disturbing elements of Gothic fiction into the homely setting of the family and the everyday, recognizable world." American critic Henry James attributed the sensation genre's appeal to its exploration of "those most mysterious of mysteries, the mysteries that are at our own doors."[22] The mysteries at our own doors are rendered all the more terrible by a phenomenon that Sigmund Freud would subsequently identify as the uncanny, the disturbingly alien nature of the intensely familiar. In the American nonfiction of murder, marital homesteads became haunted houses through the operations of the uncanny. When Alpheus Hitchcock purchased rat poison, or William Beadle sharpened the kitchen knife, or Hannah Kinney made sage tea for her ailing husband, they were engaged in deeply familiar, mundane household activities that would become terrible, alien, mysterious, once they were exposed as preludes to domestic murder.

Just as the privatization of the family enhanced the mystery, sentimentalization sharpened the horror. Narratives of domestic homicide routinely invoked the sentimental view of the family as that "sacred, social institution, ordained by Heaven to be productive of the greatest happiness to mankind," in order to emphasize the particular abomination of murder within its precincts. The domestic murderer, within this formula, committed a particularly fearful violation of social order: "when we find a man so lost to every sense of duty and feeling, as to rob his own innocent children of their mother—as to murder the partner of his bosom, whom he had chosen in his youth as a companion for life, and whom he was bound by all laws, human and divine, to protect and comfort; we are lost in astonishment at the deep depravity of human nature."[23] The domestic killer perversely chose for his (less frequently her) victim that person to whom he had the greatest social and moral obligations: "You have condemned yourself to be singled out from the mass of mankind, as one who has raised his fatal and merciless hand against her, whom every principle of religion, every dictate of morality, every kind feeling of the human heart, called upon him [sic], in the most earnest tones, to cherish and protect." Such a killer was the ultimate moral monster—"a hardened savage, and desperate villain," "a disgrace to man," "a devil in human shape."[24]

Against the new domesticity's rising requirements for closely affectionate bonds among family members, the tales of the family offered by domestic murder narratives disclosed egregious violations of the sentimental family ideal. Stories of wife-murder, by far the most common form of domestic homicide, highlighted a range of nightmares of the companionate marriage gone bad. One of these was the tale of the brutal husband who had battered his wife for months or years before his last fatal assault. Bradbury Ferguson of Exeter, New Hampshire, had abused his wife, Eliza Ann, for two or three years before her death, striking and kicking her, beating her with a chair, once dousing her and their child with cold water and driving them out into freezing winter weather, and finally shooting her in the belly with a shotgun one night when she refused to come to bed with him. John Graham of Baltimore had been known to beat his wife, Phoebe, with a stick, tongs, and a lash before he finally beat and kicked her to death; the medical examiners found extensive bruising on her face, shoulders, arms, and stomach, long parallel stroke marks on her back, and bruises of a "delicate" nature not specified in court. Stories such as these clearly foregrounded the violence of the crime, piling on the body-horror. Husbands who killed their wives after chronic abuse were typically characterized as beasts, savages, and madmen.[25]

Couples in such cases may have fought over money and household labor, the wife's supposed infidelity and disobedience, her absence from the home (usually in flight from physical abuse) and her refusal to join her husband in bed, her poor cookery, and his ill-treatment of the cat.[26] When asked why he cut his wife Lydia's throat, Samuel Perry explained, "he could not live with nor without her." Orrin Woodford said he killed his wife because "she talked to him" (he did not specify what she said).[27] The intemperance of one or both parties frequently played an important role in the abuse. "The patient, enduring wife murdered by the brutal, intoxicated husband! How frequently do we read it!" In sentencing James Ransom for the murder of his wife in 1832, the judge rhetorically asked, "What could have so perverted your nature: what could so have steeled your heart? The answer is—Spirituous liquors." He went on to explain that in the two months before the Ransom case, three intemperate men had been arraigned before him on charges of wife-murder: "As destructive as this practice is to society at large, as distressing as it is to all classes of the community, yet it is indubitably true that none are made to suffer more severely from it than married women."[28] Many wife-killers blamed their victims' chronic intemperance (sometimes confirmed and sometimes denied by other witnesses) for the violence leading to their deaths.[29]

The standard narrative of the chronic abuser was seldom cast as a tale of domestic privacy. The long-term abuses it chronicled were open and ongoing, and so disruptive that the comings and goings of neighbors and police officers tended to figure strongly. Neighbors of

Bradbury Ferguson testified that Eliza Ann had come to their homes on three or four occasions before the night of her death to hide from her husband; neighbors of John Graham had witnessed his ongoing abuse of her; during Michael McGarvey's fatal flogging of his wife in a Philadelphia tenement, several neighbors entered the room to plead unsuccessfully with him to stop. Not infrequently, abusive husbands had made death threats against their wives; in several cases, the previous abuse had been sufficiently severe to warrant brief episodes of jail time for the abuser.[30] But while these were not tales of domestic privacy, they did reveal the limits of communal surveillance over domestic conflict. The police officers summoned to protect Eliza Ann Ferguson ignored her fears for her life and asked her to honor her husband's wish that she spend one more night under his roof. "She was asked several times if she would stay, and at last replied faintly, 'I will try to.'" Her husband saw the police officers to the door, and three hours later Eliza Ann was dead.[31]

These crude tales showed how the sacred responsibilities of sentimental marriage were violated by brutality. The horror they dealt in was primarily the visceral horror of battered bodies. A more cerebral horror was at work in wife-murders planned and deliberately carried out by (usually sober) husbands who simply wanted to get rid of their wives. An example was John Hendrickson's poisoning of his nineteen-year-old wife, Maria, in Bethlehem, New York, in 1853. The trial report for this murder case recounted the Hendricksons' two-year marriage, detailing its extensive violations of the companionate ideal. According to the prosecution, Maria Van Dusen had been the educated, accomplished daughter of respectable parents who had opposed her marriage to Hendrickson, an idle rowdy, gambler, and thief. But Maria, a devotée of romantic marriage, had overridden her parents' opposition (possibly by becoming pregnant) and wedded the man she loved. Within six months, the bridegroom committed "a gross assault" on a young woman in the neighborhood and was forced to leave the area for a time. During his absence, Maria gave birth to a child, who died suspiciously in the couple's bed shortly after John's return. When John infected Maria with venereal disease, her father dismissed his son-in-law from the house where the couple lived, and subsequently disinherited him. But within a year, John persuaded Maria to reunite with him at his father's house, and three weeks later she was found dead in their bed.[32]

The case against John Hendrickson was extensive. He had been inquiring about poisons in Albany a week before Maria's death, and someone of his description had recently purchased tincture of aconite, the poison found in the dead woman's stomach. A few nights before Maria's death, John had moved their sleeping quarters from the bedroom shared with his two sisters to an attic bedroom where they slept alone. John failed to summon a physician when his wife became ill; he showed "no emotion or feeling" at his wife's deathbed; he asked anxious questions about the autopsy and was heard to say, "One thing I know, they won't find arsenic." In addition, Hendrickson was known to be sexually involved with another woman; he was discovered in the act of sending a "vile" note to a friend through a prostitute two months later; and he was found dancing in his jail cell less than a week after his wife's death. The jury found John Hendrickson guilty of murder, at a trial whose spectators included a large number of women.[33]

The coldly planned wife-murder exemplified by the Hendrickson case was represented as a more mysterious form of domestic violence than the case involving chronic physical abuse. Such murders often involved poison, a "stealthy instrument of death," and were "secret acts" "committed in darkness" behind a "veil." The husband who could plot his wife's death days in advance, the man "so hardened as to have poured poison down his wife's throat," who showed no feeling at her deathbed, the man capable of planting himself on a chest containing her vomit to conceal the evidence of his wife's death throes: such a husband was even more monstrous than overtly savage wife-batterers like Michael McGarvey or John Boies. This husband "murdered his wife in cold blood,—fiendishly, devilishly, damnably murdered her."[34] Great as was the body-horror in such a case, the moral horror was more powerful.

The strategy of the prosecution was to emphasize the defendant's ongoing emotional abuse of a devoted wife's loving heart. Maria Hendrickson, the state explained, suffered "sickness of the heart, in consciousness of unrequited love." The District Attorney continued: "A woman's love—who can tell its depth and strength? 'Man's love is of man's life, a thing apart; / 'Tis woman's whole existence' . . . When she once really loves, she loves strongly, firmly, unchangeably, even though the object of her affection should prove totally unworthy—though he should sin ever so deeply—though he should plunder, rob and murder—her trusting nature would not forsake him." Having once granted her love, however ill-advisedly, this particular true woman would never withdraw it. In return, her unworthy husband had "ruthlessly murdered" her. As Judge Marvin said in his final words to John Hendrickson, "your wife came to her death by violence from him who had sworn at the altar to love, cherish and protect her through life."[35] Hendrickson was judged guilty not just of murder, but of failure to love and cherish, and it was the latter sentimental offense that received the greater attention at his trial.

A similar story was told of John Earls's murder of his common-law wife, Catharine, in Pennsylvania in 1836. Earls, like Hendrickson, was sexually involved with another woman when he plotted his wife's death. He too chose poison as his means, dosing Catharine's hot chocolate and tea with arsenic as she lay recovering from childbirth. For his indifference to Catharine's agonized death, John was cast as "that cold and heartless man who disgraces the name of husband." And for his calculated shift of demeanor "from the threatening cruel husband" he had habitually been to "the apparently kind, dutiful and commiserating companion" of Catharine's postpartum sufferings, he was charged with sentimental hypocrisy: the change was "a gross deception! A mere cloak to his fiend-like conduct!" Only at his trial for murder, explained the prosecution, do "we now find the mask entirely torn off, and the hardened *murderer* standing disclosed in all his deformity!"[36]

The central distinction between the Earls case and the Hendrickson case was the narrative treatment of the victim. The common-law standing of the Earls marriage provided an opening for the defense to assault Catharine's character: she was a common scold, an aggressive woman without prudence or delicacy, perhaps intemperate. And since she was not properly John Earls's wife, and his affections were now turning to another, she had probably killed herself out of shame and jealousy, with an eye to casting blame on her faithless partner.[37] The contrast between this tale of Catharine Earls as a guilt-stained common-law wife and the tale of Maria Hendrickson as a virtuous "true woman" points to the all-important consideration given to the female victim's character in assessing husbands' guilt in cases of wife-murder.

But in the face of this assault on Catharine's moral character, the prosecution cleverly managed to seize the higher moral ground by focusing on the timing of the crime. With a fine attention to melo-drama, the prosecution described John's mixing the poison "for his unsuspecting wife, prostrate on her bed of confinement, with her new born babe slumbering by her side." Earls killed his wife "upon an occasion when, if ever, the sympathies of our nature are called into lively exercise—when the heart of the *savage* is softened and indi-cates *some* degree of feeling." The power of the prosecution's narra-tive proved greater than the defense's, and John Earls was convicted. In sentencing him to die for his crime, the judge suggested that he, too, accepted the prosecution's sentimental version of this domestic tale. Referring to Catharine Earls's exhumation and postmortem examination, he said, "The grave gave up its contents—that heart whose affections had clung around you for more than fifteen years, was the first to proclaim, by its ventricles filled with blood, that its pulsations had been suddenly arrested by the operation of some sudden, violent and unnatural cause."[38] The murder victim's loving heart—metaphorically damaged in life, physiologically in death—identified her killer. In the last analysis, Catharine Earls, no less than Maria Hendrickson, was deemed deserving of the companionate marriage which her cruel and faithless husband had denied her.

John Earls was the most dangerous kind of marital murderer: the nurture-killer, one who played the role of loving husband while slipping poison into an ailing wife's food and drink. Examples were abundant in the literature. Barent Becker mixed arsenic in his wife's tea and stewed cranberries; Medad McKay told his wife, Lucy, that the arsenic he fed her was medicine; Cornelius Henry Francisco administered a lethal dosage of laudanum to Maria, his wife of less than four weeks.[39] The most notorious of such cases was that of twenty-one-year-old Henry Green of Troy, New York, who killed his eighteen-year-old bride less than a week after their wedding by dosing her tea and coffee, soup, soda water, and medicinal wine with arsenic. Green's performance of the role of the solicitous husband tenderly nursing his sick wife prompted the judge to proclaim that Green's crime "stood out, and would probably stand out on the page of history, unapproached and unapproachable, unredeemed as it was in unrelenting cruelty, and horrid barbarity, by one single palliating circumstance." Green's subsequent confession could hardly have tempered this assessment: his motive had been desire for another woman. Henry Green's violation of romantic love could not have been more flagrant, and his crime was cited in subsequent murder trials, by attorneys who assumed jurors' familiarity with the case,[40] as one of the most dreadful in American criminal history.

Desire for another woman was a common motive in cases of wife-murder. In 1807, Alpheus Hitchcock of Madison County, New York, wrote love letters from his prison cell to his paramour: "must my lips never more seal a kiss, a sacred kiss, on those ruby lips of thine, my dear, dear Lois?" In Hitchcock's marriage, the new ideal of romantic love actually undercut the companionate marriage. Romantic love proved a problem as well for the reluctant marriage of Charles Getter, forced by law to marry the woman whose child he had sired, despite his passion for another. Getter sought Molly Hummer's company "on the very day of his marriage": "while his poor wife was sitting with a breaking heart beside the fragments of the then neglected wedding feast, he was soothing the feelings of another, and keeping alive the flame of lawless and unhallowed passion." Six months later, he strangled his wife. The defense responded to the prosecution's tale of a broken-hearted bride by pointing out that "the deceased was no virgin flower, plucked in all the lovely innocence of budding beauty," but rather a one-time unwed mother.[41] Nonetheless, Getter was found guilty and sentenced to hang.

No such moral ambiguity plagued the trial of Oliver Watkins for the strangling death of Roxana, a kind, obedient, and industrious wife and mother, in Connecticut in 1829. Despite his wife's pleadings, Oliver openly consorted with a widow who had kept a house of prostitution until the town council warned her out. On the day after Roxana's death, Oliver and the widow had closeted themselves alone in the room next to the one where his dead wife was laid out. In sentencing him to be executed, the judge said, "Yet neither [Roxana's] kindness nor her love would deter you from the commission of the murderous and bloody deed. You committed it in the hour of repose, while your innocent children were sleeping around you, and the infant was pressed to the mother's bosom."[42] Oliver Watkins, like a host of other wife-murderers in nineteenth-century America, was charged not only with murder but with a crime against domesticity itself.

A considerably smaller body of murder narratives concerned women who killed their husbands, beginning with the Bathsheba Spooner case in Brookfield, Massachusetts, in 1778. At thirty-two, after twelve years of marriage, Mrs. Joshua Spooner became involved with a young American soldier named Ezra Ross, and urged him to murder her husband. When he proved reluctant, she offered the job to two British soldiers for a price, and all three men ambushed Joshua at his doorstep, beat him to death, and threw his body down a well, where it was found the next day. All four participants were tried, found guilty, and executed. Bathsheba tried to "plead her belly," that is, to have the execution postponed on the grounds of pregnancy, but the jury of matrons that examined her reported that she was not pregnant. At the condemned woman's request, a postmortem examination was performed and a five-month male fetus was discovered.[43]

The Spooner case prompted much language of Gothic horror: it was a "bloody tragedy," "a most shocking, cruel murder," "scarcely to be parallelled in all history." Several factors of the crime were cited as contributing to its particular horror, including the extreme brutality of the assault, the use of hired assassins, the deliberate, secret "design to spill innocent blood," the fact that the victim was attacked at his own doorstep, and, perhaps most important, the role of a wife in murdering her husband. "Why is the life of an innocent husband

plotted against by the wife of his bosom?" rhetorically asked the Rev.
Nathan Fiske. Bathsheba Spooner was obviously no model of womanly virtue: she was an adulteress who put out a contract on her
husband's life, who in contrast to her male co-conspirators refused to
repent of her crime until the final hours of her life, and who died
pregnant, perhaps by her lover. But this husband-murder, unlike
subsequent nineteenth-century cases, generated no narrative of the
peculiar heinousness of female crime.[44]

Later treatments of husband-murder became heavily gendered
explorations of criminal guilt, spurred by the influence of new ideas
about true womanhood. Their impact was evident, for example, in
the trial of Lucretia for murdering her husband, William Chapman,
in Andalusia, Pennsylvania, in 1831. The prosecution melodramati-
cally portrayed the defendant as an infamous outrage to the ideal of
true womanhood. Hers was "a moral temperament radically diseased"; here was a woman "utterly abandoned and lost to moral
principle," whose ambition, avarice, and "licentious appetite" had
readily allied her with her seducer, Mina. She was a woman whose
"masculine intelligence and habits" had secured for her the upper
hand in her husband's house, where she dominated and abused him
out of "the most deep and loathing hatred." The prosecutor addressed the jury, "I ask you then as husbands and fathers, knowing
the loveliness of domestic love, appreciating the sanctity of domestic
obligation . . . whether you can conceive a more unnatural, a more
revolting crime than that which blasts all these, and blurs the purity
of woman's fame." Lucretia Chapman was not an angel in the house
but "a household fiend,"[45] a monstrously depraved violation of the
cult of domesticity and true womanhood.

Counsel for the defense presented an entirely different portrait of
Lucretia as "an oppressed fellow-creature—a woman—hapless, helpless, friendless, and forlorn," who had fallen victim to a "smooth
tongued villain." The defense's Lucretia Chapman was a woman of
respectable social standing, a devout Christian (who had initially
welcomed Mina into her home as an act of Christian charity), a
teacher, a devoted mother of five children, and a loving wife. The
death of her husband, according to the defense, had thrown Lucretia

and her children "helpless and unprotected, on the broad bosom of the world." Mina, with "the malignity of a demon under the mask of a sacred obligation imposed by a dying man," told Lucretia that her husband had instructed him to marry the widow and protect her children. She did plead guilty to "the charge of folly and indiscretion" in marrying Mina with such haste, but the jury should take pity on her now, for "The recollections of how miserably she has been duped, the infamy of this public exposure, the mildew on a once unspotted reputation—these will torment her pillow to the latest hour."[46]

Essential to the defense's story of her victimization as true woman was the projection of female guilt onto the lower-class women of the same household, the servants who had testified to Lucretia's adultery and ill-treatment of her husband. To destroy the credibility of these "vipers," the defense ridiculed the notion that women of their caste could possibly experience the refined distaste implied by their claimed aversion to Lucretia's misconduct, and made crude, racist puns about the black servant Ann Bantom.[47] Female evil was indeed present in the Chapman home, according to the defense, but it did not reside in the pious wife and mother who served as its high priestess. Instead, it occupied the nether regions of the house (the Chapman kitchen was in fact located in the basement), where lower-class servant-demons plotted to destroy the respectable angel of the house.

Despite the judge's highly prejudicial charge to the jury, Lucretia Espos y Mina was found not guilty. Perhaps the jury was reluctant to find any woman guilty of a capital offense; perhaps the presence of her children in the courtroom deflected a conviction; perhaps the absence of any direct evidence linking her to either the purchase of the arsenic or its introduction into William Chapman's chicken soup, lay behind the decision. The foreign-born Mina certainly provided a handy scapegoat for the crime: he was subsequently convicted of Chapman's murder and executed.[48] But given the thrust of the state's case, it is possible that the jury found Lucretia not guilty because they were unable to accept the vile narrative of domestic depravity offered by the prosecution. Given a choice between two stories—the

{153}

prosecution's tale of a demonic woman, threatening and powerful, and the defense's tale of a helpless and confiding woman, duped by a seducer—the jury may have sought some reassurance in affirming the latter.

Within ten years, the Lucretia Chapman case was being cited in a similar trial for husband-murder in Boston. In 1840, Hannah Kinney was tried for killing George T. Kinney by mixing arsenic into his sage tea. As the prosecution itself was quick to admit, Mrs. Kinney was a "very prepossessing" woman, "distinguished for personal beauty, extraordinary talents, uncommon accomplishments, and of respectable rank in society." The state conceded the defendant's fine qualities to warn jurors not to let their sympathies be turned from the victim to his killer. Citing several cases of accused female killers, including Lucretia Chapman, the District Attorney explained, "There are some who think it was the SEX, ONLY, of those defendants, which saved them from the punishment of the law." In such cases, "there are difficulties, prejudices, sympathies, anxieties and embarrassments to be overcome."[49] Despite his best efforts, however, and the considerable physical evidence of Hannah's guilt, she was acquitted of the crime.

The defense played the gender card in the Kinney case by highlighting Hannah's reported behavior at George's bedside during "his last hour." "When you shall hear the simple and touching description of that scene, at [sic] it has been described to me, if there is a man who can then believe that this woman went through a series of acts of affection, with an art and hypocrisy that surpass all human nature, he can believe more than I can." Here was a sentimental argument for the deep womanliness of Hannah Kinney's nature: she was a woman of genuine feeling, and her feeling demonstrated her innocence.[50] Mrs. Kinney, the defense argued, could not have killed her husband and then counterfeited such pathos as he lay dying. Perhaps Doctor Calvin Bachelder (who had been treating George for venereal disease) had poisoned him by accident? Maybe the arsenic found in his stomach had accidentally been added to the laboratory bottle where that organ had been stored after his autopsy? Hannah Kinney maintained that her husband, a gambler and business insolvent, might have killed himself as he had sometimes threatened to do.

When the jury brought in their verdict of not guilty, great applause broke out in the courtroom. What is most surprising about both the verdict and the applause is that Hannah Kinney, despite her "uncommon accomplishments" and "respectable rank," bore a problematic reputation. George Kinney was actually Hannah's third husband. She had divorced her first after ten years on grounds of adultery. Rumors had circulated that Hannah had poisoned her second husband (and cousin), the Rev. Enoch Freeman, who was reported to have died of cholera morbus one year after the wedding. Before marrying Freeman, she had been courted by Kinney, and there were reports that she had imprudently received his calls soon after Freeman's death. Hannah Kinney's conduct had been the subject of several investigations and disciplinary actions by her Baptist church, and she had blamed her arrest on her church enemies.

When gossip continued after her acquittal, the widow wrote *A Review of the Principal Events of the Last Ten Years in the Life of Mrs. Hannah Kinney* (1841) to defend her character. The preface to this work was a study in self-serving self-effacement: painful though it was for her to review these events, and contrary to her natural requirements for rest, tranquillity, and the fireside comforts of her sister's home ("for indeed I have no home of my own"), Kinney explained that she owed it to her children and friends to lay before the public a full statement of the facts. She prayed that God would sustain her in this endeavor, as He had sustained her in prison. The self-defense that followed demonstrated how even a woman of dubious character could use the cult of true womanhood—the *a priori* assumption that woman was morally superior to man—to save her own skin, even in the face of overwhelming evidence that she was a murderer. It may indeed have been Kinney's "SEX, ONLY"—coupled with her respectable social status—that saved her from the punishment of the law. As in the Lucretia Chapman case, it may have proved more important for the jury to contain the larger ideological danger posed by acknowledging that a respectable woman could be a killer, than to convict a flesh-and-blood woman of murder.[51]

{155}

One additional case sheds further light on the female domestic murderer. There was never any doubt that Margaret Howard killed her husband's lover in Cincinnati, Ohio, in 1849: she confessed to the crime moments after committing it. But the memoir of her life written by the judge who presided over her trial, and printed as the opening section of the trial report, made it clear that she was the primary victim in this crime. Margaret had been only fifteen years old, a student-boarder in Peoria, Illinois, when she was persuaded by gambler John Howard to elope with him. Shortly after the wedding, he imprisoned her in a room for five days without food. After the birth of their first child, a boy, John began calling his wife a "damned whore" and flourishing a bowie knife at her, locking her up and beating her, striking her with anything that came to hand including chairs, and throwing plates of food at her. When their second child, a girl, was only three weeks old, he locked away all the bedclothes in the house, leaving his wife and children to suffer without protection the cold of December. He drank constantly and soon was abusing his son as well as his wife, sometimes knocking the boy out of his chair.

According to a woman who had once lived with the Howards, "his conduct in his family, was the worst I ever knew in a man . . . the house presented one continued scene of outrage." The couple separated for a time, with Margaret keeping the children and John refusing to provide for them; when she returned to him, in midwinter, he locked them all up in an unfurnished room and deliberately extinguished the fire. Finally, he seized the children and took them to live with him and his paramour, Mary Ellen Smith. The deserted wife sank into destitution, moving from room to room, eking out a bare subsistence as a seamstress and beggar as her health and reason gave way. One afternoon in 1849, an acquaintance found her wandering the streets, with her open cloak revealing her dress stained with blood, a knife in her right hand, and her right arm to the elbow covered with blood. She said, "there is the heart's blood of the wretch who has been living with him, and been keeping me from my children." When the man asked whether she had really killed someone, she replied, "Yes; I went down and murdered her . . . Do you blame me for it? would it have been better that I should have suf-

{156}

fered on as I have suffered, or that I should have taken revenge as I have taken it?"[52]

This memoir of Margaret Howard presents an extremely sympathetic view of her life as the long-suffering wife of a cruel husband. As her memoirist commented, "The soul and heart sicken over such horrible atrocities" as were committed in the Howard household. The sympathy that pervades this memoir was expressed as well at her murder trial, at which Margaret Howard was acquitted on the grounds of insanity and committed to a mental asylum. The case for her insanity was strong: shortly after confessing the murder to one acquaintance, she had abruptly asked another man, "How came that hot blood on me? I dreamed last night of sticking a pig, and that blood spurted on me the same way, and when I did this, this afternoon, the same feeling came to my mind." Judge Brough concluded his preface to the trial report by saying, "We have thus followed Mrs. Howard from her cradle to the Lunatic Asylum, driven there by the inhuman conduct of the man who persuaded her, while but a young girl, to leave her father's protection and put her trust in him, and who swore at the altar of love, to honour and support her."[53]

Not Margaret, but John Howard, had desecrated the temple of domesticity. Margaret had acted in fierce defense of her family circle, to reclaim her beloved children. Her motive was maternal, and her choice of murder victim was probably deemed correct: the disreputable other woman, destroyer of the domestic circle. Perhaps the judge and jury would have been less inclined to pity the wife had she directed her murderous rage at her husband instead of his paramour. But her choice of victim freed jurors to treat this domestic tale as a story of a female murderer who was more victim than perpetrator. Margaret Howard belonged to a rare breed of murderer, the womanly killer.

One more category of domestic murder evoked a particularly strong horror response: the murder of a child by a parent (or guardian), in terrible violation of the sentimental ideal of child-nurture. An example was the trial of Charles Stevens, who in 1823 was accused of beating to death his eight- or nine-year-old son, Charles, with a pair of fireplace tongs, because the boy could not or would not tell the whereabouts of his mother, who had gone into hiding from her husband. The chief witness for the prosecution was Eliza Jane Stevens, seven-year-old daughter of the accused, who offered a chilling account of what had happened on the afternoon of her brother's disappearance. Her father had beaten both children with a rope in the bedroom, then sent Eliza to fetch the kitchen tongs with which he began to beat Charles, threatening to kill him for lying. Eventually he took the boy downstairs to continue the beating. From the bedchamber, Eliza had listened to her brother's cries until both the cries and the beating stopped, and she never saw her brother again. The senior Stevens fled to Portsmouth and changed his name. According to the prosecution, he had killed his son, hidden his body beneath the floor boards of the house, and later boxed and dumped it into the ocean. But the body was never recovered, and the jury found Stevens not guilty. After his acquittal, however, he was indicted for assault and battery against Eliza Jane; he pleaded guilty and received a six-month sentence.

The defense argued that Charles Stevens had legitimately whipped his son for lying, and that the boy had then run away from home. Central to their argument was the proposition that men do not suddenly become moral monsters: "That a man of respectable connexions, standing and character in society, should suddenly, and without the least known temptation of inducement, transform himself to a most atrocious villian [sic] is incredible." They thus argued simultaneously that beating the child was not an offense, and that beating him to death would have been so outrageous an offense that a man of Stevens's position could not have committed it. The Attorney General observed that, though the crime of child-murder was inconceivable, it was nonetheless committed all the time: "When passion, intoxication or jealousy take entire possession of the intellectual powers, when the mind becomes habitually depraved and the heart void of social duty, . . . we have many melancholly [sic?] instances" of child-murder. On this point, the judge, in delivering his charge to the jury, agreed with the prosecution: "This charge is so repugnant to the strong affection which nature has implanted in the parental bosom, that at first view it would seem to be absolutely incredible. But unhappily we have too much reason to believe, from the history of crimes and of mankind, that human beings, seduced by their own evil passions, instigated possibly by diabolical agency, and forsaken of God, have been left to the perpetration of crimes as dark and malignant as this."[54] Dark and malignant though it was, this crime (perhaps because of the absence of a clear *corpus delicti*) went unpunished.

In 1827, Amos and Abigail Furnald were charged and tried separately for the murder of his illegitimate son, five-year-old Alfred. The boy's mother, a young single woman, had formally identified Amos Furnald as the father, and the town had ordered him to give bond for the child's maintenance, which he provided by periodically taking Alfred into his home. There the boy was subjected to extensive abuse: he was beaten with a rawhide whip, bedded down in a box of straw where he slept in his own filth, deprived of heat and adequate nourishment (witnesses testified that Alfred had been seen chewing on shoe leather and eating from the swill pail to assuage his hunger), tossed into mud puddles, forced barefoot into the snow and pelted with snowballs, and denied schooling. Amos Furnald encouraged his wife and legitimate children to join him in torturing the bastard in their midst, and it was reported that the Furnald children once tied a rope around Alfred's neck and dragged him about the floor until the boy nearly strangled. Alfred was regularly seen with scars, bruises, and fresh blood on his face. He finally died after two months' imprisonment in a cold garret without sufficient food.

In the opening at the trial of Amos Furnald, the District Attorney made much of the "shocking" state of the victim's body and observed that "If the prisoner be guilty, he is guilty of the most deliberate and cruel murder to be found in the annals of the blackest crimes in any country." In his even more melodramatic closing, he asked the jury whether their pity would be granted to "the marble-hearted monster, who forced the tender infant from the breast of its mother, and answered her tears and agony with threats of more than savage barbarity?" or to "the deserted, and friendless, and persecuted child, withered and cut down in the morning of life—and by a death, the most agonizing which hellish malignity could invent." Death at any age was "a fearful thing to see," "but to see the healthy bloom of infancy fade by hunger, the buoyant spirit broken down by blows, the heart drooping in solitude and misery, and nakedness and frost joining to change the elastic step of youth into the tottering decrepitude of age; to see the scene closing in stifled groans, in a deserted garret, without a mother's tears or a father's sympathy" was "too horrible for a christian community ever to endure, without fixing on its author the brand of Cain."[55]

Though the jury found Amos Furnald guilty merely of manslaughter—criminal neglect without willful malice—the trial report still offered readers a horrifying account of child abuse that was a nightmarish inversion of child-centered domesticity. Amos and Abigail Furnald, like Charles Stevens Sr. and other child-killers of the period, committed crimes of violence that were also crafted into tales of domestic evil, stories of horrifying violations of the rising sentimental standards for a tender, loving child nurture. Just as little Alfred Furnald was described to jurors in the prosecution's closing for his father's trial, the dead victims of child abuse appeared posthumously before a popular readership steeped in new prescriptions for rearing children, to illustrate the terrible consequences of a parental failure to cherish childhood.[56]

———————

Popular accounts of domestic murder may be read as cultural nightmares of the new sentimental domesticity, terrible tales of transgression against the emerging norms of companionate marriage, "true womanhood," and loving child nurture. As such, these stories of deviance reinforced the new domestic ideal with their didactically sensationalistic depictions of patriarchal violence, female depravity, and child abuse. They could serve as cautionary tales to frighten readers into proper domestic conduct. Such was frequently the avowed (and implicitly apologetic) purpose set forth by editors of these publications, as well as the message delivered by prosecuting attorneys and judges through courtroom narratives of the crime.

But these narratives cannot be read solely as reaffirmations of sentimental domesticity in the face of its shocking violation. They dealt in illicit excitement, ratcheting up the melodrama to feed the public's fascination with families run amok and its desire to know all the gory details—desires that were not compatible with a respectable restatement of the family ideal. These stories were not univocal; they were filled with different voices—criminals spoke as well as judges, the defense as well as the prosecution, which often assigned different meanings to the violence. Meaning was often contested, implicitly or explicitly, most formally in the trial reports with their adversarial format, less formally in other genres. And some of these voices and perspectives actually subverted the sentimental ideal. The popular literature of domestic murder reveals a pervasive if unspoken resistance to the new values and practices of sentimental domesticity, offering a darker perspective on American family life in this period.

One illustration of the darker strains in the domestic-Gothic narrative was the popularity of stories in which wife-murderers justified their abuse of their wives by asserting patriarchal prerogative. Michael McGarvey justified whipping his wife to death on such grounds—"he had chastised her because she ought to keep her own place"—and complained to the arresting constable that "it was a damned bad country that would not allow a man to beat his wife." Wife-beater John Boies informed a concerned magistrate six months before the murder that "he had a right to whip her when and as much as he pleased." William McDonnough once told a neighbor who complained of the noisiness of the McDonnoughs' fights that "he must correct his family." A number of men who murdered their wives rather than permit them to leave the house or end the marriage similarly justified their actions by asserting their patriarchal prerogative of domestic rule. "The Last Words of Robert Bush," who killed his wife when she escaped his intemperance to live with a neighbor, offered a rambling, self-pitying account of his wife's ill treatment of him and closed by saying, "it is a pity but no wonder that the people mourn when old maids rule."[57] The point here is not that the men challenged the sentimental ideal of the companionate marriage, but that the popular press offered a forum for their voices and a popular readership made them marketable. These narratives permitted readers to have it both ways: as horrific tales of the violent consequences of an outmoded patriarchy, and as attractively illicit appeals to a cultural backlash against companionate marriage.

Even more subversive, because more formally legitimate, were the narratives commonly offered by defense attorneys at the murder trials of chronically abusive husbands: the "she-had-it-coming" defense. For these stories were offered by lawyers trying to win over jurors, and were presented with reasonable hope of their acceptance by reasonable men. When Peter Lung battered his wife to death in 1816, the defense labelled her crazy, idle, wasteful, and quarrelsome, and claimed she had died of a drunken fit. When John Banks cut his wife Margaret's throat with a razor in 1807, the defense charged her not just with drunkenness but with poor cookery (she had brought pot-liquor to her husband when he ordered coffee). William McDonnough's defense claimed that his wife had verbally abused him. Similar arguments were introduced into the trials of accused child-murderers: the beating of little Charles Stevens by his father, argued his defense, was warranted by the boy's lying; the beating of six-year-old Betsey Van Amburgh by her uncle, Stephen Arnold, in 1805 was justified by the child's obstinate refusal to read the word "gig." Though some witnesses said that Arnold beat her nearly to death before telling her the proper pronunciation, the defense claimed, "The child persisted in its perverseness, when it could and had pronounced the word right"—implying that Betsey's disobedience excused Arnold's actions.[58]

Such arguments were sometimes successful in the courtroom and often not. But they continued to be offered in court, and then distributed in print, giving readers as much an opportunity for outrage at the violation of companionate marriage and loving child-nurture, as an option to stand with the defense in questioning those ideals or at least demarcating their outer limits. When the wife was a drunkard, a scold, or a poor cook, when the child lied or proved obstinate, marital and parental affection might be set aside, these arguments suggested, and coercive patriarchy restored. At work in such courtroom narratives was not the outright condemnation of corporal punishment found in prescriptive literature, but an exploration of the realm of the permissible in the physical "correction" of wives and children.

More broadly, some accounts of domestic homicide might be read as cautionary tales against the dangers of sentimental domesticity, thus presenting their own case in favor of patriarchy. Maria Van Deusen's defiance of her parents' wishes in marrying the idle rowdy, John Hendrickson, might be read as a cautionary tale against romantic courtship, for the parental assessment of the bridegroom's character proved correct. Another example was the confession of John Zimmerman, who killed his twenty-year-old daughter in Pennsylvania in 1823. Rosina was keeping company with an Irishman, a situation Zimmerman found intolerable: "who has intercourse with the Irish, has dealings with the devil, thought I." When Rosina received her beau at the Zimmerman home and conversed with him in Gaelic, "I therefore told my Rosina to speak her father's language, that I might understand her." Suspicious that she was pregnant (she may have tried to sidestep her father's authority by this method), Zimmerman went to the woods to pray for a sign, and God commanded, "'Put your Rosina to death.' This confirmed my suspicions about my Rosina and the Irishmen [sic], nay, certain was I, my daughter had done amiss, and resolved I was to save her—to destroy her." He hastened home and beat and strangled her to death, "and thus the will of God was accomplished."[59] Zimmerman's understanding of his paternal rights and obligations was not sentimental but patriarchal: as God's representative in his own family, it was his duty to "save" his daughter from leaving his dominion for that of another man, who did not even speak her father's language, by killing her. This tale of murder issued a clear warning to romantic young women who disregarded their fathers' will in choosing their suitors.

Similarly, the many marital murders (such as Green, Hitchcock, Getter, Spooner, Chapman) prompted by one spouse's affection for a third party might have served as cautionary tales about expectations of romantic love and sexual fulfillment within the companionate marriage, for when marital love declined, disaster could strike. At the same time, some tales of domestic murder implicitly warned readers of the terrible perils of married women's expanding rights to seek separation and divorce from their husbands, even on grounds of cruelty and abuse. Bradbury Ferguson shot Eliza Ann because he would not tolerate her repeated efforts to escape his abuse in the homes of neighbors; Robert Bush killed his wife when she sought refuge in the home of a single man living nearby. When Return J. M. Ward's wife, Olive, returned home to fetch her clothes after six weeks of separation, "He at once resolved that she should never leave his house alive" and killed her with a blow from a flatiron.[60] Such tales, no matter how sentimentally sympathetic to the victim, implicitly warned readers of the terrible potential consequences of a wife's decision to leave her husband's house.

The best tale of the struggle over married women's rights was told by Guy Clark, who murdered his wife and the mother of his five children in 1832. Fanny Clark was a forceful, independent woman; she took in boarders for a while, until Guy forced her to stop; helped to place him in jail (on a charge he failed to specify); and took as a close friend a "lewd young woman" whom Clark called "Miss Co-Partner," and about whom he speculated, "O God, who could avoid thinking that there was co-partnership between them in an improper and vicious way . . . even amounting to lewdness"—possibly implying a sexual relationship between them as well as their suspected partnership in prostitution. When he "slapped her chops, and stopped her tongue," Fanny again had him jailed and this time initiated divorce proceedings against him. Guy called his wife "obstinate, turbulent, and self-willed," "highheaded and haughty, and as proud as Lucifer." He finally subordinated her by burying an axe in her skull, and then declared his innocence: "O, reader, am I guilty of murder? or has she murdered herself?" The real culprit in the case, he charged, was feminist Frances Wright: "I would give Miss Frances Wright my thanks for the sentiments she has diffused through the land of Freedom, with regard to matrimony, and would advise her to seclude herself in the Five Points or some other convenient place, if she wishes to destroy the institution of marriage, where she can carry on her practices without being bound under the galling chains of hymen." Guy Clark concluded his narrative by offering a hymn to true womanhood: "Man tarnishes his name, and brightens it again; / But if woman chance to swerve from the strictest rules of virtue, / Ruin ensues, reproach and endless shame, / And one false step forever blasts her fame." The crime that most impressed this wife-killer was his victim's alleged fall from domestic virtue.[61]

In first-person criminal claims to the patriarchal prerogative of physical violence, in the "she-had-it-coming" defense, in cautionary tales about romantic courtship and women who separated from their husbands, a diffuse resistance to sentimental domesticity was evident. But the crudest literary subversion of the sentimental ideal consisted in narratives that most graphically represented the terrible carnage of some domestic murders. In them the pornography of violence took a specifically misogynist form, focusing on the terrible damage done to the bodies of women by their husbands. Even when the surface narratives of such accounts (often reinforced by the moralistic editorial voice) were sentimental-domestic, their contents undermined the surface narratives with a titillating, prurient appeal to body-horror. The printed account of the Henry Mills familicide in 1817, for example, repeatedly invoked the conventions of sentimental domesticity in expressing outrage at the crime. But the fold-out frontispiece illustration offered a graphic black-and-white depiction of Mills's slaughter of his wife and children, embellished with red ink to represent blood gushing from the head, mouth, and breast of the dying wife and mother.[62]

Different methods of killing offered different opportunities for this misogynist pornography of violence. (Few male victims offered comparable evidence of the tortures endured before death.) One was the chronic-abuse murder: Jane Boies's body revealed fifteen axe wounds and "There appeared not a place on the body as large as the open hand which was not bruised"; Phoebe Graham's back was marked with long, narrow stroke marks apparently inflicted by a whip. Another common form was the medical postmortem report on poisoning victims, in which readers learned, for example, that the mucus membrane of Belinda Hitchcock's stomach was corroded, and that Lucy McKay's lower stomach was perforated near the intestines. Such medical details graphically reminded readers that, as in the poisoning of Catharine Earls, "The pain and agony which she suffered must have been beyond description."[63]

The most extreme examples of body-horror in the literature of domestic murder were first-person accounts by husbands who had systematically destroyed their wives' bodies by fire and dismemberment. One of the earliest of these was Edward Donnelly's murder of his wife in Carlisle, Pennsylvania, in 1808. Donnelly confessed to having beaten Catharine with a pair of fire tongs and a wagon whip, and finally killing her with a blow from the butt-end of the whip. The next morning, he built a large fire in the fireplace, burning all her flesh (he commented on how long it took for the head to be consumed), pounding her bones with an axe and then returning them to the fire, smashing the remains, and finally throwing the remaining ash outdoors. The Donnelly case was exceeded in pruriently violent detail by the *Confession of Adam Horn* to the murder and dismemberment of his wife in 1843. The middle-aged Horn, suspicious that his eighteen-year-old wife was unfaithful, killed her with two blows from a stick, then left her body in the cellar for three or four days before dismembering it. "I began by trying to take off the head, but I found that I could not succeed with the knife in getting through the bone; I accordingly got the axe and with this and the knife severed the head from the body."[64] He took the head upstairs and spent several hours burning it, then gathered up the teeth from the ashes and scattered them in the woods. He cut off the corpse's arms and legs and hid them under the bake oven behind the house, and buried the trunk in an old coffee bag in his peach orchard.

In sentencing Adam Horn to death for his crime, Judge Richard B. Magruder said, "After the revolting detail, which we have all heard during the trial, of the facts attending the commission of the crime of which you have been found guilty, it can now subserve no good purpose to recapitulate them." But the popular press was not quite so circumspect: the anthology *Annals of Murder* included a book advertisement for *The Life of Andrew Hellman, alias Adam Horn*, with an illustration of "Horn mutilating the body of his second Wife." In this print, Horn stands with a bloody knife in one hand and the severed head gushing blood in the other, while the headless corpse lies on the floor at his feet, with one severed arm lying beside it and a hatchet at its feet—an image which actually telescopes the action of the dismemberment for enhanced dramatic effect. The publishers of the *Annals of Murder* clearly believed that graphic images of chopped-up bodies could effectively sell their merchandise.[65]

The case of Return Ward, in 1857, exceeded even the Horn murder's sensationalistic appeal to body-horror. When the long-abused Olive Ward tried to separate from her husband in Sylvania, Ohio, he killed and systematically dismembered her, boiling and burning her body in a process closely detailed for pages of his printed confession. "I tore the clothes open from the throat down. I then took a small pocket knife and opened the body, took out the bowels first, and then put them in the stove upon the wood; they being filled with air, would make a noise in exploding, so I took my knife and pricked holes through them to prevent the noise; then took out the liver and heart . . . I then took out the blood remaining in the cavity of the body, by placing a copper kettle close to the same and scooping it out with my hands." He explained how he made two incisions along the sides of her trunk, then "broke off the ribs and took out the breast bone, and threw it into a large boiler; unjointed the arms at the shoulders, doubled them up and placed them in the boiler; then severed the remaining portions of the body, by placing a stick of wood under the back and breaking the back bone over the same, cutting away the flesh and ligaments with a knife." Failing in his attempt to remove the head, he placed the upper portion of the body into the boiler, and removed the legs, severing them at the knee, cutting open the thighs to remove the bones, "cutting the fleshy parts of the thighs in small strips, the more readily to dispose of them."[66] After burning what remained, he placed the ashes in a small keg, sifted out the larger pieces of bone, and scattered them in the fields around town. The printed account of the murder offered lingeringly close detail of how every body part, every internal organ, all the bones and blood, of one man's wife were destroyed, in a literary orgy of concentrated misogyny that undercut the narrative's surface appeals to sentimental domesticity. Such narratives implicitly suggested to the reader what could happen when a woman sought to break the marriage bond.

———————

One implication of the popularity of domestic murder literature in the nineteenth century is that the historical transition from the traditional patriarchal family to the modern sentimental family was rough and contested. Some families violated the sentimental ideal in terrible ways, and some murderers expressly challenged it by reclaiming their patriarchal prerogative to discipline wives and children even to the point of death. That many families did not practice the ideal is hardly surprising: cultural ideals are routinely violated, and people either openly defy or simply ignore them. The popularity of the domestic-Gothic actually suggests something more significant, pointing to pervasive fears and anxieties accompanying sentimental domesticity. It is one thing to note a discrepancy between domestic prescriptions and the actual incidence of domestic murder; this popular literature elaborately dramatized the gap between the ideal and its violation in a more immediate appeal to nineteenth-century readers.

Gothic narratives of family murder explored fault lines in the ideas and practices of American domesticity, brought out most clearly by the adversarial trial format. Murder trials asked not only "did the defendant commit this crime of murder?" but also "was he (or she) *justified* in doing it?" The courtroom emerged as an important arena for public exploration of changing domestic norms. And among the most important issues contested was the proper limitations of patriarchal authority. What happened to the husband's and father's obligation of loving affection when a wife proved a drunkard or a child, a liar? What were the proper limits on wives' rights to separation and divorce? When should the ideal of romantic courtship be suspended in deference to powerful parental opposition? How should the competing demands of the new domestic privacy and traditional communal surveillance and intervention be negotiated? These were some of the ideological fault lines that were cracked open. The darkest side of the domestic-Gothic narrative was not its demonstration that the new rules of sentimental domesticity were regularly violated, but rather its fundamental challenge to the rules themselves, suggesting disturbances in the popular understanding and acceptance of the new ideal. The general moral uncertainty of courtroom narrative took specific shape in domestic cases as a cultural contestation of the proper norms of family relationships.

Even an unambiguous acceptance of the sentimental ideal could generate conflict and personal unhappiness within real families struggling to meet its high emotional and psychological expectations of loving intimacy, mutual respect, and perfect harmony. Readers may have wondered, did other families fulfill the requirements of sentimental domesticity with all its new burdens and pressures? The resounding *no* coming from popular murder literature may have provided relief and even a secret, guilty satisfaction to some. The Asmodean impulse to expose the hidden operations of increasingly private homes might have appealed to a pervasive need to discover that other American families were really getting it wrong, that the reader, whatever the problems and conflicts of his or her own family, had relatively little grounds for feelings of domestic failure.[67]

Setting aside the reassurance such stories may have offered, the domestic-Gothic represented the family as a site of dark mysteries and unspeakable horrors. The domestic murder narrative suggested that the American home was not a haven in a heartless new commercial world, but a bastion of traditional coercion and brutal violence; that the magic circle which sentimental writers tried to draw around the separate sphere of home did not really protect its dwellers from pain and violent death. In closing the murder trial of John Earls, the prosecutor addressed the jury with delicate tact, saying, "I know it is difficult for the mind accustomed to repose on the peaceful scenes of *private life* . . . to realize the amount of wickedness with which *the world* abounds."[68] His words drew on a characteristically sentimental contrast between the "home" and the "world." But his words were belied by the entire course of the trial that preceded them, for the Earls murder demonstrated that wickedness was not merely of the "world" but present in "private life" as well. Domestic murder narratives offered their readers no "peaceful scenes of private life" formulaically invoked by this sentimental attorney, but Gothic explorations of homes destroyed by fatal violence.

The conventions of horror and mystery had endeavored to establish a vast gulf between the murderer as moral alien, and the liberally "normal" run of humanity, to reassure the morally normal that evil was not in them, but somewhere "out there"—that depravity was not of private life but of the world outside. But popular accounts of domestic murder *brought the horror and the mystery home*, deriving their greatest shock value from the revelation that the murderer-monster actually resided in the American family. Again and again, he—and less frequently but even more monstrously, she—popped up at the domestic fireside, inside the family circle, to commit terrible carnage right in the heart of the domestic sanctuary.

The domestic-Gothic tracked the horror home by the bloody footsteps on the stairs and the bloody handprint over the fireplace; traced it in the sage tea and the chicken soup; located it not only within chronically abusive families but in the homes of the newly married, and of nurturing husbands or wives tending their spouses in sickness, and of loving husbands and fathers who suddenly, inexplicably, slaughtered their entire families.[69] And the domestic-Gothic brought the mystery home, removing the roof and mapping the domestic interior to locate the crime—not in an urban brothel, roadside tavern, or pirate ship, but in the kitchens and bedchambers of ordinary houses; removing the "veil" of domestic privacy to expose the terrible transgressions enacted in the secret spaces of American homes; demonstrating the uncanny quality of that which was simultaneously most familiar and most alien. If murder could occur within apparently happy families living in ordinary American homes, then who was safe? The moral alien, the monstrous murderer, it turns out, lurked in the most intimate of human communities, plotting his crimes amongst the pots and pans, the beds and bureaus, while engaged in such mundane household tasks as fixing hot chocolate, administering medicinal wine, and sharpening the kitchen knives.

One last tale of domestic homicide to dramatize this point: in November 1807, Rufus Hill battered to death his twenty-month-old stepchild, Mary Sisson. (She was actually the daughter of his live-in lover, Rebecca Sisson, identified in the trial transcript as his second wife.) At the trial, it emerged that Hill had been battering the child for some time before her death; medical testimony revealed that at her death, the baby had a dislocated neck and four broken ribs, and her bruises clearly indicated the knuckle marks of a man's fist. The last deadly assault on Mary had taken place one evening when the child's mother was briefly absent from the house, on what proved to be an eerily coincidental errand. With a woman friend, Rebecca Sisson had gone to a neighbor's "to borrow a book relating to murder," and had explained to the lender her eagerness to return home again by saying that Hill was building a fire for them to read by.[70] While the mother stepped briefly out of her house to borrow a book on murder, her "husband" occupied himself in murdering her child.

In this quintessentially domestic-Gothic narrative, the horror and the mystery of the crime were brought *home* to the reader in the most powerful way possible. This murder had been committed by an intimate domestic companion. And the evil erupted just when the reader-in-the-text reached for a murder narrative, which she had intended to read within the presumably safe confines of her own home. Did the contemporary reader of the Rufus Hill trial transcript think, "I too am reading a book on murder, in the presumably safe confines of my home?" (the most common site of reading after the reading revolution). Is it possible that such a murder could happen here? But this case simply exaggerates the meaning embedded in all domestic-Gothic narratives, which was, "Everyone has a family: yours may harbor a murderer." The power of the domestic-Gothic was that it challenged the liberal narrative of criminal deviance as an alien phenomenon without ever fully destroying it. With a ritualistic repetitiousness, tales of domestic homicide generated astonishment that "This terrible crime of murder could happen *here*"—in the sacred haven of domesticity, the place where evil was presumed most alien.

CHAPTER SIX

Murdering Medusa

I N 1833, a young Rhode Island woman named Sally Burdick died from the effects of a botched abortion; the abortionist and the man who had secured her services were both indicted for murder. The only printed account of the case was the transcript of the pretrial examination, most of which consisted of a detailed report of the autopsy performed on the victim. The examiner, Dr. Cyrus James, recounted how he carved an inverted "Y" incision into Burdick's body, "then took the triangular part and laid it down like an apron, then taking the sides of the abdomen apart, I had a fair view of its contents." He closely described the "dark thick matter, resembling foetid matter, almost as thick as tar, smell very offensive" in her abdomen, the "double handful" of coagulated blood he removed from her abdomen, the gas of putrefaction that distended her intestines. After entering Burdick's body through his own incision, he then experimentally entered it through what he delicately called the *os externum:* noting that the opening was extremely dilated, he explained that the passage "was large enough to receive my fist without much resistance." "A large rat," he continued, "might have gone in and come out again without difficulty." He cut out the womb and laid it open to extract a six-month female fetus. And he found seven perforations made by a sharp instrument in Burdick's womb, her labia "injured and mangled," and her body in a state of uncharacteristic decay for the amount of time elapsed since death ("the sides in a gangrene state, very green, the back of florid red")—probably due to damage sustained while she was being held down for her operation.[1]

Here was a classic instance of medical body-horror, a sensational murder account which focused on the terrible physiological damage done to the victim's body. But this brief pamphlet, published in Hartford, Connecticut, in 1833, belonged more specifically to a new category: the sexual tale of murder—not a "sex-murder" in the twentieth-century sense of a crime motivated by the sexual pleasure of killing, but an account that focused on matters of sexuality; in this case, illegitimate pregnancy and its medical termination. In the late eighteenth and early nineteenth centuries, sex and sexuality emerged as major new concerns of popular murder literature. Readers were ushered into a world where pregnant single women died at the hands of inept abortionists; rape victims were murdered by their sexual assailants; rejected lovers killed their scornful sweethearts, and successful seducers killed their pregnant cast-offs; prostitutes were killed by their most favored clients; jealous husbands murdered faithless wives, and adulterous husbands killed faithful wives to mate with other women; husbands and brothers avenged the honor of their women by killing their seducers; and experimenters in sexual unorthodoxy saw their innovative arrangements erupt in deadly violence. The growing concern about sexuality in the popular literature of murder reflected rising sexual tensions and conflicts at a time of transition in sexual practices and the meanings assigned to them.

The central concern of these murder stories was the sexuality not of the murderers but of their victims, most of whom were female. The presumed mystery of their sexual histories, and the horrors of their sexual physiology, shaped the sexual narrative of murder. In peeling back the "apron"—image of domestic tidiness—of Burdick's skin to dramatically uncover the "dark," "foetid," and "offensive" horrors of her body's interior, Dr. James uncovered the secret mysteries of female nature hidden beneath the ideal of womanly purity. And in imagining a large rat—figure of filth and evil—entering her decayed vagina, he suggested (however unintentionally) a scene of

{173}

sexual torture worthy of the Marquis de Sade, suggesting an active hostility to this autopsy subject. The implication of this account and others like it was that the deepest evil of the crime lay buried in the sexuality of its victim.

Stories of sexual murder added a significant new twist to the Gothic understanding of human evil, removing the focus from the male murderer as monstrous moral alien to his female victim as monstrous sexual alien. It is thus significant that the "Gorgon head of horror" cited by Daniel Webster in the Salem murder was female.[2] She was Medusa, the mythological female monster who had writhing serpents for locks of hair, and who had killed many men by turning to stone those who gazed upon her terrible visage: "Formed to attract all eyes to thee,/And yet their withering blight to be." Perseus succeeded in killing her by refusing to look directly at her: using a bright shield as a mirror, he crept up while she and her sisters slept and cut off her head, which he carried away and later used to kill his own enemies. For this heroic act, Perseus was classified among the "just murderers" who "purify the stains of evil by force and by the shedding of blood."[3] Some nineteenth-century murderers were similarly justified for purifying the evil of female sexuality. In the context of changing views of the moral and medical nature of women, focused on their radical difference from men, Gothic horror and mystery came to center on the dangers of sexual difference. The sexual-Gothic tale of murder constructed a powerful new linkage between sex and violence in American culture, which has shaped the popular response to the crime ever since.

<hr />

In early American execution sermons, sex and sexuality had been subjects of limited concern. Sermons preached for condemned infanticides might refer to the sexual liaison that had resulted in the condemned woman's pregnancy, but offered little information concerning that relationship. Sexual uncleanness was commonly cited as one among several smaller sins that had paved the way to the ultimate crime, including disobedience, disorderly living, and drunkenness.[4] Sex was not cited as motive in the earliest execution sermons for wife-murders. And rape-murder did not enter the literature before the late eighteenth century.

But by the late eighteenth century, the sexual content of popular murder literature was expanding. Though infanticide indictments and convictions were declining, the few printed cases included more sexual detail, explaining, for example, that the maid Elizabeth Valpy had taken the sexual initiative in her relationship with fellow servant William Hardy by moving her sleeping quarters nearer to his.[5] At the same time, stories of marital murder such as the John Lewis and Francis Personel cases began to identify sexual jealousy and misconduct as motives; and after the turn of the century, sexual "crimes against nature" were cited in a few accounts of wife-murder. By the early nineteenth century, rape-murder had entered the literature. Some of the earliest of these cases involved, significantly, African-American men accused of assaulting white girls. In 1803, a slave named Cato, of Charlestown, New York, was convicted and executed for beating to death twelve-year-old Mary Akins, after she had called him "black son of a bitch," and he had tried and failed to rape her. Cato's confession made much of his general habits of lewdness, including bestiality. His account was quickly followed by the confession of John Battus to the rape-murder of thirteen-year-old Salome Talbott: "while this victim, like a lamb in the voracious jaws of a lion, lay confined on the ground, begging to be set at liberty that she might go home—I, having satiated my worse than brutal lust on her chastity—even then, was induced to take her life also."[6]

To label such murders "sex-murders" would be misleading. In modern usage, the term refers to an act of killing for sexual pleasure: "sex-murders" are understood to be motivated by sadistic sexual impulses, and typically involve acts of rape or other forms of sexual assault, sadistic rituals, and mutilation as an integral part of the crimes, often perpetrated against a series of victims killed impersonally as generic sexual objects. This modern type of "sex-murder" began to take shape as reports of the "Jack the Ripper" murders swept the English-speaking world in 1888, and was fully formalized only in the early twentieth century. The late eighteenth- and early nineteenth-century discourse on murder did not yet conceptualize any crimes as "sex-murders" in this sense. Even stories of rape-murder tended to treat the killing not as an extension of the sexual assault, but as an afterthought to escape punishment for the rape: Battus killed Talbott "for fear of a discovery of a crime already committed."[7] Though these accounts often eroticized male violence against women, they revealed no depth-psychological understanding of a "lust to kill." Rather than labelling these cases "sex-murders," it is more useful to treat them as sexual tales of murder: stories that explored sexual relationships and motivations, treated passion and sometimes the sex act itself with novelistic detail, and indulged in a pervasive tone of prurience.

Sexual narratives of murder grew in popularity after 1820, becoming increasingly varied and complex in their story lines. The sexuality portrayed in the pages of nineteenth-century murder narratives was rich in its variety. Romantic courtship, seduction and betrayal, marital intimacy, adultery (homosexual as well as heterosexual), the ménage à trois, extramarital cohabitation, spiritual marriage, group marriage, and prostitution: all were treated in the sexual narratives of murder. And all were regarded as dangerously unstable situations, loaded with possibilities for violence.

In the late eighteenth and early nineteenth centuries, the family-centered, reproductive sexual system dominant throughout the colonial era was giving way to romantic, intimate, and deeply conflicted sexuality. Within the preindustrial sexual system, the primary goal of sexuality had been reproduction, and communal injunctions against extramarital and nonprocreative sex acts were severely enforced. But in the late eighteenth century, secularization weakened state regulation of sexual morality, religious disestablishment undermined church authority over personal behavior, and commercialization disrupted the patterns of stable community life within which sexual relations had been supervised. A sharp rise in the rate of bridal pregnancies not only confirmed the breakdown of traditional familial and communal regulations on sexuality, but pointed to a youthful revolt against patriarchal control over marriage. As romantic couples developed new expectations of emotional intimacy, the physical component of courtship became a subject of increasingly self-conscious and erotically intense concern. At the same time, the emergence of family limitation through prolonged breastfeeding and coitus interruptus encouraged the pursuit of sexual pleasure apart from reproduction, reinforcing the importance of romantic love in marriage.[8]

New fears arose about the sexual vulnerability of women. Within consensual relationships unconstrained by community enforcement of moral codes, the difficulties of ensuring that pregnancy would lead to marriage grew evident. Cautionary tales of seduction began to appear in popular magazines, sentimental fiction, and ballads. These fears were especially loaded because of the ideological burden placed on womanhood by "republican motherhood," which made mothers responsible for the future of the American political system, and the doctrine of separate spheres, which affirmed and required women's moral superiority to men. The new ideals set aside earlier views of women as the "weaker vessels," more susceptible than men to succumbing to their own lustful passions. In the last decades of the eighteenth century, a new view of woman, encouraged by Protestant evangelicalism, centered on woman's "passionlessness"—not yet her complete biological lack of sexual desire, but her laudable ability to achieve virtue through self-control. "Passionlessness" offered women a means of self-protection against the potentially exploitative sexual relationships of a commercializing order, encouraging them to place limits on the new romantic intimacy by citing the purity of their womanly nature. The self-control of the passionless woman was now expected to fill the vacuum left by earlier communal controls over sexual behavior. And the "reappearance of premarital sexual restraint" evidenced in the decline of bridal pregnancy in the second quarter of the nineteenth century points to the effectiveness of this strategy.[9]

But within the new sexual system, the ideal of female passionlessness could collide with the view of sex as a means to romantic intimacy. The romantic ideal made heterosexuality an arena of heightened conflict both within marriage and without, as men and women, relegated to separate social "spheres," came to bring increasingly different expectations and experiences to their sexual encounters.

"Passionless" women might resist their suitors' sexual demands, and prudent wives concerned with family planning and the dangers of childbirth might refuse sexual relations. The presumably passionless single woman might prove to be sexually willing, and might become pregnant in the absence of effective communal pressures to ensure immediate marriage. A jealous suitor or husband might wrongly suspect a woman of betrayal. When the new ideal of romantic love came up against the realities of married life, conjugal affection sometimes waned; letters between husbands and wives "disclosed the anger, frustration, and bitterness that accompanied the often futile struggle of one spouse to regain lost intimacy"; and divorce laws in some states began to include as acceptable grounds the loss of conjugal affection. The nineteenth-century understanding of romantic love as a force beyond the control of those experiencing it, and passion as an emotion that tended to run amok, could prove a self-fulfilling prophecy when a marriage went bad because romantic interest moved to a different object.[10]

Compounding these problems was the multiplication of opportunities for sex outside marriage. The religious heterodoxy generated by the Second Great Awakening gave rise to a variety of radical notions about sexual arrangements, which were adopted in utopian communities that institutionalized such practices as polygamy, group marriage, and free love. At the same time, the world of commercial sex expanded in the context of urban boom, taking form in what contemporary observers called an urban "underworld" of commercial dance halls, assignation houses and brothels, nude theater, and the sale of "licentious" books and prints. However officially shocking such ideas and practices might have been, they did represent a mere extension of the new importance being placed on sex as a means to ends—whether spiritual perfection or physical pleasure—other than reproduction. And, as the vociferous public reaction to these new practices indicated, their mere existence contributed to the larger tensions and conflicts at work in nineteenth-century sexuality.[11]

The new world of sexuality generated a strong sense of both the promise and the potential threat of sexual intimacy. And the popular literature of murder captured both. Concerns about sexuality before marriage were expressed in tales of courtship and seduction ending in deadly violence. In 1801, twenty-one-year-old Jason Fairbanks threatened (and may have attempted) to rape eighteen-year-old Eliza Fales of Dedham, Massachusetts, after she declined his offer of marriage, and then stabbed her to death. In 1833, Joel Clough killed Mary Hamilton after she rejected his romantic attentions. Accounts of the Clough murder emphasized Hamilton's "full-blown charms" and Clough's "solemn vow . . . that she never should be the wife of another man." In 1857, schoolteacher James Eldredge courted and impregnated Sarah Jane Gould, then determined to break his engagement—possibly because he had transferred his affections to Sarah's sister, some thought—by dosing his fiancée's cold remedy with arsenic. According to the prosecution, Eldredge had "'beguiled the woman,' as did the serpent of old—he coiled his slippery folds about her—he defiled her with his filthy embrace; then, casting his baleful eyes upon another object of desire, another lamb of that flock,—*he struck his envenomed, poisoned fangs, into her bosom,*—and she drooped and perished."[12]

Some men murdered to avenge their wives' and sisters' sexual mistreatment by other men. In 1826, in Frankfort, Kentucky, Jereboam Beauchamp murdered Colonel Solomon Sharp for seducing Ann Cooke, now Beauchamp's wife, and for denying paternity by charging that Ann's infant (which died soon after birth) had been black. In 1843, Singleton Mercer murdered his sister Sarah's rapist, the wealthy Mahlon Heberton, in a sensational Philadelphia case that inspired George Lippard's *The Quaker City; or the Monks of Monk-Hall* (1845). Heberton struck up an acquaintance with Miss Mercer, the sixteen-year-old daughter of a respectable mechanic, while promenading in the city, then took her to a brothel and raped her at gunpoint. When Sarah informed her family of the assault, her brother Singleton spent several days wandering the city in a dazed state, then stalked Heberton and shot him. To the joy of the courtroom crowd, the young man was found not guilty, on grounds of both insanity and sufficient provocation. The printed murder trial included Sarah's detailed testimony concerning the rape, in a transcript interwoven with editorial comments about her extreme agitation under questioning. The assault was summarized by Mercer's defense: "Sarah struggled and cried out aloud to the last; but alarmed, almost fainting, intimidated by his *threats*, and injured by his *violence*, she was at length overpowered—when in the most brutal and violent manner he VIOLATED her PERSON—committed a RAPE upon her."[13]

Another category of stories concerned the problems of sexual intimacy within marriage: most typically, what happened when dissatisfied husbands and wives pursued the ideal of romantic intimacy into adulterous liaisons. Readers learned how John Lechler surprised his wife and his friend Haag *in flagrante*, and how Lucretia Chapman and Mina the "Spaniard" rode together in a closed carriage singing love songs and kissing. One of the most prurient of marital murders concerned a ménage-à-trois formed by Mr. and Mrs. William Stiles and their boarder, Orrin De Wolf, which came to light when Orrin was tried for William's murder in 1845. As the boarder told the story, he had first had sexual intercourse with Mrs. Stiles at the request of her husband, "Humpy" (who suffered from curvature of the spine). Eventually, the three of them shared a bed. Though De Wolf warned his partner of his gonorrhea, she raised no objections; but after she was infected, William Stiles threatened to kill De Wolf. Meanwhile, Mrs. Stiles expressed the wish that her husband were dead, and De Wolf hired a man to strangle him. De Wolf's murder trial offered an unusually seamy tale of marital infidelity. So did the trial of Abner Baker for the murder of Daniel Bates, his brother-in-law, which included the insane defendant's obscene tales of his wife's alleged dalliances with his victim, as well as with her clergyman-schoolteacher (when she was nine years old), her uncles, and others.[14]

A third category of stories concerned sexual liaisons outside the bounds of marriage. Some men murdered their live-in mistresses: in 1823, William Gross stabbed to death Kesiah Stow—the woman for whom he had abandoned his wife—because she had begun to frequent dance houses and stay out all night; in 1829, Richard Johnson shot his paramour, Mrs. Ursula Newman, for refusing to marry him, prompting the judge to comment on "how speedy can be the transition from one licentious passion to another." Others, such as Richard

Robinson and Albert Tirrell, killed prostitutes.[15] The notorious murder of New York dentist Dr. Harvey Burdell in 1857 exposed the unorthodox sexual arrangements of his boarding house, after the woman who claimed to be his secret wife and her sometime lover were charged with the crime: the press accused the victim, the defendants, and other boarders of living "on the Mormon principle generally." J. V. Craine, on trial for murder in the California Gold Country in 1855, explained that he was a follower of Andrew Jackson Davis's Harmonial Religion and, though legally married to another woman back in Kentucky, recognized in Susan Newnham his true wife according to the divine law of spiritual affinity. When Newnham's parents (and probably Susan herself) objected to the match, he shot his beloved in what he claimed was an incomplete suicide pact undertaken by the lovers, that they might together "glide gently into the spirit-world, where our happiness would be complete."[16]

These new sexual narratives of murder were part of a larger explosion of sexual discourse in the eighteenth and nineteenth centuries. Sex was something that had to be put into words; it required close scrutiny, classification, and analysis in such fields of knowledge as medicine and criminal justice—discursive developments which generated a new type of knowledge-as-power to be extended over modern bodies and their pleasures. The new "truth" about sex and its pleasures that emerged from this intensive discourse was "sexuality": a matter not just of discrete acts but of an individual's nature (mental, moral, and physiological) and development; an inquiry into every sexual impulse or response, "normal" or "perverted," an aspect of life endowed with great causal power, and subject to pathological dysfunction. *Sexuality* was thus extended to more and more of the area surrounding the sex act *per se*. The concept of "sexuality" captures the modern tendency to find sex in everything, and everything includes crimes of murder.[17] Popular tales of murder extensively explored issues of sexual nature, development, and impulse, and attributed significant causal power to *sexuality*.

Throughout the murder literature, the focus of concern was on that sex that was commonly identified as *the* sex. The detective-fiction formula "cherchez la femme" appeared first in the early nineteenth-century nonfiction of murder. As the defense attorney for wife-killer George Swearingen observed in 1829, "as if the warring facts and moral improbabilities of the case, were not enough to clothe it with 'the mysterious and horrible,' it had the usual web of all that involves plot, or mystery, or crime—*There was a woman in the case.*"[18]

Sexual stories of murder were guided by the female victim's sexual history. Some accounts took care to note the sexual chastity of the victim. *A Sketch of the Life and Adventures of Henry Leander Foote* testified to the "virgin purity" of Emily Cooper before he raped and murdered her. The editor of Joel Clough's murder trial carefully reported that throughout the proceedings, "not a blot or stain was affixed to the character of the lamented Mrs. Hamilton," who "proved to have been chaste . . . and as pure as the unclouded sky."[19] A second category of female victims included seduction victims, who were treated as objects of pity rather than censure. "Weep! Oh, parent, for confiding innocence has been betrayed," commanded the narrator of Sarah Furber's abortion-homicide. The prosecutor of James Eldredge depicted his victim as "a deceived, betrayed, confiding woman, whose only fault or weakness it was, that she loved him not wisely, but too well."[20] The standard sentimental line concerning seduction victims was that their sexual fall was owing to their womanly weakness and excessive trust, which rendered them incapable of suspecting evil in those they loved. The sentimental sympathy for the victim of a seduction, which led generations of American readers to make Susanna Rowson's *Charlotte Temple* (1791) a recurring best-seller, was enlisted by sexual murder narratives on behalf of their erring female victims.

Even stories of murdered prostitutes were partly shaped by the sentimental tale of seduction. Maria Bickford was said to have been "one of the most virtuous of her sex" as a married woman of eighteen, but her seducer's "insinuating plausibility, it will be seen, quickly drew her into the whirlpool of vice!" and "the *moral* murderer is more guilty than the *physical* one." Nevertheless, the courtroom rhetoric generated at the trial of Bickford's accused killer matter-of-factly referred to her as "a depraved and lascivious woman" (the defense), and "an unblushing harlot" (the prosecution).[21] What ultimately distinguished the Maria Bickfords from their more sympathetically viewed sisters-in-seduction was that their once-innocent natures had been utterly contaminated by the first illicit encounter. When Helen Jewett, the New York prostitute murdered in 1836, succumbed to the false promises of her respectable beau, "The kiss of the seducer rested on her lip, the embrace of the libertine was returned, and his amorous caresses polluted the deluded victim of his lust." Though she might subsequently resist descent into complete sexual degradation, "her once pure and cultivated mind" became "corrupted," and "the chaste reserve of her amiable smile" gave way to "an arch boldness of the eyes"[22] that proclaimed her nature to the world. Prostitutes fell into a third category of female sexuality: total sexual depravity.

The sexualization of the female murder victim rested, ironically, on the passionless female ideal. For all these sexual histories addressed the same question: had the victim been a properly "passionless" woman, and if not, how fully had she been polluted by her lapse? That ideal provided the yardstick for the nineteenth-century "fallen woman," an image which had no early American counterpart. The transgressions of Esther Rodgers in 1701 and Elizabeth Valpy in 1807 seem in retrospect very similar: both were single, white servants who had sex with black servants in the same household and gave birth to children from those unions. But their stories were told in dramatically different ways. Esther Rodgers, a convicted infanticide, was treated as a sinful woman whose sexual offense was a discrete sinful act embedded in a larger social pattern of sinful disobedience. Her nature was "fallen" only in the sense that all other New Englanders were fallen, and she was encouraged by her community to hope that she died as all hoped to, in Christ. A century later, Elizabeth Valpy, who was not even formally charged with her infant's murder, was treated at her lover's trial as "*a foul*, degraded, loathsome prostitute" because of her "indiscriminate and promiscuous" (but not commercial) intercourse with men "of all characters and complexions." Her promiscuity proved her prostitution, and her prostitution proved her deceitfulness, because "It is by the practice of every species of fraud" that prostitutes "conceal their diseases, their infidelities and abominations." Elizabeth Valpy was "a woman totally lost to every sense of decency and chastity"—not merely one fallen member of a fallen race, but a fallen woman, set apart from her race by her exceptionally loathsome nature.[23]

Whether a story reported the female victim's virginal innocence or total corruption, her sexual history was presumed to be a determining factor of the crime, especially in the assignment of guilt. Men who killed chaste women were typically found guilty of their crimes. Men who killed the victims of their seduction were frequently convicted. But men who killed prostitutes were acquitted; and William Hardy, Elizabeth Valpy's lover, was acquitted of infanticide when his defense cast suspicion onto a woman loosely designated a "prostitute." Nineteenth-century murder narratives searched for the sexually depraved woman. Whenever she was found, the fundamental guilt of the crime shifted off her killer's shoulders onto hers.

In the fall of 1832, at the age of thirty, Sarah Cornell was employed as a weaver in the New England mill town of Fall River, Massachusetts, not far from the Rhode Island border. Unmarried and pregnant, she informed her family and her physician that the father of her child was Methodist minister Ephraim Avery, age thirty-six, then stationed at Bristol, Rhode Island. Avery, she charged, had "seduced" her at the Thompson camp meeting in late August, demanding sex in exchange for some incriminating letters of confession she had written to him. On December 21, 1832, Sarah Cornell was found hanging from a hayrick at a farm just outside Fall River. After the first jury of inquest ruled suicide, a note was found among Cornell's possessions that read, "If I should be missing enquire of the Rev Mr Avery of Bristol he will know where I am Dec 20th S M Cornell." A second jury of inquest was called; the body was exhumed, an autopsy performed, and Avery was formally charged with murder. The prosecution argued that he had seduced Cornell and convinced her that he would support the child if she would remain quiet about its paternity; but then arranged to meet her at the Durfee farm, attempted abortion by severely battering her lower abdomen, and finally strangled her and hanged the body to make her death look like suicide.[24]

The month-long trial generated tremendous public excitement and pitted the emerging Methodist establishment, anxious to defend the character of one of its clergy, against the new industrial interests committed to salvaging the character of one of their workers. The circumstantial case against Avery was considerable: most of the physical evidence from the scene pointed to murder; Avery was spotted near the scene of the crime on the night of Cornell's death, and his alibi was uncorroborated; numerous circumstances linked him to the anonymous letters sent to Cornell by her seducer. So Avery's lawyers determined to defend their client by attacking the moral character of the dead woman, to deflect guilt for the crime onto her.

With the financial assistance of the Methodist Church, Avery's attorneys produced extensive testimony against Cornell's character, including lying, thieving, and taking assumed names, and her frequent removals from one factory town to the next under the shadow of moral suspicion. Most important were those witnesses who testified to Cornell's "lewdness": she had repeatedly been seen in compromising situations with young men and had been treated by several doctors for a "foul disease." Defense attorney Jeremiah Mason apologized that it was "a painful duty to perform—to describe a woman, to describe the dead, in a light as revolting as duty to the defendant requires." But because she was "common as the air, abandoned and profligate," the notion that she had been "ravished, almost violated!" by a Methodist minister at a camp meeting was not to be credited. The defense even argued that Cornell's fetus was older than five months (and thus could not have been fathered by Ephraim Avery) on the medical grounds that "The foetuses of women of very lewd characters are generally supposed to be smaller than those of virtuous women." The defense also produced evidence of her mental quirks and eccentricities, in support of the argument that Cornell's death was actually a suicide, "the natural death of the prostitute";[25] Cornell's promiscuity alone qualified her for this sexual label. All the apparent evidence against Avery, the defense continued, had been deliberately manufactured by Cornell before her death, to punish the clergyman who had expelled her from his Lowell church for lying and fornication. Her suicide was in reality a plot against Avery's life.

If the explicit argument of the defense was that Sarah Cornell had taken her own life, their implicit argument was that her "crimes" against the ideal of passionless womanhood were so great that she deserved a violent death. As explained by Jeremiah Mason, "That there is a charm, a refinement, a delicacy in the female sex, superior to man, no civilized community has ever doubted. It is female character, when pure and unstained, which contributes to the embellishment and refinement of society in the highest degree." But "in the same proportion as woman, when chaste and pure, excels the other sex, by just so much, when profligate, does she sink below them; and if you were to seek for some of the *vilest monsters* in wickedness and depravity, you would find them in the *female* form."[26] Sarah Cornell's sexuality rendered her, not Avery, the real moral "monster" in the case. The sexual "depravity" of a female murder victim ensured the acquittal of her probable killer.

In addressing the Cornell case, lawyers on both sides elaborated a new medical language of sexuality. The trial's investigation into the sexual past of the murder victim drew on the testimony, not only of her acquaintances, but of physicians who had variously treated her for gonorrhea, attended her in early pregnancy, performed autopsies on her corpse, or offered expert opinions on the postmortem findings. By the 1830s, the critical question of the female murder victim's sexual history had been medicalized by the courtroom appearance of the postmortem report. Had the victim been sexually assaulted? Was she pregnant at the time of her death, and was there any evidence of attempted abortion? Did she suffer from venereal disease? The tales told by the female victim's "storied body" supplemented and sometimes supplanted the more conventional social narrative of her sexual experience. When John Hendrickson poisoned his wife, Maria, in 1853, the autopsy report supplemented what was known of Hendrickson's chronic infidelity by reporting her venereal disease. In the case of James Eldredge, only the autopsy revealed that the victim had been six weeks pregnant at the time of her death.[27] The most extensive sexual autopsy reports concerned alleged abortion-homicides which offered readers a kind of medical play-within-a-play, in their dramatic representation of physicians' posthumous efforts to detect how other medical practitioners had killed their patient-victims.

The growing importance of professional medicine within sexual narratives of murder was made possible by changes in childbirth practices, as male physicians gradually began to replace female midwives in caring for women undergoing normal deliveries. In the 1760s, Dr. William Shippen, Jr. became the first American doctor to maintain a regular practice attending women in childbirth, offering his services to the women of Philadelphia's social elite after studying "male midwifery" in London and Edinburgh. Other physicians in the urban Northeast followed his lead. Their practice was given an important boost by the establishment of proprietary medical schools which recognized midwifery as a branch of medical science. By 1807, five reputable American medical schools provided courses in midwifery, though some faculty members soon donned the neologistic title "professor of obstetrics," to free their specialty from the feminine connotations of "midwife."[28]

Some male physicians deliberately campaigned to drive female midwives from their practice. Alarmed by a proposal to revive female midwifery in Boston in 1820, Dr. Walter Channing, Harvard's first professor of obstetrics (who later served as a defense witness at the Avery trial), boasted, "It was one of the first and happiest fruits of improved medical education in America, that . . . [women] were excluded from practice; and it was only by the united and persevering exertions of some of the most distinguished individuals our profession has been able to boast, that this was effected."[29] Among those exertions was an increasing application of the forceps, which countered the traditionally supportive role of the midwife with the strongly interventionist (and sometimes damaging) role of the obstetrician. Male physicians wielded them in part to justify what could seem a tenuous claim to professional expertise in competition with more clinically experienced women. (Such a claim to medical mastery was made by one physician at Alice Clifton's infanticide trial in Philadelphia in 1787: he carried a glass jar containing the dead infant, and offered to extract it *with his forceps* for the court's inspection.)[30] Until childbirth moved from home to hospital, obstetricians routinely had to share authority in the birthing room with female midwives; their triumph over their female competitors remained incomplete for most of the nineteenth century.[31]

The new medical specialists asserted their own importance by declaring the female reproductive system to be the central determinant of woman's nature. "Woman's reproductive organs are preeminent," asserted John Wiltbank in 1854. It was "as if the Almighty, in creating the female sex, *had taken the uterus and built up a woman around it*." Not only woman's entire physiological system, but her "intellectual and moral perceptivity and forces . . . are feminine as her organs are." The new medical scientists of female sexuality thus claimed a unique professional access to a total knowledge of womanhood, biological, mental, moral, psychological, even spiritual. As Dr. Charles Meigs explained to his students, their task was to "explore . . . the strange and secret influences which her organs, by their nervous constitution, and the functions, by their relation to her whole life-force, whether in sickness or health, are capable of exerting, not on the body alone, but on the heart, the mind, and the very soul of woman."[32]

In asserting the centrality of female sexuality to woman's nature, and emphasizing the *peculiarity* of that "sexual organization," nineteenth-century American obstetricians were responding to growing demands to redefine the position of women in modern society. The study of the "nature" of woman had become a major priority of scientific research. Anatomists in eighteenth-century England, France, and Germany launched a search for finer delineation of sex differences, which led to the first illustrations of a distinctively female skeleton, whose exaggeratedly wide pelvis and tiny skull testified to the gender values it was designed to carry. Scientists moved from the traditional view that women had essentially the same genitals as men only turned inward, toward a new model stressing the binary opposition between the two physiologies. Here too, new "scientific" views attached cultural meaning to physiological differences, explaining, for example, the "active" role of the sperm in reproduction as opposed to the "passive" role of the egg. Scientists in a wide range of disciplines were offering detailed expositions of the fundamental differences between women and men—anatomical, physiological, temperamental, and intellectual—in order to justify their differing social roles. Most important, they maintained that women's reproductive organs controlled their bodies, determining their emotions and dictating their proper role in society, rendering them unfit for public life.[33]

Nineteenth-century medicine did not merely sexualize woman's nature; it pathologized it. By expanding into normal childbirth, male physicians transformed a normal biological function into a pathological condition routinely demanding dramatic medical intervention.[34] Nearly all of woman's biological ailments were said to originate in her reproductive organs, "the seat of her diseases." Some physicians believed that menstruation was itself a form of disease; others, that sexual desire in a woman was a pathological condition, thus invoking medical authority to advance the passionless ideal.[35] The "controlling influence" exerted upon woman by her reproductive processes extended to her mental state. Hysteria, a "morbid state" in the male, was deemed "the natural state" in a female. Pregnancy, childbirth, lactation, and menstruation all placed women in a dangerous state of "temporary insanity" in which they were "more prone than men to commit any unusual or outrageous act"; "strange thoughts, extraordinary feelings, unseasonable appetites, criminal impulses, may haunt a mind at other times innocent and pure." When Dr. Augustus Kinsley Gardner undertook postgraduate study in Paris in 1844, his two chosen specialties were obstetrics and insanity. His activities as Parisian *flaneur*, touring the urban haunts of prostitutes and the gloomy interiors of prisons and asylums as well as hospitals, clearly reinforced his conviction of the intrinsic connections between female sexuality and insanity, and tied both these forms of deviance within his medical imagination to criminality.[36]

No wonder male practitioners argued the urgency of their medical takeover of female sexuality: in their view, women were too dangerous to be left in the unprofessional hands of their own sex. But male physicians often betrayed a revulsion against their work. Late in life, gynecologist Marion Sims admitted that, at the beginning of his career, "if there was anything I hated, it was investigating the organs of the female pelvis." Another physician routinely began his medical school lecture on women's reproductive system by "begging" his students "to accompany me in this disagreeable task." And Dr. Gardner, after his tours of Paris, emphasized the horrors of gynecological practice in a passage worthy of Gothic fiction: "Startling and fearful as may be the sight of streams of blood and clotted gore in various scenes, there are none found more appalling than [those] in the obstetrical chamber." Such revulsion must have contributed to a powerful taboo of early obstetrical practice: whenever possible, the physician was to examine his patient's reproductive organs without looking at them. Contemporary illustrations of pelvic examinations show the physician looking away from his patient or, alternatively, gazing directly into her eyes. Even during the most technically difficult interventions, physicians were assured, they would not find it necessary to watch what they were doing—"Catheterism, vaginal exploration, manipulations . . . whether manual or instrumental, delivery by the forceps and embryotomy itself, can all be performed by a competent man as well without the eye as with it"—a directive that helps explain the frequent damage caused by forceps during delivery.[37]

What lay behind such pronounced repugnance on the part of the new obstetricians was a whole complex of male attitudes towards female sexuality, which mingled fear with hatred and disgust. Expectations placed upon masculine identity in the nineteenth century, when individual economic success and social order were believed to depend on rigorous self-control, helped shape these attitudes. "The ideal of self-sovereign middle-class manhood produced an autophobic sexuality, such that erotic arousal was chronically attended by dread and was experienced as disgust and guilt when it was felt to stray beyond the boundaries of self-control"; and that dread and disgust were projected onto women as the source of sexual arousal. Beneath the passionless ideal lay the fear that women were always in danger of succumbing to sexual appetite, and thus undermining male self-command; men insisted on women's innate purity in an effort to overcome their dread of female sexual pollution.[38]

In the context of such fears, obstetrics and gynecology held out the promise of controlling women's disorder through male mastery of their sexual bodies. It was this prospect that transformed Marion Sims's initial disgust at performing pelvic exams into enthusiasm. In 1845, having improvised a kind of speculum from a metal spoon in order to treat a woman whose uterus had been displaced in a fall from a horse, Sims excitedly reported, "I saw everything as no man had ever seen before . . . I felt like an explorer in medicine who first views a new and important territory."[39] Like some Meriwether Lewis of the female reproductive system, Sims achieved mastery of "new" natural territory (new, that is, to the male practitioner) simply by exploring it. His language points to the process by which female physiology—women's "nature"—was being transformed into Nature itself, a Nature peculiarly demanding of medical intervention. Sims's career suggests why men repelled by the requirements of attending to women's sexual organs nonetheless usurped a task that had been in the hands of female practitioners for centuries.

The new medical field of obstetrics and gynecology thus generated its own Gothic language of female sexuality. Female sexuality, the new specialists affirmed, was a matter of *mystery*, with its "strange and secret influences," its dark interiority focused on its central organ, the womb (which Gardner associated with those quintessentially Gothic institutions, the prison and the mental asylum), and the "peculiarities" of its arrangements, recently reconstructed as radically alien from male sexuality. And female sexuality, according to its self-appointed professional experts, was a matter of *horror*, with its "streams of blood and clotted gore," its power to arouse mingled fear and disgust, prompting both a strong desire not to look and a need to master through looking, and its associations with dangerous forms of deviance such as insanity and criminality.

This Gothic construction of female sexuality by way of nineteenth-century medicine helped shape the popular literature of murder, most dramatically in the form of printed reports of sexual autopsies (performed only on women in the popular literature).[40] Though there may have been good forensic reasons for such postmortem examinations in cases of suspected murder, the publication of these reports as popular literature requires analysis. Abortion-homicides in particular focused readers' attention on female sexual physiology through their lengthy reports on the autopsies performed on alleged victims of the crime. Mary Anne Wilson was one such victim: a thirty-three-year-old widow of Greenfield, New Hampshire, who died in 1837 following an abortion performed by Dr. William Graves of Lowell, Massachusetts (who had testified four years earlier to Sarah Cornell's venereal disease at the Avery trial). Eliza Sowers was a factory worker of twenty-one who died in Philadelphia in 1838 after consuming abortifacients and undergoing two operations by Dr. Henry Chauncey. And Sarah Furber was a twenty-two-year-old millworker who died in 1848 after an inept surgical procedure at the hands of Dr. John McNab of Manchester, who earned public infamy by packing her corpse into a box of straw and charcoal and trying to sell it as a dissection subject to Harvard Medical College. All these "homicide" victims were subjected to postmortem explorations of their reproductive systems, the results of which were published in full medical detail.[41]

Sexual autopsies sought to penetrate the mystery of the abortion deaths by exposing and scrutinizing the female reproductive system, an operation performed physically by physicians and imaginatively by courtroom audiences and trial-report readers. The examination began with a large incision extending from sternum to navel and thence to both hipbones, which enabled the examiner to peel back the skin to expose the inner workings of the female body. The examiners then ascertained that the victim had been pregnant from the size of the womb, the site of the attached placenta, the milk that flowed through surgical incisions in the breasts ("on taking hold of the breast on that day we could draw out the milk and pump it in jets"), the color of the nipples. They next examined the reproductive organs to determine whether abortion had been attempted: in the Sowers case, examiners found mortification of the uterus and vaginal tract, laceration of the uterine mouth, and peritoneal inflammation in the abdominal cavity. In some cases, the medical examiners seemed scarcely more proficient than the physicians they were helping to prosecute: Dr. William M. Egbert, who performed the postmortem examination on Sowers, explained how "I took up the uterus, and showing it to Dr. Clark, said 'Here is the uterus'; he said, 'That can't be—it looks like an inflated bladder.'"[42]

Despite their generally clinical nature and tone, sexual autopsy reports were filled with images likely to induce horror. The opened bodies of abortion-homicides revealed severe inflammation and often putrefaction: the lining of Eliza Sowers's uterus "exhibited a bluish black appearance similar to that of gangrene in the first stage of mortification." The presence of coagulated blood, serum, "purulent fluid," and "foetid matter" were duly reported. Uterine puncture wounds were described: after examining Furber, Dr. Oliver Wendell Holmes reported, "Never in my practice have I seen anything like this puncture; hope I never shall again." Examiners commonly characterized the terrible suffering endured by the victim before death, as in the Sally Burdick case. The autopsy report on Mary Anne Wilson (exhumed twenty-one days after death and dissected in a "hearse house") depicted a virtual ghoul from Gothic fiction, describing her bloated face with its distended veins and black lips, green breasts with black nipples, abdomen distended with gas, and brick-red genitalia.[43]

At a time when female sexual physiology was believed to hold the key to woman's nature and when normal female processes were seen as gory, diseased, and even criminal, popular murder literature conveyed the idea that the secret to certain murders lay hidden in the sexual body of the female victim. The medical narrative, like the sentimental stories of a wider range of murders, searched for the true source of evil in the sexuality of the female victim—the evil figured in the large rat that Dr. Cyrus James imagined in Sally Burdick's vagina.[44] Though sentimental narrative shaped the standard story line of the abortion-homicide—the innocent young woman ruined by a heartless seducer—the medical autopsy report ultimately relocated the horror of the crime to her alien sexual physiology.

Other sexual stories of murder made reference to the intrinsic violence of the female reproductive system. In the case of the fatal battering of Phoebe Graham by her husband in Baltimore in 1804, a medical expert for the defense testified that Phoebe's severe wounds and bruises, including the long narrow stroke marks on her back, were the outward manifestations of her intemperance. "I have no doubt," Dr. Crawford confidently asserted, "but her death proceeded from drink." But the defense still had to account for "some bruises on some part of Mrs. Graham's body" which "delicacy" prevented one female witness from mentioning until prompted. When John's attorney posed the leading question, "Do you not believe they might have proceeded from uncleanliness or weakness," Mrs. Robinson staunchly replied, "I do not believe any such thing." Undaunted, the defense summoned its own witness, Nancy Taters, who testified that Phoebe had been "much afflicted with obstructions and other matters incidental to women." Just as the stroke marks on her back had emerged from the internal pathology of her intemperance, her genital bruises had emerged from the internal pathology of her reproductive system. In the end, according to the tale told by her husband's defense, Phoebe Graham's moral weakness joined with her female sexuality to kill her from within. After three minutes' deliberation, the jury returned with a verdict of not guilty.[45]

George Swearingen, sheriff of Washington County, Maryland, was tried for murdering his wife, Mary, in 1829. At the time of his wife's death, which he attributed to a fall from her horse, he was involved with a prostitute named Rachel Cunningham (because, his defense later explained, Mary was under medical instruction not to engage in "connubial intercourse").[46] The local women who laid out the body for burial observed a substantial flow of blood from the womb, and charged that violent injury had been done to it. When the women's accusation prompted an autopsy, Swearingen fled with his paramour to New Orleans, where he was captured and returned to Maryland. The medical autopsy discovered bruising on the dead woman's neck and pudendum, suggesting that she had been sexually battered and strangled.

To these charges, defense attorney John L. M'Mahon replied that Swearingen's accusers—"*the pigeon carriers of news,* the old women"—had acted out of vindictive disapproval of Swearingen's adultery, and he sneeringly condemned "the charitable tongues of the female world, *who claim the exclusive privilege of sinning against their own sex.*" Mary Swearingen, according to M'Mahon, had suffered no externally inflicted uterine injury. She was the victim, rather, of "leuco phlegmatic temperament," which made her liable to spontaneous uterine hemorrhaging and rendered her "by disease, temperament and debility, prepared for death by slight causes." The defense further suggested that the most vindictive of the townswomen, Charity Johnson, might have shoved a stick into the dead woman's vagina in order to frame George Swearingen for murder. The livid sexual bruises simply marked the beginnings of normal putrefaction, which tended to affect first such "soft and fatty parts" of the body as the neck and pudendum, releasing ammonia "which produces the unpleasant smell." In short, according to the defense, the sexual bruising on this female corpse was only the result of natural decay, and the injury to her womb was only the result of her reproductive system's natural tendency to hemorrhage or, alternatively, a posthumous assault by another woman.[47] Not sexual battery, but the natural connections between female sexuality and decay, disease, and criminal violence (by Charity Johnson) had caused Mary's death. The defense failed, however, to make its case: Swearingen was convicted of murder.

In both the Graham and the Swearingen cases, competing interpretations were offered by male physicians and the women of the neighborhood who laid out the body, some of whom probably had midwifery experience (though in the Graham case, one woman's testimony supported the defense). A similar gender competition took place at the trial of Ephraim Avery. After the first coroner's jury ruled Cornell's death a suicide, the neighborhood women who laid out her body observed severe bruising in the lower abdominal area (including "prints of fingers" on both sides of the abdomen), and concluded that Cornell had been "dreadfully abused" before her death, either by rape or attempted abortion by battering. "Oh! Mrs. Ford what has been done?" Hannah Writhington asked upon seeing the body, and Dorcas Ford replied, "rash violence." At the first autopsy, the two appointed physicians could not evaluate the abdominal bruises because modest jurors restrained them from stripping the body (though not from dissecting it). Only at the second autopsy did the same physicians examine the abdominal bruising—finding as well a "considerable" contusion above the left hip—and agreed with the neighborhood women that "The body bore marks of violence."[48]

But at Avery's trial, the defense called six expert medical witnesses to the stand, including Dr. Walter Channing, self-proclaimed enemy to female practitioners. Channing (whose testimony took three hours) and the other expert witnesses for the defense challenged the local women's opinions by pointing to the difficulty experienced by "ignorant persons" in distinguishing bruises from the marks made by the natural settling of blood after death, or suggillation, caused when the weight of Cornell's suspended body came to rest on its knees. In a sparring match with Attorney General Albert Greene, Dr. Channing refused to concede that women experienced in laying out the dead would have been sufficiently familiar with normal posthumous discoloration to distinguish it from bruising. When questioned about the neighborhood women's competence, Dr. Nathaniel Miller openly acknowledged the gendered nature of the competition: "In my opinion women are not good judges" of the matter.[49] Gravity, not physical assault, had inflicted the livid markings on Sarah Cornell's lower torso. Though all six of the defense's expert witnesses admitted under cross-examination that the markings might have been caused by violence, and though the Attorney General urged jurors to "trust to the EYES of four sensible, experienced women, to ascertain the real state of the facts," rather than to "a whole college of physicians," Avery was acquitted, and Dr. Channing's campaign against female practitioners scored another victory.[50]

Despite their differences, all three violent deaths (Phoebe Graham, Mary Swearingen, and Sarah Cornell) generated debates about whether the dead woman was a victim of sexual assault—rape, violent abortion, or sexual battery—or her own physiological processes—"obstructions and other matters incidental to women," sexually localized putrefaction, uterine hemorrhaging, the settling of the blood after death. In all three cases, neighborhood women who had laid out the victim's body insisted that sexual assault had been committed.[51] But the weight of male professional testimony lay with the defense, which argued that what appeared to the eyes of "ignorant" women practitioners as evidence of sexual assault were in reality outward manifestations of female sexual pathology and putrefaction. The sexual bodies of women were thus represented as capable of deadly violence against themselves—even, and perhaps especially, in cases that featured extensive physical evidence against male defendants.

Another case that highlighted the intrinsic violence of the female reproductive system was the death of Mary Cecilia Rogers, which was variously attributed to rape-murder, abortion-homicide, and suicide. The persistent mystery of Rogers's death and her reputation as "the beautiful cigar girl" from Anderson's tobacco shop combined to generate intense public curiosity about her sexual history. As the police interviewed one male suspect after another and the interviews were printed in the newspapers, the reading public was invited to examine the life of a beautiful young woman, independent, pursued by a number of men, and probably sexually experienced (Rogers may have had an abortion a few years before her violent death). But however much narrative attention was paid to her romantic past, it was her *body* that was believed to hold "the secrets of her sexual life, of her sexually violent death, and even of endless crimes perpetrated against her."[52]

Lurid and detailed descriptions of Rogers's badly damaged corpse were a major component of the extensive newspaper coverage of her death. These descriptions pointedly contrasted the beauty of the living woman, which had been so widely admired by the sporting men of the city, with the revolting appearance of the corpse. The *New York Post*, for example, described the body as it lay in the city "dead house" as follows:

There lay, what was but a few days back, the image of its Creator, the loveliest of his work and the tenement of an immortal soul, now a blackened and decomposed mass of putrefaction, painfully disgusting

{197}

to sight and smell. Her skin which had been unusually fair was now black as that of a negro. Her eyes so sunk in her swollen face as to have the appearance of being violently forced beyond the sockets, and her mouth which 'no friendly hand had closed in death,' was distended as wide as the ligaments of the jaws would admit and wore the appearance of a person who had died from suffocation or strangulation. The remainder of her person was alike one mass of putrefaction and corruption, on which the worms were revelling at their will.[53]

One of the final efforts to resolve the "mystery" of Mary Rogers's death attributed it, not to the sexually erring victim herself, but to another woman who lived in violation of the sexual mores of her time. George Wilkes, publisher of the *National Police Gazette*, connected the death of Mary Rogers to the notorious Ann Lohman, known as Madame Restell, who in the summer of Rogers's death was undergoing the first of her many criminal trials for practicing abortion. Instead of the sexualized murder victim herself, her sexualized surrogate carried the guilt of the murder.[54]

The theory of Rogers's suicide proved a common convention in stories of the violent deaths of sexual women. When "respectable" men such as the Rev. Avery stood charged with the murder of "fallen" women, defense attorneys axiomatically observed that "Suicide is so common a termination of their career, that it may almost be called the natural death of the prostitute. Excited by violent and unrestrained passions, driven to extreme distress and often desperation, self destruction is the ready resort of the profligate."[55] The same axiom shaped the defense of Albert Tirrell for the murder of Maria Bickford, who, in 1845, was found dead in a Boston boarding house, nearly decapitated by a razor, her body badly charred by a fire set in the room. She had been lodging with her frequent sexual companion Albert Tirrell, a "gentleman" from Weymouth, against whom there was considerable circumstantial evidence including his presence in the house that night, the couple's quarreling, his departing the house towards morning, and his immediate flight out-of-state. The defense offered a number of conflicting arguments, but most prominent was the suicide defense. A succession of physicians testified that Bickford's neck wound might have been self-inflicted. Defense attorney

Rufus Choate speculated that Bickford had reflected on her lover's imminent return to his family and on her own ruined marriage, and killed herself: "Suicide is the natural death of the prostitute."[56]

In a number of cases, the "natural" violence of female sexuality was translated into the "natural" tendency of the sexual female towards self-murder. Some narratives took this accusation one step further, charging that the apparent female victim was herself a murderer. Sarah Cornell was implicitly charged with the attempted murder of Ephraim Avery: she had killed herself and left a note implicating Avery in order to frame him, to have him executed because he had blocked her admission to the Methodist meeting. Maria Bickford was charged in print with the murders of two former lovers: "Twice were her hands imbrued in the blood of her paramours," and had she lived a few more days, she would have killed again. "By a murderer's hand she fell, as had others by her own." Most surprisingly, Tirrell's prosecutor condemned the murder victim as "an unblushing harlot and an undisguised adulteress," and quoted the passage from Proverbs, "Yea, many strong men hath been slain by [the harlot]."[57] When even the prosecuting attorney chose to invoke the murderous nature of the female victim whose accused killer he was trying to convict, the prevailing understanding of female sexual evil must have been strong indeed.

Nowhere was the threat of female sexuality developed more fully than in the many popular accounts of Helen Jewett's murder in New York City in 1836. Jewett was a beautiful twenty-three-year-old prostitute who boarded at Rosina Townsend's Palace of the Passions, where she often entertained a nineteen-year-old clerk named Richard Robinson. Early in the morning on Sunday, April 10, Rosina Townsend awoke to find the back door of the house unbarred, and a lamp from a second-floor chamber abandoned in the parlor, and went upstairs to check on her boarders. She tried Helen Jewett's door, expecting it to be locked, since she had admitted Richard Robinson (alias Frank Rivers) sometime between nine and ten o'clock the night before and delivered champagne to the couple at about eleven. But the door opened, and she found the room full of smoke from a fire in the bed where Jewett lay dead, her forehead deeply gashed and one side of her body charred. Two constables summoned to the scene discovered a bloody hatchet and a blue cloak behind the house, with matching pieces of string attached, as though the hatchet had been carried beneath the cloak before the twine broke. Robinson was arrested for her murder, and investigators subsequently discovered that the cloak was his, and the hatchet had been taken from the store where he worked.

The extensively fictional "biographies" of Robinson and Jewett that were quickly prompted by the crime documented the popular version of the life-course of the fallen woman that was to shape the courtroom narrative of the crime. Though the accounts differed in details, their central premise was that, from her initial seducer's first embrace, the fallen woman's life tended irresistibly downward through corruption and disease to early death. From a "pretty girl" Helen Jewett had developed into "a beautiful, lovely and accomplished woman." "Ripened" by the stimulation of novel-reading, "her form at sixteen had taken the contour of maturity—her faculties and functions also developed to their climax, chafed at the restraints which condemned them to inaction." She was soon liberated by her first seducer, and from that moment on, was "corrupted with the poison" of her evil associates in the "sinks of infamy" she inhabited.[58]

But Jewett remained beautiful and accomplished, and arrayed herself in expensive gowns and jewels, incurring the envy of "many a toiling maiden, who sighed within her scanty shawl, at the contrasts between the rewards of gaudy vice, and the mean requital of self-denying virtue." Her surface beauty was, however, a disguise for her underlying moral corruption: "the working maiden in her hasty glance, did not see all the loathsome labor which had bred this gaudy insect to the sun." And that corruption was inexorably drawing Jewett closer to death. Her vicious life subjected her to fatal disease: "Too soon, my dear girl," warned a relative, "may that once beautiful form be the seat of disease, and the grave receive it." On more than one occasion, Helen "thought seriously of the great panacea for the ills and miseries of life which lies in the bottom of a phial," and her brothel companion Maria Stevens—who died before

Robinson's trial—was reported to have killed herself out of remorse for her vicious life.[59]

In Jewett's case, death finally came by "the hatchet and the flame." That envious working girl had failed to see "the future picture of the burnt and blackened body, and the ghastly gashes in the brain, which were to be the epilogue of the fine show and false delight." When popular accounts described Jewett "with her transparent forehead half divided with a butcher's stroke, and her silver skin burnt to a cinder where it was not laced with blood," and when they contrasted the "mangled corpse" with the "once fascinating and innocent inmate of the boarding school," they suggested that Jewett's death was the inevitable result of her sexual fall. Readers were invited "to drop a tear o'er the murdered Ellen, who, upon the bed she had polluted, atoned for her frailties, by the hatchet of the midnight assassin, and the flame of the incendiary." Even the reported fate of Jewett's corpse conveyed a moral lesson—"Reader, would you see the lovely being who was once the pride of the boarding school, and the ornament of the place of her nativity?"—for after dissection, it had been stripped of its flesh to hang in the anatomy cabinet of a medical school.[60] Reclaimed, dissected, then publicly and ignominiously displayed: such was the ultimate fate of the polluted body of the fallen woman. The tone of satisfaction running throughout this pointed contrast between the living beauty and the butchered corpse suggested that Jewett's violent death befitted her vicious life.

Despite frequent expressions of sentimental sympathy for Jewett and the rest of the "frail sisterhood," and repeated calls for the punishment of their seducers, these accounts clearly suggested that Jewett's death was ultimately deserved. The *Lives of Jewett and Robinson* blasted prostitutes as "a troop of gaudy poisoners, teeming with disease," permitted to "stream through the streets, carrying death beneath their skirts." The woman who would "entice the wayfarer with her blandishments, and willfully and basely light a fire in his bones . . . *should be treated as a murderess.*"[61] To kill such a woman could be construed, like the slaying of Medusa, as an act of just retribution and collective male self-defense. The book suggested that Jewett was involved in killing the newborn infant of a seduction

{201}

victim. And it reported her threat against Robinson's life when she learned of his possible marriage to another.

The view of prostitutes as natural murderers was put forth immediately after Jewett's death by James Bennett, editor of the *New York Herald*, who learned of the crime within hours of the arrest and rushed to tour the brothel and view the corpse, determined to make journalistic capital of the death. "It cannot be possible," he exclaimed, "that Robinson was the [murderer]! How could a young man perpetrate so brutal an act? Is it not more like the work of a woman? Are not the whole train of circumstances within the ingenuity of a female, abandoned and desperate?"[62] Robinson's defense team adopted this position, which enabled them self-righteously to condemn Jewett's way of life without ever directly assaulting the victim (who had won popular sympathy for her reportedly genteel deportment, literary inclinations, and fine taste). The defense argued that Rosina Townsend, chief witness for the prosecution, was a far more likely murderer than Robinson. Townsend, formerly a prostitute and now a brothel-keeper, was "corrupt and rotten," a "polluted" woman leading an "infamous and abandoned course of life," whose apparently innocent testimony was like a "tender flower concealing the serpent that is beneath." Her brothel was "a pest house, where young men sicken, and go down to infamy," and where "beautiful girls" were set on "the road to an early and ignominious grave!"[63]

"Who is most capable of committing the deed," asked Price for the defense, "the young man before you, or the old hag [Townsend was thirty-nine] who had murdered dozens before (he did not say killed them outright) but the more cruel murder of consigning them to an ignominious life. Is it safe or wise to believe women at all in this court?" All the evidence in the case had been generated by "a foul conspiracy" among Townsend and two other prostitutes to frame an innocent young man for a crime which had been committed out of sexual competition for Richard Robinson (by whom, the defense did not make clear). The central strategy of the defense was to destroy the credibility of prostitutes as witnesses. In failing to call to the witness stand any of the six men present at the brothel on the night of the murder, the Attorney General permitted the defense to construct a dramatic storytelling duel between "reputable men" (Richard Robinson's associates) and "disreputable women" (Helen Jewett's companions), and thus to rest the defense on a sexual double standard. In a highly biased summation to the jury, the judge assisted this strategy by ruling out all testimony by "persons who lead most dissolute lives—who were inmates of a house of a bad description . . . a house engaged in destroying both sexes."[64] The jury was out for fifteen minutes, and returned with a verdict of not guilty.

The Jewett murder prompted a multi-layered Gothic tale of female sexuality as the true perpetrator of the crime. Stories of the Jewett murder explored the inherent pathology and violence of female sexual physiology, with repeated references to the corruption, contamination, and pollution of the fallen woman, and her susceptibility to "loathsome disease." In this case, as in the Cornell and Bickford cases, suicide was invoked as the natural death of the prostitute, as demonstrated in Jewett's alleged attempts to take her own life, and the suggestion that her sister-prostitute Maria Stevens had done so. The idea that the murder victim was herself a murderer was at work here, in the image of Jewett as a sexual cannibal and in her threat to kill Robinson. And the argument that, if the victim did not commit suicide, then another sexual female must have killed her was prominent in the Jewett accounts, most notably in the defense's argument that Rosina Townsend was the real murderer. The Jewett murder offers the supreme example of how the violent death of a fallen woman could be shaped into a Gothic narrative of sexual danger and ultimate guilt borne by the female of the species.

The generic Gothic narrative of the violent death of a fallen woman could even shape the tale of a chaste female victim. In 1849, Henry Leander Foote raped and murdered his fifteen-year-old cousin, Emily Cooper, and then killed his mother (as he explained) to protect her from hearing of his crimes. His first-person *Sketch of the Life and Adventures of Henry Leander Foote* opened with a picaresque account of his life. Born in Connecticut in 1812, Foote openly rejected God and formed an appetite for strong drink at a young age. At seventeen he took his first trip to New York, where he attended the theater, a brothel, a gambling house, and a saloon, and was introduced to "unlawful books," which had worked "the ruin of many young men and women." After a brief spell of interest in religion, he returned to his former worldliness, dabbling in a variety of occupations, and eventually enlisting with the U.S. Horse Guards to fight in the Seminole War, which he recounted and embellished with stories of the sexual torture of a white woman and the brutal rape of an Indian maiden. After his discharge in 1838, Foote travelled to South America and recorded its sexual customs with prurient detail. Back in the States, he married, but lost his wife and their new son shortly after the child's birth. At length, after a seven-year absence, he returned to Connecticut in 1842. "Since that time I have employed my time in farming, painting, drinking, sometimes to excess, and gambling. I have also visited New York, and some other cities, rather too frequently for my own good, as in former years."[65]

Only in the appendix of this lengthy account did Foote offer his "Startling Confession of the Murder of Emily H. Cooper, &c., &c., &c." He opened with a three-part diatribe: against "poisoned liquor," which he had been drinking for nearly two weeks before the murders; against prostitutes, "those fine looking women" who "array themselves in the most gay costume, adorn their persons with pearls, rings, paint, and jewels, and perfume themselves till they smell as sweet as an oriental garden" to "enchant" and "bewitch" young men; and against "licentious novels, and other bad books" which "poisoned" the minds of readers.[66]

Foote then launched into a complicated story of his visit to "the city of crime and pollution, viz. New York," a few months before his crimes. At the Bowery Theater, he was "enticed" by a prostitute who was a member of a model-artist company, which performed nude on stage. She took him back to her brothel, removed her upper garments, and offered him wine drugged with a chloroform-like substance called Cream of the Valley, which Foote refused. She then offered him a private exhibition of her model-artist "manoeuvres," which "bewitched" him; he spent the night, and in the morning stole the phial containing the drug. That evening, he tracked down a prostitute who had stolen money from him on a previous visit, administered the drug to her, stole back his money "with interest," and took back the phial of Cream of the Valley. He subsequently acknowledged his intention to administer the drug to women.[67]

Back in North Branford, Connecticut, after his New York trip, Foote's "thoughts were continually revolving upon the obscene views" he had witnessed. "A curiosity to see and examine some female in the same state of nudity was constantly haunting my mind." Remembering that his cousin Emily passed through a secluded forest on her way to school, "I resolved to make her the victim of my excited curiosity, and satisfy my wishes by a close examination of her person." He injected the prostitute's drug into a tomato, which he offered to Emily, then committed two acts which he carefully separated from one another: "But with shame! shame! do I write it, I now proceeded to examine her person, which inflamed my baser passion to an unmanageable degree; and after my eyes were satisfied, I violated and robbed her of her virgin purity." He explained, "In the first place I had no intention of doing any thing more than to satisfy my eyes; but this created a passion so strong as to overrule all better feelings, honor, and decency." Then, prompted by an almost audible voice saying that she would betray him, and held "entirely in the power of Satan," he slit her throat.[68]

After the murder, Foote realized what grief his crime would cause his mother, and resolved "to bring her sorrows to an end, and then immediately destroy my own life." But he found that he lacked the requisite hardness for matricide. So he reached once again for "the poison which had already induced me to destroy one innocent life," and drank liquor "till I was as crazy as a wounded bear." At that point his mother hid his jug. Her act "enraged" him; "It was a wrong way to deal with me, to take liquor from me to prevent my drinking"; her doing so always "caused me to behave much worse than I should otherwise have done." He came up behind her at her spinning wheel and bashed her head with a hammer, then tried to kill himself. But neighbors came to the house; doctors looked after his mother and dressed his wound; Emily's body was discovered, and Foote was taken to prison. His mother survived for twelve days, the last two without her reason. Foote explained that "She would most certainly have lost her reason, had she not received any external injury," and thanked his Saviour for taking his mother to heaven to relieve her from her sufferings.[69]

Foote's account attributed his crimes to agents, substances, and other factors outside of himself. Poisoned liquor, poisoned literature, evil sex-drugs, maternal authority, Satan, even the "Allwise Providence" which had "permitted the great enemy of souls to use me as an instrument for the destruction of innocent life"—all shared responsibility for his actions. But in this tangled web of external forces, the prime mover was the prostitute. Foote, an enthusiastic shopper in the booming sexual marketplace of New York, with its pornographic bookstores, model-artist exhibitions, and brothels, made clear that he had been "enticed" into this world by "the snares, arts, and devices of the harlot." "Once in their power," he warned, "you are not your own keeper." The enticements of the prostitute made him want to see another nude female, which led him to drug, strip, and examine his young cousin, which so excited him that he raped her, which necessitated killing her, which required that he kill his mother. Emily Cooper served as an innocent stand-in for the New York prostitutes he had encountered and triumphantly punished for injuries to himself and other men.[70] Henry Foote's story showed how the Gothic narrative of female sexuality could be accommodated to the violent death of an innocent girl as well. The narrative imperative to find the guilty woman held firm.

———

Once deemed naturally more evil than man through her depraved inheritance from Eve, the nineteenth-century woman was being recast as morally superior to man by virtue of her passionlessness. But the passionless ideal carried with it a terrible corollary succinctly captured by Ephraim Avery's defense attorney: "in the same proportion as woman, when chaste and pure, excels the other sex, by just so much, when profligate, does she sink below them." As the *Christian Reflector* said of the murder of Maria Bickford, "However amiable, and lovely, and true, a woman may have been in innocence, she is, in the degradation of lost virtue, like a fallen angel. She may retain her smiles, and charm still with her winning ways, but she is as *devilish* as she is sensual. No crime is too horrid for her to commit, if her passions be aroused."[71] Women were normally angels, but when they succumbed to sexual desire, they became fallen angels, devils, criminals. In 1701, for her act of premarital sex, Esther Rodgers had been represented as a common sinner, no different from the rest of her fallen species; in 1807, for the same transgression, Elizabeth Valpy was labelled a "*foul,* degraded, loathsome prostitute," "a woman totally lost to every sense of decency and chastity."

The new understanding of feminine evil did not simply place fallen women at the sinful end of the same moral spectrum as men. Instead, they were represented as radically distinct from men. As Avery's attorney proclaimed, "if you were to seek for some of the vilest *monsters* in wickedness and depravity, you would find them in the female form."[72] The late eighteenth-century shift in the understanding of female nature accompanied a larger shift in the understanding of human nature. Just as rising expectations of human nature generated a new sense of the "monstrosity" of those men who deviated from a human norm defined as good, free, and capable of self-government, rising expectations of female nature generated a new sense of the "monstrosity" of those women who deviated from a female norm defined as passionless and morally superior to men.

But whereas the generic label of moral monstrosity was applied to the murderer himself, the female variant invoked in sexual narratives of the crime was applied to his victim. The new gynecology of guilt demonized the female murder victim, shifting the guilt for her violent death from her killer to herself: physiologically different, with her peculiar sexual characteristics of blood and putrefaction, criminality and insanity; prone to disease, hence polluted and polluting; and, when fallen, inclined towards both suicide and murder. Within the Gothic narrative of female guilt, the sexualized victim was the real monster, whose intrinsic violence and criminality justified the violence committed against her. This was the import of the sexual narrative of murder for the larger cult of horror: it shifted the site of the monstrosity in the crime from the murderer to his victim. Sexual difference was the focal point of horror in this narrative, the gulf between male normalcy and the monstrous deviation of "that sex, through *which sin and death came into the world.*"

CHAPTER SEVEN

The Murderer as Mental Alien

O N MARCH 22, 1715, Jeremiah Meacham spent the morning on the rooftop of his house in Newport, Rhode Island, armed with a penknife, in fear that his neighbors were plotting to harm him. By afternoon, he had climbed down to shut himself up in a second-story chamber. After several hours, his wife and her sister, afraid that he would harm himself, went upstairs to plead with him to come down; he killed them with his knife and an axe, then slit his own throat, set fire to the chamber, leaped out the window, and was taken into custody. After his conviction for the two murders, the execution sermons preached on his behalf explained that Meacham had been "for some time Exercised with Grievous Hurries of Mind" which "by degrees boil'd up into a sort of a raging fury" in which he hated his home, feared his neighbors, and believed each day would prove his last. But though the Rev. Nathaniel Clap acknowledged Meacham's mental troubles, and compassionately referred to the convicted murderer as "Poor Man," he explained that Meacham had brought his troubles upon himself through sinful conduct. Despite a good religious upbringing, the man had taken up with openly wicked companions, resorted to strong drink, abandoned public worship, and had begun to speak ill of Christian practices. Because he had forsaken God, the Rev. Clap explained, God had forsaken him: "But Oh, what woes have you brought upon your own Soul! You have surrendered your Soul into the hands of Satan, the destroyer of Souls, after a dreadful manner."[1]

Over a century later, on July 22, 1845, Orrin Woodford killed his wife, Diana, with axe and knife in the kitchen of their Avon, Connecticut, home. He suspected her of trying to poison him and of participating in secret ceremonies and illicit sex with a group of men he called the "drang," whom she could summon at will by walking bareheaded to the hog pen. (Woodford had withdrawn from his religious meeting because he believed the clergyman was a member of the "drang" and sent coded sexual messages to Diana from his pulpit.) At his trial for murder, Orrin's counsel pleaded not guilty on the grounds of insanity, arguing that if delusion had overpowered his will, he could not be held legally guilty of murder. Expert medical witnesses explained his behavior as the result of monomania, evidenced not only in his suspicions of his wife, but in his habit of digging for gold and silver in the chimney, his conviction that strange men were lying around in his currant bushes, and his heavy drinking (cited not only as a symptom of mental disease but as a possible cause). Orrin Woodford was found not guilty of murder but guilty of manslaughter, and sentenced to ten years in the state penitentiary.[2]

Here were two similar episodes: two men with troubled minds abandoned religious observances, took to strong drink, grew suspicious of the people around them, and eventually killed their wives. But separated as they were by 130 years, these events were shaped into two very different cultural narratives of criminal transgression. In 1715, the Meacham episode prompted a formal story of depravity, told by a clergyman in an execution sermon. Though the Rev. Clap recognized Meacham's mental disorder and expressed sympathy for his sufferings, he treated Meacham first and last as a sinner, citing his abandonment of religion and use of strong drink as marks of his depravity. By contrast, in 1845, the Woodford episode prompted a tale of disease, told by a partnership of doctors and lawyers in a murder trial transcript. Though Woodford's attorneys and their expert medical witnesses acknowledged his vicious conduct, they interpreted his abandonment of religion and use of liquor as signs of mental illness.

The medicalization of criminal guilt had a significant role in transforming the understanding of what makes the criminal offender. The earlier depravity narrative had treated Jeremiah Meacham as a common sinner; the message of his execution sermons was, "This man, whatever his mental troubles, is fundamentally no different from you and me." By contrast, the nineteenth-century disease narrative treated Orrin Woodford as a "mental alien"—the contemporary term for the mad person—someone set apart from normal, healthy humanity by somatic disease and by the mental, physical, and moral peculiarities it generated. The message of his printed trial transcript, and of his acquittal of murder, was that "this man is not like you and me." The medicalization of criminal guilt made a significant contribution to the emergence of a modern concept of *deviance,* which, rather than seeing human frailty as a universally shared characteristic, constructed a separate category of human nature for the criminal transgressor as a monstrous aberration from the human norm. The concept of the mad murderer proved an important contribution to the sense of Gothic horror and mystery.

In a legal tradition reaching back to the ancient Hebrews, English common law held that crime consisted of both a voluntary act or omission *(actus reus)* and a certain state of mind *(mens rea).* The English doctrine of the criminally guilty mind was first formalized by the thirteenth-century ecclesiastic and common law judge Henry Bracton, who affirmed that neither madpeople nor children were capable of forming criminal intent: "They lack sense, reason and no more do wrong than a brute animal." The doctrine of *mens rea* was refined in the sixteenth century by William Lombard, who added the "natural fool" to this list of the criminally exculpable, and more importantly by Edward Coke, whose *Institutes of the Laws of England* defined four classes of the *non compos mentis:* the idiot, the person who loses memory and understanding by sickness or grief, the lunatic who sometimes has and sometimes lacks understanding, and the drunkard who temporarily loses memory and understanding through vicious conduct. But few cases of insanity were reported in English criminal law before the seventeenth century; probably only the most extreme cases of mental incapacity were deemed excusable.[3]

The definitive formulation of the *mens rea* doctrine before 1800 was Mathew Hale's, in *History of the Pleas of the Crown* (1736), which confirmed and elaborated upon the position of the court in the trial of Edward Arnold in 1724. "Crazy Ned," as he was known to acquaintances, had tried to kill Lord Onslow because he believed that Onslow had bewitched him, and tormented him by periodically entering his body. Judge Tracy confirmed that a man deprived of reason cannot be held guilty, but insisted that "it must be a man that is totally deprived of his understanding and memory, and doth not know what he is doing, no more than an infant, than a brute, or a wild beast." Because the prosecution demonstrated that Arnold could read and write, figure and bargain, make purchases and obtain employment, and that he had had no medical care for his mental condition, he was convicted and sentenced to execution (though his victim interceded on his behalf and Arnold went to prison for life instead). In keeping with the Arnold decision, Mathew Hale distinguished between partial and total insanity: though most felons are under "a degree of partial insanity" when they commit an offense, he explained, criminal exculpability required a total deprivation of understanding and memory, a complete loss of reason, in the offender. Hale's yardstick for legal responsibility was a degree of understanding comparable to that of an ordinary child of fourteen years.[4]

The total insanity or "wild beast" test set the standard for this defense in eighteenth-century England and America, determining the fate, among others, of Jeremiah Meacham (whose trial actually predated that of Arnold). According to the brief account of his trial printed with the execution sermons, Meacham pleaded that he had not been himself at the time of the murders, and was not aware of what he was doing. But the court found Meacham legally responsible for his actions on the grounds that he remembered them, and neighbors testified that he had known what he was doing at the time; and the possession of memory and understanding proved legally sufficient to bring him to the gallows. A similar understanding of *mens rea* shaped the trial in 1802 of Ebenezer Mason, who had beaten his sister's husband to death with a shovel (because the victim had criticized his work as they manured a field together). Mason defended his action by asserting that his brother-in-law was a bad man, an ugly man, and that God had commanded the deed; and the defense pleaded his want of capacity, denying that he—any more than a child, an idiot, or a lunatic—was a moral agent. But the state's questioning of witnesses was designed to demonstrate that Mason had reason and understanding; that he (like "Crazy Ned") could read and write, figure (count out money for fish hooks), and transact business (barter for onion seed), make a living (drive a team, keep cattle in winter, tend an orchard) and attend religious meeting (properly rising and sitting with the rest of the congregation), serve in the militia and keep out of harm's way; and that he could distinguish right from wrong.[5] Mason was convicted of murder and sentenced to be executed.

Jeremiah Meacham and Ebenezer Mason were held to similar legal tests of *mens rea*—requiring that total insanity alone could excuse them on grounds of mental incapacity—with the same judicial conclusion. But elements of the Mason case departed significantly from that of Meacham, and pointed towards nineteenth-century developments in the insanity defense. The editor of the printed trial report expressed doubts about the verdict, observing that "it is to be regretted, that he had not *more*, or *less* capacity. The shades do certainly intermix, in this case, in such a manner, that it is difficult to determine the line of distinction." The editor of *The Last Words of Ebenezer Mason* reported that similar doubts troubled some people who had attended the trial, and some who had read the printed transcript. In an attempt to clarify the matter, the editor went to the condemned man's cell and engaged him in a dialogue modelled on the clerical conversations with criminals that had been a staple of American criminal literature several generations earlier. The results could hardly have provided easy closure to him or his fellow doubters: Mason again explained that his victim had been ugly and bad, set forth biblical rationales for his action (observing that King David had killed and not been executed for his crime), asked who would execute the hangman for killing him, and finally descended into complete mental confusion.[6]

Even more important, the Mason accounts diverged from the depravity narrative of the Meacham case by emphasizing the defendant's mental difference from others: various witnesses testified that Ebenezer Mason was "strange," "odd," and one responded negatively to the question, "Do you think he possesses a mind like other men?" While universal human depravity had linked Jeremiah Mason to all other members of his species, mental peculiarity separated Ebenezer Mason from his fellow men and women. And Mason was not the only mentally troubled killer to prompt such a response in the late eighteenth and early nineteenth centuries. In 1793, Samuel Frost beat to death his master, Captain Allen, with a hoe, and afterwards showed no "just conception of the heinous crime of Murder," talking with "calmness and composure" of his crimes and showing no "social affection" or "moral obligation" or "compunction of mind." Rather than treating Frost as a common sinner, the broadside called him "an extraordinary character," observing that "his mind was evidently not formed altogether like those of other persons . . . He appears to have been a being cast in a different mould from those of mankind in general."[7]

A similar treatment was accorded to Caleb Adams, who in 1803 murdered six-year-old Oliver Woodworth in a dispute over a sled. The printed biography of the convicted murderer did largely conform to a depravity narrative, referring to his "depraved will and corrupt affections of the natural heart," and relating his gradual descent from profanity and Sabbath-violation to theft, vandalism, and cruelty to animals, and finally to a brutal act of murder. But within that larger framework, the clerical author made a special effort to comprehend Adams's distinctive moral nature: a vicious prenatal influence—specifically, his father's introduction of his mistress and her idiot son into the Adams home when his long-suffering wife was pregnant with Caleb—was said to have given him his "untoward cast of mind" and shaped "the form of his face, and motions of his body; which were said, to resemble the child of the woman brought into the family." In the Adams family, corruption was likened to a "disease, which is drawn insensibly in by the unwary youth, takes possession of his conscience, and like the consumption in the body, continues its flattering ravages, till it gives life and food to that worm, that never dies."[8] Not the general inheritance of humankind's depravity, but a specific family-linked strain of moral disease, was said to have infected Caleb Adams.

In all three cases, the defendants failed to meet the stringent requirements of criminal exculpability under the eighteenth-century doctrine of *mens rea,* and all three were convicted and executed for their crimes. But the printed accounts of their cases demonstrated a weakening of the older depravity narrative that had shaped the Meacham case nearly a century earlier. Frost, Mason, and Adams were puzzled over as men set apart from their fellows by their "extraordinary," "untoward," and "different" mental natures. The printed accounts of their crimes did not yet articulate a medical understanding of this mental difference. But the *disease* metaphor invoked to capture Adams's difference pointed towards the emerging criminal narrative for such offenders.

The first successful English challenge to the "wild beast" test in a major criminal trial was the case of James Hadfield, tried for attempting to assassinate the King in 1800. Hadfield was an ex-soldier, discharged as insane after sustaining severe head injuries in battle, who believed that his own death would stop God from destroying the world, and shot at the King so the state would execute him. The Attorney General set out the law of insanity according to Coke and Hale, requiring total deprivation of memory and understanding. But Hadfield's brilliant lawyer, Thomas Erskine, later to become Lord Chancellor, asserted that "no such madness ever existed in the world." Reason and "distraction," he observed, were not mutually exclusive; insane persons routinely demonstrated their knowledge, memory, and even mental acuity. To support his position, he told two separate stories of madmen who brought suit against their asylum keepers on grounds of wrongful imprisonment. In one, the madman responded to lengthy questioning without betraying any sign of mental infirmity, until his physician prompted the examiner to question him about the princess and the cherry juice; this triggered a fantastic tale of how he had been imprisoned in a high tower and deprived of ink, but managed to write letters in cherry juice, and throw them into the river surrounding the tower, where the princess awaited them in her boat. The second tale, similarly, told of a madman who appeared perfectly rational until his particular delusion was touched upon, when he fervently proclaimed that he was the Christ.[9]

Erskine thus displaced the eighteenth-century legal test for insanity, absence of reason, with a new test, the presence of delusion or derangement. The true character of madness, he argued, was delusion without frenzy or raving madness. Without realizing that he was setting a new legal standard, Chief Justice Kenyon followed Erskine's lead in his charge to the jury, explaining that "If a man is in a deranged state of mind at the time, he is not criminally answerable for his acts."[10] Hadfield was acquitted. The case did not immediately alter the course of the *mens rea* doctrine in Anglo-American courts; subsequent trials continued to cite Hale as the final authority on the matter. But Erskine's arguments were cited extensively by nineteenth-century defense attorneys, and praised for providing "a fund of illustration and reasoning on this difficult subject of insanity." And his accessible narrative examples of the subtlety of madness—the tales of the cherry-juice princess and the self-proclaimed Christ— were cited again and again in American courts of law.[11]

Though Erskine's arguments were based more on lay narratives of madness than on any systematic medical explication, they anticipated the course of nineteenth-century medical jurisprudence in broadening the realm of criminal exculpability on the grounds of mental incapacity. The new mental science rested on two basic premises: the somatic nature of insanity, understood to be a disease of the brain; and faculty psychology, which divided the mind (and thus the brain) into different faculties or functions—notably the intellect or reasoning faculty, the affections or emotional faculty, and the will or volitional faculty—each of which could be separately diseased without affecting the others. Beginning with pioneering French clinician Philippe Pinel's concept of *manie sans délire* (raving madness without delusion), the most influential practitioners of the new mental medicine in France, England, and the United States worked out the implications of these two premises in terms of *partial insanity*. Intellectual insanity could itself be partial, in patients afflicted by what Pinel's student Jean Esquirol called *monomanie*, which involved delusion in only one area of perception or action or, more crudely, on a single subject. (The characteristic act of the monomaniac, according to Esquirol, was homicide.) Nineteenth-century practitioners also recognized disorders of the affections, most notably in English alienist James C. Prichard's concept of "moral insanity" (quickly picked up by American alienist Isaac Ray), which involved no cognitive delusion but simply an impairment of the power of moral self-government. And they recognized disorders of the will, best exemplified in diagnoses of "instinctive" or "impulsive" insanity, which usually involved an involuntary, irresistible, and motiveless urge to commit violence (sometimes called "homicidal insanity") without any loss of reason.[12]

Nineteenth-century alienists by no means achieved consensus in their understanding of insanity. But collectively they contributed to a significant broadening of the insanity diagnosis, and thus of exculpability under the doctrine of *mens rea*. The distinguishing mark of nineteenth-century insanity was not the complete loss of reason required by the "wild beast" test, but a more limited and localized expression of mental disorder, which could affect some faculties and not others, and which could act intermittently across time. The new insanity could in fact be an elusive matter, difficult to detect. The monomaniac could appear perfectly sane for months or even years until someone introduced the particular subject on which his or her insanity focused; the afflicted person would then descend into insane delusion. "There are many well-authenticated cases where individuals have been insane for years upon some particular subject and their most intimate friends had no suspicion of it." The various affective and volitional disorders such as moral and instinctive insanity typically involved no delusions, no disturbance of the reasoning powers. And the homicidal maniac might lead an apparently sane life right down to the moment when the disease erupted in an insane act of violence which proved to be its first symptom. As the defense attorney for accused murderer Daniel Corey argued in 1830, insanity "may exist from birth, or for only a single day; it may extend to all subjects, or only one . . . and yet, if it exists, the subject of it cannot be punished for acts committed under its influence."[13]

Such complexities clearly called for the intervention of experts, who could read the subtle signs of mental disease and sort out mere eccentricity from full-blown lunacy. So the new mental doctors—overwhelmingly the superintendents of the mental hospitals springing up across the United States from the 1820s on—entered the criminal courtroom. Sometimes their expertise was invoked in the courtroom, in citations and readings of their published writings, such as Isaac Ray's influential *Treatise on the Medical Jurisprudence of Insanity* (1838); over time, defense attorneys became adept at citing a broadening range of European alienists including Jean Esquirol, Etienne Georget, C. C. H. Marc, John Haslam, and James C. Prichard. But after 1830, the physical presence of American alienists in the courtroom grew increasingly common. At the trial of Abraham Prescott in 1833, for example, expert medical witnesses included Dr. Rufus Wyman, superintendent of the McLean Asylum for the Insane at Charlestown, and Dr. George Parkman, who had kept his own private asylum in Massachusetts (the same Parkman who was to be murdered by John Webster); Abner Rogers's trial in 1844 included medical testimony from Dr. Brigham of the New York State Hospital, Dr. Samuel Woodward of the Worcester Mental Hospital, Dr. Luther V. Bell of the McLean Asylum, and Dr. Isaac Ray from the Maine Mental Hospital. Sometimes they testified on the basis of immediate knowledge of the defendant, sometimes not; Dr. John Butler visited Willard Clark in jail before testifying at his murder trial in 1855, whereas Dr. Isaac Ray never talked with Clark, but based his testimony on information produced in court.[14]

The alienists entered the courtroom in a significantly different capacity from that of the forensic physicians who testified to cause of death and similar issues. With their professed expertise regarding where moral responsibility ended and pathology began, alienists appeared as cultural authorities on the nature of guilt itself. From the broadest historical perspective, they were joining the lawyers in seizing from the clergy the primary task of shaping the meaning of criminal guilt in American culture. Not surprisingly, their presence generated considerable controversy over the legitimate extent of their authority. The judge in Daniel Corey's case in 1830 ruled medical testimony inadmissible on the grounds that the doctors' opinions on Corey's insanity were "no better than those of other judicious men"; the judge in Joel Clough's case in 1833 asserted that "the casuistry of doctors" could not help jurors sort out when intemperance was the cause of insanity, and when the effect. The prosecutor in Rebecca Peake's trial chided the defense for reading "copious extracts" (from works on medical jurisprudence) "from a set of moon struck authors" who assessed the human mind "through the medium of the fingers on the outward surface of the head" (a contemptuous reference to the disputed science of phrenology), in an effort "to establish that by theory which they have failed to do by proof." Alienists, according to the judge at John Haggerty's murder trial, "possess not the power to prescribe the rules which limit the extent of human responsibility for crime." Such rules were the province of the common law.[15]

But other judges summarized medical testimony with attentive care, speaking of "medical books of high authority" and "physicians whose testimony is entitled to great respect," and arguing that it was just as appropriate to consult a mental doctor regarding the sanity of a defendant, as it was to consult a sea captain regarding the seaworthiness of a ship. Defense attorneys, of course, threw their own weight behind such arguments: as one observed at Abner Rogers's trial, "If the issue before you were, whether the prisoner had a typhus fever, or some other subtle physical disease, instead of a disease of the brain, would you be satisfied to dispense with the opinion of a physician, if you could obtain it?" The alienists supported such arguments by backing up one another's testimony, and sometimes lending their specialized authority to expose the professional incompetence of generalists summoned by the prosecution. After no fewer than six medical experts (two of them from the Utica Mental Hospital) had testified to Alfred Fyler's epileptic dementia, his family physician had the temerity to diagnose Fyler as hysteric. His position was openly ridiculed by the defense, which argued that hysteria was widely known to be a female disorder, scornfully observing that "a fit of hysterics is as scarce in the male sex as jewels in a toad's head."[16]

The opposition to expert medical witnesses did not stem the tide of alienists flooding the courtroom. And their presence signalled an important moment in the history of criminal guilt in America: the transformation of an earlier *depravity* narrative of criminal transgression into a new *disease* narrative. The new narrative was devoted largely to setting forth the signs of mental disease. In an effort to demonstrate the legal exculpability of the defendant, alienists took up the earlier sense of a criminal mind "cast in a different mould from those of mankind in general" and shaped it into a fully pathologized condition of mental alienation. In so doing, they catalogued the marks of difference with far greater specificity than early American narratives had done.

Insanity, the alienists repeatedly observed, tended to be hereditary in predisposition, "a calamity visiting some of the human family from one generation to another." So the standard insanity defense was loaded with references to the defendant's mad relatives. Abraham Prescott's grandfather, aunt, cousin, and nephew were insane; Metcalf Thurston had a mad grandmother, two great-aunts, two cousins, and his mother's cousin; Alfred Fyler had a father, maternal grandmother, and two cousins who also suffered from fits, a crazy maternal aunt, and a great-uncle who was an idiot. While Jeremiah Meacham's depravity was shared by the entire human family through common descent from Adam and Eve, the new monomaniac's disease was a more particular mental doom that ran along narrower bloodlines. One authority claimed that the hereditary predisposition to insanity could be so strong that "no prominent moral cause is necessary for the production of the disease,"[17] a position which clearly exculpated the mad person from any moral guilt for his or her mental state.

Because mental disorder was believed to be somatic, insanity defenses typically reported what diseases or physical injuries had caused, or now gave evidence of (the line was often difficult to draw), a defendant's condition. John Haggerty had been hit in the head by a cart shaft, which had left a depression in the left side of his skull; Daniel Corey had repeatedly fallen on his head.[18] Abraham Prescott had suffered in infancy from a disease that caused his head to grow so large that at the age of two his father's hat nearly fit him; a postmortem examination of William Freeman showed his brain, "the organ of mind,—the seat of intellect, to be a *lifeless sponge*."[19] Most defendants pleading insanity were said to suffer from chronic, severe headache. Childhood disease was often cited as a cause of insanity, such as Singleton Mercer's lengthy bout with the croup and John Phelps's sickness of the spine and kidneys. Some defendants claimed constipation as a leading cause of their insanity. And for Margaret Howard, physiological femaleness was a primary source of the problem: "women are subject to state of constitution intimately connected with excitement of mind, rendering them at times peculiarly subject to perversion of intellect, but most commonly to irritable temper."[20]

The somatic understanding of mental disorder contributed to the close attention paid to the physical appearance of the defendant. Because Abner Rogers (who was a prisoner at Massachusetts State Prison when he killed Charles Lincoln, the warden) appeared unshaved, uncombed, slovenly, and disorderly, "his whole aspect, air and manner, conveyed to my mind, the idea of a lunatic." With his wild look, red face, and bristling hair, John Haggerty "looked frightful, like a deranged maniac." Alternatively, it was Joel Clough's dull, pale look just before he killed Mary Hamilton that was cited as evidence of his insanity.[21] The appearance of the eyes was held to be especially revealing: Orrin Woodford's wild eyes, Abraham Prescott's "idiotic, dull, lazy, indifferent" eyes, John Windsor's "insane quickness of eye," and Alfred Fyler's changed color of the iris, indicated their diseased mental condition.[22]

Such diagnostic practice owed much to the contemporary faith in the revelatory powers of physiognomy. Occasionally, phrenology was invoked as a scientific method of reading the signs of disease in the defendant's physical appearance. John Haggerty's entire brain was said to be shaped in such a way that its greatest mass lay behind his ears, where the animal passions predominated, rather than the front, where the moral and intellectual powers held sway. At his trial, Dr. William B. Fahnestock took the stand and demonstrated (on a phrenological bust designed by George Combe) the implications of the cart injury to Haggerty's skull: "The fracture passes on the lower edge of Marvellousness or Wonder, Hope and Cautiousness. It passes also between Hope and Ideality." The defense of William Miller, who in 1838 killed a peddler with an axe, introduced the testimony of noted phrenologist O. S. Fowler, who reported that the defendant's lymphatic temperament predisposed him to derangement of the animal passions, and that Miller's organs of Destructiveness, Secretiveness, and Acquisitiveness were immense. Murder defendant Henrietta Robinson was examined in her cell by Mrs. Oakes Smith, who reported that "Phrenologically her brain is low above the ears . . . She has two projections in the region of what is called Constructiveness, extending backward, which of themselves would be sufficient to throw the whole character out of balance." Albert Tirrell's alleged reading revealed "very large" Amativeness, "enormously developed" Combativeness, and "small" Human Nature.[23]

Moral causes of insanity were sometimes cited, though less frequently than physical, presumably because they might suggest the defendant's moral culpability for his or her disease. But "moral" could refer to circumstances beyond the mad person's control. One moral factor in Abraham Prescott's illness was said to be the solitude of his agricultural life. Willard Clark's monomania was attributed largely to a life of disappointments and tragedies, including romantic rejection. Margaret Howard's mental alienation arose not only from her sex, but from the emotional suffering, sickness, and destitution caused by her husband's abuse.[24] Even when "moral" causes of insanity were accompanied by bad habits—such as intemperance or the "soul-destroying and degrading habit" of masturbation—alienists often argued that such behaviors might actually have been the *result* of insanity.[25] Once again, however, cause and effect were not clearly differentiated: Dr. Nathan Benedict, who testified at Thurston's trial, observed that masturbation could be either a cause of insanity or a result.[26]

The distinctive behaviors of allegedly insane defendants came under close medical scrutiny. John Phelps, it was said at his trial, some-times acted "very queer." Metcalf Thurston was wildly erratic, alter-nating between industry and inattentiveness to his business, extrava-gant and slovenly dress, gluttony and fasting in his diet, talking fast and foolishly and standing fixed and motionless, gazing vacantly at nothing. John Windsor bored augur holes in the interior walls of his house so he could keep a close eye on his wife, whom he believed to be a witch; he sent his washing out so she could not infuse his sheets and clothing with occult poison; and he sat in court with a paper on his head to shield it from the poisonous "hot stuff" being blown on him. Even the mildest of eccentricities could be cited as evidence of madness, such as the crimson silk cap with filigree tassels worn by Abner Baker for a daguerreotype sitting, and his purchase of several fine linen cambric shirts when he was well supplied with "more suitable" ones.[27]

Of all the kinds of evidence offered for defendants' insanity, per-haps the most important was their distinctive beliefs or delusions. Daniel Corey believed that his New Hampshire farm covered a gold mine guarded by an Indian spirit in the form of a snake, a mine so vast that the precious metal was spreading all over his fields and house, making him the richest man in the world, soon to be crowned King of America. John Haggerty's delusions were apocalyptic: the Judgment Day was at hand and his own horse was the Antichrist, which he had shot dead with silver five-cent pieces after spotting it up in a tree fighting an army of saints (headed by George Washing-ton); the Son of God mounted on a white horse also appeared in the tree, along with a number of chickens (one of whom represented Martin Van Buren); a ball of fire fell from the heavens and a voice told Haggerty that he must kill his neighbor Fordney, or be killed by him, for the Day of Judgment to take place and the New World to begin. Margaret Howard had dreamed, the night before she killed her husband's paramour, that she had stuck a pig, and after the killing was confused over whether she had knifed a pig or a woman. Henrietta Robinson said she had a special swimming cork which, when held in her mouth, would keep her afloat after she had grown too tired to swim any more.[28]

Throughout the insanity narratives ran a powerful emphasis on the fundamental difference between normal and diseased minds: the testimony of Abraham Prescott's mother that "He did not act as other children" expressed a conviction crucial to his defense. The insane were set apart by their special family inheritance, the size and shape of their heads, their dress (slovenly or extravagant) and personal habits, their eyes (wild or dull) and face color (flushed or pale), their childhood diseases and digestive systems, their "queer" actions and bizarre ideas. "He acted very singularly," said an acquaintance of Willard Clark, "but I am unable to find language to explain his peculiar expressions of face and look, and his singular ways and actions, which induced me to think him insane." What this witness could not capture in language, contemporary medicine could, labelling Clark a mental "alien." But once the signs and causes of insanity had been extended to include headaches, childhood croup, constipation, eccentric dress, femaleness, a few falls on the ice, dull eyes, a low forehead, romantic disappointment, and domestic unhappiness, the demarcation between the insane and the sane proved a very fine line. And the replacement of the "wild beast" test with the new standard of partial insanity meant that many allegedly insane defendants seemed perfectly rational most of the time. As Metcalf Thurston's attorney explained, "It is popularly supposed that no man is insane unless he delivers himself up to the wildest vagaries of conduct and conversation . . . but gentlemen, there are a vast number of men who are insane upon some particular subject . . . and yet, gentlemen, you might spend with these men weeks, nay months, without being able to detect their insanity."[29]

Alienists and the lawyers who brought them to the witness stand designed a dramatic new strategy for demonstrating the mental alienation of the defendants they sought to protect. They pointed to the peculiar nature of the murder as sufficient evidence of the killer's insanity: "The circumstances of the transaction itself overthrow the presumption of sanity." For example, in the case of Rebecca Peake's murder of her stepson Ephraim, they identified "the atrocity of the crime charged upon the prisoner as evidence of mental alienation": no sane person could have poisoned a stepson and, under the guise of nursing him back to health, continued to administer arsenic until his death. In others, they cited absence of motive: "if there were no other evidence of the prisoner's insanity, than the entire absence of all motive for the act," argued Abner Rogers's attorney, "I should claim his acquittal at your hands, with the utmost confidence"; Rogers had had only three months left of his prison sentence when he stabbed the warden to death.[30] Metcalf Thurston's defense quoted Isaac Ray to the effect that "with the criminal, murder is always a means for accomplishing some selfish object . . . whereas, with the homicidal monomaniac, murder is the only object in view."[31] Defense attorneys emphasized their defendant's failure to try to conceal a crime—Haggerty killed in broad daylight on a busy street—or to flee from the scene afterwards, as evidence of mental derangement. Most subtly, they argued that the crime in question was completely out of character for the defendant, citing Andrew Combe's view that careful medical investigation was in order "when an unnatural act is committed by an individual who would previously have revolted at it."[32]

Several defense attorneys quoted French alienist Etienne Georget to clinch their case that the crime itself provided adequate evidence of insanity: "A single act of atrocity, if contrary to human nature, committed without motive, without interest, without passion, opposed to the natural character of the individual, is evidently an act of madness." The crime itself, in other words, sometimes provided the *first* indication of mental alienation.[33] With great forensic skill, Abraham Prescott's defense attorney made use of his greatest apparent disadvantage—the absence of evidence of his client's insanity before killing Sally Cochran—in order to transform it into an advantage: claiming that insanity was a difficult defense to make, he rhetorically asked, "Who will for a moment listen to the excuse of insanity for an act of such atrocity, from one whose whole life has been a regular and quiet and intelligent discharge of the duties of his humble station?" Metcalf Thurston's attorney drew this position to its logical conclusion, arguing that "In impulsive insanity the act itself is often almost the *only* evidence of insanity."[34]

Such arguments provided prosecutors with their primary target in combatting the insanity defense. "If the killing of another is of itself proof of insanity," argued the Attorney General in the case against Abraham Prescott, "without any previous or subsequent act indicating an unsound state of mind, no man could ever be punished for murder." More specifically, if the atrocity of the crime were treated as evidence of insanity, the judicial system would actually favor the more vicious murderers: "the greater the crime the greater the proof of insanity," and the likelier the acquittal on grounds of mental incompetence.[35] Willard Clark's prosecutor echoed Mathew Hale in observing that "every criminal is, at the time that he commits any heinous crime, laboring under a sort of *moral* insanity"; that did not mean that none was legally responsible for his or her actions. "The plea of insanity," observed Rebecca Peake's prosecutor, "is the ark of safety, into which criminals flee for protection, when pursued for their crimes." Alfred Fyler's prosecutor followed suit, charging that, "When great crimes are committed and the evidence is overwhelming, what other resort is there but to pretend to be insane?"[36]

In response to the perceived circularity of the insanity defense, prosecutors often chose not to argue the case on the medical turf marked out by the defense, but to return to a depravity narrative. "We have hitherto believed," explained Attorney General Sullivan in the Prescott case, "that to take the life of a human being, without just cause, afforded evidence of great and uncommon depravity of heart, but none of insanity." The alleged medical symptoms cited by the alienists, within this argument, were merely marks of old-fashioned depravity. Willard Clark's absent-mindedness, inattentiveness, and glassy-eyed stare indicated not insanity but chronic intemperance. Orrin Woodford's abuses of his wife before he killed her "had their origin, not in delusion, but in perversity of mind; not in an insane jealousy, but in a depraved wish to annoy" her. What one physician referred to as Alfred Fyler's *"severe mental agony"* after killing his wife, was better understood as "Remorse!"—sorrow over his own depraved action. Henrietta Robinson was not the romantically sympathetic Ophelia-figure depicted by the defense; rather she was a pistol-packing, bad-brandy-drinking, profane and obscene woman: not diseased but depraved.[37]

In murder trials involving the insanity defense, prosecuting attor-

{ 225 }

neys and the judges who shared their views emerged as keepers of the depravity narrative, carrying that earlier understanding of the crime into the nineteenth century. The insanity narrative, they charged, required little support "save the frailty of poor human nature in its lost estate, unless a proper discrimination is made between that which is evidence of insanity, and that which is evidence of depravity."[38] Their job, as they saw it, was to protect that distinction.

This common prosecution strategy sharply underlines the ways in which the medical narrative both assumed and sought to protect a particular *a priori* understanding of human nature. Alienists generally adhered to an Enlightenment liberalism, reinforced by the romantic faith that humankind was not only essentially good, but crafted in God's image, even perfectible. The creation of mental asylums was a major institutional expression of the movement to reform the treatment of the mentally ill.[39] The central understanding of human nature shaping the insanity narrative was, in the words of Prescott's defense, that man is "fashioned and made after the likeness and image of God and partaking of some of his attributes." Mental illness had, of course, damaged that likeness to God in the criminal defendant: Abner Baker's counsel referred to him as this "wreck of God's image now before you," who, though intelligent, gifted, promising, had been "Doomed to the greatest of earthly calamities—an eclipse of mind." Similarly, another murder defendant was identified by his defense as "but a remnant of what was once John Metcalf Thurston, and could be looked upon by those who held him near and dear as survivors are wont to gaze upon some cherished memorial of the loved and lost."[40] "Wreck" or "remnant," the mad person was affirmed to have been originally made in God's image, a creature to be pitied as the unwilling victim of a tragic lapse.

To label such a victim as a willfully depraved enemy of God and condemn him for murder, argued alienists, was to deny his humanity. Given man's likeness to God, asked Prescott's defense, "Can you believe, that the young man before you, has the hellish disposition, which would have led, while in the possession of his senses, to the commission of this crime?" The judge presiding over the trial of Joel Clough expressed his fervent liberal wish, "God grant that you may" find sufficient evidence of mental alienation, "for we would *rather, infinitely rather,* find him a maniac, than a murderer." Rebecca Peake's attorney proclaimed, "If the charge in the indictment is sustained by the proof, then may the records of human depravity be searched in vain for a crime of equal atrocity. Common charity, then, would seem to require that you should believe the prisoner insane." Defending Abner Rogers, George Tyler Bigelow pronounced, "I should have wept over the degradation and depravity of human nature, if I had been compelled to believe, that any man, however wicked or degraded, could have deliberately, and with a rational motive, committed such an awful crime."[41]

The insanity defense relegated the worst criminal offenders to a category outside human nature, defined by the concept of "alienation" or difference. Where the normative self was good, the mental alien was capable of heinous acts; where the healthy self was rational, the diseased self was subject to delusion; where the normative self was free, the aberrant self was governed by irresistible impulse or compulsion (sometimes taking the diagnostic form of "homicidal insanity"). The insanity defense created a kind of moral quarantine to contain the threat violent crime posed to the liberal faith in human nature. Not coincidentally, those who crafted the insanity defense were the keepers of the new mental asylums which, along with the new penitentiaries (to which many of those acquitted on grounds of insanity were sentenced), served as social quarantines for those same mental aliens. Just as an abstract liberal selfhood was protected by the concept of mental alienation, so live liberals were protected by the institutions designed to contain mental aliens.

Perhaps more revealingly, early nineteenth-century mental medicine effectively "quarantined" madness within the mad person's brain, in a diagnostic construction that protected the larger rational self of the mad person from a total ravaging by disease. The concept of partial insanity, in its various diagnostic forms, meant that madness could afflict one of the brain's faculties—intellect, affections, or will—while leaving the others normal and healthy. In the most common diagnosis, monomania, it meant that madness could adhere to only one subject area in the mental life of the afflicted individual—

disposition of property, alleged infidelity—while leaving other subject areas unaffected. Theoderic Beck's *Elements of Medical Jurisprudence*, a text cited in both the Rebecca Peake and the Abner Baker, Jr. cases, called monomania the most common form of criminal insanity, a claim borne out in the frequency of the diagnosis in the insanity defense. By the 1840s and '50s, even lay witnesses were characterizing the mental condition of defendants in terms clearly shaped by the monomania diagnosis: several witnesses at the trial of Margaret Howard reported that they had "always thought she was insane about her children." The grounds for the diagnosis constantly shifted: whereas some defendants were said to be insane on one *subject*, others were said to be insane in the context of one powerful *relationship* (husband to wife, mother to children), and still others were said to have been driven insane by the failure of such a relationship ("There was no cause, he said, so productive of monomania, as disappointed love").[42] In practice, the monomania diagnosis functioned less to designate a specific mental condition than to refer metaphorically to the more inclusive category of partial insanity.

The diagnosis of monomania captured a spatial understanding of partial insanity: mental disease, it affirmed, often afflicted only certain areas of mental activity. Partial insanity also assumed a temporal form, in the diagnosis of temporary or intermittent insanity.[43] In the Prescott case, Dr. George Parkman testified that "Insanity, like some other diseases, is sometimes regularly intermittent; the sufferer is quite reasonable, and then contrary on alternate days." The phrase commonly used to capture this periodicity was "paroxysm": "The disease of insanity," explained Dr. Charles Stilwell at the trial of John Windsor, "is subject to paroxysms"; in Windsor's case, according to his defense attorney, "When the paroxysm was off he was kind to his wife, and tolerant of the children." "Paroxysm" thus referred to a state of transient insanity in which the victim was not himself, and sometimes was unconscious of his actions: "Persons subject to insane paroxysms are frequently unconscious, after the paroxysms, of their conduct whilst under the influence." In some instances, paroxysmic insanity emerged only once in an otherwise normal lifetime, long enough to result in a violent crime, then disappeared forever.[44]

{228}

Perhaps the most extreme expression of intermittent insanity was invoked in a few celebrated cases before 1860 in which the defense identified the defendant as a somnambulist who had committed his crime in an altered state of consciousness. The first of these was the trial of Abraham Prescott for the murder of Sally Cochran in Pembroke, New Hampshire, in 1833. Prescott, the eighteen-year-old hired man working for Sally and Chauncey Cochran, killed Sally with a blow from a stake while picking strawberries with her on a Sunday morning in late June (Chauncey had stayed home to read about the murder trial of the Rev. Ephraim Avery). According to the prosecution, Prescott demanded sex from Sally, then killed her after she threatened to bring charges against him. The defense argued that Prescott had fallen asleep before the assault and killed Sally in a somnambulistic state. Crucial to the defense was the fact that, six months earlier, Prescott had attacked both Cochrans with an axe while they slept in their bed, then summoned Chauncey's mother and informed the neighbors of his action. Though both Cochrans were seriously wounded, they subsequently defended their assailant, calling him a good, hard-working boy who was "unconscious of hurting us" because he had been asleep at the time "and the act not intentional." And to defuse any public outrage, the Cochrans had encouraged their attending physician to submit a story to the *New Hampshire Patriot* explaining what he called "an unhappy and almost unheard-of occurrence of somnambulism."[45]

The defense argued, and the judge in his charge to the jury concurred, that "If he did the act of the 6th of January in his sleep he was not accountable for it; and it was competent for the Jury, if they felt so satisfied, to infer from it he did the act of 23d of June under a similar aberration." The defense called an impressive list of expert medical witnesses to the stand, and then played fast and loose with the medical expertise they proferred, betraying the considerable extent to which the law would bend "science" in the interest of protecting the liberal faith in human nature. Dr. Rufus Wyman and Dr. T. Chadbourne, though affirming what they termed an "analogy" or "alliance" between somnambulism and insanity, both emphasized the fundamental difference between the two mental conditions. But defense attorneys ignored that difference, using the terms somnambulism and insanity interchangeably, until the judge himself charged the jury that "Somnambulism was a species of insanity." As Prescott's defense explained, "A thousand strange phantoms come and go, without the will, or any consciousness, and these take firm possession of the mind, leading the unfortunate victim of somnambulism, or insanity, to the commission of acts the most shocking, revolting and unaccountable to him in his waking moments."[46] The primary Prescott was a good, quiet, obedient, rational boy; the diseased Prescott was a secondary self without a will, an unconscious killer who emerged only when his primary self was asleep. Despite such efforts, Prescott was convicted.

In a second notorious case of the period, defense attorneys for accused murderer Albert Tirrell argued, first, that their client did not fatally slit Maria Bickford's throat in a Boston boarding house in 1846; and second, that even if he did, he acted in a somnambulistic state evidenced by the strangled cry he gave when shaken by the man who found him wandering the streets after Bickford's death and by his confused question, "Sam, how came I here?" The Tirrell defense offered a more extensive profile of his mental condition than had been constructed thirteen years earlier for Abraham Prescott. Tirrell had suffered from this "terrible malady" of spontaneous somnambulism (as opposed to mesmeric or hypnotically induced somnambulism) from the age of six, and his paroxysms had grown more serious and more frequent over time. As a sleepwalking boy, he had committed acts of mischief and violence of which he had no memory upon awakening. As a young man, he nearly smothered his wife in bed during one attack; he frequently beat his mistress while somnambulistic, and once, while in Bickford's company in New York, nearly leaped from a third-story window.[47]

Tirrell's defense identified somnambulism as a "real mental derangement," a position accepted by Judge Dewey, who informed the jury that "Somnambulism is insanity, to be treated as such." As defense attorney Merrill put it, "In this state of body, one or more of the intellectual, and one or more of the moral faculties may be and often are in a state of activity; and though in these states we may be able to reason correctly in some respects, yet, the activity of our mind being partial, we are unable to discover the incompatibility of the circumstances we fancy to surround us." A somnambulist might rise from his bed in the middle of the night, dress himself, kill his bedmate, set fire to the room, and flee the scene, all without conscious moral intent or even the power to remember his actions. Closing for the defense, Rufus Choate intoned, "If indeed he should, in one of those dreadful dreams, or diseases, rise to kill her, it was not him that did it, it was not him that destroyed her."[48] Not Albert Tirrell—a married man of good character (a moral standing the defense insisted upon despite his indictment for adultery at the time of the murder)—not this fine, upstanding Albert Tirrell, but an alien, diseased self that emerged only when this man of excellent character was asleep, had nearly decapitated his prostitute-lover with a razor.

A third related case involved epilepsy, which was directly likened to somnambulism by expert medical witnesses, and defense attorneys sought to establish similar moral implications for its sufferers. Alfred Fyler stabbed and shot his wife, Ruth, in their home just outside Syracuse, New York, on February 22, 1854, while their six-year-old son Henry looked on. According to the Fylers' hired girl, Mary Cummins, Alfred had had sexual intercourse with her (and boasted of his exploits with former servants) and proposed to get rid of his wife if Mary would consent to live with him. Then, following Ruth's death, Alfred had confessed his crime to Mary and threatened to kill her too if she did not confirm his story that Ruth had died at the hands of burglars.

Fyler's defense, like Tirrell's, was twofold. First, he had not committed the crime: in one of the most virulently nativist criminal trials of the period, the defense blamed Ruth Fyler's murder on the "wild Irishmen" living not far from the Fyler farm, casting suspicion most prominently upon Mary Cummins herself, labelled a "harlot" for her allegedly false attack on Alfred Fyler's character. And second, even if he had committed the crime, he had done so in a state of dementia resulting from epilepsy, a condition he had suffered for years before his wife's death. A succession of relatives, neighbors, and the family physician came forward to testify to Fyler's susceptibility, inherited from his father and a maternal grandmother, to "fits," characterized by sweating, wild or vacant eyes, clammy extremities, a fast but faint pulse, stuporous silence and insensibility or delirious laughter, and convulsions or spasms in which he would throw his arms about, striking and choking anyone who tried to subdue him. The expert medical witnesses—including John Gray, superintendent of the state mental asylum at Utica—diagnosed Fyler's disease as epilepsy, and faulted that organic disease of the brain for the defendant's "undoubted symptoms of alienation of mind": epilepsy had reduced Fyler to a state of incurable dementia.[49] Led by the skillful questions of the defense, medical witnesses explained that the milder form of epilepsy that afflicted Fyler was actually more damaging to the mind than the severer form, which tended to attack the muscles rather than the brain.

According to the defense, epileptic dementia operated much like somnambulism. Because Fyler had no memory of killing his wife, he must have been unconscious at the time (if he did kill her, which the defense continued to deny even in the midst of their own medical narrative). More generally, according to both Dr. Gray and Dr. Charles Coventry (one-time manager of the Utica asylum), the larger effect of epilepsy was to destroy the power of self-control, undermining the moral faculty first and foremost, modifying the character of the epileptic "even in the absence of alienation." Even if he did not suffer a fit on the night of the killing, the defense argued, "That night the disease was there."[50]

Insanity was an alien agency that had invaded Fyler's mind and overpowered him: "Disease, like an insidious foe, had grappled with his frame. There was a serpent crawling in his brain, which was ultimately to undermine his constitution and destroy the citadel of his reason."[51] Not Alfred Fyler, but the "serpent" in his brain—the alien self which had displaced the original Alfred Fyler who loved his wife, enjoyed an unimpeachable character, and would never have bedded an Irish kitchen girl—had committed this terrible deed.

The somnambulism defense captured the broader liberal conviction that certain killers should not be held accountable for their violent act because, for them, murder was entirely out of character. This idea was invoked in the common claim that a given defendant was "not himself" at the time of the crime. This was the generic version of all partial-insanity arguments. Daniel Corey was said to be "a man educated among us, and hitherto of a moral and religious character"; Singleton Mercer was a plainly educated man from a respectable family, courteous and well respected by his employers; "the irreproachable John Windsor" had "borne for fifty years the character of an upright and inoffensive man." Because murder was a dramatic aberration for such men, they must have been insane at the time.[52]

Within the common narrative language of the insanity defense, the disease itself was often cited as the murdering agent. A number of American cases quoted Chief Justice Denman in the English case of Edward Oxford, who attempted to assassinate Queen Victoria in 1840, to the effect that "If some controlling disease was in truth the acting power within him, which he could not resist, then he will not be responsible."[53] Similarly, defense narratives often invoked mechanical metaphors to explain how the crime had happened: Daniel Corey had acted as "a mere machine of bones and muscles" in killing Matilda Nash; Metcalf Thurston had killed Anson Garrison much like an "insensible steam engine which passes over the sleeping or incautious traveller"; Willard Clark's shooting of Richard Wight was "simply mechanical; he acted without volition."[54] Whatever the metaphors invoked, in all these narratives the allegedly insane defendant had acted "under the dominion of a different and incontrolable power."[55] In a handful of cases, the defense invoked an explicit medical diagnosis of this volitional non-responsibility: homicidal or impulsive or instinctive insanity, often called "irresistible impulse." "In this disorder, the will is occasionally under the influence of an impulse, which suddenly drives the person affected to the perpetration of acts of the most revolting kind, to the commission of which he has no motive." Irresistible impulse "comes upon the intellect without a warning, and prostrates at a blow all the better faculties of our nature, poisoning the fountains of thought, unhinging the will, and making man the sport of caprice, and the slave of an ungovernable impulse."⁵⁶ Ultimately, the "irresistible impulse" case addressed issues of moral responsibility rather than medical pathology.

The mad person constructed by the new medical jurisprudence was not only alienated from the rest of humankind. He or she was self-alienated as well, morally divided into a primary liberal self—location of the "better faculties"—and a mental disease that invaded one part of the psyche, leaving a significant portion of the original, "normal" self undamaged. This definition confirmed the liberal-romantic faith in human nature. Within the complex narratives of the insanity defense, the murdering agency was not the primary self, but a spatially and/or temporally limited madness; an unconscious sleeping self, a "horrible phantom," "a serpent crawling in his brain"; a vicious secondary character which had displaced the originally respectable and moral character; the disease itself which transformed the hapless victim into a mechanical automaton; an "irresistible impulse," a "different and incontrollable power."

In the American criminal courtroom—a cultural arena of growing importance in the nineteenth century—the new field of medical jurisprudence offered its solution to the problem of radical human evil in a post-Enlightenment world: the insanity defense. The new monomaniac stood in a different relationship to the rest of humankind from that of the early American criminal, who was morally indistinguishable from every other man and woman of his community. The nineteenth-century mental alien was deemed different by nature. And his extreme mental difference distinguished him from other, undiseased criminals only by degree, for as Charles Dickens wrote, the "criminal intellect" is nothing like "the average intellect of average men" but "a horrible wonder apart." The most important ideological work done by this new construction of the criminal offender was to protect the understanding of human nature as rational and well-intentioned, by creating a kind of moral quarantine to contain the agents of the most shocking of human transgressions.

But the construction of that moral quarantine for criminal transgression carried a heavy cultural cost: the peculiarly powerful horror evoked by the spectre of the murderer as madman. Gothic horror was an emotional response to murder that arose from the great gulf separating the normal and law-abiding from the moral alien in the late eighteenth and early nineteenth centuries. In the insanity defense, moral alienation was medicalized in the concept of "mental alienation," the disease of madness. The monstrosity of the insane murderer was inscribed in his physical appearance: "it was a frightful sight," said a visitor to Alfred Fyler's jail cell, "and horrified me." It was demonstrated in the peculiar heinousness of his murderous actions: Metcalf Thurston burying an axe blade in his brother-in-law's skull as the victim sat with his daughter on his lap at the murderer's dinner table; Daniel Corey battering the elderly Matilda Nash's head with his gun, then leaving the broken stock perched on top of her bashed-in skull. It was evident in the murderer's peculiar actions following the crime: Margaret Howard rushing through the streets of Cincinnati, bloody knife in hand, her shirtwaist soaked in blood; Singleton Mercer calling for a fiddler's tune at the tavern where he was taken into police custody after shooting Mahlon Heberton to death.[57]

Once again, it was precisely the insistence on the primary goodness of human nature, and its replacement of depravity with disease as the central explanation of what drove some people to the crime of murder, that gave rise to a Gothic sense of horror. After John Haggerty's trial for murder, the extensive testimony of Dr. Baker concerning his apocalyptic delusions was printed separately, in an account that clearly indicated Haggerty's excusability on the grounds of insanity. Significantly, the preface to that testimony offered a dramatically Gothic account of the crime:

> Yes, reader, go with me for a moment to where this cry is heard—to the scene of this horrid butchery—this heart-rending tragedy—this mangling of human victims. Father, Mother, Man and Wife, parent and child, all weltering in their own blood, flowing freely from the wounds made upon them in cold, but premeditated passion: Behold! standing over their lifeless forms, without the least remorse or heartfelt anguish, erect, and in the presence of his Maker, the form of the murderer, the sinner—John Haggerty stands in a picture of

{235}

defiance; raised high above his head, and quivering in the tight grasp of this powerful man, is the axe, from the sharp edge of which trinkles [sic] the warm blood, o'er the very face of him who holds it, which only adds more horror to that expression of countenance.[58]

Insane he might be, but the murders were, in all their bloody butchery, all the more horrifying for the murderer's mad defiance and heartless lack of remorse.

To be sure, defense attorneys routinely appealed to jurors' compassion for their mentally afflicted defendants: Daniel Corey, argued his attorney, "is much more entitled to compassion and protection, than to severity." But such compassion was dramatically different from the early American sympathy invoked for the "Poor Man" Jeremiah Meacham. Whereas the compassion for Meacham was grounded in empathy, a genuine identification of all people with the universal fallen state they shared with the condemned criminal, the compassion invoked for the nineteenth-century mad person was grafted onto radical difference. Defense attorneys did sometimes warn jurors that presently normal minds might succumb to mental alienation at some future date: "If the hand of God has been invisibly visited upon the prisoner," mused Abraham Prescott's lawyer, "can we feel secure? May it not fall on us?"[59] But this warning itself appealed to jurors' presumed terror and repugnance in the face of the mental alien, that wild-eyed, bristle-haired creature before them in court. It expressly did not address present moral identification with the criminal, but envisaged the terrible threat of a similar future fate, just as the domestic murderer lurking at the fireside brought the horror home. In the end, the horror of difference—typically captured in the popular representation of the criminal madman as "monster"—overrode the compassion formally summoned in the insanity-defense narrative.

Though these murders tended to present little or no mystery concerning the nominal identity of the killer—overwhelmingly, such cases involved eyewitnesses or their near-equivalent—they addressed, at a deeper level, "that most mysterious subject, the *human mind.*" The insanity diagnosis, for all its purported scientific enlightenment, was not able to dispel that deeper mystery of the mind:

insanity "is one of those phenomena over which hangs a thick and almost impenetrable veil—its causes, its nature, the whole subject, is one which even in this advanced stage of science, is comparatively obscure." (Two allegedly insane defendants, Margaret Howard and Henrietta Robinson, lent theatrical support to this metaphorical position by coming to court heavily shrouded in veils.) As in the larger cult of mystery, it lay outside ordinary human power to fathom such obscurity: "You cannot penetrate into the recesses of his mind," explained one defense attorney for Abner Rogers. Only the providential eye commanded such power: "It belongs only to Omniscience, we believe, to penetrate the chaotic darkness of the disordered soul at such a moment, and throw light upon its hidden workings." As the editor of Orrin Woodford's trial observed, "If Woodford was a sane man, there is deep mystery about him; if insane, there is mystery still."[60]

Such difficulties attributed to ordinary men's and women's efforts to "penetrate the chaotic darkness of the disordered soul" once again affirmed the considerable distance separating their normal minds from the radically different mind of the mental alien. The operations of mental disorder were as "inscrutable, inexplicable and mysterious"[61] as was human evil itself.

Repeated references to the "hidden workings" and impenetrable "recesses" of the human mind point once again to the highly spatial nature of Gothic mystery. As it shaped the insanity defense, this sense of mystery was enhanced by the disposition of certifiedly insane defendants: incarceration in a penitentiary or a mental hospital. Both institutions served as social quarantines for madness, thus reinforcing the popular belief in the mad person's radically alien nature. In the early American period, insanity had been greeted with considerable patience and even tolerance, and most mad persons were cared for by their own families. "Distraction" was regarded as episodic rather than permanent. Minimal efforts were made to "cure" the insane of their condition, on the grounds that their condition manifested a supernatural drama involving God, Satan, and themselves. But in the first years of the nineteenth century, insanity began to take on a separate status with distinctly negative connotations; and a policy of separation and confinement emerged, initially in town almshouses and private asylums, and by the 1830s and '40s in the new state mental asylums.[62]

Some printed accounts of insanity-defense cases suggest a popular fascination with the new social quarantines. When Abner Rogers was acquitted of murder, he was sent at his request to the Worcester State Lunatic Hospital, where he committed suicide several weeks later by diving head-first through a second-story window. The editors of his printed trial report delayed publication in order to include a letter from asylum superintendent Samuel Woodward (who had testified at Rogers's trial), describing his last weeks. He had been anxious and sometimes agitated, fearful that people were trying to poison him, convinced that the hospital was feeding him on human corpses; he saw evil spirits in his room, he said, and smelled the corpses under his bed, and dared not sleep for fear of injury in the night. Such reports bore a close relationship to the popular literature of the asylum exposé, accounts of life behind bars in both the penitentiary and the mental hospital, allegedly written by former inmates. In purporting to unveil the horrors and mysteries of the new enclosures for social deviants, these works underlined the popular fascination with the gulf separating the normal reader from the alien other relegated to secret, terrifying social spaces hidden behind the asylum walls.[63]

The new construction of the murderer as madman or -woman was the purest cultural expression of the murderer as Gothic monster. Deformed in mind, morality, and physiology, the homicidal maniac committed the most horrific of all murders: the most violent, the most pointless, with the least remorse or regret. Of all the crimes incomprehensible to the liberal imagination, these "mad" murders violated most egregiously the enlightened understanding of human nature. The insanity defense represented an effort scientifically to formalize that incomprehensibility; "insanity" was proferred as the catch-all explanation for the homicide that was motiveless, shockingly unanticipated, heinous. Murders by mad people were laden with horror and mystery, the two central components of the rational person's inability to comprehend radical acts of human transgression. The madman, with his misshapen head, wild eyes, and foaming mouth, was the extreme expression of the criminal alien.

The scientific systematization of this understanding of the murderer, which began with the insanity defense in the first half of the nineteenth century, was further formalized in the late nineteenth and early twentieth centuries in the social science of criminal anthropology. Following the lead of Italian criminologist Cesare Lombroso, American physicians, academics, and penal reformers articulated the traits of "criminal man" in ways that simply extended the traits once assigned to the insane criminal to all members of the criminal "class." The "constitutional criminal" was distinguished by a separate sort of criminal brain (closely related to the brains of idiots and paranoiacs, as well as the "lower races" and animals), a criminal cranium (either very small or very large, often irregular in shape), various other anatomical deviations (eyes, ears, nose, teeth, jaws, palate, hair growth, nails, feet, mammary glands, genitalia), a distinctively criminal physiology (manifested in skin tone, pigmentation, headaches and convulsions, fainting spells and dizziness, heart and respiratory problems), and a criminal heredity.[64] With his defective brain, misshapen head, distinctive facial features, and various medical disorders, the criminal offender as constructed by the new science of criminal anthropology closely resembled the homicidal maniac of the early nineteenth century. And both variants of murderer simply captured in scientific terms the moral "monstrosity" of the criminal offender that had first been articulated in the popular crime literature of the late eighteenth and early nineteenth centuries.

The Gothic response to criminal transgression was not a remnant of an older, religious sense of human depravity. On the contrary, it was an incongruous corollary to the modern liberal view of human nature introduced by the Enlightenment. The assertion that human nature is essentially good, rational, free, and capable of self-government mandated the construction of a separate category of humanity to contain the men and women who most flagrantly challenged those assumptions by committing crimes of murder. The Gothic murderer was a moral alien, between whose monstrously deviant nature and the human norm yawned a vast gulf. Popular narratives of the crime both assumed and reinforced that sense of moral and social distance between normality and criminal deviance within two central conventions: the cult of horror, which underlined the incomprehensibility of radical human evil to normal men and women; and the cult of mystery, which assumed the ultimate unknowability of radical human evil by normal men and women. The Gothic narrative of the crime of murder played a primary role in shaping the modern response to criminal transgression, both mandating the social quarantining of criminals in penitentiaries and mental hospitals, and reinforcing the radical otherness of the criminal deviant on which that quarantining rested.

Epilogue

HE AMERICAN fascination with murder continues to flourish in contemporary popular culture. One need not look far to find evidence of it. Leading bookstore chains offer entire sections on "true-crime," shelf after shelf of best-selling paperbacks authored by journalists, prosecutors and defense attorneys, police officers and FBI agents, accused and convicted murderers, friends and relatives of murderers and their victims. Major daily newspapers, weekly newsmagazines, and the tabloid press offer regular media coverage of murders. "Reality TV"—including such shows as *Unsolved Mysteries* and *America's Most Wanted,* and the entire channel devoted to "Court TV"—explores unsolved cases, tracks suspects-at-large, and captures murder trials on camera. On the Internet, the Time-Warner True Crime Forum offers an opportunity for murder buffs to meet in cyberspace for crime chat. And in the thriving "true-crime empire," there is extensive interchange between art and life: murder fiction, film, and television constantly borrow story lines from the most sensationalistic cases; and true-crime writers return the favor, reporting, for example, that the hypnotized serial killer Arthur Shawcross took on the personality of his mother "in a scene eerily reminiscent of *Psycho.*"[1]

The true-crime empire continues to thrive in the late twentieth century because modern culture still offers no systematic and satisfying way to come to terms with human evil. "Evil," queried a cover of *Time* magazine in 1991, "does it exist—or do bad things just happen?" The question posed here is fundamentally theological: is evil a supernatural power engaged in a timeless, cosmic struggle against the forces of Good, or do bad things just happen randomly in an amoral universe devoid of any larger meaning? The author takes the secular option when he defines evil as "the Bad elevated to the status of the inexplicable."[2] After the collapse of the sacred canopy, and the withdrawal of the providential eye that, in seeing and disclosing all evil actions, once imposed upon them a transcendent moral meaning, we are left with no larger explanation for bad things that happen.

Whatever its seamier and more repugnant implications, the popularity of true-crime stories reflects a deep cultural concern about the problem of human evil. The pervasive acceptance of the inexplicability of evil shapes the central and unanswered question that reverberates throughout modern murder stories: "How could there be such evil?" When the police chief of Boulder, Colorado, distressed by intense national coverage of a faltering murder investigation, stated that the JonBenét Ramsey murder was nobody's business but Boulder's, one newsmagazine journalist defended the national coverage, saying "when I think about JonBenét Ramsey, it is not a matter of prurient curiosity; I'm wondering what to believe in . . . Evil on this scale is impossible to comprehend. To know who murdered JonBenét Ramsey is to know what world we live in, where we are."[3]

But as true-crime stories repeatedly demonstrate, to identify the murderer in contemporary culture is *not* the same as to comprehend the evil. For the dominant conventions shaping our own tales of murder remain *mystery* and *horror,* which since the late eighteenth century have continued to express and reinforce the inexplicability of radical human evil within a liberal, secular world view. Shaped by the continuing dominance of legal narrative, murder remains a "mystery," fragmentary and open-ended, resistant to full moral closure. Practically every major participant in the criminal trial of O. J. Simpson has published a book examining the police investigation and the trial, and exploring the many contingencies that went into his acquittal; all the while, the public tries to understand the moral implications of a criminal acquittal followed by the civil judgment of Simpson's accountability for Ron Goldman's violent death.[4] True-crime literature and television invite readers and viewers to examine the facades and interiors, maps and floor plans of crime scenes, and time tables of the defendant's movements, in an effort to reconstruct for themselves just what happened. They offer photographs of murder weapons, bloodstains, and other physical evidence, to enable them to explore for themselves "the shadowy events surrounding the mysterious murder." Even in cases resulting in confessions, the dominant narrative demands that some mystery remain: *Missing Beauty*, the story of a Tufts University professor's murder of a Boston prostitute, closes with the still-unresolved question of where he disposed of her body, a question provocatively highlighted in the book's title.[5]

Contemporary murder also remains overwhelmingly a matter of *horror*. Reviewers praise works that offer "a haunting horror story told in compelling detail." True-crime accounts follow the tradition, established in the late eighteenth century, of competitively claiming, "it's the most horrible crime scene I have ever seen." They still linger on the carnage and gore, follow the autopsy reports with care, and pay particular attention to cases involving torture, dismemberment, and multiple victims. Whereas nineteenth-century murder literature offered occasional sketches of the murder victims, true-crime books almost invariably provide "eight pages of shocking photographs," "eight pages of chilling photos," or "twelve pages of dramatic photos!" which often include pictures of the bloody corpse. The horrific shock of corpse-discovery remains a focal point: "On the roof landing at the top of the stairwell, they came upon a sight of overwhelming horror."[6] Most important, the horror response invoked by contemporary crime continues to feature speechlessness and noncomprehension: the crime depicted is "too horrible to imagine." Horror merges with mystery in the repeated observation, "It was almost impossible to believe that it had happened [horror], let alone to consider who might have been responsible [mystery]."[7]

Contemporary popular culture is still troubled by the moral impli-

Sensational (handwritten margin note)

cations of its own sensationalism, haunted by the pornographic quality of this endless pursuit of ever more grisly murders. But this relentless barrage of murder stories is due to the inability of any single tale of murder to explain "how could there be such evil?" True-crime literature is engaged in an endless exploration of a question to which we have no satisfying answer. All it can do is to repeat over and over again, with each horrifying revelation of some new case, that murder is fundamentally a mystery—resistant to full knowledge and moral comprehension—and a horror—unspeakable, unimaginable, inexplicable. The simple investigative question, "How did this happen?" shades invariably into the deeper moral question, "How could this possibly have happened?" often amplified by the anguished cry of whatever community was the site of the crime, "How could this happen *here?*" A terrible murder occurs, generating large quantities of stories; we consume those stories, and they impress upon us the reality of human evil. But they offer little or no explanation of the evil. To seek answers, we go on reading: new murders are committed, new tales seem to promise answers, and the cycle of inexplicability continues.

At the heart of the issue is the relationship between the reader and the murderer. The cult of horror still labels murderers "monsters," alien creatures utterly apart from the normal men and women around them. "He was a monster," wrote Ann Rule of serial sex-killer Jerome Brudos. Robert Ressler entitled his memoir, *Whoever Fights Monsters: My Twenty Years Tracking Serial Killers for the FBI;* while, at the other end of the manhunt, "Son of Sam" identified himself as "Mr. Monster."[8] True-crime stories make some effort to explain how monsters are made: "What happens to change a chubby-cheeked, freckled five-year-old into a monster?"[9] The answer, typically, involves childhood neglect, abandonment, and abuse, overbearing mothers and absent or inept fathers. But through their sheer inadequacy, such environmental explanations tend to reinforce the basic assumption that a great moral distance separates normal men and women from monstrous murderers. Contemporary tales of murder often promise readers a mental "*journey* into darkness" with the true-crime work serving as the reader's "*passport* into perversion."[10] Evil, they imply, is not native to the reader's country; it is territorially foreign. And they reassure readers that such crimes are ultimately "beyond all imagining," "unspeakable," "unthinkable."[11] That which the evil killer can perform, the presumably moral reader cannot even imagine: and in that failure lies the reader's moral safety.

But at the same time, true crime quietly undermines that sense of moral distance from the monster. Tales of murder routinely emphasize the immediate community's astonishment upon learning that someone they know and trust is the murderer they seek. "He was Jimmie Ray Slaughter, army veteran, a trusted Oklahoma City nurse—and devoted family man." He was "the magnetic, all-American Jeffrey MacDonald," or "a quiet and reclusive bachelor with a lopsided grin and a diffident manner." He was high school coach Gabby Moore, who "wasn't temperamental. He wasn't mean. He was a great guy . . . I still can't understand what happened." Ann Rule spent months writing a book about an unknown serial killer before learning that he was "the stranger beside me," her co-worker on the phone lines at Seattle's Crisis Clinic: "Ted has been described as the perfect son, the perfect student, the Boy Scout grown to adulthood . . . He is all of these things, and none of them. Ted Bundy fits no pattern at all; you could not look at his record and say: 'See, it was inevitable that he would turn out like this.' In fact, it was incomprehensible."[12] When All-American boys, grown-up Boy Scouts, and beloved high-school coaches commit murder, we experience the "terrifying resonance when the most chilling facts curl out of those things we think we know and trust the most." Murder, we are warned, lurks in the "green stucco house on Ocean Breeze Drive" and the "luxurious Boulder, Colorado, home," in the "well-heeled Fresno community" and the "quiet Houston suburb."[13] These are not foreign countries, but native soil.

True-crime stories thus impress upon us "the cruelty and evil of some who walk among us."[14] But at a deeper level, they suggest that evil is not entirely alien to the hearts and minds of true-crime readers. For if the killer is so deeply alien to us, why must we repeatedly imagine ourselves walking in his footsteps, accompanying him to the crime, witnessing his murderous violence, revisiting the scene, examining his weapons, gazing upon his victim? Our fascination with the "monster" betrays our uneasy sense that our intense interest implicates us, if only as voyeurs, in the crime, however much we assert the inhumanity of the murderer. This ambivalent engagement with the murderer is captured in an increasingly popular model for the detective: the FBI profiler, who uses crime-scene photos to imagine himself into the mind of the killer in order to draw up his social and psychological profile. The model for this detective is former Special Agent John Douglas, who in two recent books has claimed credit for the Investigative Support Unit's system for profiling serial killers through intense crime-scene analysis. *"Put yourself in the position of the hunter [meaning, the murderer],"* Douglas invites his readers. "That's what I have to do." A growing body of fictional detectives follow Douglas's lead: most notably, Jack Crawford in Thomas Harris's *Red Dragon* and *The Silence of the Lambs.* Crawford's protegé, Will Graham, calls serial killer Hannibal Lecter a "monster," but after he successfully captures Lecter using Crawford's "mindhunting" technique, Lecter tells him, "The reason you caught me is that we're *just alike!"*[15]

New England Puritans believed that the only reliable safeguard against committing murder was to acknowledge common sinfulness with the murderer, and to be grateful for the restraining hand of divine Providence. Two recent tales of crime return, by strikingly different routes, to a similar position. The film *Seven,* one of the most disturbing horror films ever made, places two New York homicide detectives on the trail of a serial killer who is working on his criminal masterpiece: seven grisly murders staged as "sermons" on the seven deadly sins. Detective William Somerset (played by Morgan Freeman) is a thirty-four-year veteran on the force, a quiet, brooding, solitary man who is about to retire, having seen enough evil to last a lifetime. Detective David Mills (played by Brad Pitt) is his replacement, a hot-tempered young man eager to launch a one-man crusade to clean up the evil of New York City. As body after body turns up, Somerset the Calvinist warns Mills, "You know, this isn't going to have a happy ending." When Mills carelessly says he'll be happy just to catch the killer, Somerset replies, "If we catch John

Doe, and he turns out to be the devil, I mean if he's Satan himself, that might live up to our expectations. But he's not the devil. He's just a man." When Mills labels their prey insane, Somerset warns, "It's dismissive to call him a lunatic," and "We're talking about everyday life here. You can't afford to be this naive." Evil, in Somerset's view, is mundane, human, and ineradicable; for Mills, it is exceptional, aberrant, and stoppable.

In the film's final scene, John Doe completes his criminal masterpiece by deliberately turning the crusader Mills into a murderer. It is Mills who commits the seventh murder, shooting John Doe after learning that the sixth victim was the young detective's beautiful, pregnant wife. Before he pulls the trigger, Somerset warns him, "It's what he wants . . . David, if you kill him, he will win." But John Doe has read Mills's nature too well: his prevailing sin is Wrath, and in his tempestuous battle against evil without, he has failed to come to terms with the evil within. He has indeed proved too "naive" in Somerset's term, too quick to see evil as an occasional, exceptional phenomenon located outside himself. The film concludes with Somerset's words, "Ernest Hemingway once wrote, 'The world is a fine place, and worth fighting for.' I agree with the second part." *Seven* paradoxically enlists the horror genre to undermine the liberal world view which had been its historical foundation.

But *Seven* ultimately remains within the horror genre, and it is likely that many viewers fall in with Mills rather than Somerset, rejoicing when he executes the monster (who has threatened to escape full punishment by pleading insanity). A more dramatic departure from the Gothic narrative of murder is offered in *Dead Man Walking* (1993) by Sister Helen Prejean, a member of the Sisters of St. Joseph of Medaille and a community organizer in the projects of New Orleans. In this powerful work, a *New York Times* best-seller, she tells the story of her service as spiritual adviser to two murderers on death row at the Louisiana State Penitentiary, Angola. Her book thus returns to the seventeenth-century New England genre of the execution sermon, especially the recorded dialogue between the condemned criminal and the minister come to offer spiritual solace and counsel while he awaits death.

{ 247 }

The crimes for which Patrick Sonnier and Robert Lee Willie await execution are horrific. Sonnier and his brother had attacked a teenage couple parked on a lovers' lane, raping the girl and then shooting her and her boyfriend in the head; Willie and a friend had raped and stabbed to death one teenage girl, raped another, and stabbed and shot her boyfriend, leaving him partially paralyzed. But Sister Prejean sticks closely to the orthodox Christian theology of the execution sermon. Her primary concern is that the condemned criminals confess their sins, express contrition (she has an almost Protestant unconcern for the sacrament of Communion), and die without harboring hate for those who wish them dead—on the ideal model of Christ as "Executed Criminal."[16] In Tim Robbins's film *Dead Man Walking* (1995), this focus on the full confession and reconciliation of the murderer Matthew Poncelet (a composite of Sonnier and Willie) is even more central than in Prejean's book. Poncelet resists Sister Helen's appeals for confession until the final half-hour before his execution, and then confesses to rape and murder, winning his adviser's pronouncement, "You are a Son of God." At his execution by lethal injection, Poncelet is strapped to a cross-shaped table which is then rotated to an upright position so he can address the audience in the same posture as the "Executed Criminal."

Prejean's own spiritual challenge in this process is not to shrink from the murderers in horror, not to regard them as monsters. All around her, true-crime storytellers cast the condemned men's crimes as inconceivably evil—"It's hard to imagine that there may be somebody in this fine community of ours who could contemplate, much less carry out, this vilest of vile deeds"—and refer to them as "that monster" and "God's mistake." And Prejean herself initially experiences horror upon learning of their crimes: "I look down at the name in horror. Do I really want to know such a man? . . . The details of the depravity stun me." But throughout her relationships with both men, she struggles to think of them as human beings while never forgetting or condoning their crimes. Preparing her appeal for Sonnier's life before the Pardon Board, she says, "I'll acknowledge the evil Pat has done and make very clear that I in no way condone his terrible crime, but I'll try to show that he is not a monster but a human being like the rest of us in the room."[17] For Sister Helen Prejean, the legislation of the death penalty directly depends on the popular perception of the murderer as subhuman monster; her battle against that perception is part of her opposition to capital punishment.

The foundation for Prejean's insistence on a common humanity is her own conviction of sin. "Why do I feel as if I have murdered someone myself?" she wonders, and concludes it is because she is befriending a murderer. She acknowledges that she, like the murderer, is capable of cruelty, recalling that she once helped some neighbor boys torture an opossum by beating it with a stick. Then she draws a line between herself and the murderer: "I can't bear myself when I hurt someone," she says, "But this is my sensitivity, not Sonnier's. Maybe he doesn't care about the pain he inflicts on others." She feels remorse for her evil actions, while the murderer does not. But Sister Prejean's spiritual work on death row does bring Sonnier to some sense of contrition, thus accomplishing, in her view, his moral reconciliation with the larger human community. The endpoint of Prejean's ritual of reconciliation is, however, dramatically different from that of the New England Puritans: it comes to a passionate opposition to capital punishment, which is the central message of *Dead Man Walking*. As she explains to the captain in charge of the death house, "What he [Sonnier] did was evil. I don't condone it. I just don't see much sense in doing the same to him."[18]

In conventional political parlance, Sister Helen Prejean's opposition to capital punishment makes her a "liberal," and more pejoratively, a bleeding-heart liberal; one murder victim's family calls her and the other nuns who protest executions the "sob sisters."[19] Theologically speaking, however, Prejean is not liberal but orthodox. Historically, her views on crime—evil is mundane, human, and ineradicable—link her to seventeenth-century Puritanism even if her views on punishment do not. In a sense, Sister Helen Prejean follows Puritan views on crime to their logical conclusion in insisting on an end to the death penalty, which in modern society involves identifying "monsters" and attempting to exterminate them. In any case, in reaching for the long-outmoded genre of the execution sermon to address these issues, she offers a rare escape from the still-dominant conventions of the Gothic narrative of murder.

The popularity of *Seven* and *Dead Man Walking* may reflect some cultural movement towards a new critique of the concept of criminal deviance that has held sway since the early nineteenth century. Sister Prejean would clearly have sided with Detective Somerset in the climactic scene of *Seven*. What Prejean and the fictional Somerset have in common is their refusal to participate in the Gothic response to crimes of murder. They will not label murderers as moral aberrations, subhuman monsters. The murderer, they agree, is not the devil; he's just a man, subject to sin as they themselves are subject to sin. And on the grounds of their common humanity both condemn his execution, seeing it as yet one more killing in an endless, meaningless chain of killings. Significantly, neither Detective Somerset nor Sister Prejean is particularly engaged with the challenge of satisfactorily explaining human evil. It is enough simply to acknowledge its universality.

Notes · Index

Notes

Introduction

1. Hayden White, "The Value of Narrativity in the Representation of Reality," in W. J. T. Mitchell, ed., *On Narrative* (Chicago: University of Chicago Press, 1981), p. 23.

1. The Murderer as Common Sinner

1. [John Rogers,] *Death the Certain Wages of Sin to the Impenitent* (Boston: Printed by G. Green and J. Allen for Samuel Phillips, 1701). On infanticide, see Peter C. Hoffer and N. E. H. Hull, *Murdering Mothers: Infanticide in England and New England, 1558–1803* (New York: New York University Press, 1981).
2. Pieter Spierenburg, *The Broken Spell: A Cultural and Anthropological History of Preindustrial Europe* (New Brunswick: Rutgers University Press, 1991), chap. 7; Lawrence Stone, "Interpersonal Violence in English Society, 1300–1980," *Past & Present* 101 (November 1983):22–33; Ted Robert Gurr, "Historical Trends in Violent Crime: A Critical Review of the Evidence," *Crime and Justice: An Annual Review of Research* 3 (1981):295–353; J. M. Beattie, "The Pattern of Crime in England 1660–1800," *Past & Present* 62 (1974):47–95; J. M. Beattie, *Crime and the Courts in England 1660–1800* (Princeton: Princeton University Press, 1986); Karen Halttunen, "Humanitarianism and the Pornography of Pain in Anglo-American Culture," *American Historical Review* 100, 2 (April 1995):303–334.
3. Lincoln B. Faller, *Turned to Account: The Forms and Functions of Criminal Biography in Late Seventeenth- and Early Eighteenth-*

Century England (Cambridge: Cambridge University Press, 1987), pp. 22, 73.

4. David D. Hall, *Worlds of Wonder, Days of Judgment: Popular Religious Belief in Early New England* (Cambridge, Mass.: Harvard University Press, 1990), pp. 72, 80, 176; Spierenburg, *Broken Spell*, pp. 132–134.

5. Margaret Spufford, *Small Books and Pleasant Histories: Popular Fiction and Its Readership in Seventeenth-century England* (Athens, Ga.: University of Georgia Press, 1982), p. 154; J. A. Sharpe, "'Last Dying Speeches': Religion, Ideology, and Public Execution in Seventeenth-Century England," *Past & Present* 107 (1985):144–167; Faller, *Turned to Account*.

6. Eliphalet Adams, *A Sermon Preached on the Occasion of the EXECUTION of Katherine Garret* (New London: T. Green, 1738), p. 25; Rogers, *Death the Certain Wages of Sin*, p. 153. On the execution sermon, see Daniel A. Cohen, *Pillars of Salt, Monuments of Grace: New England Crime Literature and the Origins of American Popular Culture, 1674–1860* (New York: Oxford University Press, 1993), Parts I and II; Hall, *Worlds of Wonder*, pp. 178–184; Ronald A. Bosco, "Lectures at the Pillory: The Early American Execution Sermon," *American Quarterly* 30 (Summer 1978):156–176; Daniel E. Williams, "Rogues, Rascals and Scoundrels: The Underworld Literature of Early America," *American Studies* 24 (Fall 1983):5–19; Daniel E. Williams, "'Behold a Tragick Scene Strangely Changed into a Theater of Mercy': The Structure and Significance of Criminal Conversion Narratives in Early New England," *American Quarterly* 38 (Winter 1986):827–847.

7. Rogers, *Death the Certain Wages*, p. 147; Adams, *Sermon Preached on the Occasion*, p. 42; Cotton Mather, *Pillars of Salt* (Boston: B. Green and J. Allen, 1699), Preface.

8. Harry S. Stout, *Preaching and Religious Culture in Colonial New England* (New York: Oxford University Press, 1986); Donald M. Scott, *From Office to Profession: The New England Ministry 1750–1850* (Philadelphia: University of Pennsylvania Press, 1978), chap. 1; Richard D. Brown, *Knowledge Is Power: The Diffusion of Information in Early America, 1700–1865* (New York: Oxford University Press, 1989), p. 279.

9. Hall, *Worlds of Wonder*, p. 31; Roger Chartier, *The Cultural Uses of Print in Early Modern France*, trans. Lydia G. Cochrane (Princeton: Princeton University Press, 1987), introduction; Natalie Zemon Davis, "Printing and the People," in *Society and Culture in Early Modern France* (Stanford: Stanford University Press, 1975), pp. 189–226.

10. Increase Mather, *Sermon Occasioned by the Execution of a Man* (Boston: Joseph [oblit.], 1686), p. 9; Benjamin Colman, *The Hainous Nature of the Sin of Murder* (Boston: John Allen, 1713), p. 6.

11. Nathaniel Clap, *Sinners Directed to Hear & Fear* (Boston: J. Allen for N. Boone, 1715), p. 39. Samuel Checkley, *Murder a Great and Crying Sin* (Boston: T. Fleet, 1733), p. 3.

12. Clap, *Sinners Directed*, p. 39; Increase Mather, *Sermon Occasioned*, p. 24.

13. The Calvinist clergy played a key role in justifying capital punishment for crimes including murder from the seventeenth century on; see Cohen, *Pillars of Salt*, chap. 5.

14. Cotton Mather, *The Sad Effects of Sin* (Boston: John Allen, 1713), p. 23.

15. *The Westminster Confession of Faith* and *The Shorter Catechism* both quoted in H. Shelton Smith, *Changing Conceptions of Original Sin: A Study in American Theology Since 1750* (New York: Charles Scribner's Sons, 1955), p. 2. Also see Charles Lloyd Cohen, *God's Caress: The Psychology of Puritan Religious Experience* (New York: Oxford University Press, 1986), chap. 1.

16. Rogers, *Death the Certain Wages*, p. 95; Samuel Willard, *Impenitent Sinners Warned* (Boston: B. Green & J. Allen, 1698), p. 48.

17. John Williams, *Warnings to the Unclean* (Boston: B. Green and J. Allen, 1699), p. 42; Joshua Moodey, *An Exhortation to a Condemned Malefactor*, included in Cotton Mather, *The Call of the Gospel Applyed* (Boston: R.P., [1686]), p. 87; Thomas Foxcroft, *Lessons of Caution to Young Sinners* (Boston: S. Kneeland and T. Green, 1733), pp. 49 and 50.

18. Willard, *Impenitent Sinners Warned*, p. 26; Cotton Mather, *Pillars of Salt*, p. 107; Increase Mather, *Sermon Occasioned*, p. 20; Cotton Mather, *Warnings from the Dead* (Boston: Bartholomew Green, 1693), p. 73. Also see Cohen, *Pillars of Salt*, chap. 4.

19. Foxcroft, *Lessons of Caution*, p. 60; William Shurtleff, *The Faith and Prayer of a Dying Malefactor* (Boston: J. Draper for D. Henchman, 1740), p. ii.

20. Williams, *Warnings to the Unclean*, p. 21; Samuel Moody, *Summary Account of the Life and Death of Joseph Quasson* (Boston: Gerrish, 1726), p. 37; Cotton Mather, *Tremenda* (Boston: B. Green, 1721), p. 26.

21. Thomas Shepard, *The Sincere Convert*, and *The Diary of Samuel Sewall*, both quoted in Hall, *Worlds of Wonder*, pp. 134 and 216. On this point, see Faller, *Turned to Account*, pp. 54, 81; David J. Rothman, *The Discovery of the Asylum: Social Order and Disorder in the New Republic* (Boston: Little, Brown, 1971), pp. 15–18; Richard Slotkin, "Narratives of Negro Crime in New England, 1675–1800," *American Quarterly* 25 (March 1973):3–31.

22. Arthur Browne, *Religious Education of Children Recommended* (Boston: S. Kneeland and T. Green, 1739), p. 15; Mather Byles, *The Prayer and Plea of David* (Boston: Samuel Kneeland, 1751), p. 16; Shurtleff, *Faith and Prayer*, p. 17; Clap, *Sinners Directed*, pp. 36–37.

23. Foxcroft, *Lessons of Caution*, p. 35; Cotton Mather, *Valley of Hinnom*, (Boston: J. Allen for Robert Starke, 1717), p. 1. Increase Mather was more informative but scarcely less brief in his explanation that James Morgan's victim provoked him with "ill language," prompting Morgan to "run the Spit into his bowels"; *Sermon Occasioned*, p. 18.

24. Mather, *Pillars of Salt*, p. 68.

25. "Rebekah Chamblit's Declaration, Dying Warnings and Advice," in Foxcroft, *Lessons of Caution*, following sermon; *A Faithful Narrative of the Wicked Life and Remarkable Conversion of Patience Boston* (Boston: S. Kneeland and T. Green, 1738).

26. Cotton Mather, *A Vial Poured Out upon the Sea* (Boston: T. Fleet, 1726), p. 1, and Benjamin Colman, *It Is a Fearful Thing to Fall into the Hands of the Living God* (Boston: John Philip and Thomas Hancock, 1726), p. 30; Mather, *Tremenda*, p. 34.

27. Byles, *Prayer and Plea of David*, p. 18; Willard, *Impenitent Sinners Warned*, p. 27.

28. Moodey, *Exhortation to a Condemned Malefactor*, p. 78; Foxcroft, *Lessons of Caution*, p. i; Adams, *Sermon Preached on the Occasion*, p. 39; Rogers, *Death the Certain Wages*, p. 118.

29. Foxcroft, *Lessons of Caution*, pp. i, 55. On the criminal conversion narratives, see Cohen, *Pillars of Salt*, chap. 3; and Williams, "'Behold a Tragick Scene.'"

30. Shurtleff, *Faith and Prayer*, pp. 25–30; Rogers, *Death the Certain Wages*, pp. 139 and 153.

31. Nathanael Clap, *Some of the Last Words of Several Dying Persons Considered*, bound with *The Lord's Voice, Crying to His People* (Boston: B. Green, 1715), p. 134; Rogers, *Death the Certain Wages*, p. 68.

32. Increase Mather, *Sermon Occasioned*, p. 27; Cotton Mather, *Valley of Hinnom*, p. 2; Moody, *Summary Account*, p. 1.

33. John Demos, ed., *Remarkable Providences 1600–1760* (New York: George Braziller, 1972), pp. 20–22.

34. Foxcroft, *Lessons of Caution*, p. ii; Cotton Mather, *Speedy Repentance Urged* (Boston: Samuel Green, 1690), p. 82; John Webb, *The Greatness of Sin Improv'd by the Penitent* (Boston: S. Kneeland and T. Green, 1734), p. 23.

35. Rogers, *Death the Certain Wages*, p. 118. See Bosco, "Lectures at the Pillory"; and Williams, "'Behold a Tragick Scene'"; Cohen, *Pillars of Salt*, pp. 48–49.

36. The social function of the execution sermon as jeremiad suggests that murders committed by members of these social groups may have received disproportionate attention at the printing press.

{256}

37. Foxcroft, *Lessons of Caution*, p. i.
38. Sharpe, "'Last Dying Speeches'", p. 162. See Michel Foucault, *Discipline and Punish: The Birth of the Prison*, Alan Sheridan, trans. (New York: Pantheon, 1977); Pieter Spierenburg, *The Spectacle of Suffering: Executions and the Evolution of Repression from a Preindustrial Metropolis to the European Experience* (Cambridge: Cambridge University Press, 1984); Peter Burke, *Popular Culture in Early Modern Europe* (New York: Harper & Row, 1978), pp. 197–198. More useful to my own interpretation are Faller, *Turned to Account*, pp. xi, 245; and Randall McGowen, "The Body and Punishment in Eighteenth-century England," *Journal of Modern History* 59, 4 (December 1987):651–679.
39. Colman, *Hainous Nature*, p. 24; Moody, *Summary Account*, pp. 27, 25.
40. Rogers, *Death the Certain Wages*, p. 118; John Dunton, quoted in Edwin Powers, *Crime and Punishment in Early Massachusetts 1620–1692: A Documentary History* (Boston: Beacon Press, 1966), p. 298. Dunton's observation suggests a sharp contrast between the solemnity and compassion of the New England execution audience, and the "carnivalesque" qualities of the English audience which was typically festive, boisterous, ribald, and drunk; see Thomas W. Laqueur, "Crowds, Carnival and the State in English Executions, 1604–1868," in *The First Modern Society: Essays in English History in Honour of Lawrence Stone*, ed. A. L. Beier, David Cannadine, James M. Rosenheim (Cambridge: Cambridge University Press, 1989), pp. 305–355.
41. Foxcroft, *Lessons of Caution*, n.p.; Cotton Mather, *Pillars of Salt*, p. 62.
42. Cotton Mather, *Valley of Hinnom*, pp. 2 and 22; Cotton Mather, *Pillars of Salt*, p. 77.
43. Lincoln Faller, *Turned to Account*, chaps. 3 and 5. Also see Cynthia Herrup, "Law and Morality in Seventeenth-century England," *Past & Present* 106 (1985):102–123.
44. Samuel Davies, quoted in Smith, *Changing Conception*, p. 8.
45. Thomas Tillam, "Upon the first sight of New England, June 29, 1638," quoted in Andrew Delbanco, *The Death of Satan: How Americans Have Lost the Sense of Evil* (New York: Farrar, Strauss, and Giroux, 1995), p. 32.
46. See Chadwick Hansen, *Witchcraft at Salem* (New York: George Braziller, 1969), chap. 11; Richard Slotkin, *Regeneration through Violence: The Mythology of the American Frontier, 1600–1850* (Middletown: Wesleyan University Press, 1973), chap. 5; John Putnam Demos, *Entertaining Satan: Witchcraft and the Culture of Early New England* (New York: Oxford University Press, 1982); Hall, *Worlds of Wonder*, chap. 2.
47. Hall, *Worlds of Wonder*, p. 80; Alan Macfarlane, "The Root of All Evil,"

in David Parkin, ed., *The Anthropology of Evil* (Oxford: Basil Blackwell, 1985), pp. 57–76.

48. See Hall, *Worlds of Wonder*, p. 18.

49. Thomas Hooker, "A True Sight of Sin," in Perry Miller and Thomas H. Johnson, eds., *The Puritans*, rev. ed., vol. 1 (New York: Harper Torchbooks, 1963), p. 292; Thomas Shepard, "Journal," quoted in Charles E. Hambrick-Stowe, *The Practice of Piety: Puritan Devotional Disciplines in Seventeenth-Century New England* (Chapel Hill: The University of North Carolina Press, 1982), p. 166.

50. Cotton Mather is quoted in Edmund S. Morgan, *The Puritan Family: Religion and Domestic Relations in Seventeenth-Century New England* (New York: Harper and Row, 1966), p. 97. Also see Slotkin, *Regeneration through Violence*, chaps. 4 and 5; and Hambrick-Stowe, *Practice of Piety*, chap. 8.

51. Cotton Mather, quoted in Hansen, *Witchcraft at Salem*, p. 171; also see Mather, *The Wonders of the Invisible World* (Boston, 1693), p. 55.

52. Quoted in Demos, ed., *Remarkable Providences*, p. 371; and in Chadwick Hansen, *Witchcraft at Salem* (New York: George Braziller, 1969), p. 19.

53. Benjamin Colman, quoted in Delbanco, *Death of Satan*, p. 31; Delbanco, *Death of Satan*, p. 43.

54. David Thomas Konig, *Law and Society in Puritan Massachusetts: Essex County, 1629–1692* (Chapel Hill: University of North Carolina Press, 1979), p. 175.

55. Robbins is quoted in David H. Flaherty, *Privacy in Colonial New England* (Charlottesville: University Press of Virginia, 1972), p. 159; Emil Oberholzer, Jr., *Delinquent Saints: Disciplinary Action in the Early Congregational Churches of Massachusetts* (New York: Columbia University Press, 1956).

56. Roger Thompson, *Sex in Middlesex: Popular Mores in a Massachusetts County, 1649–1699* (Amherst: University of Massachusetts Press, 1986), p. 198; trial witness quoted on p. 7. Also see Konig, *Law and Society in Puritan Massachusetts*, p. 124; Jules Zanger, "Crime and Punishment in Early Massachusetts," *William and Mary Quarterly* 22 (1965):471–477; George Lee Haskins, *Law and Authority in Early Massachusetts: A Study in Tradition and Design* (New York: The Macmillan Co., 1960), pp. 204–211; Powers, *Crime and Punishment*, chaps. 6–8.

57. See Eli Faber, "Puritan Criminals: The Economic, Social, and Intellectual Background to Crime in Seventeenth-Century Massachusetts," *Perspectives in American History* 11 (1977–78), pp. 129, 137–142; Powers, *Crime and Punishment*, p. 414; John P. Demos, *A Little Commonwealth:*

Family Life in Plymouth Colony (Oxford: Oxford University Press, 1970), pp. 70, 184; Rothman, *Discovery of the Asylum*, chap. 2.

58. *Faithful Narrative of Patience Boston*, p. 35.

59. On execution sermons as "sensationalism," see Hall, *Worlds of Wonder*, esp. pp. 56–57, 133–137, 183; Williams, "Rogues, Rascals and Scoundrels," pp. 6–8.

60. Clap, *Sinners Directed*, p. 39; Rogers, *Death the Certain Wages*, p. 14;. Increase Mather, *Sermon Occasioned*, p. 12. A few exceptions proved this rule.

61. Hall, *Worlds of Wonder*, pp. 84, 131, 195.

62. Phillipe Ariès, *The Hour of Our Death*, trans. Helen Weaver (New York: Alfred A. Knopf, 1981), chap. 2; Spierenburg, *Broken Spell*, pp. 125–162; David E. Stannard, *The Puritan Way of Death: A Study in Religion, Culture, and Social Change* (New York: Oxford University Press, 1977), chap. 5; Charles O. Jackson, ed., *Passing: The Vision of Death in America* (Westport, Conn.: Greenwood Press, 1977)

63. In applying the sociology of *deviance* to Puritan "crime waves," Kai Erikson has superimposed a modern analysis of the criminal transgressor upon a culture which did not embrace this understanding of the sinner as moral alien; see *Wayward Puritans: A Study in the Sociology of Deviance* (New York: Wiley, 1966).

2. The Birth of Horror

1. *A Brief Narrative of the Life and Confession of Barnett Davenport* ([Hartford?], 1780), p. 10.

2. Ibid., pp. 11, 12, 9.

3. Ibid., pp. 10, 14.

4. Ibid., p. 10.

5. Samson Occom, *A Sermon Preached at the Execution of Moses Paul* (New London: T. Green, [1772]); Aaron Bascom, *A Sermon Preached at the Execution of Abiel Converse* (Northampton: William Butler, 1788); Elijah Waterman, *A Sermon, Preached at Windham* (Springfield, Mass.: Henry Brewer, [1803]); Sylvanus Conant, *The Blood of Abel, and the Blood of Jesus* (Boston: Edes and Gill, 1764), p. 19; Joshua Spaulding, *A Sermon Delivered at Salem* (Salem: Dabney and Cushing, 1787), p. 19.

6. *Account of a Horrid Murder, Committed by Captain William Corran* (Philadelphia, 1794); *The American Bloody Register* (Boston: Russell, 1784).

7. *A Poem on the Execution of Samuel Frost* (broadside) (Worcester: Isaiah Thomas [?], 1793); *A Tribute to the Memory of Catherine Berrenger* (broadside) (n.p., 1800).

NOTES TO PAGES 36–38

8. *A Narrative of the Life Together with the Last Speech, Confession, and Solemn Declaration of John Lewis* (New Haven: James Parker, 1762); *An Authentic and Particular Account of the Life of Francis Burdett Personel* (New York, 1773).

9. *The Trial of Alice Clifton* [N.p., n.d.]. For a detailed discussion of the emergence of the printed trial report, see chap. 4.

10. David D. Hall, "The Uses of Literacy in New England, 1600–1850," in William L. Joyce, David D. Hall, Richard D. Brown, John B. Hench, eds., *Printing and Society in Early America* (Worcester: American Antiquarian Society, 1983), pp. 1–47; Cathy N. Davidson, ed., *Reading in America: Literature and Social History* (Baltimore: The Johns Hopkins University Press, 1989), Introduction, pp. 1–26 (John Adams is quoted on p. 9); Richard D. Brown, *Knowledge Is Power: The Diffusion of Information in Early America, 1700–1865* (New York: Oxford University Press, 1989); William J. Gilmore, *Reading Becomes a Necessity of Life: Material and Cultural Life in Rural New England, 1780–1835* (Knoxville: University of Tennessee Press, 1989), pp. 198, 203.

11. Gilmore, *Reading Becomes a Necessity*, p. 157.

12. See Robert Darnton, "What Is the History of Books?" in Davidson, ed., *Reading in America*, pp. 27–52; Gilmore, *Reading Becomes a Necessity;* Hall, "The Uses of Literacy"; Davidson, introduction to *Reading in America*.

13. See Brown, *Knowledge Is Power;* Harry S. Stout, *Preaching and Religious Culture in Colonial New England* (New York: Oxford University Press, 1986); Donald M. Scott, *From Office to Profession: The New England Ministry, 1750–1850* (Philadelphia: University of Pennsylvania Press, 1978), chap. 2; Robert A. Ferguson, *Law and Letters in American Culture* (Cambridge, Mass.: Harvard University Press, 1984). The Trumbull quote is from Ferguson, p. 102.

14. Lennard J. Davis, *Factual Fictions: The Origins of the English Novel* (Philadelphia: University of Pennsylvania Press, 1996), p. xi; Samuel Richardson is quoted on p. 182. Also see J. Paul Hunter, *Before Novels: The Cultural Contexts of Eighteenth-Century English Fiction* (New York: W. W. Norton, 1990); John Bender, *Imagining the Penitentiary: Fiction and the Architecture of Mind in Eighteenth-Century England* (Chicago: University of Chicago Press, 1987); Terry Castle, *Masquerade and Civilization: The Carnivalesque in Eighteenth-Century English Culture and Fiction* (Stanford: Stanford University Press, 1986); Leopold Damrosch, Jr., *God's Plot and Man's Stories: Studies in the Fictional Imagination from Milton to Fielding* (Chicago: University of Chicago Press, 1985).

15. "Real life" is Samuel Richardson's term, quoted in Davis, *Factual Fic-*

tions, p. 182; Bender, *Imagining the Penitentiary*, p. 155; Ian Watt, *The Rise of the Novel* (Berkeley: University of California Press, 1964), p. 200.

16. Bender, *Imagining the Penitentiary*, p. 186; Paul Ricoeur, quoted in Peter Brooks, *Reading for the Plot: Design and Intention in Narrative* (New York: Vintage Books, 1985), p. 13.

17. See Hunter, *Before Novels*, chap. 12; Bender, *Imagining the Penitentiary*, (Hume is quoted on p. 6); Gilmore, *Reading Becomes a Necessity*, p. 15; Brooks, *Reading for the Plot*, p. 6.

18. *Narrative of Lewis*, pp. 3–4; *Trial of Clifton*, p. 9; *The Confession of Mary Cole* (New York: n.p. [1813?]), p. 10; *Banks' Life and Death. The Only Correct Account of the Life, Trial, and Confession of John Banks* (New York: n.p., 1807), p. 10.

19. *The Trial of Alpheus Hitchcock*, reported by George Richards, Jr. (Utica: Seward and Williams for George Richards, Jr., 1807), p. 42; *Trial of John Graham* (Baltimore: Frayer & Clark, [1804]), p. 21.

20. *Confession of John Joyce* (Philadelphia: No. 12 Walnut St., 1808), p. 7; *A Sketch of the Proceedings and Trial of William Hardy* (Boston: Oliver and Munroe, 1807).

21. *Murders. Report of the Trial of James Johnson* (New York: Southwick and Pelsue, 1811); *Trial of Edward Tinker* (Newbern [N.C.]: Hall and Bryan and T. Watson, 1811); *Horrid Massacre!! Sketches of the Life of Captain James Purrinton* (Augusta: Peter Edes, 1806). For a detailed treatment of the Purrinton murders in their neighborhood context, see Laurel Thatcher Ulrich, *A Midwife's Tale: The Life of Martha Ballard, Based on Her Diary, 1785–1812* (New York: Alfred A. Knopf, 1990), chap. 9.

22. *Horrid Massacre!!*, p. 4; *Impartial Account of the Trial of Ebenezer Mason* (Dedham: Mann, 1802); Enoch Huntington, *A Sermon Preached at Haddam* (Middletown, Conn.: Moses H. Woodward, 1797), pp. 23–24.

23. Bender, *Imagining the Penitentiary*, p. 11; also see Patricia Meyer Spacks, *Imagining a Self: Autobiography and Novel in Eighteenth-Century England* (Cambridge, Mass.: Harvard University Press, 1976). For murder accounts that included letters from the murderer, see *The Confession of John Battus* (n.p., [1804?]), pp. 16–29; *A Brief Account of the Trial of Winslow Russell* (n.p., [1811?]), p. 19; John W. Kirn, *Sketch of the Trial of Mary Cole* (Norwich: Israel Brumley, 1813), pp. 8–10.

24. *Authentic and Particular Account of the Life of Francis Burdett Personel*. Also see *The Dying Confession of Charles Cunningham* (Northampton [Mass.], 1805).

25. For the influence of Locke in eighteenth-century America, see Jay Fliegelman, *Prodigals and Pilgrims: The American Revolution Against Patriarchal Authority, 1750–1800* (New York: Cambridge University

NOTES TO PAGES 42–46

Press, 1982); Henry F. May, *The Enlightenment in America* (Oxford: Oxford University Press, 1976), part I; Donald H. Meyer, *The Democratic Enlightenment* (New York: G. P. Putnam's Sons, 1976).

26. Meyer, *Democratic Enlightenment* p. 43.

27. By Lemuel Briant, 1749; see May, *Enlightenment in America*, p. 56.

28. Joseph Haroutunian, *Piety versus Moralism: The Passing of the New England Theology* (New York: Harper and Row, 1970); Meyer, *Democratic Enlightenment*, chap. 3; May, *Enlightenment in America*, chap. 3.

29. *Trial of Mason*, p. 9; *Trial of Tinker*, p. 41.

30. *Trial of Russell*, pp. 5–6; *The Life and Confession of Cato* (Johnstown: Romeyn, 1803); *Trial of Cole*; Moses C. Welch, *Sketch of the Circumstances of the Birth, Education and Manners of Caleb's Life*, bound with Waterman, *Sermon Preached at Windham*, pp. 20, 27.

31. *Narrative of the Life of John Lewis*; Thaddeus Maccarty, *The Guilt of Innocent Blood Put Away* (Worcester: Isaiah Thomas, 1778), p. 36.

32. *Trial of Tinker*, p. 59; *Trial of Hitchcock*, p. 49. The Tinker trial also included usage of the term by a witness who was not a legal professional, p. 15.

33. *Horrid Massacre!!*, p. 16; Conant, *Blood of Abel*, p. 21; *An Account of the Trial of Joseph Andrews* (New York, 1769), p. 6; Henry Channing, *God Admonishing His People of Their Duty* (New London: T. Green, 1786), p. 5; *Trial of Hardy*, p. 18. On eighteenth-century views of the "passions" vs. the "sentiments," see Gilmore, *Reading Becomes a Necessity*, p. 40.

34. *Confession of John Joyce*, pp. 12–13; Huntington, *Sermon Preached*, pp. 23–24; *Murder—Horrible Murder!! Clarksburg, Virginia* [Morgantown? 1805?], (broadside).

35. *The Trial of Stephen Arnold* (Cooperstown [N.Y.]: Phinney, [1805]); *Narrative of Davenport*, pp. 11, 10; *Last Speech and Confession of Henry Halbert* (Philadelphia: Anthony Ambruster, [1765]), p. 5; *Confession of Joyce*, p. 14.

36. James Dana, *Men's Sins Not Chargeable on God* (New Haven: T. & S. Green, [1783]), p. 21; also see *Horrid Massacre!!*, p. 18; *Trial of Clifton*, p. 9.

37. Nathan Fiske, *A Sermon Preached at Brookfield* (Boston: Thomas & John Fleet, 1778), p. 6; *Narrative of Davenport*, p. 12.

38. *Trial of Graham*, p. 17; *Trial of Tinker*, pp. 42–43; *Confession of Joyce*, p. iii; *A Correct and Concise Account of the Interesting Trial of Jason Fairbanks* (Boston, [1801?]), p. 8. Also see *The Confession of John Battus, A Mulatto . . .* (n.p., [1804?]), p. 11; and *The Trial of David Lynn, Prince Kein, Jabez Meiggs [et al.]* (Augusta: Peter Edes, 1809), p. 36.

39. *A Narrative of the Life of William Beadle* (Hartford: Bavil Webster, 1783, p. 19; *Confession of Battus*, p. 19.

40. Jonathan Plummer, *Murder!! Death of Miss Mack Coy, and the Young Teazer* (Boston: [Coverly, 1813]), broadside; Welch, *Sketch of Caleb's Life*, p. 27; *Trial of Tinker*, p. 43. Also see *Report of the Trial of Dominic Daley and James Halligan* (Northampton: S. & E. Butler, booksellers; T. M. Pomroy, printer, [1806]), pp. 33–34.

41. Some execution sermons did anticipate this notion of the subhumanity of the murderer; see Nathaniel Clap, *Sinners Directed to Hear & Fear* (Boston: J. Allen for N. Boone, 1715), pp. 39–40; Cotton Mather, *Speedy Repentance Urged* (Boston: Samuel Green, 1690), p. 1; John Rogers, *Death the Certain Wages of Sin* (Boston: Printed by G. Green and J. Allen for Samuel Phillips, 1701), p. 69. But their overriding emphasis was that the murderer acted out of a depraved nature shared with the rest of his fellows; and their references to the murderer as monster worked within their larger understanding of "that ugly Monster Sin" that afflicted all humankind; see Cotton Mather, *Tremenda* (Boston: B. Green, 1721), p. 2.

42. Quoted in Elizabeth MacAndrew, *The Gothic Tradition in Fiction* (New York: Columbia University Press, 1979), p. 23. Emphasis added.

43. *Trial of Tinker*, pp. 76, 84; *The Last Words of Ebenezer Mason* (Boston, [1802]), introduction; *Trial of Mason* (Dedham: Mann, 1802).

44. See David D. Hall, *Worlds of Wonder, Days of Judgment: Popular Religious Belief in Early New England* (Cambridge, Mass.: Harvard University Press, 1990), chap. 2.

45. MacAndrew, *Gothic Tradition*, pp. 24, 4. For a full discussion of the psychological narrative of evil, in the form of the insanity defense, see chap. 7.

46. *The Confession and Dying Words of Samuel Frost* (Worcester: Isaiah Thomas [1793]), broadside.

47. Charles Chauncy, *The Horrid Nature, and Enormous Guilt of MURDER* (Boston: Thomas Fleet, 1754), pp. 12, 17; Fiske, *Sermon Preached*, p. 8.

48. *Trial of Tinker*, p. 63.

49. Conant, *Blood of Abel*, p. 32 (the "Pity" also invoked by this account seems to have been for the victim, not her killer); Fiske, *Sermon Preached*, p. 6.

50. *Confession of Cole*, p. 3.

51. *Narrative of Lewis*, p. 4; Channing, *God Admonishing His People; Confession of Joyce; Biography of Mr. Jason Fairbanks and Miss Eliza Fales* (Boston: Pandamonium Press, 1801), broadside.

52. *The Interesting Trials of the Pirates* (Newburyport: Herald Press, [1797]); *The Trials of Samuel M. Mayo and William Love* (Augusta [Me.]: Chronicle Office, 1807); *Trial of James Anthony* (Rutland [Vt.]: Fay & Davison, [1814]).

53. *Trial of Anthony*, p. 18; *Horrid Massacre!!*, p. 6.

54. *A Correct Account of the Trials of Charles M'Manus, John Hauer [et al.]* (Harrisburgh: John Wyeth, 1798), p. 128; Holloway Whitfield Hunt, *Sermon Preached at the Execution of Matthias Gotlieb* (Newton, N.J., 1796), p. 7; *A Mournful Tragedy* (N.p., n.d.), broadside; *Correct Trial of Fairbanks*, p. 5.

55. Plummer, *Murder!! Death of Miss Mack Coy; Murder. Narrative of the Trial, Conviction and Execution of Captain William Corran* (Halifax, printed July 27, Newport, reprinted, September 12, 1794), pp. 5–6.

56. *Trial of Clifton*, p. 1; *Report of the Trial of Susanna* (Troy: Ryer Schermerhorn, 1810), pp. 6–7; Fiske, *Sermon*, p. 5. Fiske's sermon was a new literary form ideally suited for such attention: the funeral sermon for the murder victim, which was preached in the presence of the corpse. Also see "Extracts from the Rev. Mr. Marsh's Sermon at the Funeral of his [William Beadle's] Wife and Children," in *Narrative of Beadle* (1783), p. 18.

57. *A Narrative of the Life of William Beadle* (Bennington, Haswell, 1794) identified "Esquire Mitchell" as one of two men who were first on the scene of the familicide; see pp. 34–40, and the discussion below.

58. Italics mine. [Stephen Mix Mitchell], *A Narrative of the Life of William Beadle* (Hartford: Bavil Webster, 1783); *Narrative of Beadle* (1794); and *A Narrative of the Life of William Beadle* (Windsor: Alden Spooner, 1795).

59. *Narrative of Beadle* (1783), pp. 17, 9.

60. *Narrative of Beadle* (1794), pp. 37, 38. The *Narrative* similarly dealt with the reaction of the crowds who came to view the bodies after word of the murders got out, observing that "The very inmost souls of the beholders were wounded at the sight, and torn by contending passions," and emphasizing the "agitation of mind which must be the consequence of being near such a scene of horror," p. 10.

61. *Narrative of Beadle* (1783), pp. 19, 20.

62. Ibid., p. 18.

63. Channing, *God Admonishing*, pp. 29–30; *Confession of Cole*, p. 4; *Trial of Daley and Halligan*, p. 7. By 1806, the corpse-discovery scene had acquired sufficient cultural power to shape midwife Martha Ballard's response to the Purrinton familicide in her own neighborhood: "My son went in and found a Candle, which he lit and to his great surprise said Purington, his wife & six Children Corps! . . . My husband went and returned before sunrise when after taking a little food he and I went on to the house there to behold the most shocking scein that was Even seen in this part of the world." Ulrich, *Midwife's Tale*, p. 291.

64. *Confession of Joyce*, p. 6; Channing, *God Admonishing*, p. 5; *Trial of Hardy*, p. 23.

65. See Malcom Ware, "Sublimity in the Novels of Ann Radcliffe: A Study of the Influence upon Her Craft of Edmund Burke's *Enquiry into the Origin of Our Ideas of the Sublime and Beautiful*" (Upsala: A. B. Lundequistska Bokhandeln, 1963), p. 16.

66. *Narrative of Beadle* (1783), p. 10; (1794), p. 37. Speaking of the scene of the Beadle familicide, Mitchell reported that "description can do no more than faintly ape and trifle with the real figure," p. 10.

67. Wheland, *Narrative of the Horrid Murder,* p. 6; *Horrid Massacre!!,* p. 5; *Report of the Trial of Jason Fairbanks* (Boston: Russell and Cutler, 1801), p. 73; *Trial of Daley and Halligan,* p. 3.

68. *Biography of Fairbanks and Fales; Trial of Jameson and M'Gowan,* p. 21.

69. Moses Baldwin, *The Ungodly Condemned in Judgment* (Boston: Kneeland & Adams, 1771); Chauncy, *Horrid Nature,* p. 17.

70. *Confession of Battus,* pp. 3, 8, 10–12, 18, 19, 22.

71. For an excellent discussion of this transformation of the criminal into moral alien, see Cynthia B. Herrup, "Law and Morality in 17th-century England," *Past & Present* 106 (February 1985):102–123. Also see Roy Porter, *Mind-Forg'd Manacles: A History of Madness in England from the Restoration to the Regency* (Cambridge, Mass.: Harvard University Press, 1987); Keith Thomas, "Other Modes of Thought" (a review of Porter), *Times Literary Supplement* 4418 (December 4–10 1987):1339–1340; George L. Mosse, *Nationalism and Sexuality: Respectability and Abnormal Sexuality in Modern Europe* (New York: Howard Fertig, 1985).

72. Meyer, *Democratic Enlightenment,* p. 7; Andrew Delbanco, *The Death of Satan: How Americans Have Lost the Sense of Evil* (New York: Farrar, Straus and Giroux, 1995), p. 64; May, *Enlightenment in America,* p. 60.

73. Quoted in Meyer, *Democratic Enlightenment,* p. 10.

3. The Pornography of Violence

1. *Life of the Celebrated Salem Murderer, Richard Crowninshield* (N.p., 1845), p. 2; *The Trial in the Case of the Commonwealth, versus John Francis Knapp* [Salem? 1830?] [entry #570 in Thomas McDade, *The Annals of Murder: A Bibliography of Books and Pamphlets on American Murders from Colonial Times to 1900* (Norman, Ok.: University of Oklahoma Press, 1961); McDade numbers will be cited when necessary to distinguish similar accounts, pp. 5–6, 14]. Also see Howard A. Bradley and James A. Winans, *Daniel Webster and the Salem Murder* (Columbia, Mo.: Artcraft Press, 1956).

2. Samuel McCall, quoted in Bradley and Winans, *Daniel Webster and the Salem Murder,* p. 219. Webster delivered similar speeches at both trials, which were recorded with variations by a range of reporters, and finally

edited for publication by Webster himself; my treatment draws from all versions printed at the time of the case.

3. *The Most Important Testimony Adduced on the Trial of John Francis Knapp* (Providence: H. H. Brown, 1830) (McDade 566), p. 33; *Trial of George Crowninshield, J. J. Knapp, Jun. and John Francis Knapp* (Boston: Beals and Homer, and Francis Ingraham, 1830) (McDade 571), pp. 92–93; *Trial of John Francis Knapp* (Boston: Dutton & Wentworth, 1830) (McDade 572), p. 57.

4. James B. Twitchell, *Dreadful Pleasures: An Anatomy of Modern Horror* (New York: Oxford University Press, 1985); *Life of Crowninshield*, p. 2.

5. [William Wollaston], *The Religion of Nature Delineated* (London, 1724), p. 139; David B. Morris, *The Culture of Pain* (Berkeley: University of California Press, 1991), p. 48; James Turner, *Reckoning with the Beast: Animals, Pain, and Humanity in the Victorian Mind* (Baltimore: Johns Hopkins University Press, 1980); also see John Kirkup, "Surgery Before General Anaesthesia," in *The History of the Management of Pain: From Early Principles to Present Practice*, Ronald D. Mann, ed. (Park Ridge, N.J.: Parthenon, 1988), pp. 23, 28. For general discussions of the new humanitarian sensibility, see Keith Thomas, *Man and the Natural World: A History of the Modern Sensibility* (New York: Pantheon, 1983); G. J. Barker-Benfield, *The Culture of Sensibility: Sex and Society in Eighteenth-Century Britain* (Chicago: University of Chicago Press, 1992); and Paul Langford, *A Polite and Commercial People: England 1727–1783* (New York: Oxford University Press, 1989), chap. 10; Judith Shklar, *Ordinary Vices* (Cambridge, Mass.: Harvard University Press, 1984). On the "civilizing process," see Norbert Elias, *The Civilizing Process: The History of Manners*, Edmund Jephcott, trans. (New York: Urizen Books, 1978); Pieter Spierenburg, *The Broken Spell: A Cultural and Anthropological History of Preindustrial Europe* (New Brunswick: Rutgers University Press, 1991); John F. Kasson, *Rudeness and Civility: Manners in Nineteenth-Century Urban America* (New York: Hill and Wang, 1990). On the decline of casual criminal violence, see Lawrence Stone, "Interpersonal Violence in English Society, 1300–1980," *Past & Present* 101 (November 1983):22–33; Ted Robert Gurr, "Historical Trends in Violent Crime: A Critical Review of the Evidence," *Crime and Justice: An Annual Review of Research* 3 (1981):295–353; J. M. Beattie, "The Pattern of Crime in England 1660–1800," *Past & Present* 62 (February 1974):47–95; Spierenburg, *Broken Spell*, chap. 7. For a more detailed treatment of these developments, see Karen Halttunen, "Humanitarianism and the Pornography of Pain in Anglo-American Culture," *American Historical Review* 100 (April 1995):303–334.

6. Ronald S. Crane, "Suggestions toward a Genealogy of the 'Man of

Feeling,'" *Journal of English Literary History* 1 (1934):205–230; Frans de Bruyn, "Latitudinarianism and Its Importance as a Precursor of Sensibility," *Journal of English and Germanic Philology* 80 (1981):349–368; David B. Davis, *The Problem of Slavery in Western Culture* (Ithaca, N.Y.: Cornell University Press, 1966), pp. 348–364.

7. See Ernest Lee Tuveson, *The Imagination as a Means of Grace: Locke and the Aesthetics of Romanticism* (Berkeley and Los Angeles: University of California Press, 1960), chap. 2; John K. Sheriff, *The Good-Natured Man: The Evolution of a Moral Ideal, 1660–1800* (University, Ala.: University of Alabama Press, 1982), chap. 1; Basil Willey, *The English Moralists* (New York: Norton, 1964), chap. 14; and Willey, *The Eighteenth Century Background: Studies on the Idea of Nature in the Thought of the Period* (Boston: Beacon Press, 1961), chap. 4; Janet Todd, *Sensibility: An Introduction* (London and New York: Methuen, 1986), chap. 2; John Mullan, *Sentiment and Sociability: The Language of Feeling in the Eighteenth Century* (New York: Oxford University Press, 1988), chap. 1.

8. See John Dwyer, *Virtuous Discourse: Sensibility and Community in Late Eighteenth-Century Scotland* (Edinburgh: J. Donald, 1987); Gladys Bryson, *Man and Society: The Scottish Inquiry of the Eighteenth Century* (Princeton: Princeton University Press, 1945); *The Origins and Nature of the Scottish Enlightenment*, R. H. Campbell and Andrew S. Skinner, eds. (Edinburgh: J. Donald, 1982); *A Hotbed of Genius: The Scottish Enlightenment 1730–1790*, David Daiches, Peter Jones, and Jean Jones, eds. (Edinburgh: University Press, 1986). Hume is quoted in Louis I. Bredvold, *The Natural History of Sensibility* (Detroit: Wayne State University Press, 1962), p. 23; and in Willey, *English Moralists*, p. 25. Hutcheson is quoted in T. D. Campbell, "Francis Hutcheson: 'Father' of the Scottish Enlightenment," in *Origins and Nature*, Campbell and Skinner, eds., 168–169.

9. Ann Jessie Van Sant, *Eighteenth-Century Sensibility and the Novel: The Senses in Social Context* (New York: Cambridge University Press, 1993); Todd, *Sensibility*; R. F. Brissenden, *Virtue in Distress: Studies in the Novel of Sentiment from Richardson to Sade* (New York: Barnes and Noble, 1974); Mullan, *Sentiment and Sociability*; Bredvold, *Natural History of Sensibility*; Dwyer, *Virtuous Discourse*, chap. 6; J. M. S. Tompkins, *The Popular Novel in England 1770–1800* (London: Methuen, 1932), esp. chap. 3.

10. See Turner, *Reckoning with the Beast*; Myra C. Glenn, *Campaigns against Corporal Punishment: Prisoners, Sailors, Women, and Children in Antebellum America* (Albany: State University of New York Press, 1984); Thomas, *Man and the Natural World*; Robert W. Malcolmson, *Popular Recreations in English Society 1700–1850* (Cambridge: Cambridge Uni-

versity Press, 1973), esp. chaps. 3 and 7; Richard D. French, *Antivivisection and Medical Science in Victorian Society* (Princeton: Princeton University Press, 1975); *Vivisection in Historial Perspective*, Nicolaas A. Rupke, ed. (London: Croom Helm, 1987).

11. See Michel Foucault, *Discipline and Punish: The Birth of the Prison*, Alan Sheridan, trans. (New York: Pantheon, 1977); Pieter Spierenburg, *The Spectacle of Suffering: Executions and the Evolution of Repression: From a Preindustrial Metropolis to the European Experience* (Cambridge: Cambridge University Press, 1984); Randall McGowen, "The Body and Punishment in Eighteenth-Century England," *Journal of Modern History* 59, 4 (December 1987):651–679; and "Civilizing Punishment: The End of the Public Execution in England," *Journal of British Studies* 33 (July 1994):257–282; Michael Ignatieff, *A Just Measure of Pain: The Penitentiary and the Industrial Revolution* (New York: Pantheon, 1978); Martin J. Wiener, *Reconstructing the Criminal: Culture, Law, and Policy in England, 1830–1914* (Cambridge, England: Cambridge University Press, 1990), chap. 3; Michael Meranze, *Laboratories of Virtue: Punishment, Revolution and the Transformation of Authority in Philadelphia, 1760–1835* (Chapel Hill: University of North Carolina Press, 1996); David Brion Davis, "The Movement to Abolish Capital Punishment in America, 1787–1861," in his *From Homicide to Slavery: Studies in American Culture* (New York: Oxford University Press, 1986), pp. 17–40; Louis P. Masur, *Rites of Execution: Capital Punishment and the Transformation of American Culture, 1776–1865* (New York and Oxford: Oxford University Press, 1989).

12. Anne Digby, *Madness, Morality and Medicine: A Study of the York Retreat, 1796–1914* (Cambridge, England: Cambridge University Press, 1985); *Madhouses, Mad-Doctors, and Madmen: The Social History of Psychiatry in the Victorian Era*, Andrew Scull, ed. (Philadelphia: University of Pennsylvania Press, 1981); Mary Ann Jimenez, *Changing Faces of Madness: Early American Attitudes and Treatment of the Insane* (Hanover, N.H.: University Press of New England, 1987); Gerald N. Grob, *Mental Institutions in America: Social Policy to 1875* (New York: Free Press, 1973); Nancy Tomes, *A Generous Confidence: Thomas Story Kirkbride and the Art of Asylum-Keeping, 1840–83* (Cambridge: Cambridge University Press, 1984); Samuel Tuke, *Description of the Retreat: An Institution Near York for Insane Persons of the Society of Friends*, introduction by Richard Hunter and Ida Macalpine (London: Dawsons of Pall Mall, 1964), p. 148.

13. Anti-flogging petition to Parliament in 1834, quoted in J. R. Dinwiddy, "The Early Nineteenth-Century Campaign Against Flogging in the Army," *English Historical Review* 97 (April 1982):317. Also see Myra C.

Glenn, "The Naval Reform Campaign against Flogging: A Case Study in Changing Attitudes toward Corporal Punishment, 1830–1850," *American Quarterly* (Fall 1983):408–425; Harold D. Langley, *Social Reform in the United States Navy, 1798–1862* (Urbana: University of Illinois Press, 1967), chaps. 6 and 7.

14. See J. H. Plumb, "The New World of Children in Eighteenth-Century England," in Neil McKendrick, John Brewer and J. H. Plumb, *The Birth of a Consumer Society: The Commercialization of Eighteenth-Century England* (Bloomington: Indiana University Press, 1982), pp. 286–315; Jay Fliegelman, *Prodigals and Pilgrims: The American Revolution against Patriarchal Authority, 1750–1800* (Cambridge, England and New York: Cambridge University Press, 1982); Donald R. Raichle, "The Abolition of Corporal Punishment in New Jersey Schools," *Corporal Punishment in American Education: Readings in History, Practice, and Alternatives,* Irwin A. Hyman and James H. Wise, eds. (Philadelphia: Temple University Press, 1979), pp. 62–88.

15. Lewis Perry, *Radical Abolitionism: Anarchy and the Government of God in Antislavery Thought* (Ithaca, N.Y.: Cornell University Press, 1973); Peter Brock, *Pacifism in the United States from the Colonial Era to the First World War* (Princeton: Princeton University Press, 1968); Donna T. Andrew, "The Code of Honour and Its Critics: The Opposition to Duelling in England, 1700–1850," *Social History* 5 (October 1980):409–434; Malcolmson, *Popular Recreations in English Society,* esp. chaps. 3 and 7; Spierenburg, *Broken Spell,* chap. 7; Elliott J. Gorn, *The Manly Art: Bare-Knuckle Prize-Fighting in America* (Ithaca, N.Y.: Cornell University Press, 1986).

16. Steven Bruhm, "Aesthetics and Anesthetics at the Revolution," *Studies in Romanticism* 32 (Fall 1993):403, 404; F. F. Cartwright, *The English Pioneers of Anaesthesia (Beddoes, Davy, and Hickman)* (Bristol, Eng.: J. Wright, 1952); M. H. Armstrong Davison, *The Evolution of Anaesthesia* (Baltimore: Williams & Wilkins, 1965), pp. 73–96; James E. Eckenhoff, *Anesthesia from Colonial Times: A History of Anesthesia at the University of Pennsylvania* (Philadelphia: Lippincott, 1966); Martin S. Pernick, *A Calculus of Suffering: Pain, Professionalism, and Anesthesia in Nineteenth-Century America* (New York: Columbia University Press, 1985); Daniel De Moulin, "A Historical-Phenomenological Study of Bodily Pain in Western Man," *Bulletin of the History of Medicine* 48 (1974):540–570.

17. Turner, *Reckoning with the Beast,* p. 80. On p. 79, he quotes Frances Power Cobbe, "The Rights of Man and the Claims of Brutes"; see her *Studies New and Old of Ethical and Social Subjects* (Boston, 1866), p. 220.

18. Dr. Jacob Bigelow quoted in James J. Farrell, *Inventing the American Way of Death, 1830–1920* (Philadelphia: Temple University Press, 1980),

pp. 106, 148, 171; Stanley E. French, "The Cemetery as Cultural Institution: The Establishment of Mount Auburn and the 'Rural Cemetery' Movement," in Charles O. Jackson, ed., *Passing: The Vision of Death in America* (Westport, Conn.: Greenwood Press, 1977), p. 73; Neil Harris, "The Cemetery Beautiful," in Jackson, ed., *Passing,* pp. 102–111.

19. Philippe Ariès, *The Hour of Our Death,* trans. Helen Weaver (New York: Alfred A. Knopf, 1981), pp. 368, 375. "Delicious pain" is from William Wordsworth, "Sonnet, on seeing Miss Helen Maria Williams weep at a Tale of Distress," quoted in Todd, *Sensibility,* p. 63; "pleasing Anguish" is Scottish moralist David Fordyce, *The Elements of Moral Philosophy* (1754), quoted in Crane, "Suggestions toward a Genealogy," p. 205; Godwin quoted in Todd, *Sensibility,* p. 139.

20. [Edmund Burke], *A Philosophical Enquiry into the Origin of Our Ideas of the Sublime and Beautiful* (London, 1757), p. 13. On Gothic fiction, see *The Gothic Imagination: Essays in Dark Romanticism,* G. R. Thompson, ed. (Pullman: Washington State University Press, 1974); Elizabeth MacAndrew, *The Gothic Tradition in Fiction* (New York: Columbia University Press, 1979); David Punter, *The Literature of Terror: A History of Gothic Fictions from 1765 to the Present Day* (London: Longmans, 1980); Devendra P. Varma, *The Gothic Flame* (London: Arthur Baker, 1957); Twitchell, *Dreadful Pleasures;* Cathy N. Davidson, *Revolution and the Word: The Rise of the Novel in America* (New York: Oxford University Press, 1986), chap. 8; Donald A. Ringe, *American Gothic: Imagination and Reason in Nineteenth-Century Fiction* (Lexington, Ky.: University Press of Kentucky, 1982). See also Mario Praz, *Romantic Agony,* 2nd ed. (New York: Oxford University Press, 1951); Philip P. Hallie, "Horror and the Paradox of Cruelty" (Middletown, Conn.: Wesleyan University, 1969); Lowry Nelson, Jr., "Night Thoughts on the Gothic Novel," *Yale Review* 52 (1962):236–257.

21. The first usage cited in the *OED* of the term "sensationalism" meaning "addiction to what is sensational in literature or art" is from 1865; see *Oxford English Dictionary,* 2nd edition, vol. 14 (Oxford, 1991), p. 976. Also see Richard D. Altick, *Deadly Encounters: Two Victorian Sensations* (Philadelphia: University of Pennsylvania Press, 1986), pp. 4–6 (William Wordsworth is quoted on p. 3); Thomas Boyle, *Black Swine in the Sewers of Hampstead: Beneath the Surface of Victorian Sensationalism* (New York: Viking, 1989); David S. Reynolds, *Beneath the American Renaissance: The Subversive Imagination in the Age of Emerson and Melville* (New York: Knopf, 1988); Winifred Hughes, *The Maniac in the Cellar: Sensation Novels of the 1860s* (Princeton: Princeton University Press, 1980); Jane P. Tompkins, *Sensational Designs: The Cultural Work of American Fiction, 1790–1860* (New York: Oxford University Press, 1985).

22. James R. Brice, Esq., *Secrets of the Mount-Pleasant State Prison* (Albany, 1839), p. 69. On these popular American genres, see Karen Halttunen, "Gothic Mystery and the Birth of the Asylum: The Cultural Construction of Deviance in Early Nineteenth-Century America," in Karen Halttunen and Lewis Perry, eds., *Moral Problems in American Life: New Essays on Cultural History* (Ithaca, N.Y.: Cornell University Press, 1998).

23. Peter Wagner, *Eros Revived: Erotica of the Enlightenment in England and America* (London: Secker & Warburg, 1988), p. 7; Roger Thompson, *Unfit for Modest Ears: A Study of Pornographic, Obscene and Bawdy Works Written or Published in England in the Second Half of the Seventeenth Century* (Totowa, N.J.: Rowman and Littlefield, 1979); David Foxon, *Libertine Literature in England 1660–1745* (New Hyde, N.Y.: University Books, 1966); *The Invention of Pornography: Obscenity and the Origins of Modernity, 1500–1800*, Lynn Hunt, ed. (New York: Zone Books, 1993); Walter Kendrick, *The Secret Museum: Pornography in Modern Culture* (New York: Viking, 1988).

24. Wagner, *Eros Revived*, chap. 3; Ivan Bloch, *Sexual Life in England Past and Present*, trans. William H. Forstern (London: Arco in association with Rodney Book Service, 1958); Steven Marcus, *The Other Victorians: A Study of Sexuality and Pornography in Mid-Nineteenth-Century England* (New York: Basic Books, 1985), esp. chap. 6; Ian Gibson, *The English Vice: Beating, Sex and Shame in Victorian England and After* (London: Duckworth, 1978); Antony E. Simpson, "Vulnerability and the Age of Female Consent: Legal Innovation and its Effect on Prosecutions for Rape in Eighteenth-century London," *Sexual Underworlds of the Enlightenment*, G. S. Rousseau and Roy Porter, eds. (Chapel Hill: University of North Carolina Press, 1988), pp. 181–205; Reynolds, *Beneath the American Renaissance*, pp. 211–224; Timothy J. Gilfoyle, *City of Eros: New York City, Prostitution, and the Commercialization of Sex, 1790–1920* (New York: W. W. Norton, 1992), chaps. 6 and 7.

25. See Richard D. Brown, *Knowledge Is Power: The Diffusion of Information in Early America, 1700–1865* (New York: Oxford University Press, 1989), especially chap. 10 and the conclusion; Daniel A. Cohen, *Pillars of Salt, Monuments of Grace: New England Crime Literature and the Origins of American Popular Culture, 1674–1860* (New York: Oxford University Press, 1993), chap. 1; David Ray Papke, *Framing the Criminal: Crime, Cultural Work and the Loss of Critical Perspective, 1830–1900* (Hamden, Conn.: Archon Books, 1987), chap. 2. Rising murder rates ensured plenty of material for the expanding media; see Roger Lane, *Murder in America: A History* (Columbus: Ohio University Press, 1997), chap. 4.

26. Papke, *Framing the Criminal*, chap. 3; Dan Schiller, *Objectivity and the News: The Public and the Rise of Commercial Journalism* (Philadelphia: University of Pennsylvania Press, 1981), esp. chaps. 1 and 2; Michael Schudson, *Discovering the News: A Social History of American Newspapers* (New York: Basic Books, 1978), chap. 1.

27. *A Minute and Correct Account of the Trial of Lucian Hall, Bethuel Roberts, and William H. Bell* (Middletown, Conn.: Charles H. Pelton, 1844), p. 6; *Serious Reflections on the Execution and Death of Michael Powars* (Boston: E. G. House, 1820), p. 3; *Report of the Trial of Edward E. Bradley* (Hartford: Case, Tiffany, 1857), p. 154; *Trial of David F. Mayberry* (Janesville, Wisc.: Baker, Burnett & Hall, 1855), p. 22; Carroll E. Smith, *The Fyler Murder Case* (Syracuse: Smith & Hough, 1855), p. 6; William B. Sprague, *Wicked Men Ensnared by Themselves* (Springfield [Mass.]: Tannatt, 1826), p. 3.

28. *An Account of the Apprehension, Trial, Conviction, and Condemnation of Manuel Philip Garcia and José Demas Garcia Castillano* (Norfolk: C. Hall, 1821), p. 8; *The Life and Confessions of Daniel Davis Farmer* (Amherst, N.H.: Elijah Mansur, 1822), p. 17.

29. *Trial of Richard P. Robinson* (New York, n.d.), p. 5; also see *The Trial of Albert J. Tirrell* (Boston: Boston Daily Mail, 1846) (McDade 990), p. 23; *The Trial for Murder, of James E. Eldredge* (Ogdensburgh, N.Y.: Hitchcock, Tillotson & Stilwell's Steam Presses, 1857), p. 89; *Trial of Mrs. Margaret Howard* (Cincinnati, Ohio, 1849), p. 13. "Antoine Le Blanc," *Tragedies on the Land, Containing an Authentic Account of the Most Awful Murders*, ed. Henry K. Brooke (Philadelphia: John B. Perry and New York: N. C. Nafis, 1841), p. 183. At Alfred Fyler's trial, "About five hundred women were present throughout, and many hundreds of the sterner sex were unable to obtain entrance to the Court-room"; Smith, *Fyler Murder*, p. 122. Also see *The Life and Confessions of Mrs. Henrietta Robinson, the Veiled Murderess!* (Boston: Dr. H. B. Skinner, 1855), p. 16; *Trial of John Hendrickson, Jr.* (Albany: David M. Barnes & W. S. Hevenor, 1853), p. 90; *Trial of Reuben Dunbar* (Albany: P. L. Gilbert, 1850), p. 50.

30. "Antoine Le Blanc," *Tragedies on the Land*, p. 183; *Trial of Mayberry*, p. 5; "Trial of Joel Clough," *Confessions, Trials, and Biographical Sketches of the Most Cold Blooded Murderers* (Boston: George N. Thomson, 1837), p. 302; *Trial of Professor John W. Webster* (Boston: John A. French, Boston Herald Steam Press, 1850) (McDade 1067), p. 13; *Trial of Albert John Tirrell* (Boston: Published at the *Times* Office, 1846) (McDade 991), p. 11.

31. *Trial, Sentence, Confession and Execution of Joel Clough* (New York:

Christian Brown, [1833]), p. 23; *The Authentic Confession of Jesse Strang* (New York: E. M. Murden & A. Ming, 1827), p. 17; *Trial and Sentence of John Johnson* (New York: Joseph Desnoues, 1824), p. 36.

32. *Trial, Confession, and Execution of Peter Robinson* (New York: The Reporter, 1841), p. 16; *The Manheim Tragedy: A Complete History of the Double Murder of Mrs. Garber and Mrs. Ream* (Lancaster: Evening Express Office, 1858), pp. 50, 51, 55–56.

33. *A Vindication of the Result of the Trial of Rev. Ephraim K. Avery*, p. 25; *Trial of Daniel Davis Farmer* (Concord: Hill and Moore, 1821), p. 41; *Trial of Tirrell* (McDade 991), p. 17; *Trial of Mayberry*, pp. 7–8.

34. George Carroll, *The Manchester Tragedy* (Manchester, N.H.: Fisk & Moore, 1848), p. 11.

35. *Manheim Tragedy*, p. 6; *Murder Most Foul! A Synopsis of the Speeches of Ogden Hoffman, Thomas Phenix, Hugh Maxwell, Judge Edwards, &c. on the Trial of Robinson* (New York: R. H. Elton, 1836); *Awful Disclosures! The Life and Confessions of Andress Hall* (Troy: J. C. Kneeland, 1849); *Confessions, Trials, and Biographical Sketches; Tragedies on the Land; Annals of Murder, or, Daring Outrages, Trials, Confessions, &c.* (Philadelphia: John B. Perry, and New York: Nafis & Cornish, 1845).

36. "The Murder of Francis Baker, Esq. by Isaac B. Desha," *Tragedies on the Land*, p. 69; *Serious Reflections on Powars*, p. 9; "Joel Clough, the Murderer of Mrs. Mary W. Hamilton," *Tragedies on the Land*, p. 159; *Account of Garcia and Castillano*, p. 28.

37. *Trial of Farmer*, p. 10; *Trial of Knapp* (McDade 572), p. 3; *Fyler Murder*, pp. 5–6; *Trial of Hall, Roberts, and Bell*, p. 6.

38. See, for ex., *Trial, Confession, and Execution of Robert M'Conaghy* (Philadelphia, 1841).

39. *Trial of Eldredge*, p. 129; also see *Trial of Henry G. Green* (Troy, 1845); *The Trial of Alpheus Hitchcock* (Utica: Seward and Williams, 1807); *Report of the Trial and Conviction of John Earls* (Williamsport, 1836), p. 110.

40. See *Trial of Amos Furnald* (Concord: Jacob B. Moore, 1825), p. 16; "The Case of John Johnson," *Tragedies on the Land*, p. 13; *Trial of Mayberry*, p. 24; *Speech of John V. L. M'Mahon, on Behalf of . . . George Swearingen* (Baltimore: Lucas and Deaver, 1829), pp. 43–44.

41. *Confession of Edward Donnelly* (Philadelphia, 1808); *The Confession of Mary Cole* (New York, [1813]), p. 4; *Trial, Confession, and Execution of Peter Robinson*, p. 15; Carroll, *Manchester Tragedy*, p. 12.

42. *Account of Garcia and Castillano*, pp. 6–7; *The Confession of Adam Horn* (Baltimore: James Young, 1843), pp. 18–20; *The Triple Murderer. Life and Confessions of Return J. M. Ward* (Toledo: Hawes, 1857), pp. 26, 18.

43. Holloway Whitfield Hunt, *A Sermon, Preached at the Execution of Matthias Gotlieb* (Newton, N.J., 1796), p. 3; *Life of Michael Powers* (Boston: Russell & Gardner, 1820), p. 19.

44. *A Report of the Evidence and Points of Law, Arising in the Trial of John Francis Knapp* (Salem: W. & S. B. Ives, 1830) (McDade 567), p. 27; *Trial of Earls*, pp. 28–29.

45. *Trial and Execution of Thomas Barrett* (Boston: Skinner & Blanchard, 1845), pp. 7–8; *Fyler Murder*, p. 5; *Trial of Earls*, p. 179.

46. *Trial of Bradley*, p. 11; *Trial of Isaac Spencer* (Bangor: Nourse & Smith, 1835), p. 10; *The Life of Eliza Sowers* (Philadelphia: P. Augustus Sage, 1839), p. 27; *Trial of Farmer*, p. 15; *Trial of Bradley*, pp. 11, 14; *Trial of Webster* (McDade 1067), p. 19.

47. *Narrative of the Murder of James Murray* (New York: S. King, 1824), p. 65; *Authentic Confession of Strang*, p. 20; *Trial of Eldredge*, p. 23; *Trial of Dr. Valorous P. Coolidge* (N.p., n.d.), p. 12.

48. *The Confession of Mina* (Doylestown, Penn., 1832), p. 24; William Goodwin, *Death Cell Scenes* (New Haven: J. H. Benham, 1850), pp. 26–29; "Lives and Trial of Gibbs and Wansley," *Confessions, Trials, and Biographical Sketches*, p. 209; *Trial of Mayberry*, p. 48; *Manheim Tragedy*, pp. 54, 62; *Authentic Confession of Strang*, p. 19; *Trial of M'Conaghy*, p. 15.

49. Richard Bushman, *The Refinement of America: Persons, Houses, Cities* (New York: Knopf, 1992).

50. *Report of the Trial of Dominic Daley and James Halligan* (Northampton: S. & E. Butler, booksellers; T. M. Pomroy, printer [1806]), "Advertisement," n.p; *The Fate of Murderers. A Faithful Narrative of the Murder of Mrs. Sarah Cross* (Philadelphia, 1808), p. 6; *Narrative of the Murder of James Murray*, p. iii; *Manheim Tragedy*, pp. 3, 4.

51. See, for example, *The Confession of Jereboam O. Beauchamp* (Bloomfield, Ky., 1826), p. 134; *The Last Hours of Charles R. S. Boyington* (Mobile, Ala.: printed at the Commercial Register Office, 1835), preface; *Impartial Account of the Trial of Ebenezer Mason* (Dedham: Mann, 1802), pp. iii–iv, 26; *The Dying Confession of John Lechler* (Lancaster, Penn.: M. M'Kelly, 1822), p. 3; *Life and Awful Confession of Reuben Dunbar!* (N.P., n.d.], p. 8; *Trial of Daley and Halligan*, "Advertisement"; *A Report of the Trial of James Jameson, and James M'Gowan* (Harrisburgh: John Wyeth, 1806), p. 3; *Confession of Donnelly*, p. 12; *Trial of Hendrickson*, introduction, n.p.; *Trial of Lucretia Chapman* (Philadelphia: G. W. Mentz & Son, 1832), p. 1.

52. *Cold Blooded Murderers*, p. v.

53. *A Sketch of the Life and Adventures of Guy C. Clark* (Ithaca: n.p., 1832), preface. *Speech of M'Mahon . . . Swearingen*, p. 11.

54. See Noel Perrin, *Dr. Bowdler's Legacy: A History of Expurgated Books in England and America* (New York: Atheneum, 1969).

55. Terry Heller, *The Delights of Terror: An Aesthetics of the Tale of Terror* (Urbana: University of Illinois Press, 1987), pp. 72, 85.

56. Punter, *Literature of Terror*, p. 410.

57. See, for ex., "The Shocking Murder of the Young and Beautiful Evelina Cunningham," *Tragedies on the Land*, p. 122; and "The Murder of a Wife by Her Husband," *Annals of Murder*, p. 24.

58. Rhys Isaac, *The Transformation of Virginia, 1740–1790* (Chapel Hill: University of North Carolina Press, 1982), p. 122; Walter J. Ong, *The Presence of the Word: Some Prolegomena for Cultural and Religious History* (New Haven: Yale University Press, 1967), esp. pp. 133–135; Ian Watt, *The Rise of the Novel: Studies in Defoe, Richardson and Fielding* (Berkeley: University of California Press, 1957), esp. chap. 6; Jack Goody and Ian Watt, "The Consequences of Literacy," in Jack Goody, ed., *Literacy in Traditional Societies* (Cambridge: Cambridge University Press, 1968); Davidson, *Revolution and the Word*, p. 14.

59. See Henri F. Ellenberger, *The Discovery of the Unconscious: The History and Evolution of Dynamic Psychiatry* (New York: Basic Books, 1970); and Lancelot Law Whyte, *The Unconscious before Freud* (New York: Basic Books, 1960), chaps. 4–7.

60. Sprague, *Wicked Men Ensnared*, p. 41; *The Trial of Alpheus Livermore and Samuel Angier* (Boston: Watson & Bangs, 1813), p. 36 (actual quote is "shocking scenes"); *A Correct Account of the Trials of Charles M'Manus, John Hauer, Elizabeth Hauer* (Harrisburgh: John Wyeth, 1798), p. 110.

61. "The Murder of Elizabeth Topping, by Her Husband, Thomas Topping," *Annals of Murder*, pp. 29–30.

62. *Tragedies on the Land*, p. 23; *A Correct Copy of the Trial & Conviction of Richard Johnson* (New York: Christian Brown [1829?]), title page; *Annals of Murder*, n.p. (book advertisement).

63. *Serious Reflections of Powars*, p. 9; *Trial of Barrett*, p. 2; "Attempt of a Husband to Burn his Wife," *Annals of Murder*, p. 34.

64. *Trial of Crowninshield, Knapp, and Knapp* (McDade 571), pp. 92–93;. *Trial of Earls*, p. 166.

65. *Trial of Clough*, pp. 17, 16; *Confessions, Trials, and Biographical Sketches*, p. 304.

66. Mirjam Westen, "The Woman on a Swing and the Sensuous Voyeur: Passion and Voyeurism in French Rococo," in Jan Bremmer, ed., *From Sappho to De Sade: Moments in the History of Sexuality* (London: Routledge, 1989), pp. 69–83; Lennard J. Davis, *Factual Fictions: The Origins of the English Novel* (New York: Columbia University Press, 1983), esp. chap. 3.

67. "The Trial and Sentence of Michael M'Garvey, for the Murder of His Wife," *Tragedies on the Land,* p. 149.
68. Twitchell, *Dreadful Pleasures,* p. 291; Lucy Fischer and Marcia Landy, "*Eyes of Laura Mars:* A Binocular Critique," in Gregory A. Waller, ed., *American Horrors: Essays on the Modern American Horror Film* (Urbana: University of Illinois Press, 1987), pp. 62–78 (quote is on p. 74); John Berger, *Ways of Seeing* (London: BBC and Penguin Books, 1973), p. 10.
69. *Life and Awful Confession of Reuben Dunbar!* (N.p.,n.d.), p. 6; *A Confession of the Awful and Bloody Transactions in the Life of Charles Wallace* (New Orleans: E. E. Barclay & Co., 1851), p. 9; "Life and Confession of John W. Cowan," in *Confessions, Trials, and Biographical Sketches,* p. 252; Henry Foote, *A Sketch of the Life and Adventures of Henry Leander Foote* (New Haven: T. J. Stafford, 1850), p. 44; *Awful Disclosures! . . . Hall,* p. 13.
70. Edward N. Kirk, *The Murderer: A Discourse Occasioned by the Trial and Execution of John W. Webster* (Boston: Tappan, Whittemore & Mason, 1850), p. 4; *Life, Letters, and Last Conversation of John Caldwell Colt* ([New York]: Published at the *Sun* office, 1841), p. 7; Goodwin, *Death Cell Scenes,* pp. 7–8.
71. *Confession of Beauchamp; Life, Letters . . . Colt;* Patricia Cline Cohen, "Unregulated Youth: Masculinity and Murder in the 1830s City," *Radical History Review* 52 (1991):33–52; *Murder Most Foul!,* p. 3.
72. *Trial of Tirrell* (McDade 990), p. 36; Cohen, *Pillars of Salt,* p. 238; Louis C. Jones, *Murder at Cherry Hill: The Strang-Whipple Case, 1827* (Albany: Historic Cherry Hill, 1982), p. 113.
73. *Trial of Knapp* (McDade 572), p. 57; *Trial of M'Conaghy and Confession of Robinson,* p. 13; *Confessions, Trials, and Biographical Sketches,* pp. 255, 391.
74. *Report of the Trial of Abraham Prescott* (Concord [N.H.]: M. G. Atwood, and Currier and Hall, 1834), p. 54.

4. The Construction of Murder as Mystery

1. Henry Channing, *God Admonishing His People of Their Duty* (New London: T. Green, 1786), pp. 29–30.
2. Frank Kermode, "Novel and Narrative," in Glenn W. Most and William W. Stowe, eds., *The Poetics of Murder: Detective Fiction & Literary Theory* (New York: Harcourt Brace Jovanovich, 1983), pp. 175–196 (quote on p. 180); Alfred D. Hutter, "Dreams, Transformations, and Literature: The Implications of Detective Fiction," in Most and Stowe, eds., *Poetics of Murder,* pp. 230–251 (quote on 231–232). Also see David

Lehman, *The Perfect Murder: A Study in Detection* (New York: Free Press, 1989), p. 1; Dennis Porter, *The Pursuit of Crime: Art and Ideology in Detective Fiction* (New Haven: Yale University Press, 1981), chap. 2 (quote on p. 24).

3. See Terry Eagleton, *Literary Theory: An Introduction* (Minneapolis: University of Minnesota Press, 1983), p. 105; Most and Stowe, Introduction, *Poetics of Murder;* Tzvetan Todorov, "The Typology of Detective Fiction," *The Poetics of Prose,* trans. Richard Howard (Ithaca, N.Y.: Cornell University Press, 1977), pp. 42–52.

4. "Edgar Allan Poe invented the detective story": Martin Priestman, *Detective Fiction and Literature: The Figure on the Carpet* (New York: St. Martin's Press, 1991), p. 36.

5. Benjamin Colman, *The Hainous Nature of the Sin of Murder* (Boston: John Allen, 1713), p. 6. Also see John Williams, *Warnings to the Unclean* (Boston: B. Green and J. Allen, 1699), p. 17; Nathaniel Clap, *Sinners Directed to Hear & Fear* (Boston: J. Allen for N. Boone, 1715), p. 39; Sylvanus Conant, *The Blood of Abel, and the Blood of Jesus* (Boston: Edes and Gill, 1764).

6. Cotton Mather, *Pillars of Salt* (Boston: B. Green and J. Allen, 1699), p. 61; also see his *Terribilia Dei* [Boston, 1697], p. 45; and *A Faithful Narrative of the Wicked Life and Remarkable Conversion of Patience Boston* (Boston: S. Kneeland and T. Green, 1738), p. 8. For a legal-historical treatment of the corpse-touching test as the "law of the bier," see Joseph S. Sickler, "The Law of the Bier or Bier Right," in *Rex et Regina vs. Lutherland* (Woodstown, N.J.: Seven Stars Press, 1948). The work reprinted here, *Blood Will Out . . . Trial of Thomas Lutherland* (Philadelphia: Will. Bradford, 1692), demonstrates the practice of this test in the colony of West Jersey; see p. 7.

7. David D. Hall, *Worlds of Wonder, Days of Judgment: Popular Religious Belief in Early New England* (Cambridge, Mass.: Harvard University Press, 1990), pp. 176–177. See, for ex., William Shurtleff, *The Faith and Prayer of a Dying Malefactor* (Boston: J. Draper for D. Henchman, 1740), p. ii. For a discussion of a related providential test of guilt in a bestiality case, see Gail Sussman Marcus, "'Due Execution of the Generall Rules of Righteousness': Criminal Procedure in New Haven Town and Colony, 1638–1658," in David D. Hall, John M. Murrin, Thad W. Tate, eds., *Saints and Revolutionaries: Essays on Early American History* (New York: W. W. Norton, 1984), pp. 99–137 (115).

8. Samuel Checkley, *Murder a Great and Crying Sin* (Boston: T. Fleet, 1733), p. 11. Also see Increase Mather, *Sermon Occasioned by the Execution of a Man* (Boston: Joseph [oblit.], 1686), p. 24; Joshua Moodey, *An Exhortation to a Condemned Malefactor* (Boston, 1685/6) bound with

Cotton Mather, *Call of the Gospel Applyed* (Boston: R. P., [1686]), p. 92; Shurtleff, *Faith and Prayer*, p. 25.

9. See John H. Langbein, "The Criminal Trial before the Lawyers," *The University of Chicago Law Review* 45, 2 (Winter 1978): 263–316; and "Shaping the Eighteenth-Century Criminal Trial: A View from the Ryder Sources," *The University of Chicago Law Review* 50, no. 1 (Winter 1983):1–136; J. M. Beattie, *Crime and the Courts in England 1660–1800* (Princeton: Princeton University Press, 1986), pp. 362–376; Glanville Williams, *The Proof of Guilt: A Study of the English Criminal Trial* (London: Stevens & Sons, 1963), chap. 1; Marcus, "Due Execution," p. 108. For a transcript of a nonadversarial trial held in the American colonies, see *Blood Will Out.*

10. See Marcus, "Due Execution," pp. 111–112, 126; John M. Murrin, "Magistrates, Sinners, and a Precarious Liberty: Trial by Jury in Seventeenth-Century New England," in Hall, Murrin, Tate, eds., *Saints and Revolutionaries*, pp. 152–206.

11. Cotton Mather, *Tremenda* (Boston: B. Green, 1721), p. 34.

12. See *Blood Will Out;* and *Some Account of the Trial of Samuel Goodere, Esq.* (Boston, 1741), an English trial printed in Boston. Nathaniel Clap's execution sermon for Jeremiah Meacham included a brief summary of his trial; see *Sinners Directed. An Account of the Trial of Joseph Andrews for Piracy and Murder* [New York, 1769], which opens like a trial account, but moves quickly into a straightforward narrative of the piracy and the murders. Daniel A. Cohen observes that few criminal cases other than piracy trials prompted printed reports in New England before the early nineteenth century; see *Pillars of Salt, Monuments of Grace: New England Crime Literature and the Origins of American Popular Culture, 1674–1860* (New York: Oxford University Press, 1993), pp. 14–15.

13. See *The Trial of William Wemms, James Hartegan, William M'Cauley, [et al.]* (Boston: J. Fleeming [1770]) (reprinted in 1807 and 1824); *The Trial of Alice Clifton* [N.p., n.d.]; *The Trial of John Kease, Patrick Kinnon and John Campbell* (Philadelphia, 1787); *A Correct Account of the Trials of Charles M'Manus, John Hauer, Elizabeth Hauer, [et al.]* (Harrisburgh: John Wyeth, 1798); *The Narrative of Whiting Sweeting* (Lansingburgh [N.Y.]: Sylvester Tiffany, 1791). Thomas McDade identifies the Sweeting narrative as "probably the most frequently reprinted murder pamphlet in American criminal history"; see his *The Annals of Murder: A Bibliography of Books and Pamphlets on American Murders from Colonial Times to 1900* (Norman, Ok.: University of Oklahoma Press, 1961), p. 283.

14. See, for ex., *The Trial of Jereboam O. Beauchamp* (New York: Joseph

M'Cleland, 1826); George Carroll, *The Manchester Tragedy* (Manchester, N.H.: Fish & Moore, 1848); *The Confession of Adam Horn* (Baltimore: James Young, 1843).

15. See, for ex., *Examination of Dr. J. K. Hardenbrook, Before the Police Court of Rochester* (Rochester, N.Y., 1849); *The Closing Speech of Z. Collins Lee, Esq.* (Baltimore: Bull & Tuttle, 1838); *The Closing Argument in the Case of the People vs. Reuben Dunbar* (Albany: Joel Munsell, 1851); *The Horrid Murder of John Carson, Committed by Richard Smith. The Judge's Charge to the Jury* (Philadelphia, 1816); *John Gordon's Petition* [for clemency to the governor of Rhode Island] [N.p., n.d., probably 1844]; *The Commutation of the Punishment of William Miller* (New York: Christian Brown, 1828); *Review, Opinions, &c., of Dr. Charles A. Lee, and Others, of the Testimony of Drs. Salisbury and Swinburne* (New York, 1855); Lysander Spooner, *Illegality of the Trial of John W. Webster* (Boston: Bela March, 1850).

16. These figures are based on a categorization and counting of the 1126 bibliographic entries in McDade, *Annals of Murder.* From 1800 to 1859, trial reports outnumbered the mixed legal narratives by almost three to one, and outnumbered the trial fragments and commentaries by almost five to one. After 1860, this dominance of the trial report over other legal narratives diminished.

17. See Stephen Botein, "The Legal Profession in Colonial North America," in Wilfrid Prest, ed., *Lawyers in Early Modern Europe and America* (London: Croom Helm, 1981), pp. 129–146; Gerard W. Gawalt, *The Promise of Power: The Emergence of the Legal Profession in Massachusetts 1760–1840* (Westport, Conn.: Greenwood Press, 1979); Richard D. Brown, *Knowledge Is Power: The Diffusion of Information in Early America, 1700–1865* (New York: Oxford University Press, 1989), chap. 4; Kermit L. Hall, *The Magic Mirror: Law in American History* (New York: Oxford University Press, 1989), chaps. 1–3; Lawrence M. Friedman, *A History of American Law* (New York: Simon and Schuster, 1973), pp. 81–88, 95–96; John M. Murrin, "The Legal Transformation: The Bench and Bar of Eighteenth-Century Massachusetts," in *Colonial America: Essays in Politics and Social Development,* eds. Stanley N. Katz and John Murrin (New York: Alfred A. Knopf, 1983), pp. 540–572. On the connection between law and letters, see Robert A. Ferguson, *Law and Letters in American Culture* (Cambridge, Mass.: Harvard University Press, 1984); and Donald Weber, *Rhetoric and History in Revolutionary New England* (New York: Oxford University Press, 1988).

18. Langbein, "Shaping the Eighteenth-Century Criminal Trial," p. 130.

19. Ferguson, *Law and Letters,* p. 69.

20. *The Trial of William Freeman* (Auburn, N.Y.: Derby, Miller & Co., 1848) was 508 pages long; *A Brief Narrative of the Trial for the Bloody and Mysterious Murder of the Unfortunate Young Woman, in the Famous Manhattan Well* [N.p., n.d., probably c. 1800), was 16 pages; *Trial of William S. Beckley* [Cincinnati, Ohio, 1859] was 12 pages; *Trial of Sarah Jane Pinkerton* [Boston? 1848?] was 8 pages.

21. *Report of the Case of John W. Webster* (Boston: Charles C. Little & J. Brown, 1850) (McDade 1060); *A Full and Correct Report of the Trial and Conviction of Prof. John W. Webster* (Boston: H. B. Skinner, 1850) (McDade 1057); *Report of the Trial of Jason Fairbanks* (Boston: Russell and Cutler, 1801); *A Deed of Horror! Trial of Jason Fairbanks* (Salem: W. Carlton, [1801]). The preface to *The Trial of Stephen Arnold* (Cooperstown: E. Phinney, [1805?]) explained (with unusual editorial scrupulosity) that, while trial testimony had been taken down nearly verbatim and compared with the notes taken by the Chief Justice, the arguments of counsel were condensed because copies of their statements could not be obtained from either the prosecution or the defense; p. iii.

22. See, for ex., *Report of the Trial of Levi Weeks . . . Taken in Shorthand by the Clerk of the Court* (New York: John Furman, 1800); *Trial of John Blaisdell . . . Reported by a Member of the Bar* (Exeter, [N.H., c. 1822]); *Trial of Daniel Davis Farmer . . . Reported by Artemas Rogers & Henry B. Chase, Counselors at Law* (Concord [N.H.]: Hill and Moore, 1821); *Report of the Trial of Abner Rogers, Jr. . . . By George Tyler Bigelow and George Bemis, Esqrs., Counsel for the Defendant* (Boston: Charles C. Little and James Brown, 1844); *A Full Report of the Trial of Orrin Woodford . . . By N. H. Morgan, Keeper of the Hartford County Jail* (Hartford: Elihu Geer, 1846); *Trial of Reuben Dunbar . . . Reported Exclusively for the Albany Morning Express, by Jacob C. Cuyler* (Albany: P. L. Gilbert, 1850); *Trial, of the Rev. Ephraim K. Avery* (Penn-Yan, N.Y.: Printed at the Democrat Office, 1833) (McDade 51).

23. See, for ex., *Trial of David Lynn, Jabez Meigs, Elijah Barton, [et al.] . . . Taken in Shorthand, by John Merrick, Esq.* (Hallowell: Ezekial Goodale, 1810); *Testimony. State of Maine vs. George Knight . . . By J. D. Pulsifer, Phonographic Reporter* (Lewiston: Waldron and Dingley, 1857); *Trial of Professor John W. Webster . . . Stenographic Report* (Boston: John A. French, Boston Herald Steam Press, 1850) (McDade 1067).

24. William E. Du Bois, *Trial of Lucretia Chapman* (Philadelphia: G. W. Mentz & Son, 1832), "Advertisement" on p. 1; *Trial, Sentence, Confession and Execution of Joel Clough* (New York: Christian Brown, [1833]), p. 3.

25. For the Strang and Webster editions, see McDade *Annals of Murder*, pp. 277–278; 312–316. For editorial justifications, see *Trials of M'Manus et al.*, p. 3; *Report of the Trial of Dominic Daley and James Halligan*

(Northampton: S. & E. Butler, booksellers; T. M. Pomroy, printer, [1806]), "Advertisement," n.p.; *Trial of Arnold*, pp. iii–iv; *Trial of Lynn et al.*, p. 4; *The Most Important Testimony Adduced on the Trial of John Francis Knapp* (Providence: H. H. Brown, 1830); *Trial of Chapman*, p. 1.

26. Conant, *Blood of Abel*, p. 23. The Rev. Holloway Hunt's execution sermon for Matthias Gotlieb was prefaced with a detailed discussion of the findings of the coroner's inquest; see Holloway Whitfield Hunt, *A Sermon, Preached at the Execution of Matthias Gotlieb* (Newton, N.J., 1796), p. 3.

27. Moses Baldwin, *The Ungodly Condemned in Judgment* (Boston: Kneeland & Adams, 1771), p. 17; Enoch Huntington, *A Sermon Preached at Haddam* (Middletown, Conn.: Moses H. Woodward, 1797), pp. 21, 15; Moses C. Welch, *The Gospel to be Preached to All Men* (Windham: John Byrne, 1805), p. 16. Also see Thaddeus Maccarty, *The Guilt of Innocent Blood Put Away* (Worcester: Isaiah Thomas, 1778), p. 22.

28. *Trial of Wemms et al.; Trial of John Graham* ([Baltimore, Md.] Fryer & Clark, [ca. 1804]); *A Sketch of the Proceedings and Trial of William Hardy* (Boston: Oliver and Munroe, 1807).

29. See, for ex., *An Impartial Account of the Trial of Mr. Levi Weeks, for the Supposed Murder of Miss Julianna Elmore Sands* (New York: M. M'Farlane, 1800); *The False Prophet! The Very Interesting and Remarkable Trial of Matthias . . . for the Alleged Murder of Mr. Elijah Pierson* (New York: W. Mitchell, 1835); *A Sketch of the Life of R. P. Robinson, the Alleged Murderer of Helen Jewett* (New York, 1836); *Report of the Trial of James M. Williams for the Alleged Murder of Vanness Wyatt* (Concord: William Butterfield, 1862).

30. Langbein, "The Criminal Trial before the Lawyers," and "Shaping the Eighteenth-Century Criminal Trial"; Beattie, *Crime and the Courts in England;* Williams, *Proof of Guilt,* chap. 1; Lawrence M. Friedman, *Crime and Punishment in American History* (New York: Basic Books, 1993), pp. 134, 136.

31. *Trial of Richard P. Robinson* (New York: n.p., n.d.); *The Correct, Full and Impartial Report of the Trial of Rev. Ephraim K. Avery* (Providence: Marshall and Brown, 1833) (McDade 36); *Trial of Farmer; The Trial for Murder, of James E. Eldredge* (Ogdensburgh, N.Y.: Hitchcock, Tillotson & Stilwell's Steam Presses, 1857).

32. See *The Trial of James M. Bickford* (Malone: J. J. and J. K. Seaver, 1854), p. 14; *Trial, Confession, and Execution of Robert M'Conaghy* (Philadelphia: n.p., 1841), p. 4; *Closing Argument . . . Dunbar,* p. 14.

33. *Report of the Trial of Edward E. Bradley* (Hartford: Case, Tiffany and Co., 1857), p. 174.

34. See *Trial of John Hendrickson, Jr.* (Albany: David M. Barnes & W. S.

Hevenor, 1853); *The Fyler Murder Case* (Syracuse: Smith & Hough, 1855); and *Trial of Bradley*.

35. *Report of the Trial of the Rev. Ephraim K. Avery* (New York: William Stodart, n.d.) (McDade 44), p. 4; *Trial of Chapman*, p. 112; *A Minute and Correct Account of the Trial of Lucian Hall, Bethuel Roberts, and William H. Bell* (Middletown, Conn.: Charles H. Pelton, 1844), p. 7 (emphasis added). For a useful discussion of circumstantial evidence see Charles Hoffmann and Tess Hoffmann, *Brotherly Love: Murder and the Politics of Prejudice in Nineteenth-Century Rhode Island* (Amherst: University of Massachusetts Press, 1993), chap. 3.

36. David Richard Kasserman, *Fall River Outrage: Life, Murder, and Justice in Early Industrial New England* (Philadelphia: University of Pennsylvania Press, 1986), pp. 96–97; *The Trial of Charles Stevens* (Kennebunk: James K. Remich, 1823).

37. *Trial of Fairbanks; Trial of John Graham*.

38. See, for ex., the medical testimony in *Trial of Avery* (McDade 36).

39. *Trial of James Anthony* (Rutland: Fay & Davison, [1814]). Alice Clifton, a slave tried for infanticide in 1787, testified that the child had been born dead; that she had cut the child's throat to keep it from crying and revealing its existence to her masters; that she had killed it by command of the child's father, who had promised to purchase her and make her a fine lady if she would do so; and that she had cut the throat of her stillborn child so that the father would keep his promise to her; see *Trial of Clifton*.

40. *The Trial in the Case of the Commonwealth, versus John Francis Knapp* [Salem? 1830?] (McDade 570), pp. 12–13.

41. W. Lance Bennett and Martha S. Feldman, *Reconstructing Reality in the Courtroom: Justice and Judgment in American Culture* (New Brunswick: Rutgers University Press, 1981), pp. 3, 9.

42. See Lawrence M. Friedman, "Law, Lawyers and Popular Culture," *The Yale Law Journal* 98 (July 1989):1579–1606.

43. See Karen Halttunen, "'Domestic Differences': Competing Narratives of Womanhood in the Murder Trial of Lucretia Chapman," in Shirley Samuels, ed., *The Culture of Sentiment: Race, Gender, and Sentimentality in Nineteenth-Century America* (New York: Oxford University Press, 1992), pp. 39–57.

44. *Report of the Trial of John Boies* (Dedham: H. & W. H. Mann, [1829?]), quote on p. 4.

45. *Trial of Hendrickson*, p. 172.

46. For "Murder Will Out!" see *Trial of Hendrickson*, p. 158; *Report of the Trial and Conviction of John Earls* (Williamsport: Packer and Cummings, 1836), p. 179; *Trial of Edward Tinker* (Newbern [N.C.]: Hall &

Bryan and T. Watson, 1811), p. 27. For "blood of the sacrifice," *Trial of Chapman*, p. 121. Also see *Trial of Farmer*, p. 72; *Closing Argument . . . Dunbar*, p. 21; *Trial of Jameson and M'Gowan*, p. 3.

47. *Trial of Medad M'Kay* (Albany: Websters and Skinners, 1821), p. 8; *Trial of Chapman*, p. 121.

48. "But Providence has so ordered the affairs of men, that it most frequently happens, that great crimes committed in secret leave behind them some traces, or are accompanied by some circumstances which lead to the discovery and punishment of the offender: therefore the law has wisely provided that you need not have, in cases of this kind, direct proof"; *Summit County Common Pleas. Judge Humphreville, Presiding. State of Ohio against James Parks* (n.p., 1853[?]), p. 27.

49. *Trial of Earls*, p. 166; emphasis added.

50. *Trial of Eldredge*, p. 106; *Trial of Farmer*, p. 65; *A Report of the Evidence and Points of Law, Arising in the Trial of John Francis Knapp* (Salem: W. & S. B. Ives, 1830), p. 20.

51. *Trial of Hendrickson*, p. 152; *Trial of Earls*, p. 179.

52. *The Trial of Albert J. Tirrell* (Boston: Daily Mail, 1846) (McDade 990), p. 5; *Trial of Eldredge*, p. 23; Edward N. Kirk, *The Murderer. A Discourse Occasioned by the Trial and Execution of John W. Webster* (Boston: Tappan, Whittemore & Mason, 1850), p. 26. This legal narrative of circumstantial evidence has proved an enduring feature of detective fiction; as contemporary writer Ross Macdonald observed, "The web of causality is almost infinitely exact. There are no coincidences in life." Quoted in Lehman, *Perfect Murder*, p. 29.

53. *Trial of John Francis Knapp* (Boston: Dutton and Wentworth, 1830) (McDade 572), p. 57.

54. *Trial of Hendrickson*, p. 158; also see *Trial of Farmer*, p. 60; Hammond, *Closing Argument . . . Dunbar*, p. 20. Confessed murderer Andress Hall himself pondered the psychological force that Poe called "the imp of the perverse," the urge to betray guilt. Having stolen some gold beads from his victim, he traded them for a bracelet in New York City; the beads provided the strongest evidence against him at his trial. "I [sic] seems strange to me that I did not dispose of those beads before," he wrote. "I often thought of it, and when going to knew York [sic], I went to the stern of the boat and even lifted my arm to throw them overboard, but did not"; *Awful Disclosures! The Life and Confessions of Andress Hall* (Troy: J. C. Kneeland, 1849), p. 14.

55. *Trial of Dunbar*, p. 40; *Trial of Chapman*, p. 125; *Trial of Tirrell* (McDade 990), p. 29; *Trial of Bradley*, p. 174; *Speech of John V. L. M'Mahon, on Behalf of . . . George Swearingen* (Baltimore: Lucas and Deaver, 1829), p. 7.

56. *A Brief Narrative of the Trial for the Bloody and Mysterious Murder; Full Report of the Trial of Dr. John McNab, of Barnet, Vermont, and Others Implicated in the Misterious [sic] Abduction and Murder* (n.p., 1848?); *Trial of Stephen and Jesse Boorn . . . with some other Interesting Particulars, Relating to this Mysterious Affair* (Rutland, Vt.: Fay and Burt [1819]). Also see *The Princeton Murder. The Burdell Mystery Unraveled* (New York: National Police Gazette Office, 1863); *The Udderzook Mystery!* (Philadelphia: Barclay, 1873).

57. *Strictures on the Case of Ephraim K. Avery* (Providence: William Simons, Jr.—Herald Office, 1833), p. 5; *Mystery Developed; or, Russell Colvin, (Supposed to be Murdered,) in Full Life* (Hartford: William S. Marsh; R. Storrs, 1820), p. 13; "Horrible Murder of Samuel Adams," in *Annals of Murder, or, Daring Outrages, Trials, Confessions, &c.* (Philadelphia: John B. Perry; New York: Nafis & Cornish, 1845), p. 3.

58. *An Account of the Apprehension, Trial, Conviction, and Condemnation of Manuel Philip Garcia and José Demas Garcia Castillano* (Norfolk: C. Hall, 1821), p. 5.

59. *Narrative of the Murder of James Murray* (New York: S. King, 1824), p. 13.

60. Howard Haycraft, *Murder for Pleasure: The Life and Times of the Detective Story* (New York: D. Appleton-Century Co., 1941), pp. 12 and 5.

61. See James F. Richardson, *The New York Police: Colonial Times to 1901* (New York: Oxford University Press, 1970); Wilbur R. Miller, *Cops and Bobbies: Police Authority in New York and London, 1830–1870* (Chicago: University of Chicago Press, 1973); Roger Lane, *Policing the City: Boston 1822–1885* (Cambridge, Mass.: Harvard University Press, 1967); Samuel Walker, *Popular Justice: A History of American Criminal Justice* (New York: Oxford University Press, 1980); Eric H. Monkkonen, *Police in Urban America 1860–1920* (Cambridge: Cambridge University Press, 1981); Pauline Maier, "Popular Uprisings and Civil Authority in Eighteenth-Century America," *William and Mary Quarterly* 27 (1970):3–35; David R. Johnson, *American Law Enforcement: A History* (St. Louis: Forum Press, 1981), chaps. 1 and 2.

62. See Amy Gilman Srebnick, *The Mysterious Death of Mary Rogers: Sex and Culture in Nineteenth-Century New York* (New York: Oxford University Press, 1995), chap. 5.

63. *Fyler Murder*, pp. 5–6.

64. *Narrative of Sweeting; The Address of Abraham Johnstone* (Philadelphia, 1797); *The Life and Adventures of Ambrose Gwinett* (Philadelphia: Robert Bell, 1784). Subsequently, a defense attorney cited Gwinett's story to persuade jurors of the limitations of circumstantial evidence. Acknowledging that the tale came "from the pack of the pedlar" rather

than "the library of the lawyer," and admitting that he did "not vouch for the authenticity of the narrative," he asserted that Gwinett's story was nonetheless "an ingenious illustration of the danger of yielding to presumptive evidence, where the life of man is at stake." *Trial of Daley and Halligan*, pp. 59, 62.

65. *The Life, Trial & Execution of John Dahmen* (N.p.: L. Cuthberg, 1825), p. 4; *The Confession of Jereboam O. Beauchamp* (Bloomfield, Ky.: n.p., 1826).

66. See, for ex., *Account of Garcia and Castillano*, in which the "Confession of Garcia" charged Castillano with the crime; and *The Confession of Mina* (Doylestown, Penn.: N.p., 1832), in which the condemned man charged his wife with the murder of her previous husband, p. 18.

67. *Tribune*, November 18, 1842; quoted in John Walsh, *Poe the Detective: The Curious Circumstances Behind "The Mystery of Marie Roget"* (New Brunswick: Rutgers University Press, 1968), p. 55. For an excellent study of this case, see Srebnick, *Mysterious Death*.

68. Srebnick's *Mysterious Death* offers a multilayered and richly insightful study of the Rogers murder. She argues that three distinct narratives shaped the literary response to the Rogers case. "As a tragic narrative, her death was used to show the triumph of evil over good in the perpetual war between the competing forces of urban life; as a narrative of violent death, her story provided titillation at the same time as it provoked fear, rage, and cries for retribution; and, as a source of mystery, her death inspired literary quests for detection and understanding"; pp. 167–168.

69. On Poe's treatment of the case, see Srebnick, *Mysterious Death*, chaps. 6 and 7; Walsh, *Poe the Detective;* William K. Wimsatt, "Poe and the Mystery of Marie Roget," *PMLA* 56 (March 1941):230–248; Samuel Copp Worthen, "Poe and the Beautiful Cigar Girl," *American Literature* 20 (November 1948):305–312; Ned Buntline [Edward Zane Carrol Judson], *The Mysteries and Miseries of New York: A Story of Real Life* (New York: Berford, 1848), Book V, p. 69; *A Confession of the Awful Bloody Transactions in the Life of the Fiend-like Murderer of Miss Mary Rogers* (New Orleans: E. E. Barclay, 1851).

70. *Annals of Murder*, p. 48.

71. D. Wilson, *Henrietta Robinson* (New York: Miller, Orton & Mulligan, 1855), p. 69. Also see *Life and Confession of Mrs. Henrietta Robinson, the Veiled Murderess!* (Boston: Dr. H. B. Skinner, 1855), pp. 3–4, 15.

72. *Veiled Murderess!*, front and back covers.

73. The placement of these illustrations reinforces an argument made by Dennis Porter about how detective fiction (and, by my extension, murder-mystery narrative) exaggerated the nature of all novel-reading as

an act of "decipherment and discovery"; *Pursuit of Crime*, p. 52. For other "veiled ladies" at murder trials, see *Trial of Mrs. Margaret Howard* (Cincinnati, Ohio, 1849), p. 13; and *The Veiled Lady; or, the Mysterious Witness in the McFarland Trial* (Philadelphia: C. W. Alexander [1870?]).

74. *Life, Trial and Execution of Edward H. Ruloff [sic] . . . A Man Shrouded in Mystery!* (Philadelphia: Barclay, 1871); E. H. Freeman, *The Veil of Secrecy Removed. The Only True and Authentic History of Edward H. Rulloff* (Binghamton: Carl & Freeman, 1871); *"The Barrel Mystery"* (Chicago: Norris & Hyde, 1859); *The Great "Trunk Mystery"* (Philadelphia: Barclay, 1871).

75. *The Life and Death of Mrs. Maria Bickford* (Boston: Silas Estabrook, 1846), p. 16; *The Dying Confession of John Lechler* (Lancaster, Penn.: M. M'Kelly, 1822), pp. 11–12; *Awful Disclosures!*, p. 12.

76. *Confession of Horn*, p. vi. Such ambiguity makes this account "fantastic," a genre defined by the reader's hesitation between a natural and a supernatural understanding of events; see Tzvetan Todorov, *The Fantastic: A Structural Approach to a Literary Genre*, trans. Richard Howard (Ithaca: Cornell University Press, 1975).

77. See Jeffrey B. Russell, *A History of Witchcraft: Sorcerers, Heretics, and Pagans* (London: Thames and Hudson, 1980), pp. 12–13.

78. *Trial of Stephen and Jesse Boorn*, p. 16.

79. *Mystery Developed*, p. 13. For a useful discussion of the Boorn case as mystery, see Gerald W. McFarland, *The "Counterfeit" Man: The True Story of the Boorn–Colvin Murder Case* (Amherst: University of Massachusetts Press, 1990), chap. 5.

80. The workings of detective fiction lend support to the reader-centered criticism of Stanley Fish and Roland Barthes, which treats texts not as static artifacts but in terms of the transactions that occur between a text and a reader who takes an active role in processing that text, always constructing and dismantling hypotheses about the work's meaning; see Porter, *Pursuit of Crime*, pp. 6, 229; Priestman, *Detective Fiction*, p. 21; Stanley Fish, "Literature in the Reader: Affective Stylistics," *New Literary History* 2, no. 1 (1970):123–162.

81. On the active narrative role of trial jurors, see *Trial of Hendrickson*, p. 120; *Closing Argument . . . Dunbar*, p. 22; *Trial of Knapp* (McDade 570), p. 7.

82. The first marginal comment is in *Report of the Trial of Daniel H. Corey* (Newport, [N.H.]: French & Brown, 1830) (copy at American Antiquarian Society): the reader corrected a date and the names of a medical authority and a judge, and crossed out a line that was extraneous to the trial. The second is noted by Thomas McDade in his entry for

Statement of James E. Eldredge (Canton, New York: S. P. Remington, 1859) in *Annals of Murder*, p. 85. The third is in *Trial of Chapman* (copy at American Antiquarian Society).

83. "The Mysterious Fate of Mary Cecilia Rogers," *Annals of Murder*, p. 48; *Trial of Chapman*, p. 121. Also see *Trial of Tinker*, p. 91; *Account of Garcia and Castillano*, p. 30.

84. Channing, *God Admonishing*, pp. 29–30; *Fyler Murder*, pp. 5–6; *Trial of Hall*, p. 6.

85. *Trial of Farmer*, p. 60; also see *Trial of Bickford*, pp. 14–16.

86. *The Trials of Samuel M. Mayo and William Love* (Augusta: Chronicle Office, 1807), pp. 4–5; *The Triple Murderer* (Toledo: Hawes & Co., 1857), p. 18.

87. *Trial of Bickford*, p. 14; *State of Ohio against Parks*, p. 10; *Trial of M'Conaghy*, p. 4.

88. *Trial of M'Conaghy*, p. 4; *Trial of Bickford*, p. 15.

89. *Most Important Testimony . . . Knapp*, p. iv; *Trial and Execution of Thomas Barrett* (Boston: Skinner & Blanchard, 1845), p. 5; *Trial of Chapman*, pp. 35, 70; *Triple Murderer*, p. 18; *Facts Relating to the Murder of Joseph Green* [Rutland, Vt.: Fay & Davison, 1814], broadside; *Awful Disclosures!*, p. 14; *Trial of Eldredge*, p. 24.

90. *Trial of Bradley*, p. 174.

91. *Confession of Horn*, p. v.

92. For a literary analysis of the "storied body," see Peter Brooks, *Body Work: Objects of Desire in Modern Narrative* (Cambridge, Mass.: Harvard University Press, 1993).

93. *Trial of Bradley*, p. 157.

94. Ibid., pp. 5–6, 9, 152, 157.

95. Ibid. pp. 173–174; emphases added.

96. *Life of Michael Powers* (Boston: Russell & Gardner, 1820), p. 19.

97. For the bludgeon illustration, see *Report of the Evidence . . . Knapp*, frontis. The illustrated hand is in *Trial of Hall et al.*, p. 26; the heading reads, "We here insert a very exact representation of the RIGHT HAND of HALL, as it appeared after it was cut and when he was arrested." The facsimile letters of the Rev. Avery were printed in *A Fac-simile of the Letters Produced at the Trial of the Rev. Ephraim K. Avery* (Boston: Pendleton's Lithography, 1833).

98. *Trial of Anthony*, p. 4.

99. *Account of Garcia and Castillano*, pp. 5–6; *Fyler Murder*, pp. 11, 176.

100. *The Manheim Tragedy* (Lancaster, Penn.: Evening Express Office, 1858), opposite p. 7; *Trial of Tirrell* (McDade 990), obverse of title page; *Fyler Murder*, opposite p. 122.

101. The fictional practice of including diagrams of the crime was initiated

by author Charles Felix in *The Notting Hill Mystery* (1862); see Julian Symons, *Bloody Murder: From the Detective Story to the Crime Novel* (New York: Viking, 1985), chap. 3.

102. *Report of Evidence . . . Knapp*, n.p.; *Trial of Hall et al.*, n.p.; *Trial of Dunbar*, opposite p. 3; *Trial of Thomas O. Selfridge* (Boston: Russell & Cutler, Belcher and Armstrong, and Oliver and Munroe [1807]), p. 170; *Trial of Rev. Mr. Avery*, reported by Benjamin F. Hallett (Boston: Daily Commercial Gazette and the Boston Daily Advocate, 1833) (McDade 52), (included as loose-leaf foldout). Also see *Trial of Bickford*, opposite p. 1; *Trial of Woodford*, p. 8; *Trial of Charles Getter* (Philadelphia: Alexander's, 1833), opposite title page; and *Report of the Trial of Abraham Prescott* (Concord: M. G. Atwood, and Currier & Hall, 1834), p. 155.

103. *Manheim Tragedy*, p. 7; J. Winston Coleman, Jr., *The Beauchamp-Sharp Tragedy: An Episode of Kentucky History During the Middle 1820's* (Frankfort, Ky.: Roberts Printing Company, 1950), opposite p. 16; *Trial of Knapp* (McDade 572), frontis; *Trial of Hall et al.*, p. 18; *Fyler Murder*, p. 12. Also see *The Trial of Samuel Perry* (Utica: William Williams, 1826), p. 5.

104. See *Tragedies on the Land*, p. 129; *The Lives of Helen Jewett and Richard P. Robinson* [New York: (George Wilkes?), 1849] p. 118; *Confessions, Trials, and Biographical Sketches of the Most Cold Blooded Murderers* (Boston, 1837), p. 304.

105. *Trial of Anthony; Trial of Robinson; Report of the Trial of Joel Clough* (Boston: Beals, Homer & Co., 1833); *Trial of Knapp*, (McDade 570), p. 14.

106. See *Trial of Eldredge*, p. 23; *Trial of Hendrickson*, p. 153; *Lives of Jewett and Robinson*, pp. 40–42; *Trial of Albert J. Tirrell*, reported by J. E. P. Weeks, Esq. (Boston: Times Office, 1846) (McDade 991), p. 32.

107. *Appendix to the Report of the Trial of John Francis Knapp* (Salem, 1830), p. 38.

108. *Trial of Avery* (McDade 36), p. 9; *The Trial of Alpheus Hitchcock* [Utica: Seward and Williams (for George Richards, Jr.), 1807], p. 42; *Strictures . . . Avery*, p. 49.

109. See Frank Morn, *"The Eye That Never Sleeps": A History of the Pinkerton National Detective Agency* (Bloomington: Indiana University Press, 1982).

110. Eino Railo, *The Haunted Castle: A Study of the Elements of English Romanticism* (London: George Routledge & Sons, 1927); Edith Birkhead, *The Tale of Terror: A Study of the Gothic Romance* (London: Constable, 1921); Devendra P. Varma, *The Gothic Flame* (London: Arthur Baker, 1957); Donald A. Ringe, *American Gothic: Imagination and Rea-*

son in Nineteenth-Century Fiction (Lexington: University Press of Kentucky, 1982).

111. See Stuart M. Blumin, "George G. Foster and the Emerging Metropolis," introduction to *New York by Gas-Light* (1850) (Berkeley: University of California Press, 1990), pp. 1–61; David S. Reynolds, *Beneath the American Renaissance: The Subversive Imagination in the Age of Emerson and Melville* (New York: Alfred A. Knopf, 1988), chap. 2; Michael Denning, *Mechanic Accents: Dime Novels and Working-Class Culture in America* (London: Verso, 1987), chap. 6.

112. See, for example, Jonathan H. Green, *Secret Band of Brothers* (Hicksville, N.Y.: Exposition Press, 1980) (originally printed 1847), p. x (originally, the title page); John B. Gough, *Sunlight and Shadow* (Hartford: A. D. Worthington, 1881), p. 292; *Memoir and Select Remains of the Late Rev. John R. M'Dowall* (New York: Leavitt, Lord, 1838), p. 266; George Barrell Cheever, *The Dream: or, the True History of Deacon Giles' Distillery, and Deacon Jones' Brewery* (New York, 1848). On the Gothic dimensions of reform literature, see Karen Halttunen, "Gothic Imagination and Social Reform: The Haunted Houses of Lyman Beecher, Henry Ward Beecher, and Harriet Beecher Stowe," in Eric J. Sundquist, ed., *New Essays on Uncle Tom's Cabin* (Cambridge: Cambridge University Press, 1986).

113. David Brion Davis, "Some Themes of Countersubversion: An Analysis of Anti-Masonic, Anti-Catholic, and Anti-Mormon Literature," in Davis, ed., *The Fear of Conspiracy: Images of Un-American Subversion from the Revolution to the Present* (Ithaca: Cornell University Press, 1971), pp. 9–22. On the relationship between this Gothic spatial sensibility and the emergence of the prison and the mental institution, see Karen Halttunen, "Gothic Mystery and the Birth of the Asylum: The Cultural Construction of Deviance in Early Nineteenth-Century America," in *Moral Problems in American Life: New Essays on Cultural History*, ed. Karen Halttunen and Lewis Perry (Ithaca, N.Y.: Cornell University Press, 1998).

114. Stuart M. Blumin, "Explaining the New Metropolis: Perception, Depiction, and Analysis in Mid-Nineteenth-Century New York City," *Journal of Urban History* 11 (1984):9–38.

115. Blumin, ed., *New York by Gas-Light*, p. 6; *A Letter from Richard P. Robinson* (New York, 1837), p. 6.

116. Blumin, ed., *New York by Gas-Light*, p. 72.

117. *The Burdell Murder Case* (New York: Stearns, 1857), p. 28; this was a quote from the New York *Herald*, February 15. For middle-class readers in particular, this sense of mystery surrounding urban murders may have been enhanced by the disproportionate number of working-

NOTES TO PAGES 125–128

class and immigrant men who committed these crimes; see Eric Monkkonen, "Diverging Homicide Rates: England and the United States, 1850–1875," in Ted Robert Gurr, ed., *Violence in America*, vol. 1 (Newbury Park, 1989), pp. 80–101; Roger Lane, *Violent Death in the City: Suicide, Accident, and Murder in Nineteenth-Century Philadelphia* (Cambridge, Mass.: Harvard University Press, 1979); and Roger Lane, *Murder in America: A History* (Columbus: Ohio State University Press, 1977), chap. 4.

118. Jacques Barzun and Wendell Hertig, *A Catalogue of Crime*, quoted in Ian Ousby, *Bloodhounds of Heaven: The Detective in English Fiction from Godwin to Doyle* (Cambridge: Harvard University Press, 1976), p. 1; Arthur Conan Doyle, "A Case of Identity." As Dennis Porter has argued, a main point of interest in detective fiction has always been its exploitation of the reader's desire to peer into other people's private lives. "The crime is a gap by means of which the reader is permitted to enter the closed world behind the yew hedge or the apartment. The detective story gratifies because it legitimates activities considered taboo in its reader's lives": looking under beds, eavesdropping on private conversations, reading personal correspondence, and generally enjoying "without guilt the luxury of watching without being seen." Porter, *Pursuit of Crime*, pp. 240 and 41.

119. *Trial of Knapp* (McDade 570), pp. 5–6; *Account of Garcia and Castillano*, p. 30; *Triple Murderer*, p. 22, emphasis added; *Trial of Hendrickson*, p. 156. For remote rural murders, the Gothic spatial sensibility took a different form. The prosecution of John Blaisdell for the murder of John Wadleigh in Exeter, New Hampshire in 1822 emphasized that the "inhuman deed" was committed "in a remote and solitary situation," "on a dark and tempestuous night," at a spot where the nearest house was "more than a hundred rods" from "this scene of wickedness"; "a thick wood, increasing the surrounding darkness, stood near." "No one could be expected to interrupt him in his murderous work." *Trial of Blaisdell*, pp. 7, 52.

120. See Robert Sullivan, *The Disappearance of Dr. Parkman* (Boston: Little, Brown, 1971); Simon Schama, *Dead Certainties (Unwarranted Speculations)* (New York: Alfred A. Knopf, 1991), part 2; Helen Thomson, *Murder at Harvard* (Boston: Houghton Mifflin, 1971).

121. *The Boston Tragedy!* (Boston: n.p., 1850), p. 3.

122. *Awful Disclosures and Startling Developments* (N.p., 1849), p. 9; *The Boston Tragedy!*, p. 12.

123. *The Boston Tragedy!*, p. 13.

124. *Awful Disclosures and Startling Developments*, cover.

125. Ibid., p. 11.
126. *Report of the Case of Webster* (McDade 1060), after p. 36 and after p. 50; *The Parkman Murder. Trial of Prof. John W. Webster* (Boston: Daily Mail Office [1850]) (McDade 1059), pp. 24–25; *Trial of Webster* (McDade 1067), p. 13.
127. See *Trial of Webster* (McDade 1067), pp. 18, 22–23; *Trial of Webster* (McDade 1060), between pp. 80–81.
128. At least three editions of the trial report included both these drawings: see *Trial of Webster* (McDade 1067), pp. 14 and 25; *Trial of Professor John W. Webster* (New York: Stringer & Townsend, 1850) (McDade 1066), pp. 11 and 21; *Report of the Trial of Prof. John W. Webster* (Boston: Phillips, Sampson, 1850) (McDade 1062), pp. 54 and 309.
129. *Awful Disclosures and Startling Developments*, p. 16.
130. *The Extraordinary Confession of Dr. John White Webster* (Boston: Hotchkiss, 1850), p. 5.
131. Sullivan, *Disappearance of Parkman*, p. 204.
132. Schama, *Dead Certainties*, p. 281; Sullivan, *Disappearance of Parkman*, chap. 13.
133. Quoted in Schama, *Dead Certainties*, p. 269.
134. Ibid., p. 265; Sullivan, *Disappearance of Parkman*, pp. 143–145.
135. *Awful Disclosures and Startling Developments*, p. 4.
136. On this latter point, see Sullivan, *Disappearance of Parkman*, pp. 194–198.
137. Ousby, *Bloodhounds of Heaven*, pp. 48, 99, 103, 21.
138. Detective fiction was, as Michel Foucault and D. A. Miller have argued, an expression of the modern will to achieve power through surveillance; see Foucault, *Discipline and Punish* (New York: Pantheon, 1977); and Miller, *The Novel and the Police* (Berkeley: University of California Press, 1988). But in the larger scheme of popular criminal discourse, detective fiction was an act of wish-fulfillment just as the Pinkerton logo was.
139. *Trial of Chapman*, p. 112.

5. Murder in the Family Circle

1. Edgar Allan Poe, "The Black Cat," *Tales of Mystery and Imagination*, introduction by Graham Clarke (London: J. M. Dent, 1984), pp. 563–572 (quotes from pp. 563 and 564).
2. See John Rogers, *Death the Certain Wages of Sin to the Impenitent* (Boston: B. Green and J. Allen for Samuel Phillips, 1701); Cotton Mather, *Warnings from the Dead* (Boston: Bartholomew Green, 1693),

p. 73; Thomas Foxcroft, *Lessons of Caution to Young Sinners* (Boston: S. Kneeland and T. Green, 1733); John Williams, *Warnings to the Unclean* (Boston: B. Green and J. Allen, 1699), p. 56.

3. Cotton Mather, *Pillars of Salt* (Boston: B. Green and J. Allen, 1699), p. 85; Nathaniel Clap, *The Lord's Voice, Crying to His People* (Boston: B. Green, 1715), p. 68; Cotton Mather, *Tremenda* (Boston: B. Green, 1721), p. 3; Cotton Mather, *Speedy Repentance Urged* (Boston: Samuel Green, 1690), p. 58; Cotton Mather, *Tremenda*, p. 33.

4. Nathaniel Clap, *Sinners Directed to Hear & Fear* (Boston: J. Allen for N. Boone, 1715), p. xi; Mather, *Tremenda*, pp. 26, 34.

5. See, for ex., *Report of the Trial and Conviction of John Earls* (Williamsport, 1836); *Trial of Henry G. Green* (Troy: Budget Office, 1845).

6. On the Spooner case, see *The Dying Declaration of James Buchanan, Ezra Ross, and William Brooks* [Worcester, Mass. 1778]; Thaddeus Maccarty, *The Guilt of Innocent Blood Put Away* (Norwich: John Trumbull, 1778); *The Lives, Last Words, and Dying Speech of Ezra Ross, James Buchanan, and William Brooks* [Worcester? 1778?]; *The Rev. Mr. Maccarty's Account of the Behaviour of Mrs. Spooner* [N.p., 1778]. Also see William E. Du Bois, *Trial of Lucretia Chapman* (Philadelphia: G. W. Mentz & Son, 1832); *Trial of Mrs. Hannah Kinney* (Boston: Times and Notion Office, 1840).

7. *An Account of the Trial of Jesse Wood* [N.p., n.d.]; *Trial of Amos Furnald* (Concord [N.H.]: Jacob B. Moore, 1825); *Sketch of the Trial of Mary Cole* (New Brunswick, 1812); *Life of Benjamin D. White* (Batavia [N.Y.], 1843).

8. Stephen Arnold beat to death his six-year-old niece in 1805; see *A Brief Relation of the Cruel Murder of Betsy Van Amburgh* (New Jersey, 1805). Rufus Hill killed his stepdaughter; see *The Trial of Rufus Hill* [N.p., n.d.]. Rebecca Peake killed her stepson Ephraim Peake; see *Trial of Mrs. Rebecca Peake* (Montpelier [Vt.]: E. P. Walton & Son, 1836). Reuben Dunbar killed his stepfather's two nephews, Steven and David Lester, in 1850; see *Trial of Reuben Dunbar* (Albany: P. L. Gilbert, 1850). Robert McConaghy killed the mother and five siblings of his wife in 1840; see *Trial of Robert McConaghy* (Philadelphia [ca. 1840]). John Metcalf Thurston killed his sister's husband in 1851; see *Trial of John Metcalf Thurston* (Owego, N.Y.: Hiram A. Beebe, 1851).

9. *A Narrative of the Life, Together with the Last Speech, Confession and Solemn Declaration, of John Lewis* (New Haven: James Parker, at the Post-Office, 1762).

10. *A Narrative of the Life of William Beadle* (Hartford [Conn.]: Bavil Webster, 1783), p. 18.

11. On the Yates case, which inspired Charles Brockden Brown's *Wieland;*

or, The Transformation (1798), see Alan Axelrod, *Charles Brockden Brown: An American Tale* (Austin: University of Texas Press, 1983), chap. 3; *A Succinct Narrative of the Life and Character of Abel Clemmens* (Morgantown: J. Campbell, 1806); *Horrid Massacre!! Sketches of the Life of Captain James Purrinton* (Augusta: Peter Edes, 1806); *Narrative of the Life and Dying Confession of Henry Mills* (Boston: N. Coverly, 1817); *The Life and Confession of John W. Cowan* (Cincinnati: Kendall and Henry, 1835); *The Life and Confession of Isaac Heller* (Liberty: C. V. Duggins, 1836). Thomas M. McDade believes the Henry Mills case to be fictitious; see *The Annals of Murder: A Bibliography of Books and Pamphlets on American Murders from Colonial Times to 1900* (Norman: University of Oklahoma Press, 1961), p. 202.

12. *Horrid Massacre!!*, p. 4.

13. John Demos, *A Little Commonwealth: Family Life in Plymouth Colony* (New York: Oxford University Press, 1970); Edmund S. Morgan, *The Puritan Family: Religion and Domestic Relations in Seventeenth-Century New England* (New York: Harper and Row, 1966); Philip Greven, Jr., *Four Generations: Population, Land, and Family in Colonial Andover, Massachusetts* (Ithaca, N.Y.: Cornell University Press, 1970); Steven Mintz and Susan Kellogg, *Domestic Revolutions: A Social History of American Family Life* (New York: Free Press, 1988), chaps. 1 and 3; David J. Rothman, *The Discovery of the Asylum: Social Order and Disorder in the New Republic* (Boston: Little, Brown, 1971).

14. Nancy F. Cott, *The Bonds of Womanhood: "Woman's Sphere" in New England, 1780–1835* (New Haven: Yale University Press, 1977); Nancy F. Cott, "Passionlessness: An Interpretation of Victorian Sexual Ideology, 1790–1850," *Signs* 4 (1978):210–236; Kathryn Kish Sklar, *Catharine Beecher: A Study in American Domesticity* (New Haven: Yale University Press, 1973) ("family state" is quoted on p. 265); Carl N. Degler, *At Odds: Women and the Family in America from the Revolution to the Present* (New York: Oxford University Press, 1980), chap. 2 ("God's appointed agent" is quoted on p. 27); Barbara Welter, "The Cult of True Womanhood, 1820–1860," *American Quarterly*, 18 (1966):131–175; Mary P. Ryan, *Cradle of the Middle Class: The Family in Oneida County, New York, 1790–1865* (New York: Cambridge University Press, 1981).

15. See Lawrence Stone, *The Family, Sex and Marriage in England, 1500–1800* (New York: Harper and Row, 1977); Randolph Trumbach, *The Rise of the Egalitarian Family: Aristocratic Kinship and Domestic Relations in Eighteenth-Century England* (New York: Academic Press, 1978); Jay Fliegelman, *Prodigals and Pilgrims: The American Revolution Against Patriarchal Authority, 1750–1800* (Cambridge: Cambridge University Press, 1982); Mintz & Kellogg, *Domestic Revolutions*, chaps. 1 and 3;

Greven, *Four Generations;* Daniel Scott Smith, "Parental Power and Marriage Patterns: An Analysis of Historical Trends in Hingham, Massachusetts," in Michael Gordon, ed. *The American Family in Social-Historical Perspective,* 2nd ed. (New York: St. Martin's Press, 1978), pp. 87–100.

16. Herman R. Lantz et al., "Pre-Industrial Patterns in the Colonial Family in America: A Content Analysis of Colonial Magazines," *American Sociological Review* 33 (1968):420; Daniel Blake Smith, *Inside the Great House: Planter Family Life in Eighteenth-Century Chesapeake Society* (Ithaca, N.Y.: Cornell University Press, 1980) (quote is on p. 138); Jan Lewis, *The Pursuit of Happiness: Family and Values in Jefferson's Virginia* (Cambridge: Cambridge University Press, 1983), chap. 5; Ellen K. Rothman, *Hands and Hearts: A History of Courtship in America* (New York: Basic Books, 1984), chaps. 1 and 2.

17. Degler, *At Odds,* chap. 2; Mintz and Kellogg, *Domestic Revolutions,* chap. 3; John D'Emilio and Estelle B. Freedman, *Intimate Matters: A History of Sexuality in America* (New York: Harper and Row, 1988); Nancy F. Cott, "Eighteenth Century Family and Social Life Revealed in Massachusetts Divorce Records," *Journal of Social History,* 10 (Fall 1976):20–43; Cott, "Divorce and the Changing Status of Women in Eighteenth Century Massachusetts," *William and Mary Quarterly,* 3rd ser., 33 (1976):586–614; Nelson Manfred Blake, *The Road to Reno: A History of Divorce in the United States* (New York: Macmillan, 1962), chap. 5; Elizabeth Pleck, *Domestic Tyranny: The Making of Social Policy Against Family Violence from Colonial Times to the Present* (New York: Oxford University Press, 1987), chap. 1; Carol Zisowitz Stearns and Peter N. Stearns, *Anger: The Struggle for Emotional Control in America's History* (Chicago: University of Chicago Press, 1986) (Alcott quote on p. 39).

18. Bernard Wishy, *The Child and the Republic: The Dawn of Modern American Child Nurture* (Philadelphia: University of Pennsylvania Press, 1968); Myra C. Glenn, *Campaigns against Corporal Punishment: Prisoners, Sailors, Women, and Children in Antebellum America* (Albany: State University of New York Press, 1984) (quote on "rod of correction an ordinance of God," p. 8); Peter Gregg Slater, *Children in the New England Mind: In Death and in Life* (Hamden, Conn.: Archon Books, 1977) (Child is quoted on p. 151); Mintz and Kellogg, *Domestic Revolutions,* chaps. 1 and 3 ("the only effective and lasting government" is quoted on p. 47).

19. Ryan, *Cradle of the Middle Class,* esp. chap. 4 ("silken threads" is from the *Mother's Magazine,* 1833, quoted on p. 159); Glenn, *Campaigns against Corporal Punishment,* chap. 2; John Demos, "The Changing

Faces of Fatherhood," in *Past, Present, and Personal: The Family and the Life Course in American History* (New York: Oxford University Press, 1986), pp. 41–67; Ruth Bloch, "American Feminine Ideals in Transition: The Rise of the Moral Mother, 1785–1815," in *Feminist Studies* 4 (1978):98–116; Robert V. Wells, "Family History and the Demographic Transition," *Journal of Social History* 9 (Fall 1975):1–20.

20. *The Triple Murderer* (Toledo, Oh.: Hawes, 1857), p. 22; *Trial of John Hendrickson, Jr.* (Albany: David M. Barnes & W. S. Hevenor, 1853), p. 156.

21. Zephania Swift, *A Vindication of the Calling of the Special Superior Court . . . for the Trial of Peter Lung* (Windham, Conn.: J. Byrne, 1816), p. 26; Carroll E. Smith, *The Fyler Murder Case* (Syracuse: Smith & Hough, 1855), p. 44; *Trial of Hendrickson*, p. 31; *Trial of Kinney*, p. 11.

22. Quoted in Jenny Bourne Taylor, *In the Secret Theatre of Home: Wilkie Collins, Sensation Narrative, and Nineteenth-century Psychology* (London: Routledge, 1988), p. 1.

23. C. E. Potter, *Report of the Trial of Bradbury Ferguson* (Concord [N.H.]: Morrill Silsby, 1841), p. 70; *The Trial of Alpheus Hitchcock*, reported by George Richards, Jr. (Utica: Seward and Williams, 1807), p. 5. Also see *Speech of John V. L. M'Mahon, on Behalf of . . . George Swearingen* (Baltimore: Lucas & Deaver, 1829), p. 19.

24. *Report of the Trial of William F. Comings* (Boston: Samuel N. Dickinson, 1844), p. 123; *An Authentic Account of the Trial of John Banks* (n.p., n.d.), pp. 3, 151.

25. *Trial of Ferguson; Trial of John Graham* ([Baltimore, Md.]: Fryer & Clark [ca. 1804]), p. 28.

26. For examples of cases centering on these issues, see the following: on money and household labor, *Trial of Banks;* on sexual infidelity, *A Full Report of the Trial of Orrin Woodford*, by N. H. Morgan (Hartford: Elihu Geer, 1846); *Trial of William M'Donnough* (Boston: Thomas G. Bangs, [1817]); on marital disobedience, *Trial of Ferguson;* on intemperance, *The Trial of Samuel Perry* (Utica: William Williams, 1826); *Trial of Graham;* "Trial of Michael M'Garvey," *Tragedies on the Land, Containing an Authentic Account of the Most Awful Murders* (Philadelphia: John B. Perry and New York: N. C. Nafis, 1841), pp. 143–151; on chronic absence, *Trial of Ferguson;* on wives' refusal to join their husbands in bed, *Trial of Medad M'Kay* by M. T. C. Gould (Albany: Websters & Skinners, 1821); on the wife's poor cookery, *Vindication of the Calling . . . Lung; Trial of Banks;* on the husband's ill-treatment of the cat, *Trial of Woodford.*

27. *Trial of Perry*, p. 7; *Trial of Woodford*, p. 15.

28. "The Murder of a Wife by Her Husband" (James Adams), *Annals of*

Murder, or, Daring Outrages, Trials, Confessions, &c. (Philadelphia: John B. Perry; New York: Nafis & Cornish, 1845), p. 24; *Trial, Sentence and Execution of James Ransom* ([New York]: 211 Water St., [1832]), p. 15.

29. *Trial of Banks; Vindication of the Calling . . . Lung;* "Trial of M'Garvey"; *Trial of Boies; Trial of Graham.*

30. On the first, see *Trial of M'Kay; Trial of Woodford; Report of the Trial of John Boies* (Dedham [Mass.]: H. & W. H. Mann [n.d.]); on the second, see *Trial of Banks; Vindication of the Calling . . . Lung;* and *Trial of Ferguson.*

31. *Trial of Ferguson,* p. 15. An important factor in the lack of privacy in these cases was the social position of the perpetrators, most of whom were lower class. Peter Lung was a common laborer and Michael McGarvey a carter; Medad McKay was said to be of poor and humble condition; John Banks was an apple vendor; William McDonnough lived in a tenement. And a high proportion of these wife-murderers were immigrants, frequently Irish; see, for ex., *Trial of Boies,* p. 34.

32. For a quick summary of these marital episodes, see the prosecutor's opening, *Trial of Hendrickson,* pp. 2–11.

33. *Trial of Hendrickson,* pp. 153, 158, 90. On the medical testimony at the Hendrickson trial, see *Review, Opinions, &c., of Dr. Charles A. Lee, and Others, of the Testimony of Drs. Salisbury and Swinburne* (New York, 1855).

34. *Trial of Hendrickson,* pp. 145, 156, 172, 12, 153, 120.

35. Ibid., pp. 119–120, 127, 172.

36. *Trial of Earls,* pp. 110, 166, 169.

37. Ibid., pp. 124, 151.

38. Ibid., pp. 155, 179.

39. *The Trial of Barent Becker* (n.p. 1815); *Trial of M'Kay* (who was acquitted); *Trial of Cornelius Henry Francisco* (n.p., [1837?]).

40. *Confession of Henry G. Green* (Troy: R. Rose and F. Belcher, 1845), p. 48. For a reference to the Green trial, see *Trial of Hendrickson,* p. 117.

41. *Trial of Hitchcock,* pp. 24, 25; *Trial of Charles Getter* (Philadelphia: Alexander's General Printing Office, 1833) (McDade 335), pp. 5, 55; also see *The Trial of Charles Getter* (Easton: F. W. Muller, 1833) (McDade 336). The Rev. Jacob Harden likewise killed his wife, whom he married under pressure by her parents after he had ruined her reputation; see *Life, Confession, and Letters of Courtship of Rev. Jacob S. Harden* (Hackettstown, N.J.: E. Winton, 1860).

42. *The Trial and a Sketch of the Life of Oliver Watkins* (Providence: H. H. Brown, 1830), p. 31.

43. See Maccarty, *Guilt of Innocent Blood,* pp. 36–39.

44. Nathan Fiske, *A Sermon Preached at Brookfield* (Boston: Thomas & John Fleet, 1778), p. 5; Maccarty, *Guilt of Innocent Blood*, p. 24; Fiske, *Sermon Preached at Brookfield*, pp. 8, 7, 10; Maccarty, *Guilt of Innocent Blood*, pp. 36–39.

45. *Trial of Chapman*, pp. 112, 118, 193.

46. Ibid., pp. 155, 151, 142, 76.

47. Ibid., pp. 168, 170–171. For a more detailed discussion of this case, see Karen Halttunen, "'Domestic Differences': Competing Narratives of Womanhood in the Murder Trial of Lucretia Chapman," in Shirley Samuels, ed., *The Culture of Sentiment: Race, Gender, and Sentimentality in Nineteenth-Century America* (New York: Oxford University Press, 1992), pp. 39–57.

48. See *The Confession of Mina* (Doylestown, Penn., 1832).

49. *Trial of Kinney*, pp. 3, 5.

50. *Trial of Kinney*, pp. 27–28.

51. *A Review of the Principal Events of the Last Ten Years in the Life of Mrs. Hannah Kinney* (Boston: J. N. Bradley & Co., 1841), pp. 3–4. Kinney's first husband, Ward Witham, responded to this publication with his *Brief Notice of the Life of Mrs. Hannah Kinney* (n.p., 1842), which charged her with repeated acts of adultery, including an illicit relationship with her third husband while she was married to her second. The exception that proves the rule with respect to the difficulty of convicting socially respectable women of husband-murder was the case of Elizabeth Van Valkenburgh, a lower-class woman convicted and executed for the murder of two consecutive husbands in 1846; see *The Awful Confession of Elizabeth Van Valkenburgh*, bound with *Testimonium Dr. Baker et Aliorum Fecit in the Trial, in quaem est Confession of John Haggerty* ([Lancaster, Penn.: J. S. Jones], 1846).

52. *Trial of Mrs. Margaret Howard* (Cincinnati, 1849), pp. 7, 29.

53. Ibid., pp. 8, 26, 12.

54. *The Trial of Charles Stevens* (Kennebunk: James K. Remich, 1823), pp. 31, 32, 34.

55. *Trial of Amos Furnald* (Concord [N.H.]: Jacob B. Moore, 1825), pp. 16, 17, 105, 112.

56. The specific horror of child-murder was less powerful when the victim was grown: see, for ex., *Trial of Peake; An Account of the Trial of Jesse Wood* [N.p., n.d.].

57. "Trial of M'Garvey," pp. 147, 148; *Trial of Boies*, p. 9; *Trial of M'Donnough*, p. 11; *The Trial of Robert Bush* (Springfield [Mass.], 1828), p. 15. For a social history of murderous husbands as "failed patriarchs," see Randolph Roth, "The Indulgence of Passion: Murders of Husbands and Wives in Northern New England, 1790–1865," in Christine

Daniels, ed., *Over the Threshold: Intimate Violence in Early America, 1640–1865* (New York: Routledge Press, forthcoming).

58. *Vindication of the Calling . . . Lung*, p. 12; *A Full and Particular Narrative of the Life, Character and Conduct of John Banks* (New York, 1807), p. 10; *Trial of M'Donnough*, p. 49; *Trial of Stevens*, p. 27; *The Trial of Stephen Arnold* (Cooperstown [N.Y.]: E. Phinney [1805?]), p. 19.

59. "The Unprecedented Crime of John Zimmerman," *Tragedies on the Land*, pp. 29, 30.

60. *Triple Murderer*, p. 16.

61. *A Sketch of the Life and Adventures of Guy C. Clark* (Ithaca, 1832), pp. 35, 32, 37, 34, 43, 44.

62. *Narrative of the Life and Dying Confession of Henry Mills* (Boston: H. Trumbull, 1817) (a probable fiction; see McDade, *Annals of Murder*, p. 202).

63. *Trial of Boies*, p. 7; *Trial of Graham*, pp. 39–40; *Trial of Hitchcock*, pp. 15–16; *Trial of M'Kay*, p. 18; *Trial of Earls*, p. 110.

64. *Confession of Edward Donnelly* (Philadelphia, 1808); *The Confession of Adam Horn* (Baltimore: James Young, 1843), p. 18.

65. *Confession of Horn*, p. 30; *Annals of Murder*, n.p.

66. *Triple Murderer*, pp. 20–21.

67. See Steven Mintz, *A Prison of Expectations: The Family in Victorian Culture* (New York: New York University Press, 1983); John Demos, "Images of the Family, Then and Now," in *Past, Present, and Personal*, pp. 24–40; Helena M. Wall, *Fierce Communion: Family and Community in Early America* (Cambridge, Mass.: Harvard University Press, 1990), esp. p. 148.

68. *Trial of Earls*, p. 100.

69. The domestic scene of the crime actively enhanced its horror. "The corpse, wrote W. H. Auden, 'must shock not only because it is a corpse but also because, even for a corpse, it is shockingly out of place, as when a dog makes a mess on a drawing room carpet.' The incongruity of the corpse on the drawing room carpet is its shock value. On the other hand, once our eyes get used to the sight, the result turns out to be a domestication of homicide"; David Lehman, *The Perfect Murder: A Study in Detection* (New York: Free Press, 1989), p. 9.

70. *Trial of Hill*, p. 8.

6. Murdering Medusa

1. *A Report of the Examination of David Gibbs, Fanny Leach, and Eliza P. Burdick* (Hartford: Hanmer and Comstock, 1833), p. 8.

2. *Trial of George Crowninshield, J. J. Knapp, Jun. and John Francis Knapp* (Boston: Beals and Homer, and Francis Ingraham, 1830), p. 93.

3. "The Medusa, As Copied from an Antique Gem," by Mrs. A. R. St. John, in M. A. Dwight, *Grecian and Roman Mythology*, 2nd ed. (New York: George P. Putnam, 1849), pp. 308, 305. Also see Thomas Bulfinch, *The Age of Fable; or Beauties of Mythology* (Boston: J. E. Tilton, 1863), pp. 161–162.

4. See, for ex., Eliphalet Adams, *A Sermon Preached on the Occasion of the Execution of Katherine Garret* (New London: T. Green, 1738), pp. 28–30, 43–44.

5. *A Sketch of the Proceedings and Trial of William Hardy* (Boston: Oliver and Munroe, 1807); also see *The Trial of Alice Clifton* [N.p. (1787)]; and *Report of the Trial of Susanna* (Troy, N.Y.: Ryer Schermerhorn, 1810). On the decline of prosecutions and convictions for infanticide, see Peter C. Hoffer and N. E. H. Hull, *Murdering Mothers: Infanticide in England and New England* (New York: New York University Press, 1981).

6. *Confession of Edward Donnelly* (Philadelphia, 1808), p. 3; Moses C. Welch, *The Gospel to be Preached to All Men* (Windham: John Byrne, 1805), p. 30; *The Life and Confession of Cato* (Johnstown [N.Y.]: Abraham Romyen, 1803); *The Confession of John Battus* [Dedham, Mass., 1804?], pp. 10, 11.

7. Deborah Cameron and Elizabeth Frazer, *The Lust to Kill: A Feminist Investigation of Sexual Murder* (Oxford: Polity Press, 1987), p. 22; *Confession of Battus*, p. 11; also see *Trial and Execution of Thomas Barrett, Who First Committed a Rape on the Person of Mrs. Houghton . . . and Then Foully Murdered Her to Conceal His Crime* (Boston: Skinner & Blanchard, 1845). For a brilliant study of sexual murder narratives in nineteenth-century England, see Judith R. Walkowitz, *City of Dreadful Delight: Narratives of Sexual Danger in Late-Victorian London* (Chicago: University of Chicago Press, 1992).

8. T. Walter Herbert, *Dearest Beloved: The Hawthornes and the Making of the Middle-Class Family* (Berkeley: University of California Press, 1993), p. 139; John D'Emilio and Estelle B. Freedman, *Intimate Matters: A History of Sexuality in America* (New York: Harper and Row, 1988); John C. Spurlock, *Free Love: Marriage and Middle-Class Radicalism in America, 1825–1860* (New York: New York University Press, 1988); Ellen K. Rothman, *Hands and Hearts: A History of Courtship in America* (New York: Basic Books, 1984); Daniel Scott Smith and Michael Hindus, "Premarital Pregnancy in America, 1640–1971: An Overview and Interpretation," *Journal of Interdisciplinary History* 4 (Spring 1975):537–570; Robert V. Wells, "Illegitimacy and Bridal Pregnancy in Colonial America," in Peter Laslett, Karla Oosterveen, and Richard M. Smith, eds., *Bastardy and Its Comparative History* (Cambridge, Mass.: Harvard University Press, 1980), pp. 349–361; Daniel Scott Smith, "The Long

Cycle in American Illegitimacy and Prenuptial Pregnancy," in Laslett et al., *Bastardy,* pp. 362–378; Daniel Scott Smith, "Parental Power and Marriage Patterns: An Analysis of Historical Trends in Hingham, Massachusetts," *Journal of Marriage and the Family* 35 (August 1973):419–428; Michael Grossberg, *Governing the Hearth: Law and Family in Nineteenth-Century America* (Chapel Hill: University of North Carolina Press, 1985); Daniel Scott Smith, "Family Limitation, Sexual Control, and Domestic Feminism in Victorian America," *Feminist Studies* 1 (1973):40–57; Karen Lystra, *Searching the Heart: Women, Men, and Romantic Love in Nineteenth-Century America* (New York: Oxford University Press, 1989).

9. Smith and Hindus, "Premarital Pregnancy in America," p. 550; Nancy F. Cott, *The Bonds of Womanhood: "Woman's Sphere" in New England, 1780–1835* (New Haven: Yale University Press, 1977); and Cott, "Passionlessness: An Interpretation of Victorian Sexual Ideology, 1790–1850," *Signs* 4 (Winter 1978):219–236; Linda K. Kerber, *Women of the Republic: Intellect and Ideology in Revolutionary America* (Chapel Hill: University of North Carolina Press, 1980); Ruth Bloch, "The Gendered Meanings of Virtue in Revolutionary America," *Signs* 13 (Autumn 1987):37–58; Jan Lewis, "The Republican Wife: Virtue and Seduction in the Early Republic," *William and Mary Quarterly* (1987):689–721.

10. Lystra, *Searching the Heart,* p. 10; Nancy F. Cott, "Divorce and the Changing Status of Women in Eighteenth-Century Massachusetts," *William and Mary Quarterly,* 33 (1976):586–614; Janet Farrell Brodie, *Contraception and Abortion in Nineteenth-Century America* (Ithaca: Cornell University Press, 1994), p. 34; Jan Lewis and Kenneth Lockridge, "'Sally Has Been Sick': Pregnancy and Family Limitation among Virginia Gentry Women," *Journal of Social History* 22 (Fall 1988):5–19.

11. D'Emilio and Freedman, *Intimate Matters;* Louis J. Kern, *An Ordered Love: Sex Roles and Sexuality in Victorian Utopias—The Shakers, the Mormons, and the Oneida Community* (Chapel Hill: University of North Carolina Press, 1981); Lawrence Foster, *Religion and Sexuality: Three American Communal Experiments of the Nineteenth Century* (New York: Oxford University Press, 1981); Spurlock, *Free Love;* Timothy J. Gilfoyle, *City of Eros: New York City, Prostitution, and the Commercialization of Sex, 1790–1920* (New York: W. W. Norton, 1992).

12. Daniel A. Cohen, *Pillars of Salt, Monuments of Grace: New England Crime Literature and the Origins of American Popular Culture, 1674–1860* (New York: Oxford University Press, 1993), chap. 8; "Joel Clough, The Murderer of Mrs. Mary W. Hamilton," *Tragedies on the Land, Containing an Authentic Account of the Most Awful Murders* (Philadelphia: John

B. Perry; and New York: N. C. Nafis, 1841), p. 164; *The Authentic Confession of Joel Clough* (Philadelphia: Robert P. Desilver, 1833), p. 6; *The Trial for Murder, of James E. Eldredge* (Ogdensburgh, N.Y.: Hitchcock, Tillotson & Stilwell's Steam Presses, 1857), p. 118.

13. *The Confession of Jereboam O. Beauchamp* (Bloomfield, Ky., 1826); *A Full and Complete Account of the Heberton Tragedy* (New York [c. 1849]), p. 28.

14. *The Dying Confession of John Lechler* (Lancaster, Penn.: M. M'Kelly, 1822), p. 5; William E. Du Bois, *Trial of Lucretia Chapman* (Philadelphia: G. W. Mentz & Son, 1832), pp. 21–22; *Trial of Orrin De Wolf* (Worcester: Thomas Drew, Jr. [1845]); *Life and Trial of Dr. Abner Baker, Jr.* (Louisville, Ky.: Prentice and Weissinger, 1846). For another case of a husband's murdering his wife's lover, see Nat Brandt, *The Congressman Who Got Away with Murder* (Syracuse: Syracuse University Press, 1991).

15. *The Only True Confession. The Last Words and Dying Confession of Wm. Gross* (Philadelphia, 1823); *A Correct Copy of the Trial & Conviction of Richard Johnson* (New York: Christian Brown [1829?]), pp. 15–16; Patricia Cline Cohen, *The Murder of Helen Jewett: The Life and Death of a Prostitute in Nineteenth-Century New York* (New York: Alfred A. Knopf, 1998). Specific contemporary accounts of these crimes will be footnoted below.

16. *The Burdell Murder Case* (New York: Stearns & Co., 1857), p. 28; *The Conspirators' Victims, or, the Life and Adventures of J. V. Craine* (Sacramento: [Gardiner and Kirk], 1855), p. 19. For a vividly detailed study of murder in a perfectionist religious community, see Paul E. Johnson and Sean Wilentz, *The Kingdom of Matthias: A Story of Sex and Salvation in 19th-Century America* (New York: Oxford University Press, 1994).

17. Michel Foucault, *The History of Sexuality*, trans. Robert Hurley, vol. 1 (New York: Pantheon, 1978), p. 151.

18. *Speech of John V. L. M'Mahon, on Behalf of . . . George Swearingen* (Baltimore: Lucas & Deaver, 1829), p. 3.

19. *A Sketch of the Life and Adventures of Henry Leander Foote* (New Haven: T. J. Stafford, 1850), p. 42; *Trial of Joel Clough*, p. 3.

20. *Manchester Tragedy*, p. 8; *Trial of Eldredge*, p. 13.

21. *The Authentic Life of Mrs. Mary Ann Bickford* (Boston, 1846), p. 48; *Trial of Albert John Tirrell* (Boston: Times' Office, 1846) (McDade 991), p. 19; *The Trial of Albert J. Tirrell* (Boston: Boston Daily Mail, 1846) (McDade 990), p. 5.

22. *The Life of Ellen Jewett* (New York, 1836), pp. 7, 23–24 (Jewett was variously called "Helen" and "Ellen"); *The Lives of Helen Jewett, and Richard P. Robinson* (New York, 1849), p. 30.

23. John Rogers, *Death the Certain Wages of Sin to the Impenitent* (Boston: B. Green and J. Allen for Samuel Phillips, 1701); *Trial of Hardy*, pp. 27, 28, 29.

24. On this case, see David Richard Kasserman, *Fall River Outrage: Life, Murder, and Justice in Early Industrial New England* (Philadelphia: University of Pennsylvania Press, 1986); and William G. McLoughlin, "Untangling the Tiverton Tragedy: The Social Meaning of the Terrible Haystack Murder of 1833," *Journal of American Culture* 7 (1984):75–84.

25. *Trial of Rev. Mr. Avery* (Boston: Daily Commercial Gazette and the Boston Daily Advocate, 1833) (McDade 52), p. 96; *The Arguments of Counsel in the Close of the Trial of Rev. Ephraim K. Avery* (Boston: Daily Commercial Gazette and the Boston Daily Advocate, 1833), pp. 25, 30, 27; *Report of the Trial of the Rev. Ephraim K. Avery* (New York: William Stodart [n.d.]) (McDade 44), p. 20.

26. *Arguments of Counsel . . . Avery*, p. 25.

27. *Trial of Hendrickson; Trial of Eldredge*. On the "storied body," see Peter Brooks, *Body Work: Objects of Desire in Modern Narrative* (Cambridge, Mass.: Harvard University Press, 1993).

28. Richard W. Wertz and Dorothy C. Wertz, *Lying-In: A History of Childbirth in America* (New Haven: Yale University Press, 1989); Judith Walzer Leavitt, *Brought to Bed: Childbearing in America 1750–1950* (New York: Oxford University Press, 1986); Catherine M. Scholten, "'On the Importance of the Obstetrick Art': Changing Customs of Childbirth in America, 1760–1825," in Judith Walzer Leavitt, ed., *Women and Health in America: Historical Readings* (Madison: University of Wisconsin Press, 1984), pp. 142–154.

29. Jane B. Donegan, "'Safe Delivered,' But by Whom? Midwives and Men-midwives in Early America," in Leavitt, ed., *Women and Health*, p. 311.

30. *Trial of Clifton*, p. 10.

31. Wertz and Wertz, *Lying-In*; Leavitt, *Brought to Bed*; Scholten, "Importance of the Obstetrick Art"; Judith Walzer Leavitt and Whitney Walton, "'Down to Death's Door': Women's Perceptions of Childbirth in America," in Leavitt, *Women and Health*, pp. 155–165; Mary Poovey, "'Scenes of an Indelicate Character': The Medical 'Treatment' of Victorian Women," in Catherine Gallagher and Thomas Laqueur, eds., *The Making of the Modern Body: Sexuality and Society in the Nineteenth Century* (Berkeley: University of California Press, 1987), pp. 137–168. For a richly detailed discussion of how one eighteenth-century midwife (sometimes uneasily) shared birthing rooms with male physicians, see Laurel Thatcher Ulrich, *A Midwife's Tale: The Life of Martha Bal-*

lard, Based on Her Diary, 1785–1812 (New York: Alfred A. Knopf, 1990), esp. pp. 175–181.

32. Wiltbank is quoted in Carroll Smith-Rosenberg, "Puberty to Menopause: The Cycle of Femininity in Nineteenth-Century America," *Disorderly Conduct: Visions of Gender in Victorian America* (New York: Oxford University Press, 1985), p. 184; Ann Douglas Wood, "'The Fashionable Diseases': Women's Complaints and Their Treatment in Nineteenth-Century America," in Leavitt, ed., *Women and Health,* pp. 223–224; G. J. Barker-Benfield, *The Horrors of the Half-Known Life: Male Attitudes Toward Women and Sexuality in Nineteenth-Century America* (New York: Harper Colophon Books, 1976), p. 83.

33. Londa Schiebinger, "Skeletons in the Closet: The First Illustrations of the Female Skeleton in Eighteenth-Century Anatomy," in Gallagher and Laqueur, eds., *Making of the Modern Body,* pp. 42–82; Thomas Laqueur, *Making Sex: Body and Gender from the Greeks to Freud* (Cambridge, Mass.: Harvard University Press, 1990).

34. In the United States more than anywhere else, childbirth came to be viewed as "a potentially diseased condition that *routinely* requires the arts of medicine to overcome the processes of nature"; Wertz and Wertz, *Lying-In,* p. xvi. Ironically, "it is probable that physicians' techniques created new problems for birthing women and actually increased the dangers of childbirth" (Leavitt, *Brought to Bed,* p. 57), by infecting obstetrical patients with puerperal fever passed from diseased patients, damaging birthing mothers and fetuses through misuse of the forceps, and steadily expanding the repertoire of medical interventions. The linkage of obstetrics with disease was clearly made in the academic titles of medical school faculty: "professor of obstetrics and diseases of women and children"; Leavitt, *Brought to Bed,* p. 170.

35. Smith-Rosenberg, "Puberty to Menopause," pp. 183–184; Cott, "Passionlessness." As Foucault observed, the new medical specialists understood the female body "as being thoroughly saturated with sexuality" and "integrated into the sphere of medical practices, by reason of a pathology intrinsic to it"; Foucault, *History of Sexuality,* p. 104.

36. Carroll Smith-Rosenberg, "The Hysterical Woman: Sex Roles and Role Conflict in Nineteenth-Century America," in Smith-Rosenberg, *Disorderly Conduct,* p. 206; Wertz and Wertz, *Lying-In,* p. 57; Barker-Benfield, *Horrors of the Half-Known Life,* p. 83, chap. 20.

37. Barker-Benfield, *Horrors of the Half-Known Life,* pp. 93, 281; Smith-Rosenberg, "Puberty to Menopause," p. 190; Donegan, "Safe Delivered," p. 313.

38. Herbert, *Dearest Beloved*, p. 143; Barker-Benfield, *Horrors of the Half-Known Life*, esp. chaps. 6 and 15; Stephen Nissenbaum, *Sex, Diet, and Debility in Jacksonian America: Sylvester Graham and Health Reform* (Westport, Conn.: Greenwood, 1980).

39. Quoted in Barker-Benfield, *Horrors of the Half-Known Life*, p. 95.

40. For ex., though murder victim George Kinney suffered from venereal disease and secondary symptoms, according to his physician, were apparent, the autopsy report indicated that "There are no appearances of the disease (venereal) on the post mortem examination. We did not examine with that reference." See *Trial of Mrs. Hannah Kinney* (Boston: Times and Notion Office, 1840), p. 10.

41. *Examination of Dr. William Graves* [N.P., (1837)]; *The Life of Eliza Sowers* (Philadelphia: P. Augustus Sage, 1839); George Carroll, *The Manchester Tragedy* (Manchester, N.H.: Fish & Moore, 1848); *Full Report of the Trial of Dr. John McNab* (N.p. 1848?). Before the American Medical Association launched its campaign against abortion at mid-century, the procedure was legal in most states until "quickening" (fetal movement) occurred, usually in the second trimester; see Brodie, *Contraception and Abortion*, pp. 33, 253–254; Carroll Smith-Rosenberg, "The Abortion Movement and the AMA, 1850–1880," in *Disorderly Conduct*, pp. 217–244. But charges of murder against practitioners who inadvertently killed their patients suggest some earlier opposition to the procedure.

42. *Life of Sowers*, pp. 16, 17.

43. Ibid., p. 16; *Examination of Graves*, pp. 18–19; *Examination of Gibbs, Leach, and Burdick*, pp. 10, 8; *Manchester Tragedy*, p. 20.

44. In one case, the forensic legitimacy of sexual postmortem examinations was called into question by a physician testifying for the defense: Benjamin Shurtleff of Boston, who counted some six thousand midwifery cases to his credit, explained that "the work is all hidden and secret; the fact is the drum sounds well, but when we cut it open we don't find the cause of the sound." But Shurtleff's position—that the mystery of female sexuality defied the Asmodean opening of the female body—was the exception that proved the rule. See *Examination of Graves*, p. 27.

45. *Trial of John Graham* ([Baltimore, Md.]: Fryer & Clark, [ca. 1804), pp. 40, 28, 29, 38.

46. *Speech of M'Mahon . . . Swearingen*, p. 104.

47. Ibid., pp. 84, 58, 50, 44.

48. *Trial of Avery*, (McDade 52), pp. 47–49, 52, 30, 35; *A Report of the Examination of Rev. Ephraim K. Avery*, by L. Drury ([Providence], 1833), p. 34; *The Correct, Full and Impartial Report of the Trial of Rev.*

Ephraim K. Avery (Providence: Marshall and Brown, 1833) (McDade 36), p. 16.

49. *Trial of Avery* (McDade 52), p. 107; *Arguments of Counsel . . . Avery*, p. 200; *Trial of Avery* (McDade 44), p. 19.

50. *Arguments of Counsel . . . Avery*, p. 74.

51. This gender competition was a general pattern, not an unbroken rule: two male physicians in the Avery trial testified that Sarah Cornell had been sexually assaulted before death; and a woman testified to Phoebe Graham's chronic female problems at John Graham's trial, suggesting that no sexual assault had taken place.

52. Amy Gilman Srebnick, *The Mysterious Death of Mary Rogers: Sex and Culture in Nineteenth-Century New York* (New York: Oxford University Press, 1995), p. 12.

53. Ibid., p. 76.

54. See Ned Buntline [Edward Zane Carrol Judson], *The Mysteries and Miseries of New York: A Story of Real Life* (New York: Berford, 1848), Book V, p. 70.

55. *Arguments of Counsel . . . Avery*, p. 27.

56. *Trial of Tirrell* (McDade 990), p. 30; also see *Eccentricities & Anecdotes of Albert John Tirrell* (Boston, 1846), p. 14.

57. *The Life and Death of Mrs. Maria Bickford* (Boston, 1845), p. 23; also see the fictionalized account, *Julia Bicknell: or, Love and Murder!* (Boston: Henry L. Williams, 1845), pp. 26–27; *Trial of Tirrell* (McDade 991), pp. 5, 8. "It hardly seemed clear from Parker's opening argument who was the greater victim in the case—and who ought to be on trial: 'young man' Tirrell or 'harlot' Bickford"; Cohen, *Pillars of Salt*, p. 218.

58. *Life of Jewett*, pp. 6, 7, 11; *Lives of Jewett and Robinson*, p. 6.

59. *Lives of Jewett and Robinson*, pp. 40, 76; *Life of Jewett*, pp. 36–37.

60. *Life of Jewett*, pp. 10, 7, 45, 46; *Lives of Jewett and Robinson*, pp. 40, 119.

61. *Lives of Jewett and Robinson*, p. 79; emphasis added.

62. James Gordon Bennett, *New York Herald*, April 14, 1836, quoted in Cohen, *Murder of Helen Jewett*, p. 21.

63. *Trial of Richard P. Robinson* (N.p., n.d.), p. 21; *Murder Most Foul! A Synopsis of the Speeches . . . on the Trial of Robinson* (New York: R. H. Elton, 1836), pp. 122, 3, 4, 13.

64. *Murder Most Foul!*, pp. 4, 12, 22, 23.

65. *Life and Adventures of Foote*, pp. 7, 14, 27.

66. Ibid., pp. 35–37.

67. Ibid., pp. 38, 39.

68. Ibid., pp. 40–44.

69. Ibid., pp. 45, 46, 48.

70. Ibid., pp. 39–43.

71. *Arguments of Counsel...Avery*, p. 25; Cohen, *Pillars of Salt*, p. 204. Also see *Julia Bicknell*, p. 28.
72. *Arguments of Counsel...Avery*, p. 25; emphasis added.

7. The Murderer as Mental Alien

1. Nathaniel Clap, *The Lord's Voice, Crying to His People* (Boston: B. Green, 1715) (quote p. 68); and Clap, *Sinners Directed to Hear & Fear* (Boston: J. Allen for N. Boone, 1715) (quote p. iii).
2. *A Full Report of the Trial of Orrin Woodford* by N. H. Morgan (Hartford: Elihu Geer, 1846).
3. See Jacques M. Quen, "Anglo-American Criminal Insanity: An Historical Perspective," *Journal of the History of the Behavioral Sciences* 4 (1974):313–323; Quen, "An Historical View of the M'Naghten Trial," *Bulletin of the History of Medicine* 4 (1968):43–51; James C. Mohr, *Doctors and the Law: Medical Jurisprudence in Nineteenth-Century America* (New York: Oxford University Press, 1993), chap. 10; Anthony Platt and Bernard L. Diamond, "The Origins of the 'Right and Wrong' Test of Criminal Responsibility and Its Subsequent Development in the United States: An Historical Survey," *California Law Review* 54 (1966):1227–1260.
4. Quen, "Anglo-American Criminal Insanity" and "Historical View of the M'Naghten Trial"; Platt and Diamond, "Origins of the 'Right and Wrong' Test."
5. Clap, *Sinners Directed*, pp. vi–vii; *Impartial Account of the Trial of Ebenezer Mason* (Dedham: H. Mann, 1802). The so-called "right and wrong" test of insanity, commonly attributed by many legal historians to the "M'Naghten Rules" of 1844, was actually invoked routinely well before the M'Naghten case (including the Edward Arnold case). See Platt and Diamond, "The Origins of the 'Right and Wrong' Test."
6. *Trial of Mason*, p. 25; *The Last Words of Ebenezer Mason* (Dedham: Printed and sold at the Minerva Office, 1802), pp. iii, 11.
7. *Trial of Mason*, pp. 14, 15; *The Confession and Dying Words of Samuel Frost* (Worcester: Mr. Thomas's Printing Office [n.d.]), broadside.
8. Elijah Waterman, *A Sermon Preached at Windham... Also, a Sketch of ... Caleb's Life... By Moses C. Welch* (Windham [Conn.]: John Byrne, 1803), pp. 7, 20, 27, 9.
9. Quen, "Anglo-American Criminal Insanity"; quote on "no such madness," p. 317.
10. Quoted in Quen, "Anglo-American Criminal Insanity," p. 318.
11. *Report of the Trial of Abner Rogers, Jr.* by George Tyler Bigelow and George Bemis, Esqrs. (Boston: Little, Brown, 1844), pp. 64–66; *Report*

of the Trial of Daniel H. Corey by Joel Parker (Newport [N.H.]: French & Brown, 1830), p. 28; *Life and Trial of Dr. Abner Baker, Jr.* by C. W. Crozier (Louisville, Ky.: Prentice and Weissinger, 1846), p. viii.

12. See Mohr, *Doctors and the Law;* Janet A. Tighe, "Francis Wharton and the Nineteenth-Century Insanity Defense: The Origins of a Reform Tradition," *American Journal of Legal History* 27 (July 1983):223–253; Norman Dain, *Concepts of Insanity in the United States, 1789–1865* (New Brunswick: Rutgers University Press, 1964); John Starrett Hughes, *In the Law's Darkness: Isaac Ray and the Medical Jurisprudence of Insanity in Nineteenth-Century America* (New York: Oceana Publications, 1986); Smith, *Trial by Medicine;* Robert J. Waldinger, "Sleep of Reason: John P. Gray and the Challenge of Moral Insanity," *Journal of the History of Medicine and Allied Sciences* 34 (April 1979):163–179; Eric T. Carlson and Norman Dain, "The Meaning of Moral Insanity," *Bulletin of the History of Medicine* 36 (March-April 1962):130–140; Raymond de Saussure, "The Influence of the Concept of Monomania on French Medico-Legal Psychiatry (from 1825 to 1840)," *Journal of the History of Medicine* 1 (1946):365–397.

13. *Trial of Mrs. Rebecca Peake* (Montpelier [Vt.]: E. P. Walton & Son, 1836), p. 37; *Trial of Corey*, p. 58.

14. *Report of the Trial of Abraham Prescott* (Concord [N.H.]: M. G. Atwood, and Currier and Hall, 1834) (McDade 769); *Trial of Rogers; Report of the Trial of Willard Clark* by H. H. McFarland (New Haven: Thomas H. Pease, [1855]), pp. 66, 76.

15. *Trial of Corey*, p. 51; *Report of the Trial of Joel Clough* (Boston: Beals, Homer, 1833) (McDade 188), p. 43; *Trial of Peake*, p. 74; *Testimonium Dr. Baker et Aliorum Fecit in the Trial, in Quaem est Confession of John Haggerty* (Lancaster, Penn.: D. G. McGowan, [1846]), p. 18.

16. *Number One. Murder Trials and Executions in New Hampshire. Report of the Trial of Abraham Prescott* (Manchester, N.H.: Daily Mirror Office, 1869) (McDade 770), p. 35; *Trial of Clark*, p. 212; *Trial of Rogers*, pp. 93–94; *The Fyler Murder Case* by Carroll E. Smith (Syracuse: Smith & Hough, 1855), p. 164.

17. *Trial of Corey*, p. 31; *Trial of Abraham Prescott* (Concord: Printed at the Statesman Office for C. and A. Hoag, 1834) (McDade 771), p. 5; *Trial of John Metcalf Thurston* (Owego: Hiram A. Beebe, 1851), p. 20; *Fyler Murder*, pp. 108, 110, 126; *Trial of Peake*, p. 50. Also see *In the Court of Oyer and Terminer for the County of Albany. John H. Phelps ads. The People* (Albany: Weed, Parsons, 1855), p. 16; *Trial of Capt. John Windsor* (Milford, Del.: J. H. Emerson, 1851), p. 25; *Trial of Rogers*, p. 143.

18. *Report of the Trial and Conviction of John Haggerty* (Lancaster: John H. Pearsol, 1847), p. 19; *Trial of Corey*, p. 60.

19. *Trial of Prescott* (McDade 771), p. 7; *Trial of Thurston*, p. 51. Also see *The Trial of William Freeman* (Auburn [N.Y.]: Derby, Miller, 1848). This postmortem exam was cited in the trial of Willard Clark, which reported that "His [Freeman's] brain was dissected and found rotten"; *Trial of Clark*, p. 98.

20. *A Full and Complete Account of the Heberton Tragedy* (New York, 1843), p. 22; *Phelps ads. The People*, p. 16; *Trial of Thurston*, pp. 33, 43; *Trial of Mrs. Margaret Howard* (Cincinnati: E. E. Barclay, 1849), p. 46.

21. *Trial of Rogers*, p. 138; *Trial of Haggerty*, p. 23; *Trial of Clough*, p. 44.

22. *Trial of Woodford*, p. 17; *Trial of Prescott* (McDade 771), p. 8; *Trial of Windsor*, p. 29; *Fyler Murder*, p. 162.

23. *Trial of Haggerty*, p. 41; Platt and Diamond, "Origins of the 'Right and Wrong' Test"; *Life and Confession of Mrs. Henrietta Robinson, the Veiled Murderess!* (Boston: Dr. H. B. Skinner, 1855), p. 4; *Eccentricities and Anecdotes of Albert John Tirrell* (Boston, 1846), pp. 14, 15.

24. *Trial of Prescott* (McDade 769), p. 55; *Trial of Clark*, p. 133; *Trial of Howard*, p. 44.

25. On intemperance, see *Trial of Woodford*, pp. 25, 32; on masturbation, see *Trial of Rogers*, p. 214; and *Trial of Thurston*, pp. 29, 33–36, 43.

26. *Trial of Thurston*, p. 34.

27. *Phelps ads. The People*, p. 21; *Trial of Thurston*, p. 43; *Trial of Windsor*, p. 7; *Life and Trial of Baker*, p. xiii.

28. *Trial of Corey*, pp. 14, 32, 75; *Testimonium Dr. Baker . . . Haggerty*, pp. 7–9, 11–13; *Trial of Howard*, p. 26; *Veiled Murderess!*, p. 15.

29. *Trial of Prescott* (McDade 771), p. 7; *Trial of Clark*, p. 34; *Trial of Thurston*, p. 11.

30. *Trial of Clark*, p. 101; *Trial of Peake*, p. 58; *Trial of Rogers*, p. 200.

31. *Trial of Thurston*, p. 53; also see *Trial of Corey*, p. 66.

32. *Life and Trial of Baker*, p. vii.

33. *Trial of Prescott* (McDade 769), p. 98; also see *Trial of Peake*, pp. 59, 49.

34. *Trial of Prescott* (McDade 769), p. 87; *Trial of Thurston*, p. 34; emphasis added.

35. *Trial of Prescott* (McDade 769), p. 127; *Trial of Prescott* (McDade 771), p. 15; see also *Trial of Woodford*, p. 61.

36. *Trial of Clark*, p. 90; *Trial of Peake*, p. 72; *Fyler Murder*, p. 151.

37. *Trial of Prescott* (McDade 769), p. 127; *Trial of Clark*, p. 95; *Trial of Woodford*, p. 64; *Fyler Murder*, p. 152; D. Wilson, *Henrietta Robinson* (New York: Miller, Orton & Mulligan, 1855), p. 187. Prosecutors frequently charged alienists with casting the net of mental incompetence far too widely, with dire results for the criminal justice system. Willard Clark's prosecutor condescendingly explained that "The physician who makes dyspepsia his particular study, will be prone to trace dyspepsia in

every case of disease. And so, too, he who makes disease of the mind his entire study, will discover something of that in almost every case of irregularity of conduct; and hence there are those who assert that every impulse is, to a certain extent, insanity"; *Trial of Clark*, p. 149. Also see *Testimonium Dr. Baker . . . Haggerty*, p. 19.

38. *Trial of Peake*, p. 72.

39. John L. Thomas, "Romantic Reform in America, 1815–1865," *American Quarterly* 17 (Winter 1965):656–681; David J. Rothman, *The Discovery of the Asylum: Social Order and Disorder in the New Republic* (Boston: Little, Brown, 1971), chaps. 5, 6, and 9.

40. *Trial of Prescott* (McDade 769), p. 29; *Life and Trial of Baker*, p. 49; *Trial of Thurston*, p. 55.

41. *Trial of Prescott* (McDade 769), pp. 28–29; *Trial of Clough*, p. 43; *Trial of Peake*, p. 59; *Trial of Rogers*, p. 200.

42. *Trial of Howard*, p. 33 (also see *Trial of Windsor*, p. 27); Wilson, *Henrietta Robinson*, p. 172.

43. The diagnosis of temporal insanity sometimes accompanied monomania, and sometimes displaced it. In the Abner Rogers case, the defense quoted Esquirol on monomania's tendency to end abruptly (because Rogers's madness had seemingly abated after several days); *Trial of Rogers*, p. 79. In the case of Orrin Woodford, the jailer testified that his view of Woodford's disease had changed over time, moving from an initial impression that his insanity was periodic to a belief that his mind was deranged on a single subject, the alleged bad conduct of his wife; *Trial of Woodford*, p. 21.

44. *Trial of Prescott* (McDade 770), p. 21; *Trial of Windsor*, pp. 31, 40; *Phelps Ads. The People*, p. 39; also see *Trial of Thurston*, p. 34. Dr. Rufus Wyman cited a young man who, "suddenly seized with a paroxysm of derangement without any premonitions," rushed into a Boston shop and tried to stab a woman; after one week's care in an asylum, he achieved full recovery; *Trial of Prescott* (McDade 771), p. 8.

45. *Trial of Prescott* (McDade 770), p. 7; ibid. (McDade 771), p. 9.

46. Ibid., (McDade 770), pp. 16, 18, 22; ibid. (McDade 771), p. 16; ibid. (McDade 769), pp. 51–52.

47. *Trial of Albert John Tirrell* (Boston: Published at the "Times" Office, 1846) (McDade 991), pp. 16–23, 30.

48. Ibid., pp. 38, 21, 31.

49. *Fyler Murder*, pp. 159, 165, 28, 60, 116–117, 52.

50. Ibid., pp. 90, 128, 104, 131.

51. Ibid., p. 124.

52. *Trial of Corey*, p. 58; *Account of the Heberton Tragedy*, pp. 22–23; *Trial of Windsor*, pp. 35, 37. Also see *Trial of Howard*, p. 26; *Trial of Woodford*,

p. 24; *Trial of Clough*, pp. 45–46. Such arguments sometimes took gendered form in the argument from "female character," as in Rebecca Peake's defense that "Such a deed of atrocity is too much for the female heart. Woman is naturally timid, gentle, affectionate and forgiving. In her bosom no harbor is to be found for vengeance, and fiendlike malice"; *Trial of Peake*, p. 58.

53. *Trial of Windsor*, p. 47; *Trial of Rogers*, p. 102; *Trial of Clark*, p. 135; *Trial of Thurston*, p. 52. For a discussion of the Oxford case, see Quen, "Anglo-American Criminal Insanity," p. 319.

54. *Trial of Corey*, p. 59; *Trial of Thurston*, p. 52; *Trial of Clark*, p. 73.

55. *Trial of Corey*, p. 66; also see *Trial of Rogers*, p. 190.

56. *Trial of Thurston*, pp. 48, 50; *Trial of Rogers*, p. 187.

57. *Fyler Murder*, p. 60; *Trial of Thurston*; *Trial of Corey*, pp. 7–8; *Trial of Howard*, p. 29; *Account of the Heberton Tragedy*, p. 13.

58. *Testimonium Dr. Baker . . . Haggerty*, p. 3.

59. *Trial of Corey*, p. 62; Clap, *The Lord's Voice*, p. 68; *Trial of Prescott* (McDade 771), p. 14.

60. *Trial of Prescott* (McDade 769), p. 117; *Trial of Clark*, p. 90; *Trial of Howard*, p. 13; *Veiled Murderess!*; *Trial of Rogers*, pp. 193 and 88; *Trial of Woodford*, p. 6.

61. *Trial of Woodford*, p. 50.

62. See Mary Ann Jimenez, *Changing Faces of Madness: Early American Attitudes and Treatment of the Insane* (Hanover: University Press of New England, 1987).

63. *Trial of Rogers*, pp. 284–286. See Karen Halttunen, "Gothic Mystery and the Birth of the Asylum: The Cultural Construction of Deviance in Early Nineteenth-Century America," in *Moral Problems in American Life: New Essays on Cultural History*, eds. Karen Halttunen and Lewis Perry (Ithaca: Cornell University Press, 1998).

64. Marie-Christine Leps, *Apprehending the Criminal: The Production of Deviance in Nineteenth-Century Discourse* (Durham, NC: Duke University Press, 1992), part I; Arthur E. Fink, *Causes of Crime: Biological Theories in the United States 1800–1945* (New York: A. S. Barnes, 1938), chaps. 5 and 6.

Epilogue

1. Kate McClare, of the *Boca Raton News*, calls Ann Rule "the ruler of the whole true-crime empire" in a review of *You Belong to Me and Other True Cases*, excerpted in the front of Ann Rule, *A Fever in the Heart and Other True Cases* (New York: Pocket Books, 1996); John Douglas and Mark Olshaker, *Mindhunter: Inside the FBI's Elite Serial Crime*

Unit (New York: Pocket Books/Simon & Schuster, 1995), p. 351. Alfred Hitchcock's *Psycho* was itself modelled on the Ed Gein case in 1957; see Harold Schechter, *Deviant: The Shocking True Story of Ed Gein, the Original "Psycho"* (New York: Pocket Books/Simon & Schuster, 1989).

2. Lance Morrow, "Evil," in *Time*, June 10, 1991, p. 50.

3. Carlton Smith, *Death of a Little Princess: The Tragic Story of the Murder of JonBenét Ramsey* (New York: St. Martin's Press, 1997), pp. 290, 208.

4. See Vincent Bugliosi, *Outrage* (New York: W. W. Norton, 1996); Christopher Darden, with Jess Walter, *In Contempt* (New York: Regan Books, 1996); Alan M. Dershowitz, *Reasonable Doubts* (New York: Simon & Schuster, 1996); Robert L. Shapiro, with Larkin Warren, *The Search for Justice* (New York: Warner Books, 1996); Jeffrey Toobin, *The Run of His Life: The People v. O. J. Simpson* (New York: Simon & Schuster, 1997).

5. Smith, *Death of a Little Princess*, back cover; Teresa Carpenter, *Missing Beauty* (New York: Pinnacle Books, 1997). Most true-crime paperbacks offer maps, floorplans, and photographs of the scene, the corpse, the weapon, etc.; for ex., see Wilt Browning, *Deadly Goals: The True Story of an All-American Football Hero Who Stalked and Murdered* (New York: St. Martin's Press, 1996), after p. 140; Carlton Smith, *Seeds of Evil: A True Story of Murder and Money in California* (New York: St. Martin's Press, 1997), after p. 122; Ann Rule, *Lust Killer* (New York: New American Library, 1988), after p. 120; Rule, *Fever in the Heart*, after p. 140.

6. Joe McGinniss, *Fatal Vision* (New York: New American Library, 1983), back-cover review from *Newsweek;* Bill G. Cox, *Over the Edge* (New York: Pinnacle Books, 1997), p. 32 and back cover; Stephen G. Michaud and Hugh Aynesworth, *The Only Living Witness: A True Account of Homicidal Insanity* (New York: New American Library, 1983), front cover; Lyn Riddle, *Ashes to Ashes* (New York: Pinnacle Books, 1997), back cover; Douglas and Olshaker, *Mindhunter*, p. 158.

7. Riddle, *Ashes to Ashes*, p. 27; Smith, *Seeds of Evil*, p. 131.

8. Ann Rule, *Lust Killer* (New York: New American Library, 1988), p. 18; Robert Ressler, *Whoever Fights Monsters: My Twenty Years Tracking Serial Killers for the FBI* (New York: St. Martin's Press, 1993); Douglas and Olshaker, *Mindhunter*, pp. 141–142.

9. Rule, *Lust Killer*, p. 233.

10. John Douglas and Mark Olshaker, *Journey Into Darkness* (New York: Pocket Star Books, 1997); Ann Rule, *If You Really Loved Me* (New York: Pocket Books, 1991), frontispiece review from *Seattle Times/Seattle Post Intelligencer.*

11. Schechter, *Deviant*, back cover; Smith, *Death of a Little Princess*, back

cover; Ann Rule, *Small Sacrifices* (New York: New American Library, 1988), back cover.

12. Cox, *Over the Edge*, back cover; McGinniss, *Fatal Vision*, back cover; Schechter, *Deviant*, p. x; Rule, *Fever in the Heart*, p. 21; Ann Rule, *The Stranger Beside Me* (New York: New American Library, 1986), p. xv.

13. McGinniss, *Fatal Vision*, frontispiece review from *Chicago Sun-Times*; Rule, *If You Really Loved Me*, photo caption after p. 308; Smith, *Death of a Little Princess*, back cover; Smith, *Seeds of Evil*, back cover; Riddle, *Ashes to Ashes*, back cover.

14. Douglas and Olshaker, *Mindhunter*, front-cover review from *The New York Times Book Review*.

15. Douglas and Olshaker, *Mindhunter*, p. 12 (emphasis in original); Douglas, *Journey into Darkness;* Thomas Harris, *Red Dragon* (New York: Bantam Books/G. P. Putnam's Sons, 1981), p. 67; Thomas Harris, *The Silence of the Lambs* (New York: St. Martin's Press, 1988).

16. Sister Helen Prejean, *Dead Man Walking: An Eyewitness Account of the Death Penalty in the United States* (New York: Vintage Books, 1993), pp. 25, 62.

17. Ibid., pp. 15, 138, 176, 4, 17, 119, 62.

18. Ibid., pp. 20, 11, 76.

19. Ibid., p. 175.

Index

Harvard University Press is a member of Green Press Initiative (greenpressinitiative.org), a nonprofit organization working to help publishers and printers increase their use of recycled paper and decrease their use of fiber derived from endangered forests. This book was printed on recycled paper containing 30% post-consumer waste and processed chlorine free.